COWBOY APOCALYPSE

RACHEL WAGNER

COWBOY APOCALYPSE

RELIGION AND THE MYTH OF THE VIGILANTE MESSIAH

NEW YORK UNIVERSITY PRESS
NEW YORK

NEW YORK UNIVERSITY PRESS
New York
www.nyupress.org

© 2025 by New York University
All rights reserved

Library of Congress Cataloging-in-Publication Data
Names: Wagner, Rachel, author.
Title: Cowboy apocalypse : religion and the myth of the vigilante messiah /
Rachel Wagner.Description: New York : New York University Press, 2025. |
Includes bibliographical references and index.
Identifiers: LCCN 2024012779 (print) | LCCN 2024012780 (ebook) |
ISBN 9781479831623 (hardback) | ISBN 9781479831630 (ebook) |
ISBN 9781479831647 (ebook other)
Subjects: LCSH: Cowboys in popular culture. |
Cowboys—Mythology. | West (U.S.)—In popular culture. |
Popular culture—Religious aspects—Christianity.
Classification: LCC P96.C695 W34 2025 (print) | LCC P96.C695 (ebook) |
DDC 305.9/636213—dc23/eng/20240607
LC record available at https://lccn.loc.gov/2024012779
LC ebook record available at https://lccn.loc.gov/2024012780

This book is printed on acid-free paper, and its binding materials are chosen for strength
and durability. We strive to use environmentally responsible suppliers and
materials to the greatest extent possible in publishing our books.

Manufactured in the United States of America

10 9 8 7 6 5 4 3 2 1

Also available as an ebook

For Jim, who survived the war in Vietnam,
then threw his medal on the Capitol steps
and said "no more."

For my children, who deserve a world
in which they will not be shot.

CURES FOR APOCALYPSE
Rachel Wagner

Strawberry plants on every joint of earth.
Enough for everyone.
Bare hands in chilly stream.
Strummed music. Dance.
Strangers that hug.
Milkshakes.
A long long sleep.
Damp blankets spread beneath a dewy moon.
Lasagna made with peas.
Blue beetles perched on trees.
I'd like a million monarch butterflies.
So many bees.
Please, I'd like the whales to sing.
Pick people up, please, off the ground.
Love them. Wrap your coat around them.
Sincere apologies. Repeat as needed.
So many tears, and room for all of them.
I've seen the way you look at me,
The way you catch your breath.
These days, I don't put lightning bugs in jars.

CONTENTS

Introduction 1

1 13 Ways of Looking at a Gun 25

2 The Bones: Cowboy Apocalypse as Story 49

3 Shooting the Cowboy Apocalypse 81

4 A White Man's Frontier: *The Walking Dead* 110

5 "Eat Leaden Death, Demon": First-Person Shooter as End-Time Ritual 129

6 Witnessing the Future: *Doomsday Preppers* 151

7 The NRA in the Game: The Man behind the Gun 174

8 Souvenirs of Apocalypse 197

9 Live-Action Role-Play: Real Players, Real Bullets 215

Conclusion: Otherwise 237

Epilogue: On "Madmen" 265

Acknowledgments 269

Bibliography 271

Index 295

About the Author 307

INTRODUCTION

The photo is of me, at about two years old. I've got a perfect replica of my grandfather's gun strapped around my waist. I'm looking at the camera in defiance, as if I know the gun is powerful and it makes me powerful too. Being a girl, it was transgressive to wear it—especially in the early 1970s. But why did my parents have me pose for this shot? Was it my mother, in a visual nod to second-wave feminism? Was it my father, amused at a *girl* holding a weapon like that? Or was it my grandfather, whom I adored and who adored me? Maybe he thought it made me look strong. I really don't know. But to my eyes, looking back, I find the photo horrifying, a sign of how embedded guns are in U.S. culture—and how easily guns and toys get mixed up together.

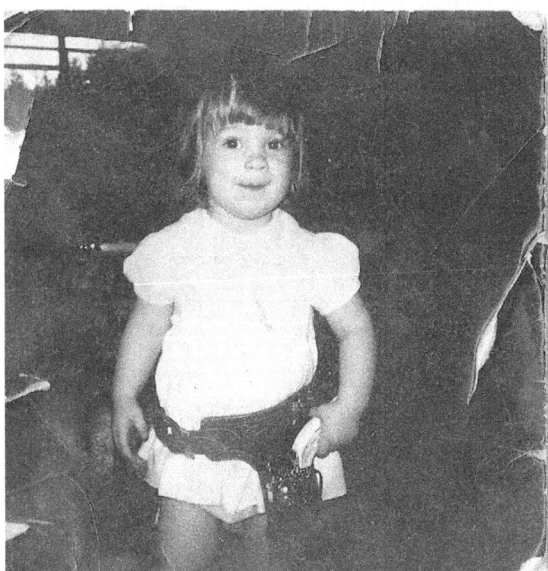

Personal photograph of author as child holding a gun.

To understand better why guns matter so much in the United States, this book considers what I call the *cowboy apocalypse*. The cowboy apocalypse is a complete mythic narrative arc. It crafts a story of America's frontier beginnings, blending it with the imagination of the world's imminent ending. As I define it, the cowboy apocalypse is a pervasive story expressed in the idiom of armed white men accustomed to being in charge. In this new version of the frontier story, non-white enemies can again be defeated and the wilderness tamed, but only by employing more gun violence. The gun, as a symbol of violent colonization, reflects the continuing force of frontier ideals in a contemporary environment.

The cowboy apocalypse depends on a self-proclaimed gun-wielding messiah who performs radical salvation with a gun. He doesn't save *the* world. He saves *his* world. We see this story replayed in television shows like *Doomsday Preppers* and *The Walking Dead*, and in movies like *The Young Ones* and *Amerigeddon*, enacted in videogames and live-action role-plays, and in political actions like the raid on the United States Capitol in January 2021. The cowboy apocalypse's fans engage in live-action *real* play, as they authenticate beliefs through violence. Pervasive media like the countless representations of the cowboy apocalypse can have powerful ideological impacts, shaping our habits and our beliefs. They can shape the ways we engage with material reality itself, including bodies and bullets.

The desire for a different world is an understandable impulse. Refugees flood national borders. Climate change damages our planet. We are running out of fossil fuels. We are poisoning our own water. For many, the world feels out of control. Whether we like it or not, it is no longer feasible to wall ourselves off from others. Sociologist Ulrich Beck draws attention to humanity's interdependence:

> [E]veryone is living in a direct and universal proximity with everyone else.... The conjecture that what is common to all human beings today is the longing for a world that is a little less unified is not unfounded. This negative solidarity based on the fear of global destruction once again exhibits the communicative logic of the world risk society ... [but] systemic closures are no longer an option because we are all bound into this World Wide Web of the production and definition of risk. (Beck 2009, 6)

As we become more connected, some people experience a sense of claustrophobia, wishing to live in a world that is less unified. This is the appeal of the cowboy apocalypse. To foresee—to even *now* see—the world as a post-apocalyptic wasteland is to reject the web of connection that binds our fates together and to imagine a world in which individual strengths are sufficient for survival. This dystopian fantasy presumes tough guys will be just fine.

Today, the would-be cowboy messiah carves out a retreat on a mountaintop or builds a bomb-proof bunker in his backyard. He creates a personal Eden by farming off-grid, surrounding his land with booby traps to keep out the urban rabble. Within the perimeters of this tiny paradise, abundance is measured by canned goods, seed packets, and fresh water. Hoarding, bunker-building, and target shooting offer a ritual architecture that renders the outside world unnecessary. Bullets are stored as symbolic indicators of future battles. Read in this context, the cowboy apocalypse is the expression of a desire to be in a purified post-apocalyptic world where faith in God is replaced with faith in oneself. But just as cowboy apocalypticism reflects what its proponents desire in the future, it also tells us something about what its proponents desire *right now*—namely, relief from contemporary challenges like globalization, resource depletion, racial tensions, feminism, and immigration.

The cowboy apocalypse draws on two foundational influences: Christian apocalypticism and American frontier mythology. This hybrid provides a contemporary story that accounts for America's beginnings and its endings. The popular trope of the "good guy with a gun" is born from this powerful alchemy, resulting in a mode of imminent apocalypticism that imagines an end to global cooperation, celebrating the vigilante gun owner as an earthbound savior figure.

The most famous account of early frontier mythology comes from Frederick Jackson Turner, a nineteenth-century academic who penned a racist rhapsody celebrating the West. Turner's essay was so influential that its argument has become known simply as the Turner thesis, now shorthand for the view that the West was a vacant, verdant wilderness in need of taming. Turner claimed that the settling of the frontier shaped the very character of settler Americans, who were able to leave behind European values by being tempered in the harshness of the West. He describes the "winning of the wilderness" as the development of "progress out of the primitive and economic conditions of the frontier" (Turner 1920, 1). This kind of reasoning is an echo of the Puritan work ethic, which suggests that those who work hardest are most loved by God.

For Turner, the frontier was the "meeting point between savagery and civilization" (3). It was a defining line that moved progressively westward as white settlers developed into plucky, self-reliant individuals using violence for what they deemed the greater good. Turner describes how the "American intellect" was shaped by the frontier:

> That coarseness and strength combined with acuteness and inquisitiveness; that practical, inventive turn of mind, quick to find expedients; that masterful grasp of material things, lacking in the artistic but powerful to effect great ends; that restless, nervous energy; that dominant individualism, working for good and for evil, and withal that buoyancy and exuberance which comes with freedom—these are the traits of the frontier, or traits called out elsewhere because of the existence of the frontier. (37)

These traits show up today in the imagination of the white American cowboy, especially the good guy with a gun. For Turner, the frontier encouraged grit and self-determination. Without moving west, said Turner, America could not fulfill its destiny. It is no accident that the idea of "whiteness" emerged around this same time, as settlers from distinctive European origins sought a shared identity to unite against the peoples already living in the land. White settlers were buoyed by Turner's exuberant "American intellect" to explain their own avarice.

The cowboy myth was cultivated in the self-serving ideology of folks like Turner. It was nurtured in the hills of Wyoming, Oregon, and Colorado, tempered in the wars with Mexico, and washed in the blood of Indigenous peoples. Cowboy history is complex, but the myth is simple: it is a European settler's story of control. In *Cowboy: The Enduring Myth of the Wild West*, writer Russell Martin (1983) shows how the cowboy myth transformed the "flesh-and-blood trail boys" into the "proud and strapping characters" who were made "symbolically important" for their directed use of violence (26). Real cowboys focused on moving cattle. The mythic cowboy was a "mountain fighter and adventurer who rode nowhere without his six-shooters strapped to his hips" (31). Cowboys were the eponymous boot-strappers. Their guns were a sign of ingenuity and self-sufficiency, not merely tools of the trade.

The ideological purposes of the frontier narrative are laid bare in its inherent contradictions. The West was empty, but filled with hostile foes. It was unsettled, yet needed to be cleared of Indigenous residents, who were presumed to be aggressive and lazy at the same time. In 1859, Horace Greeley justified this treatment by claiming the average Indian was both a "slave of appetite and sloth" and "never emancipated from the tyranny of one animal passion save by the more ravenous demands of another" (Greeley 2006, 152).

As later white writers would also do, Greeley lumps all Indigenous people together as if tribal identities are irrelevant. This move makes their dismissal, mistreatment, and murder easier to manage. The six-shooter cowboys of myth are portrayed as "bitter enemies" of the "redskins," who were "vile, treacherous, and sub-human" (Martin 1983, 240). "Indians" were encountered most on the moving western edge of America, a force to be pushed back to make room for settler development. Only if the Indigenous peoples of America were viewed as inferior to other human beings could they be so "wantonly hated, mistreated, and killed" (240).

The religious implications of this story of conquest are not lost on historian Elliott West (2012), who sees settling as "salvation in movement, rebirth through travail" (268).

> **Long ago, with the first European settlement on the Atlantic Coast, people from an old world came into a new one. It was a wilderness, full of unforeseen dangers and undreamt-of challenges. The people came brimming with hope and ideals and set out with a great determination. (280)**

The vestiges of this frontier myth are found today in language describing guns as tools of self-defense against wild enemies embedded in

America's landscape. Settlers viewed Indigenous land as "a wasteland that [only] humankind—cowboy kind—[could] bring under control" (Martin 1983, 71). Violence against Indigenous people was presented as *necessary*. America's fascination with the good guy starts here. The "good guy" fights a heroic battle against a "brutal" and "inhuman" enemy to satisfy God's great plans for America (West 2012, 240). This story resurfaces painfully today, applied to the immigrant and refugee poor at America's borders and to anyone not assimilated into America's story of civilized "whiteness."

The notion of a wide-open wilderness put there for the cowboy to master hides the terrible treatment of Indigenous people. Yet the idea has become essential to cowboy identity. "If the cowboy is ever left with no open land to head into, to test himself against, our mythic horseman may well have to dismount and unsaddle his horse, never to ride again" (Martin 1983, 66). For the cowboy dream to be kept alive, the frontier must remain open, in need of the cowboy's beneficent hand:

> **For if the land were no longer capable of inducing hardship and surprise, if the fickle weather could be harnessed, if predators and varmints could be corralled once and for all, if horses could truly be trusted and if cows had a lick of sense, then there would be nothing wild about the West at all and nothing special about being a cowboy. (78)**

Without peril, the cowboy can't demonstrate his mettle. No wonder cowboys still look for a fight. No wonder the southern U.S. border is a hot spot for vigilante activity. To admit the frontier story was a farce exposes the brazen theft of land and the genocide of Indigenous people. Instead of conquering wide-open spaces, today's cowboy is in *retreat* as unruly enemies come (he thinks) to conquer *him*.

We see the early appeal of the cowboy myth in the popularity of Buffalo Bill's "Wild West and Congress of Rough Riders of the World" in the nineteenth century, established as the frontier was closing. Buffalo Bill, well-known as a frontier scout, formed a theatrical troupe in the 1870s that performed Western-themed shows. By 1883, Bill's show was "a circuslike combination of pageantry and parades, feats of skill and daring, and 'authentic' reenactments of frontier events"

(Martin 1983, 16). It was an "extravaganza" that featured Indian attacks, stagecoach robberies, and fake shootouts (Winkler 2013, 164). The live action show manufactured reality in a way that written stories could not, shaping an action-packed portrait of the West that featured Indian aggression contrasted with white cowboy virtue (White and Limerick 1994, 29).

In early cowboy performances like Buffalo Bill's shows, we find "marauding redmen who burned barns and farmhouses, ambushed wagon trains, raped and killed, and finally were wiped out by a cowboy culture that revered civilization and had the courage to protect its entrance into the West" (Martin 1983, 259). Buffalo Bill's audience "needed raw and blatant representations of victor and vanquished to explain the winning of the West" (259). Buffalo Bill's show was an early form of "reality staged as theater," as actual historical figures and real events were integrated into the lopsided narrative. When the Sioux defeated General Custer in the Battle of the Little Bighorn, Bill left his show clad in a ridiculous Mexican *vaquero* outfit made of black velvet and silver buttons, serving as a scout for the 5th Cavalry. Claiming vengeance for the death of Custer in a skirmish at War Bonnet Creek, he captured and scalped the Cheyenne leader Hay-o-wei, or "Yellow Hand." Bill wore the costume and displayed Yellow Hand's scalp—the *actual flesh*—in a show called "The Red Right Hand; or the First Scalp for Custer" (White and Limerick 1994, 34). The scalp became a prop that authenticated Buffalo Bill's stories and provided proof of Indigenous savagery (34).

Half of the Indian actors in Buffalo Bill's re-creation of the Battle of the Little Bighorn had participated in the battle but subjected themselves to Buffalo Bill's rescripting of events (Martin 1983, 232). Sitting Bull, a Sioux medicine man, became famous in Bill's shows. Other Sioux performed "tricks and feats of horsemanship," while "taking part in mock battles between the 'Indian warriors' and the 'veterans of the United States cavalry'" (232). Buffalo Bill made Indigenous people inhabit gross "imitations of themselves" in which they performed "white versions of events" to authenticate Bill's version of history (White and Limerick 1994, 35). Indigenous people played the role of "murderous Indian enemies" intent on "attacking helpless white women and children or badly outnumbered white men" (29). Such portrayals were common, justifying a violent campaign of expansion that, "peppered with a sense of religious mission, transformed alien peoples—Blacks, Native Americans, and Mexicans" into barbarians who could be met only with annihilation (Hosley 1996, 50).

Cowboys, on the other hand, were valorized. In Buffalo Bill's shows, cowboys weren't drunkards or hooligans, but "fine, upstanding young men with indomitable spirits, great courage, energy, skills, and self-confidence" (Martin 1983, 282). The cowboys in Bill's shows were "badly abused conquerors" who really had no choice but to massacre Indigenous people and settle on their land (White and Limerick 1994, 27).

In Buffalo Bill's show, the "rifle and the bullet" played a starring role, personified as "the pioneer of civilization" (White and Limerick 1994, 9). Prescient of the NRA slogan, Russell Martin describes the violent logic employed by Buffalo Bill's cowboys: "The only way to put a stop to unwarranted shooting is to do some shooting of your own." Cowboys, Buffalo Bill's shows suggested, would only kill the "bad guys" who "got it coming to them" (Martin 1983, 283). And in Buffalo Bill's shows, these bad guys were almost always Indigenous people. Simply by existing in the territory the settlers desired, they automatically deserved the violence directed at them.

Buffalo Bill's depictions were frankly racist, but there is some truth to the image of manly cowboys shooting at each other in dusty streets. In some frontier towns, there was no official law enforcement, and the gun itself became a symbol of social order. The Colt six-shooter and the Winchester carbine rifle were commonly called "peacemakers," and the Colt revolver was sometimes called "Judge Colt and his jury of six" (271). If the legal system was weak and bad guys needed dispatching, "an individual simply had to do it alone, with the aid of an iron pistol and fast lead bullets" (275). Myth and reality blended in the story of the cowboy bringing order through violence. As Martin notes, the cowboy myth already had "succeeded in equating violence in defense of law with virtue" (281).

Many towns *did* have local law enforcement and strict gun laws. Frontier town law typically "forbade people from toting their guns around," and in many towns, only local law enforcement was allowed to carry firearms (Winkler 2013, 165). Guns were checked at entry points or left at livery stables or police stations in exchange for tokens (165). A study of homicides in Dodge City showed only fifteen killings in nine of the city's busiest years. Similarly, in Tombstone, only five people were killed in its most violent year, and three were outlaws (163).

The most common nineteenth-century gun control law was a ban on concealed firearms. Kentucky, Louisiana, Indiana, Virginia, Alabama, and Ohio adopted bans of concealed weapons between 1813 and 1859 (Winkler 2013, 166). According to historian Clayton Cramer, these bans were intended to control violence in towns and prevent deadly duels (cited in Winkler 2013, 167). If a cowboy wanted to carry his guns attached to his body, "he'd have to be out in the wilderness, away from town folk" (166). Even John Wayne wouldn't have been allowed to amble about, fully armed, and shoot up frontier towns like in the movies.

John Wayne is an obvious inheritor of Buffalo Bill's cowboy image. In his cowboy movies, Wayne is presented as "the hard man" who is nonetheless gentle with family and friends. He's a ready-made armed hero who "perceives evil and eradicates it" (Savage 1979, 28). Wayne's cowboy character is "happy to fight with fists and guns and anything else that was handy." He "swore, spat, and swilled whiskey on occasion" but was a "moralist nonetheless, a hero in common man's clothes" (Martin 1983, 35). This portrayal presumes the cowboy to be a virtuous man willing to engage in violent behavior for the sake of good. For Wayne's cowboy characters, there is "no accommodation, no compromise, only the sort of wisdom that allows consideration of the world in stark contrasts of black and white" (Savage 1979, 28).

Cowboy heroes did not agonize over whether violence was justified. They simply "knew right from wrong, by God, and were always ready to shoot it out to prove it" (Martin 1983, 272). Wayne bought fully into the rivalry between cowboys and Indians, saying in an interview that Americans did not do anything wrong in "taking this great country away" from its original inhabitants. Echoing the Turner thesis, Wayne declared that "there were great numbers of people who needed new land, and the Indians were selfishly trying to keep it for themselves" (Martin 1983, 259).

The cowboy myth can be distinguished from stories about real cowboys who were less like John Wayne and more like your average farmhand—industrious, quiet, lonely, independent, leading a "drab and passionless" life herding cattle across boring, uneventful plains (Martin 1983, 40). Real-life cowboys were lower-class men who worked in harsh conditions on horseback managing cattle and had little contact with Indigenous peoples, interacting mainly when trading goods or asking permission to drive cattle over Indigenous-occupied land (240). There are still ordinary cowboys around—in Montana, Texas, Oklahoma, and anywhere wide-ranging fields are used for the cultivation of cattle. Real-life cowboys were "vagabond boys of every race who were intrigued by the prospect of money and adventure that could be found on the back of a horse" (30).

The real cowboy's roots are grounded in the lives of peoples with diverse histories and culture. The word "buckaroo" is an Anglicization of the Spanish *vaquero*, or cattle driver, and reveals the foundational quality of Texas and Mexican cattle management in the cultivation of the cowboy image (101). Black cowboys like Isom Dar, Nat Love, and Bill Pickett don't show up in our mythic compositions of the West (Savage 1979, 9). The cowboy apocalypse myth is distinct from stories like these, just as it is distinct from other cowboy myths like the cowboy as honorable protector, or the *gaucho* cowboy as generous, brave, and mischievous.

Whereas *actual* cowboys led lives of hard work and little excitement, *mythic* cowboys sought adventure. Whereas *actual* cowboys provided a model of simplicity, devotion, and honor, *mythic* cowboys define themselves (and their guns) as forces of ultimate good. By drawing on existing tropes but redesigning them to cope with the anxieties of twenty-first-century life, the cowboy apocalypse is a resurgence of Western tropes twisted to serve new ends. This transformation took time, though. It drew on fierce antagonisms following the Civil Rights Movement, tapping into racist backlash in the 1980s and 1990s as the political anger of white evangelicals met with apocalyptic expectation and militant defenders of the Second Amendment made common cause with conspiracy theorists and self-declared vigilantes. Mediated retellings of the cowboy apocalypse story show the emergence of this hybrid as a declaration of war by angry white men seeking retribution for a loss of power. The gun is its most potent prop.

The cowboy apocalypse is defined by frontier mythology as its past, but apocalypticism defines its future. Apocalypticism is the determined imagination of a troubled present reality transformed into a hoped-for world to come. Biblical scholar Carol Newsom describes the ancient Jewish and Christian apocalyptic mindset this way, but if you add dust and boots it applies as easily to the cowboy apocalypse:

> [T]he structure of the [cosmic] plot is known in advance. Good will triumph over evil. Indeed, the moral satisfaction of reading or hearing an apocalypse is the experience of feeling the danger of evil, imagining it vividly, even while knowing that it is already doomed, and that good will be established forever. (Newsom 2016, xi)

Newsom keys into the rhetorical pleasure of apocalypse, especially its tendency to imbue people with a sense of moral superiority. People invested in apocalypticism feel confident that although others less worthy will suffer, they will be ushered into a better world beyond. Apocalypticism depends on this sense that the future cannot be reined back from its current trajectory, nor *should* it be, since the future it careens toward will be better. Many ancient apocalyptic authors seem to have hoped for such a transformation. These weren't pipe dreams; they were intense hopes resting in a conviction that God would intercede soon.

The theological gravity of human passivity in traditional apocalypticism cannot be overstated. It is one of the defining features of ancient apocalyptic literature, serving to magnify God's greatness and power. It is God who will judge, while humans wait and hope. In the cowboy apocalypse, God's vengeance is replaced by the human, gun-toting messiah. For today's cowboy messiahs, there is expectation of a turning point, when the undesirable present gives way to a more desirable future in which guns (instead of God) will be the means to power.

There is a kind of theological resignation in the earthly focus of the cowboy apocalypse: the best we can hope for is to rebuild from the ashes through leadership of self-designated righteous men. God isn't going to help, but in this refreshed frontier the cowboy messiah will no longer be constrained by rules telling him how to behave. What he thinks is right will simply *be* right. This is what makes apocalyptic thinking so attractive. It provides reflexive reinforcement for preexisting values. In the impending collapse of civilization, bullets—not angels—will keep evil at bay.

Apocalyptic discourse is characterized by a refusal to see our present world as ultimate reality. Instead, it "looks toward an alternative reality in which righteousness prospers while evil is either punished or abolished" (Carey 2005, 6). In its mythic plot of good and evil, apocalypse is "an organizing principle imposed on an overwhelming, seemingly disordered universe" (Rosen 2008, xi). Apocalypses offer comfort because they invite readers to see the world destroyed to make room for a better one, in which those now oppressed gain freedom from (or over) their enemies. Readers who see the world as "corrupt beyond repair" can imagine it ending soon. Indeed, they "desperately desire for that to be the case," says religion scholar Cathy Gutierrez. They impose this expectation onto history itself and place themselves in the midst of a story awaiting (and sometimes enacting) the apocalypse (2005, 48).

In an interpretation of the biblical book of Revelation, communication scholar Stephen O'Leary describes a dialectic between "now" and "not-yet"—between the present and the hoped-for future. This tension creates a situation in which the apocalyptic text can be "read as prediction" and "experienced as enactment" (1998, 70). Reading the text can *feel* authenticating for those who *already* believe its vision of the future. For O'Leary, reading the apocalyptic text is a "symbolic enactment that constitutes its own proof" (88). O'Leary says that, for those inclined, performative desire can lead to self-authentication of belief: "successfully arguing a case for an imminent End is to bring the End closer by performing it rhetorically" (87). Reading the text can be ritual authentication itself.

In the same way, contemporary fans watch movies playing out the imminent cowboy apocalypse or read novels predicting it and can use these texts to affirm their own beliefs about the future. The "now" and the "not-yet" slip together, as prediction and fulfillment coalesce. The future is already destined, with a story that is laid atop current events to *make* that future feel destined. So they live now as if they were *already* in the future they want—to convince themselves it is indeed on the way. In a kind of circular logic, apocalyptic expectations authenticate apocalyptic expectations, which seem *more real* than the world as it now is. Such expectations can be understood as a form of what performance theorist Richard Schechner has called "make belief."

Schechner draws a distinction between "make believe" and "make belief." Make-believe, he explains, is an imaginative act that retains self-aware boundaries between real and play. People engaging in "make believe" readily admit they are pretending. "Make belief," however, is the blurring of the boundaries between real and play. When engaging in "make belief," a person enacts "the effects they want the receivers of their performances to accept 'for real'" (Schechner 2002, 35). Make-belief is a performative *as-if.* It creates the appearance of the real as a means of *generating* its acceptance as real. For the cowboy apocalypse, this means believing with full conviction in an imminent end could bring *about* that end. Make-belief is performative desire. It is commitment and determination. One might even call it stubbornness. Many traditional religious beliefs depend on just this kind of leap of faith.

We can see a lot of make-belief in the fandom of the cowboy apocalypse. The more complicated and difficult the world grows, the more some people desire entry into a post-apocalyptic space, investing in that future through the purchase of consumer objects like guns and supplies, and living out desire in ritualized activities like videogames, live-action role-play, and in some cases, violent acts. The more invested one is in apocalyptic storytelling, the more one is primed to interpret the world in that light. And whereas most fans of the cowboy apocalypse never cross over into the realm of make-belief, some do. For them, to aim a gun in real life at someone they have already decided is a bad guy is proof of their commitment.

Apocalypses work by promising a different future just around the bend. Biblical scholar J. J. Collins maintains that apocalypses "involve a transcendent eschatology that looks for retribution beyond the bounds of history," delaying justice by imaginatively postponing it into a space beyond ordinary time (1998, 11). Apocalyptic discourse "refuses to acknowledge the present world of perception and experience as the ultimate reality. Instead, it looks toward an alternative reality in which righteousness prospers while evil is either punished or abolished" (Carey 2005, 6). If justice cannot be achieved in this life, it will in the next. In the cowboy apocalypse, we see a similar move. If justice cannot be achieved in the world as it is now, cowboy messiahs look toward apocalyptic transformation.

Resilience and grit are rewarded in post-apocalyptic space as the cowboy messiah defends himself against angry hordes determined to steal his resources. Enemies are shot, tricked, betrayed, and sent to a violent end. The cowboy apocalypse appears in many forms. In this book, we will move from less embodied forms to highly embodied forms of the cowboy apocalypse, as we consider together how the gun and the fan's body are integrated into different mediations of the story. As interactivity increases, the gun becomes an essential prop in the performance of ritual enactment. And as the gun becomes materialized, so the actual bodies of other people—presumed enemies—become props dragged into a ritualized story they would rather not inhabit.

Scholars Robert Joustra and Alissa Wilkinson point out that today's most popular apocalyptic stories "rarely refer to God, or gods, or shared beliefs" (2016, 54). Nonetheless, these new apocalypses are "as religious as any ancient, medieval, or even early modern incarnation" (60). Whether they reference God explicitly or not, apocalypticists produce a grand narrative—an overarching story about the world—that suits their own desires. They engage in the "ultimate act of deconstruction" (59) as they picture the world's destruction to cope with fears, frustrations, and unsatisfied desires. They place themselves at the center of the story with agency to determine what comes afterward.

A human-centered vision of the end times imagines us still stuck here, but on a radically transformed earth. The shift is substantial not just in terms of how one pictures judgment, but also how one visualizes rewards for the righteous. The *elsewhere* of apocalypse cannot be heavenly because hope for the future is no longer heavenly. The rioters who descended on the Capitol on January 6, 2021, certainly saw *themselves* as pious judges trying to bring about a new world. Their role-play was *real*, their fiction transformed to fact by force and angry fiat.

When the world falls apart, the good guy with a gun makes things right again. We have removed God and "swapped *ourselves* into the position of apocalypse-enactor" (Joustra and Wilkinson 2016, 2). This shift places "the human person at the center of the universe as the creator of meaning" (2). Instead of locating our reasons for existence in a "metaphysical dimension," we assert the power "to make and decide" what is meaningful (5). In the cowboy apocalypse, the cowboy messiah designates *himself* divine. We see this plot played out again and again in videogames and films, and sometimes in real life, when the desire for justice is grafted onto the present through apocalyptic expectation authenticated by violence.

The gun is the most important symbol in the cowboy apocalypse. It is a nimble ambassador across mediated worlds, spilling its effects in all directions. The gun leaps from novels to films to violent videogames, and into the dangerous worlds of television shows like *The Walking Dead* (2010). It slips from gritty films like *The Road* (2009) into dystopian reality shows like *Doomsday Preppers* (2012). It even shows up in weekend survivalist events where participants aim but do not shoot at their fellow role-play apocalypticists. The gun has the potential to cross from the mediated space of the screen into the real lives of users, taking material form within the hands of the most hardcore fans of the cowboy apocalypse. The gun's material reality, in this case, can serve as authentication of the story it evokes. When viewed in the context of apocalypse, guns are otherworldly guides that pass from this world to the expected world to come. The gun exists *here* and *there*, *now* and *then*.

Media studies professor Eugene Thacker argues that today the supernatural is alive and well "via the panoply of media objects that satellite us and that are embedded into the very material fabric of our bodies, cities, and lives" (2014, 95–96). The supernatural is "as immanent as our media are—distributed, ubiquitous, in the 'cloud' and enveloping us in its invisible, ethereal bath of information and noise" (96). We hunger for escape, and transmedia offers it. Our fascination with mediated realities is a kind of religious impulse, drawing us to an otherwise and an elsewhere that may seem more desirable than the here and now. Even for those who do not believe in heaven, the draw of otherworldly spaces is alluring. Mediated storyworlds invite our imaginary habitation in them, offering an escape and a defining script for how to live.

While the gun is a symbol at the center of cowboy apocalypse fandom, not all who value guns are cowboy apocalypse fans. Some people keep a gun in their home in case somebody breaks in. Some people rely on guns for hunting. Some people carry a gun because they fear being attacked for their skin color, gender, religious beliefs, or sexual identity. Failure to think about *how* we engage with gun fandom can lead to distractions, like blaming videogames for what actual guns do. The cowboy apocalypse is always *ideologically* problematic. But only occasionally do actual guns aimed at actual people enact its narrative. What is more, it is a substantially different thing to read apocalyptic stories than to play apocalyptic videogames. It's a different thing again for apocalyptic survivalists to shoot at each other in the woods. And yet another thing to imagine oneself a good guy emboldened to save the world armed with an AR-15. And yet all of these are modes of fetishizing the gun as a symbol of salvation. For gun owners looking to distinguish themselves from those who employ the gun as a symbol of rejection of others, clarity about their relationship to cowboy apocalypticism may be a useful means of differentiation. What if you play videogames, but don't go to a shooting range? What if you own a gun, but don't *actually* hope for the end of the world? The cowboy apocalypse obliterates the present by investing ritually in a longed-for future. The gun, as authentication of this future, serves as material evidence.

Because the cowboy apocalypse is experienced in different sorts of media, using the notion of transmedia makes sense. The same core story is spun across novels, films, plays, fan fiction, merchandise, live events, and even theme parks. Preeminent media scholar Henry Jenkins defines transmedia storytelling as:

> . . . **a process where integral elements of a fiction get dispersed systematically across multiple delivery channels for the purpose of creating a unified and coordinated entertainment experience. Ideally each medium makes its own unique contribution to the unfolding of the story. (Jenkins 2007)**

As the same story is dispersed, it is experienced in different ways, some more interactive than others, with each iteration taking advantage of the medium in which it is told. Transmedia is participatory, because it is "designed above all to be immersive" (Rose 2012, 2). In other words, it is intended to seduce us into wishing it were real.

The cowboy apocalypse can be deeply immersive or less immersive, deeply interactive or less interactive. A live-action role-play is more immersive than a television show. A videogame is more interactive than a movie. There is a difference between videogame gunslinging in *Red Dead Redemption* and the kind of riveting gun fan devotion that prompts someone to aim an actual rifle at another human being. Fans can demonstrate their commitment to the cowboy apocalypse by a willingness to consume as many versions of it as possible, for example, by purchasing *Walking Dead* prepping supplies and becoming active in online discussion boards.

People who are deeply dedicated to transmedia fandoms long to inhabit the fandom's imaginary space, integrating it in their own lives through performative activities like wearing costumes, buying props, or engaging in role-plays. The more they buy, the more they read, the more they watch, the deeper their sense of immersion and completion will be. They might engage in costumed role-play with similarly devoted fans to increase a sense of being transported to another time and place. They might come to believe elements of the fictional story, letting the narrative wash over and transform reality itself. This kind of experience is what scholars call "pervasive play," in which the whole point is to soften the distinction between reality and game. Belief is participatory. Or to put it another way, the deepest forms of participatory fandom are a kind of belief.

Transmedia worldbuilding is an attractive substitute for the real world, because in transmedia worlds, our experiences can all be tied together into a neat core narrative. Transmedia is the promise of order in an otherwise fragmented world, unity in a time of fragmentation. In a way, then, transmedia can be viewed as a cultural manifestation of the desire for a world with a single set of rules and a shared set of key characters. The cowboy apocalypse certainly fits this bill. Transmedia can be viewed as a quasi-religious impulse clad in the sometimes garish, sometimes gorgeous mode of videogames, films, books, and live-event role-play. With its tendency to weave between the real world and a fantasy world, the cowboy apocalypse is one of the most compelling examples of transmedia around.

This book considers the theoretical and ideological underpinnings of the cowboy apocalypse, moving through exemplary forms of its transmediated nodes. The popularity of the myth makes it impossible for Americans to avoid. Building on the equally ubiquitous myths of the American West, the cowboy apocalypse draws out themes from Christian apocalypticism and American exceptionalism to craft a vision of the future that resists the interdependence of our time.

The cowboy apocalypse is a powerful myth that is relayed through a host of different media platforms, rituals, live events, and social practices. It offers an imagined salve to the world's ills by positing a fictional post-apocalyptic space in which the self-appointed cowboy messiah sees himself roaming a refreshed frontier, armed to the teeth, defeating evil and protecting his family. This myth is rehearsed again and again in American movies, television shows, videogames, and even live events like gun shows and role-play events.

Chapter 1 looks at the gun as an object of interpretive attention. It draws on cultural studies, gamer studies, anthropology, ritual theory, the social sciences, tourist studies, religious studies, and other related fields to explore thirteen key ways the gun can be understood as a cultural object. Instead of looking at specific types of guns, it considers the gun as a broad category of objects referenced visually in films, crafted into plastic toys and film replicas, and wielded as a deadly weapon defended by the constitutional "right to bear arms." This chapter paves the way for those that follow, which analyze the cowboy apocalypse in performative contexts ranging from books to television shows to survivalist camps—with the gun as a meaningful object that moves between them.

Chapter 2 considers the gun as it appears in books. It evaluates post-apocalyptic novels featuring white men who watch the world fall apart but survive through a combination of survivalist preparation, willingness to shoot, and an instinct about who to trust. Although books can certainly invite reader immersion, they don't allow for much interactivity. Any representation of guns is experienced passively by the reader, who cannot pull the trigger. This limitation is reflected in the fixedness of the book itself, which doesn't allow for the reader to change the plot or make different choices. Novels show us one possible world, but they define that world with such determinism that to read them is to give oneself over, at least temporarily, to the author's vision of things. This kind of determinism can be comforting in its inevitability, but disappointing in its personal agency. Guns are not actually used; they have textual and symbolic import, but no direct power for the reader.

Chapter 3 considers the cowboy apocalypse in film. Famous cowboy figures like John Wayne and Clint Eastwood are enshrined in Western films that have powerfully shaped American consciousness. In recent decades, though, the cowboy myth increasingly has blended with apocalyptic imagery, producing films with angry men with guns wandering in a wasteland. The cowboy becomes the cowboy *messiah* when he uses his gun to cope with perceived enemies. This chapter demonstrates how the visual screening of the cowboy apocalypse offers a more immersive mode of engagement than reading a novel—especially for hardcore cowboy apocalypse fans who perceive their own guns as a kind of movie prop that can be used in real life.

Chapter 4 turns to television. As a compelling example of the cowboy apocalypse, *The Walking Dead* situates itself in the grisly aftermath of apocalyptic change. The medium of serialized television presents the new gun-infused frontier environment as stretching inexorably into the future—with a seemingly endless supply of transmediated spin-offs. Despite its ridiculous zombie premise, *The Walking Dead* depicts an environment where violence is the only means of survival. In its desolate landscape, groups of armed people survive behind walls, attempting to stave off the endless flow of the dead. *The Walking Dead* is an anticipative dirge for our globalized world and a painful expression of desire for a return to a simplified frontier environment. Like other iterations of the cowboy apocalypse, *The Walking Dead* imagines a future in which retributive violence will be celebrated by gritty men who survive against impossible odds. Perhaps predictably, *The Walking Dead* presents women as having to learn to act (and shoot) like the men or be dependent on men for survival.

Chapter 5 moves to more interactive modes as we explore the relationship between the U.S. military-industrial complex and the development of violent videogames. As we move from literary and screened images of guns to interactive simulations of gun activity, we see more engagement with visual violence and more agency for the user. The cybernetic military-driven past of videogame development hard-bakes a kind of apocalypticism into first-person shooter videogames, but blends these with the instigation of a messianic player who is responsible for virtual violence to "win" and "save" others. Looking at videogames, we see how the brinkmanship of military-inspired game design and the violence of the cowboy apocalypse blend to offer a ritualized enactment of violence that does not force players to become violent, but which *does* invite an ideological engagement that represents other people as one-dimensional props and encourages their violent dispatch.

Chapter 6 looks at gun fandom at the heart of the reality television show *Doomsday Preppers*. In the show, non-actors show what they believe will happen after society's collapse, including how they will use their firearms to kill their less prepared enemies. The performance of the cowboy apocalypse hovers on the edge between onscreen and offscreen, as serious preppers are filmed for entertainment purposes. These preppers seem to believe their own predictions, but they are also performing for the camera. They present themselves as a chosen remnant, remarkable for their prescient consumer practices and vigilante training. Preppers occupy the *future* while living in the present. Participants' stories about how to survive apocalypse are remarkably consistent, suggesting producers are keenly aware of how seriously the cowboy apocalypse is taken by some viewers.

Chapter 7 considers what the spillover into real life can look like in the apocalyptic rhetoric of the National Rifle Association (NRA) in its home-grown videogames and in its public rhetoric. Because it is a game that is *lived*, the apocalyptic rhetoric of the NRA is inescapably embodied, marking this as a dangerous form of cowboy apocalypticism. A version of the good-guy-with-a-gun story is retold by the NRA whenever there is a shooting on American soil, even when the story doesn't fit. This shift from virtual to embodied is pivotal in our analysis of how the cowboy apocalypse can be dangerous—and marks the NRA as a more troubling means of transmediation for the cowboy apocalypse than videogames. The most dangerous mediations of the cowboy apocalypse myth are the *material* forms that invite gun owners to see themselves as good guys living out the story on the streets, wielding *actual* firearms, and willing to enact *real* violence. While the NRA's star has descended in recent years, the history of gun fandom is incomplete without considering the role the organization has played in recent decades developing the core performative elements of the cowboy apocalypse.

Chapter 8, using elements of trauma theory and tourism studies, attends to how objects can signify what cannot be articulated due to pain and loss. If the cowboy apocalypse is a story obsessively replayed in American media as a means of perpetuating a hegemonic tale of white male order, then trauma theory helps us shift our focus onto the victims of gun trauma. Just as guns can be powerful symbols of masculine authority and power, so they can also be symbols of the ongoing violence of white supremacy in America. In the cowboy apocalypse, guns point toward an imagined post-apocalyptic future of white male rule. In our own real world, though, they also point to a past of slave patrols, Ku Klux Klan actions, and white vigilante crime. Sometimes objects point to a story that cannot be told except by victims. This chapter considers how guns look from the other end of the barrel.

Building on insights about self-declared vigilante saviors wielding actual firearms, Chapter 9 uses live-action role-playing (larping) to examine the faltering distinction between fiction and real life in the kind of extreme play that motivated the rioters on January 6, 2021. Extreme larping pushes the envelope of performativity, using the conceit of *as-if* as a protective screen for morally problematic actions like playing at rape, or asking players to pretend they are throwing other players into a crematorium. Alternate reality games (ARGs) borrow the role-play premise but place players on *actual* streets with people who may not know they are in the game. This kind of slippage between playful performativity and transgressive activity was on full display at the insurrection at the Capitol. The rioters engaged in *extremist* role-play: the militia-style activity of self-declared gun enthusiasts who play according to preconceived plot lines. Whereas the NRA and their media outlets retroactively impose the good-guy scenario onto actual shootings, the insurrectionists were *prompted* to act based on self-designated messianic function. Those who take the cowboy apocalypse as a real story and wish to authenticate it may make the final shift from fictional engagement with the mythos of the cowboy apocalypse to lived authentication of it.

The transmediated cowboy apocalypse places the story of the self-empowered, gun-wielding messianic cowboy at the center and spins it into as many modes of engaging consumption as Americans will devour. It idealizes the frontier by erasing the horrors of Indigenous genocide. It ignores the story of American slavery and celebrates a form of toxic white male supremacy. And it makes the actual gun a prop in this dangerous story. So the final chapter focuses on the approaches of those people who have been targeted as enemies in the cowboy apocalypse—the "them" to the cowboy messiah's "us." It draws from authors and artists offering critical insights relating to feminism, critical race theory, queer theology, globalization, religious pluralism, and Afrofuturism.

The dangers of mythmaking through the cowboy apocalypse lie not so much in its fictionalized expressions (though even these can habituate racist patterns) but in the *lived* expression of that myth as it is authenticated through violent performance in America's gun-saturated culture. These alternative thinkers imagine a nonviolent, gender-complex, anti-colonialist, anti-racist future. The self-ordained messiah of the cowboy apocalypse, though, is a man who knows by instinct when to shoot and believes he can tell who deserves to die. This is a recipe for the kind of violence we see in America every day.

Some studies place the gun in a long line of American hunting implements. Others consider the gun within military history. There are paeans of praise for the gun, manuals for using guns, and analyses of guns as a threat to health and safety. People tend to look at the gun as either an object of devotion or a terrifying threat. Here, I consider how the gun can be viewed as an enacted symbol of American culture, as well as a material item that is displayed, celebrated, feared, ritualized, and utilized by actual human beings who endow it with powerful meaning. Because gun culture impacts all Americans, we *all* have the right to set policies around it, whether we own guns or not. This book is more than history or cultural analysis; it is a call to action to become critically aware of how embedded these stories are in our culture, and how the stories imprint themselves violently on our bodies. Your voice matters, even more so if you have been a victim of gun violence.

Some people argue that only gun owners have something valuable to say about guns because only they understand a gun's heft and power. But potential victims have something to say, too. As someone who lives in a culture awash in gun violence, I am as invested in the question of gun rights as anyone else in the United States. As a professor of religion and media, I aim with this book to figure out what is going on with our American fascination with guns and how this fascination relates to religion and American popular culture. Why are guns so central to American identity? What role do guns play in the stories we tell in our movies, television shows, videogames, interactive hobbies, and ritualized obsessions? Why do guns so often play a starring role in American stories of disaster, apocalypse, and endings? And why is it so hard to think about controlling access to them?

Myths like the cowboy apocalypse are ways of ordering the world, shaping how we see ourselves and what we imagine is possible. To understand our own myths is to understand what we, as a people, want and value—and what we fail to grasp. Guns are woven into the fabric of American history, and they continue to shape its hazardous present (Dizard et al. 1999, 6). The gun, as a phantom limb, says "no" to compromise, to vulnerability, to open flows, and even to conversation itself. In a world where some believe there is *too* much communication, the gun creates a protective perimeter around its brandisher. The gun is antiseptic, purging the surrounding environment through the promise of violence. The gun's purpose is to *halt* exchange and dialogue. According to the chilling logic of the cowboy apocalypse, the more connected people become, the more bullets we need.

As you read, I invite you to ask where you find yourself within this fraught story. How does the cowboy apocalypse shape *your* life? Do you have habits of viewing others that are shaped by the sometimes racist, sometimes sexist apocalyptic stories obsessively replayed in American media? How likely are you to see yourself as the good guy who shoots the bad guy? How might such presumptions shape your everyday interactions? If you pick up a real gun, do the widely rehearsed stories of American justice on the apocalyptic frontier impact at whom you take aim? We all have a role to play in this American drama, and that means we have the right to reject those stories and practices which dehumanize others.

13 WAYS OF LOOKING AT A GUN

Wallace Stevens's poem "Thirteen Ways of Looking at a Blackbird" is a set of aphorisms. In the eleventh stanza, the blackbird is a distracting illusion startling the passenger until he redirects his focus:

> He rode over Connecticut
> In a glass coach.
> Once, a fear pierced him,
> In that he mistook
> The shadow of his equipage
> For blackbirds.
> (STEVENS 1923/1991)

Wallace Stevens writes of the ways we can shift our focus and see a thing anew. In this stanza, the blackbird disappears as a thing altogether and reappears only as an error in perception. It is with a similar mode of startled redirection that we now focus on guns as things that invite us to blink again for a larger field of view. Many of us think we know what a gun is. But there are at least thirteen ways of looking at a gun and probably many more.

A gun, says professor Jimmy Taylor, "isn't always a gun." Sometimes it is "an antique, a cultural artifact, an aesthetically pleasing sculpture, the memory of loved ones living and deceased, the embodiment of familial pride, and even a god of sorts" (2009, 69). Guns can be lovingly cared for "as if they possess human or even super-human qualities" (93). But guns aren't always positive symbols. Wielding a gun can be a way of saying that one lives in a state of threat and the world is filled with evil. The critical question is what stories a gun owner believes and how he expresses that devotion. The gun is "capable of unleashing awful power," but it is also an object "around which living histories are built and rituals conducted" (142).

Guns are at the center of American culture, as symbolic as apple pie, baseball, and Bibles. Four in ten Americans report they live in a household with a gun, according to a 2023 survey by the Pew Research Center. Six in ten say gun violence is a serious problem in America (Schaeffer 2023). People love guns for backyard target shooting, for hunting, and for their value as historical artifacts. For some, a gun is a family heirloom. The Gun Violence Archive reports that in 2023, over 43,000 people in the United States died from gun violence. In the same year, over 900 children were killed or injured (gunviolencearchive.org). There were 657 mass shootings. For most people who have experienced gun violence, guns represent violence, loss, and grief.

The gun may also be, for those who embrace the cowboy apocalypse, a powerful symbol of how the world *should* be. Even without being fired, the gun is a means of establishing a fixed perimeter, of walling people out, of *refusing* communication. Symbolically, then, the gun is a form of radical, directional flow intended to *prevent* flow of dialogue. It's a material and symbolic reaction against interdependence through the individualization of its own violent authority. It's a movement from the world to the atomized self. Not everyone who owns a gun participates in the symbolism of the cowboy apocalypse. But for those who do, the gun hammers out a violent rejection of global engagement through a form of personalized apocalyptic disruption. When utilized within the cowboy apocalypse, the gun enacts a ritual of refusal. When fired at another person, the gun is a form of speech that kills.

Guns are made for ending things. They are the ultimate means of silencing someone for good. Scholar and activist Roxanne Dunbar-Ortiz says that although "nearly anything, including human hands, may be used to kill, only the gun is created for the specific purpose of killing a living creature" (2018, 15). For the cowboy apocalypticist, the gun is a single-syllable shout through a proxy mouth saying only "no." The gun is a one-keyed typewriter.

In the cowboy apocalypse, the gun is a sacramental object that binds the gun holder to an imagined, imminent future in which violence is the means to a good life. Guns become a ritualized way of asserting dominance, and a means of imagining oneself tasked with saving the world. But there are so many different views about guns and so many ways to use them. The demand to view all gun enthusiasm as the same is a red herring intended to prevent condemnation of those ways of appreciating guns that are deadly.

The world of the gun, says Jimmy Taylor, is "a busy and expressive world" (2009, 30). To begin to view this world, I offer thirteen ways of looking at a gun, an imperfect approach that I nonetheless hope will begin a more nuanced conversation. In this chapter, I draw on numerous, sometimes unrelated, fields of study for making sense of the gun's stubborn centrality in American culture. I begin with terms typically used by gun owners themselves and move to more complex notions that consider the gun within the larger social fabric in which it is placed, symbolically and literally. The overarching presumption of this chapter is that guns are never *just* guns. They are always a layered, symbolic means of expression, part of a larger cultural search for fixed meaning in a destabilizing world.

1. Gun as Tool

Gun owners commonly refer to their guns as tools, separate from their users and with specific neutral, machinic functions. Consider this description of semiautomatic weapons from the *NRA Guide to the Basics of Personal Protection in the Home*:

> The popularity of semi-automatic arms stems from several factors. First, they generally have considerably greater cartridge capacity than revolvers of similar size, allowing more shots to be fired before reloading is necessary. When reloading is required, the semi-automatic can be reloaded with a full magazine much more quickly than a revolver's cylinder can be filled, even with speedloaders. Also, although the initial shot from a typical double-action semi-automatic is fired using a long and heavy trigger pull similar to that of a double-action revolver, each subsequent shot is fired by a short, light, single-action pull, which is generally considered to contribute to accuracy. (*NRA Guide* 2000, 185)

Nothing here is *technically* wrong, but the description is entirely passive. The gun *is* loaded. It *is* fired. Obviously, the writers realize that real people use these weapons. But when viewed as a tool, the gun is *described* in passive, neutral ways, disconnected from the person who fires it.

Some people compare guns to other tools to demonstrate neutrality. Don Burtchin, president of a gun club in Tucson, says a gun is "just a tool like a hammer" and can be used or misused (Kahler 1999, 160). For Carolyn Chute, a political activist, writer, and militia leader in Maine, a gun is like a plow or a canning jar (George 1999, 442). In Jack Schaefer's 1949 novel *Shane*, the namesake character says: "A gun is just a tool. No better and no worse than any other tool, a shovel—or an axe or a saddle or a stove or anything. . . . A gun is as good—and as bad—as the man who carries it" (49).

But tools are designed for specific purposes—and not all tools are the same. A shovel or a stove *could* be used as a weapon. People are more likely to use guns for shooting than for cooking. The NRA guide quoted above says a handgun is "unquestionably the most effective defensive tool available" when someone has invaded your home (*NRA Guide* 2000, vii). A gun *might* be used for purposes like target practice, hunting animals, or even simple enjoyment. There is a reason soldiers carry guns instead of canning jars. "Guns are made to kill, and except for hunting, that usually means killing other humans or oneself" (Dunbar-Ortiz 2018, 175).

Anthropologist Arjun Appadurai's work on the social role of objects is helpful here. Our tendency is "to regard the world of things as inert and mute" (1986, 4). Objects are set in motion and animated by how people talk about them and use them. Appadurai says objects, like persons, have social lives (3). Their meanings "are inscribed in their forms, their uses, [and] their trajectories" (5). When viewed this way, guns are things-in-motion within a specific context. Objects acquire a social history that shapes how they are seen. Guns are tools, but they are not *just* tools.

2. Gun as Deterrent

Guns are often described as deterrents against crime. In nineteenth-century Florida, in the years after land was forcibly taken from Native Americans, the gun was described as the "only obstacle to the butchery" of one's family (quoted in Hosley 1996, 62). The gun is what made the cowboy a "deadly antagonist," not only against Native Americans, but also against "rustlers, bandits, and renegades" (Courtwright 2009, 87). In pioneer contexts, the gun was how people stayed safe in hostile conditions. The history of guns from the Native American perspective would surely look different.

On the frontier, guns were a proxy for law since they "could quickly punish" (Martin 1983, 271). The Colt six-shooter and the Winchester carbine rifle were called "peacemakers" and the Colt was called "Judge Colt and his jury of six" (271). If the legal system was weak, "then an individual simply had to do it alone, with the aid of an iron pistol and fast lead bullets" (275). An editorial in 1852 declared wars could be decreased through the production of more guns, urging science to devote its attention to "the efficiency of warlike implements, so that the people and nations may find stronger inducements than naked moral suasion to lead them towards peace" (Hosley, 52). The abolitionist preacher Henry Ward Beecher saw the gun as having peacemaking abilities, calling the breech-loading rifle more moral than "a hundred Bibles" (Hosley, 52).

Today, we see a similar logic at work in the National Rifle Association's claims that the ideal gun user is a "real-life hero who defends the defenseless" and who "cares deeply about 'American virtues,' particularly American freedom" (Stroud 2016, 15–16). Former executive vice president of the NRA Wayne LaPierre claims the sight of a firearm alone is enough to deter most criminal attacks (LaPierre 2010). Potential criminals, he says, won't attack if they fear their potential victims might be armed. This preemptive reasoning has religious implications. Just as Calvinists could comfort themselves in assurance of salvation by pointing to the material comfort they amassed, so today's gun owners can look at a pile of weapons and see a sign of their own latent heroism. In a nod toward predestination, each bullet is *already* a bad guy taken down. LaPierre's view of the gun as deterrent depends on religiously minded assumptions: that some people are fundamentally bad; that some others are fundamentally good; and that the good people have the ability to recognize the bad ones on sight. LaPierre's reliance on the gun is also evidence of his doubt that God will miraculously intervene in the darkness of human affairs. When faith fades, the gun steps in.

3. Gun as Symbol

Actor Charlton Heston called the gun an extraordinary symbolic tool representing human dignity and liberty. He pointed to the smoking muskets of the ragtag rebels who fought for American independence (Dizard et al. 1999, 202–203). For him and others, guns are the "symbol of what makes this country great" (Davidson 1998, 43). One NRA executive says that to those who love them, guns are "a symbol of freedom" (44). The gun symbolizes American values touted by the Turner thesis and associated with the frontier: masculinity and a sense of empowerment.

Taylor (2009) describes how guns are used in rites of passage for men. A family member passes down a gun to signify the transition to manhood, for example. Guns are tightly linked with male initiation rituals involving tests of fortitude such as wilderness survival (39). Guns can be masculine accessories appealing to men who feel embattled in today's world (13). Jay Mechling (2008) notes the longstanding phallic association, pointing to the common military chant: "This is my rifle, this is my gun, this is for shooting, this is for fun". (198)

Professor of sociology Jennifer Carlson describes the symbolic power of carrying concealed guns. Just having a gun on you is "a way to 'do something' in the face of state inefficacy and to assert oneself as a useful, relevant man willing to protect" (2015, 112). But guns also symbolize the worst horrors of the twenty-first century: the massacres at Sandy Hook, the Pulse nightclub, the Las Vegas concert, and Marjory Stoneman Douglas High School. For some, the gun is a "symbolic reclamation of white, masculine authority, a throwback to a time when 'white' equated to both 'right' and 'might'" (27). The symbolism of the gun is not fixed or universal; instead, it is shaped powerfully by the different experiences of people who live with and around guns.

4. Gun as Totem

According to French sociologist Émile Durkheim, humans define themselves in relation to groups to which they belong. Durkheim (1915) proposes the shared identity of a group can be represented in the form of a totem that sits at the center of a society's religious practices. The totem represents the group's solidarity, its wholeness. For Durkheim, it also represents moral values, which are defined by what is best for the group. His view is overly simplistic, but his notion of the totem has had real staying power, providing insight in recent years to everything from rock stars to baseball. Read as totem, the gun gives owners a sense of belonging and purpose and can be a means by which some readings of history gain sacrosanct status.

Fans of guns are drawn together in live events like shooting competitions or gun shows. The Brady Act of 1986 allowed guns to be sold between individual hobbyists, making gun shows increasingly popular in the years to follow (Violence Policy Center 1996). In 1996, the NRA sponsored its first annual National Gun Collectors Show and Conference in Nashville Tennessee. Today, gun shows take place nearly every weekend of the year. There are close to five thousand gun shows every year in the United States (Schreier 2012). These events offer a "forum for the reaffirmation of traditions" that some Americans believe "embody our hard-won freedoms—freedoms that seem beleaguered to many, whether or not they own guns" (Dizard et al. 1999, 7). Writer Osha Gray Davidson explicitly calls the gun a totem, saying it has the ability of "mystically linking owners to their ancestors, and even more important, to our collective American forefathers"—or at least, linking them to the stories they would *like* to tell (1998, 44).

This pronounced sense of identity helps explain why so many researchers feel they must honor—alongside their subjects—the totem of the gun. Professor of sociology Angela Stroud enrolled in a concealed carry training class despite never having owned a gun before because she "wanted to understand how cultural discourses inform the worldview of people who obtain CHLs [concealed handgun licenses]" (2016, 19). She felt in-depth interviews alone would be insufficient to understand what motivated people to carry concealed weapons. Another researcher reports that "if you actually hold a gun, more of them [research subjects] will talk to you" (quoted in Taylor 2009, 32). Taylor uses a "thick description" style of "characterizing data in motion," getting to know gun owners while shooting alongside them (32).

Sociologist Richard Mitchell took a similar approach, spending time in the backwoods with preppers. One night around the campfire, Mitchell and his compatriots, including Klan members, shared racist stories. They imagined violent solutions to the "queer problem." Mitchell himself, to earn their trust, participated in the storytelling under the light of a flaming cross, though he says he feels awful about it: "If there are researchers who can participate in such business without feeling, I am not one of them nor do I ever hope to be" (1991, 180). Mitchell's troubling account, more than any other, confirms my conviction in taking an approach that doesn't require participation in the totemic activities of racism and gun worship.

Here I take another approach, drawing on religious scholar Robert Orsi's method for approaching religious difference, as described in his book *Between Heaven and Earth* (2005). Orsi studied Catholic piety but found himself concerned when one of his subjects invited him to pray. Orsi doesn't believe in prayer, so engaging in it seemed disingenuous. Besides, he was a researcher. Orsi argues that to respectfully study the faith of others, one does not have to "believe what practitioners believe and do what they do." Instead, we must only "acknowledge the human project, within the framework of different histories and different ways of being in the world." If we take this approach, study "becomes not a matter of taking notes but of comparing them," of observing oneself in relation to the other, whatever they believe (174). This is neither neutral observation nor sympathetic performance of belief. Instead, it is the conscious awareness of difference. To study gun culture, I don't have to shoot guns or even like them. I have a *right* to study them because they so populate the stories we tell about them, and because beliefs about them shape public policy. In this sense, I hope to fulfill Orsi's goal of "respecting one's own culture" while being "attentive to the conscious and unconscious motivations of our inquiries" (175).

5. Gun as Ritual Object

"You would get a far better understanding," Warren Cassidy of the NRA says, "if you approached us as if you were approaching one of the great religions of the world." This might explain why any new gun control measure so easily "takes on the quality of a holy war for firearms owners" (Davidson 1998, 44). For those who view the world as corrupted by evil, guns are ritual objects of purification. Religious studies scholar Brent Plate has said ritual objects can function as fetish objects, that is, "material objects endowed with magical powers that must be treated with proper respect" (2014, 11). Guns seem to fall into this category.

Richard Mitchell's embedding with survivalists induced him to act out end-time scenarios with them in the woods with their guns. For some of these people, survivalism was less about readiness than it was "an encompassing game of make-believe" (1991, 214). Expecting society to collapse soon, they practiced for when the SHTF (shit hits the fan). Indeed, Mitchell says, "when survivalists play out their dystopian creations, they are not far from the powerful imaginative actualizations of sacred performance in archaic culture . . . or millenarian rituals of more modern times" (215). Mitchell's compatriots carried assault rifles, but they had received "mechanical vasectomies" and were "capable of noisy banging but in reality, impotent" (67). The survivalist story they told was placed within expectant "schemes for maximizing personal competence, actualization, and relevance" as they imagined their identity as if on "the cutting edge of . . . the new frontier" (10). Survivalist games like these are "temporary enchantments," in which worlds are "crafted and momentarily admired" (215). Guns—like other religious objects—are "privileged sites for rendering religious worlds present in the movements of bodies in space and time" (Orsi 2005, 74).

The gun, like other ritual objects, is cherished, cleaned, caressed, and cradled. Samuel Colt's guns were produced by machines, but he hired engravers to decorate barrels, grips, and frames and encouraged sellers to buy presentation cases made of exotic woods (Hosley 1996, 68). This craftsmanship was celebrated anew in 2011, when Colt's Manufacturing Company partnered with the NRA to issue a "one-of-a-kind Colt Model 1911 Master Engraved 100th Anniversary Edition" that had over three hundred hours' worth of "hand engraving, authentic ivory grips and 24 karat gold inlays." The NRA Foundation auctioned the gun at their 2011 Annual Meeting, where it sold for $60,000.

Religious people have traditionally looked to physical objects like images, statues, beads, foods, stones, oil, candles, and water as tools with which to materialize the immaterial. Why not guns too? Plate (2014) writes of religious objects that are "put to use in highly symbolic, sacred ways" and have the power to "link us with a world beyond our own skin" (4). Religious objects play a role in the "practice of making the invisible visible, of concretizing the order of the universe." They have the ability to render invisible dynamics "visible and tangible, present to the senses in the circumstances of everyday life" (Orsi 2005, 73–74). Religious objects can "hold the power of [a] holy figure" and "make it present" (49). Guns, as religious objects, have the power to make other worlds tangible.

6. Gun as Souvenir

Writer Susan Stewart says that a souvenir is a kind of "microcosmic thought," an evocative set of memories aroused through the agency of a special object:

> **We might say that this capacity of objects to serve as traces of authentic experience is, in fact, exemplified by the souvenir. . . . We do not need or desire souvenirs of events that are repeatable. Rather we need and desire souvenirs that are reportable, events whose materiality has escaped us, events that thereby exist only through the invention of narrative. (1993, 135)**

The souvenir brings memories to life in the stories we tell about it. So what happens when we think of the gun as souvenir?

The study of dark tourism is a few decades old, though dark tourism itself is not new. Dark tourism is characterized by a fascination with death and atrocity, as people are drawn to physical locations where horrible events occurred. For example, people who tour the Manson house are given a piece of masonry from "the very fireplace that was located right next to the bodies of Tate and Sebring" (Podoshen et al.

2015, 320). We could consider dark souvenirs associated with the murders at Auschwitz. We could even view as souvenirs the body parts that serve as relics enshrined in churches associated with the deaths of famous religious figures.

Not all guns are dark souvenirs, but some are. This way of thinking forces us to consider how guns accrue value, and how they may be used to trigger memories of traumatic events. Think of the gun used to shoot Trayvon Martin as a dark souvenir. In 2012, George Zimmerman killed the unarmed Black teenager in a Florida suburb with a 9 mm handgun and was eventually acquitted of murder charges. In 2016, Zimmerman advertised the sale of his gun by telling bidders: "I am honored and humbled to announce the sale of an American Firearm Icon. The firearm for sale is the firearm that was used to defend my life and end the brutal attack from Trayvon Martin on 2/26/2012" (Varandani 2016). A gun of this type is typically worth only a few hundred dollars. Zimmerman received over $100,000 for it (Vasilogambros 2016). What made the gun special was its souvenir status, specifically the way it offered tangible evidence of Zimmerman's story of heroism and survival.

For Stewart (1993), the souvenir is always partial because it can never fully recreate the experience to which it alludes. It remains "impoverished" but is "supplemented by a narrative discourse ... which articulates the play of desire" (136). Zimmerman's gun evokes the narrative of Zimmerman's "attack." The narrative provides context for the object, evoking a disturbing nostalgia that in this case can only be read as viciously racist. Zimmerman's gun will be parsed differently by white supremacists and Black Americans. One of these groups seems more likely to value the gun as a souvenir, and to pay for the right to step into its story.

An increasing interest in dark sites reflects an increased insecurity about death and is encouraged by "the globalized, sensationalized, media-driven environment we are in" (Podoshen et al. 2015, 316). Memorial objects, explanatory plaques, or other markers have sprung up at the sites of mass shootings, inviting dark tourists to get a "simulation-oriented dark tourism experience" as they imagine themselves in these violent spaces (320). Sites of extreme loss can evoke negative emotions like "distress, horror, fear, anger, anguish, grief, guilt and shame" (Isaac 2015, 329). To view the gun as souvenir is to ask how the gun's identity shapes the way people think about it and the stories they tell.

7. Gun as Toy

Professor of American studies Jay Mechling says the Daisy BB gun he owned as a child stirred in him a desire for real guns, which seemed like "powerful talismans, something always just outside [his] reach" (2008, 192). Like a souvenir, a toy gun physically embodies a larger narrative, but the story evoked is usually imaginary. A toy, says Susan Stewart, is a device for fantasy, a point of beginning for narrative. A toy "opens an interior world, lending itself to fantasy and privacy in a way that the abstract space, the playground, of social play does not" (1993, 56). To "toy" with something is to "manipulate it, to try it out within sets of contexts, none of which is determinative" (56). Toys are for experimentation, for imagining what is possible.

Mechling says we should not worry about children playing with guns because they shoot at each other "in a play frame" (2008, 204). He extends this interpretation to adults playing with guns in paintball games or war reenactments (203–204). For Mechling, children know they are playing and can distinguish that experience from actual violence. Playing with guns isn't practicing violence, he says; it's fun.

But things aren't quite so simple. Think, for example, of the recent active shooter drills at an elementary school in Indiana. The Indiana State Teachers Association reports that during the active shooter drill, "four teachers at a time were taken into a room, told to crouch down and were shot execution style with some sort of projectiles—resulting in injuries to the extent that welts appeared, and blood was drawn" (Indiana State Teachers Association 2019). The weapon used was a toy: an airsoft gun, the fully automatic Rival Nemesis, capable of shooting foam balls at seventy miles per hour. Mechling's presumption of a "play frame" doesn't really work here. While it's true participants knew this was a drill, and while nobody was badly hurt, this occupies a space somewhere between obvious play and something more serious. Not all "play" is fun, and not all "frames" are fixed.

Toy guns are modeled on the real thing, and by design invite a kind of play that points toward the real thing. Even though they don't shoot real bullets, toy guns can be as symbolic, as totemic, and as ritually powerful as real guns. When toy guns are used to evoke the experiences of mass shootings, they gesture toward the real, no matter how brightly colored the plastic barrel might be.

8. Gun as Person

In the early nineteenth century, sailors on frigates named their cannons. A historian writing in 1817 about the USS *Chesapeake* says the guns had names like Raging Eagle, Viper, or Mad Anthony "engraven on small squares of copper-plate" (William James, quoted in USS Constitution Museum 2014). On the frigate USS *President*, the cannons were also named, with Bibles affixed to them. One Bible says in a flyleaf: "every gun of the . . . Frigate was named after some general or patriot of the United States" (USS Constitution Museum, 2014). Affixing Bibles to cannons associates firepower with divine will, a practice imitated on AR-15 discussion forums when gun owners say they name their weapons things like Deterrence, Doombringer, or Breath of God.

Guns are personified as loyal companions. An 1857 broadside advertising Colt's guns describes his weapons as "easily taken care of . . . Treat them well, and they will treat your enemies badly." The gun will serve its owner faithfully: "If you buy a Colt's Rifle or Pistol, you feel certain that you have one true friend, with six hearts in his body, and who can always be relied upon" (Hosley 1996, 67). Daniel Boone named his rifle Tick Licker for its accuracy. Davy Crockett is said to have named all his rifles Betsy.

Other people also give their guns female names. One gun owner calls his gun Marge "because she's just like a slightly disgruntled housewife—kinda sexy and edgy, yet always by your side." If you "set her off," though, she "has one heck of a bark" (Reich 2011). Another named his gun "Sarah McGlocklan because she'll put a hater in the arms of an angel" (Trevor 2015). Commitment to one's gun resembles commitment to one's lover. Rifle owner Mark Olis says: "I call my Remington 11–87 Special Purpose . . . Black Death . . . It has killed every turkey I've ever taken . . . I love that thing" (Reich 2011).

The practice of giving guns agency through personification sits in stark tension with the claim that "guns don't kill people" because they *have* no agency. If Mark's gun kills turkeys all by itself, what does Mark do? The claim that guns act violently all by themselves, like the claim that people act violently all by themselves, is too simple. It actually *matters* what kind of weapon a person is holding, just as it matters *why* that person holds the weapon.

9. Gun as Network

French philosopher Jean Baudrillard remarked in 1968 that industrialization had produced such a proliferation of new objects that "we lack the vocabulary to name them all" (1996, 3). There are almost as many criteria of classification as there are objects themselves (3–4). Firearms are mass-produced, with ever increasing efficiency in design. But today's guns are nothing like the ones used by colonial settlers. The first revolvers, rifles, and cannons have more in common with a spitball and straw than they do with today's semiautomatic rifles. If we trace the history, we find the term "gun" is less an objective label than a trail of desire from those first clumsy rifles to the AR-15s of today.

French anthropologist Bruno Latour says "things do not exist without being full of people, and the more modern and complicated they are, the more people swarm through them" (2000, 10). Objects are networked, in that they are made of many vectors of experience, materiality, desire, and usage. Latour says if we want to understand an object, we must consider as many of these vectors as we can. He uses the example of a projector, which we consider as a single thing until it breaks. Then we notice that it consists of dozens of parts, acting as one thing. Once repaired, the projector is again an assembly of lightbulb, lens, screws, and power supply that share a destiny as one thing.

Latour similarly considers a key in a door. A key mediates between a person and a lock, which itself sits within a door that blocks that person from where they want to go. The key might open the door, but only if the person knows how to operate it, and when or where to use it. Latour knew that people bring *themselves* to objects as they use them. People alter things, caress them, break them, repurpose them, and so on. Things are never just things; they're networks that include their users.

In one essay, Latour speaks explicitly about guns as social objects, refusing simplistic claims on gun control. One group, he says, instrumentalizes the gun at the expense of the person: "Guns kill people!" The other group instrumentalizes the person at the expense of the gun: "Guns don't kill. People do!" According to Latour, each gun is tightly networked with the world around it. We can't only blame the gun, since it is clearly held by a human who must choose to shoot it. Nor can we only blame the human, because it matters if that human is holding a gun or not and it matters if that human is filled with rage, sorrow, or gratitude. Instead, we should think of the gun and the person holding it as a sort of hybrid unit, a network of sorts (Latour 1999).

Latour's writing on pipettes is also helpful in understanding guns (1994). He considers two kinds of pipettes in a lab, one type that requires precision and an automated one. The second pipette is "itself skilled," and levels the playing field for people using it. Latour calls this process the "socialization of nonhumans," in which inanimate objects are pulled into the human stream, creating hybrid actors (53). If we apply this "socialization" to the analysis of guns, the gun and the person holding it should be viewed as *one networked thing*. Only when placed within the hands of someone wishing to fire it does a gun-human hybrid become an operational machine.

The distribution of skill matters, too. A rifle that must be reloaded frequently interacts with its human partner differently than an AR-15 that shoots whole rounds without pausing. It really *does* matter who is holding a gun and why. And it really *does* matter if someone is holding a machine gun or a spoon. A gun is a network of a million moments, of numerous human bodies, of designers and workers, and of course the desires of the person who might shoot it. Guns are comprised of components that, only when partnered together, can perform the function for which they were designed.

10. Gun as Computer Program

Some guns exist only in virtual spaces. Virtual guns are not as threatening as real guns, for the simple reason that they can't shoot real bullets. A virtual gun is a copy without an original. Virtual shooting does not indicate that any material damage has been done, but simply that a particular kind of interface has taken place between the embodied player and the images onscreen. Military activities may involve virtual guns that shoot real bullets (drones with virtual counterparts, for example). But their ability to shoot real ammunition renders them actually not virtual at all.

Virtual guns are merely images that move in exciting ways. The most a virtual gun *might* do is encourage certain habits of mind in the player and *maybe* instigate a desire for real-life shooting. But hefting a real gun is not the same as shooting a virtual one:

> **When one swings a real weapon, the weight and length is easily felt by body schema processes, and if one hits something with the weapon as a consequence of a full swing, the impact can be literally stunning for the somatosensory system and muscles and joints. . . . All of these crucial sensory inputs will be missing from the [bodily action of a videogame player] . . . in physical space. (Gregersen and Grodal 2009, 76)**

Videogames scholar Victor Navarro describes the doubling of the human body in a videogame, in which the avatar invites identification (2012, 63). The virtual body's actions are experienced as authentic because the player uses his real body to express what he wants his virtual body to do. But this action is not a perfect parallel. To shoot a virtual gun, the player mashes buttons or pulls a plastic trigger or clicks a mouse and the virtual gun responds with a visual blast. The screen remains between the embodied actor and his virtually mirrored correspondents. Shooter videogame guns are as much about *absence* as they are about presence. Virtual bullets have no material manifestation whatsoever in the player's living room.

And yet to play a videogame is to become, in a sense, a virtual gun. The virtual body and the virtual gun become one object, controlled by the real-life player. Rather than just watching the avatar shoot, the player is "embodied by the shooting mechanic and the point-of-view" (65). While functionally melded with the gun, the player navigates a series of experiences that require shooting the gun repeatedly. The game becomes a "routinized, ceaseless hunt with violence an inevitable endpoint" (Rehak 2003, 118). This violence, though, is never completed because avatars die and return and games are replayed. So while virtual guns can't shoot anyone, first-person shooter games place the gun at their symbolic center and require repeated imagination of gun violence. To what extent such habits of imaginative experience may shape real-life choices is one of the most difficult and most important questions we can ask.

Another way of thinking about guns as computer programs is to look at guns that can be "printed" using a material printer. In 2012, Cody Wilson formed Defense Distributed, an "open-source gunsmith organization," and he released plans for the Liberator, a 3D-printable gun made of thermoplastic with a metal firing pin. The plans were downloaded over a hundred thousand times in the weeks after their release. Federal authorities temporarily forced the company to stop sharing the plans. Most plans are for pistols, but Defense Distributed also released parts for a semiautomatic weapon (All3dp.com). In addition, Wilson made available plans for printing a machine called the Ghost Gunner, a home-based desktop milling machine that can create the aluminum frame of the M1911, a popular handgun.

Defense Distributed has defended their right to release the plans online by pointing to the constitutional right to freedom of speech. The case was settled in 2018, resulting in the plans again being distributed freely online. Is sharing plans for gun printing online a form of free speech? Is printing the material gun a mode of free speech? What about *shooting* the "printed" gun? Which of these is "speech"? How do we know?

11. Gun as Prop

The study of props and fandom looks at how people materialize aspects of otherworldly spaces. Props are characterized by a desire to render the mediated as material. For media professor Matt Hills, props convey a sense of boundary crossing. Hills (2014) uses quasi-religious language when he refers to prop building as "framing immateriality." Once incarnated, a prop occupies "an interspace between materiality and what might be termed *soul*." The prop sits at the junction between fictional and real, making the nonmaterial material.

Industry-crafted memorabilia offer a way of imagining entry into a desired fictional space. Communication scholar Ian Peters (2014) looks at "feelies," factory-produced objects marketed for collectors. Feelies, Peters says, are "media paratexts" that are "both extensions of and separate from the games or worlds that inspired them." An artifact feely is a life-size reproduction of "objects from within the game space." Players hold the object "in the physical realm exactly as a character in the virtual realm can." Feelies work like ritual objects that simultaneously exist in this world and a world beyond.

Media professor Lincoln Geraghty considers prop reverence a kind of nostalgia, as fans "collect, salvage and reclaim from the past" (2014, 3). Nostalgia, in this sense, is about "creating a reflexive and tangible identity in the present" by identifying with the past (4). Replica guns, based on those used by characters in films, fall into this category. Players who handle a replica may experience a sense of "spatial and temporal proximity" with the film or videogame from which it comes. A prop can acquire a pseudo-authentic layer that makes it seem *more* real than its virtual counterpart because of its passage from virtual to material space (Peters 2014).

Prop fandom might include reenactments of Civil War battles using replica guns, or fans who dress in furs to imagine themselves living on the frontier. Taylor (2009) has extensively studied "cowboy clubs," interviewing gun owners and exploring their commitment to role-play experiences (35). To use guns as props can be viewed as a performance of desire for entry into an idealized frontier past or a post-apocalyptic future. Props facilitate ontological bridging between everyday life and an imagined beyond, allowing the fan to hold material evidence of a desired world in their hands. For believers, the gun binds *now* with *then*, the undesirable present with a wished-for future. Orsi (2005) says sacred souvenirs "stand for otherwise inaccessible places, times, experiences" (59). Ritual objects promise contact with a greater reality by offering themselves up for immediate touch. They incite a sense of yearning.

Cultural anthropologist Birgit Meyer invites us to think about media as material invitations to a "beyond conventionally referred to as spirits, gods, demons, ghosts, or God" (2020). Meyer proposes otherworldly realms are *made* real by active engagement with media that we believe can access those spaces. Meyer refers to images that "re-present" and thereby also "render present—what is invisible and absent through a performative act" (Meyer 2015, 334). Religious seeing is mediation that makes the space to which a "sensational form" or prop points seem real. To interact with sensational forms is not merely to *receive* information from an otherworldly space—but also to be invited to participate in translating the invisible into the visible as the sensational form is activated (346). Types of mediating sensational forms can include bones, plants, and statues; but also texts, images, films, and even—as I suggest here—guns.

12. Gun as Sacrament

When I say guns can function sacramentally, I don't mean anything explicitly Christian by it, except that Christianity offers a functional model for the kind of world-bridging at work with the gun in the cowboy apocalypse. For believers, the sacrament of the Eucharist is two things at once: bread and body. And it exists in two places: on earth and in heaven. The gun can function sacramentally in this way, as something that is both *here* and *now*, but which points to a desirable *there* and *then*.

Drawing on Catholic belief in transubstantiation, Robert Orsi looks at how objects are recruited to describe the intersection of this world and a heavenly one. Presence is when "the transcendent [breaks] into time," when the "particularity of here" meets the "beyond-all-places" of *there* (2005, 51). When the sacred takes material form in the sacrament, it can be "negotiated and bargained with, touched and kissed, made to bear human anger and disappointment" (74). Orsi says the notion of presence is hard to appreciate since "modern prohibitions" against presence are all around us (2016, 43). Today, people are less likely to see objects as sacraments, resisting supernatural implications. This dearth of presence, Orsi suggests, has "generated an enduring and intense longing for it" (43). What makes sacraments desirable is the promise of contact with a greater reality. Props also have this quality, as we have seen. What would it mean to view the sacrament as a kind of prop? What does it mean to view a prop as a kind of sacrament?

More pointedly, what does it mean to think of guns in terms of "presence"? If sacred objects communicate the presence of something beyond the material world, then to think of the gun sacramentally is to see it as a link between here and a world beyond. The gun can become what Orsi calls a "capillary of presence," binding the unbearable present with a wished-for future: "Our short lives acquire not only purpose but also grandeur and drama when they are set against the horizon of sacred history, the story that goes from the origins of the world to its end" (204). As disturbing as it may be to think this way, guns can function sacramentally for those who see them as tangible authentication. This is a hegemonic fantasy with teeth.

13. Guns as Media

The gun is a mode of mediation in its own right. It is a perfect material instantiation of what scholars Galloway, Thacker, and Wark (2013) call "excommunication." In religious contexts, excommunication consists of the exile of a member of the community. The excommunicant is forbidden further contact and "considered dead" to others (15). Galloway, Thacker, and Wark appropriate the religious term "excommunication" for their own theory of how people accomplish the intentional exclusion of others—that is, how they communicate a refusal to communicate. What happens when communication fails—when messages get garbled, remain undelivered, or when mediation is intentionally shut down? (10). They call this phenomenon "excommunication" and examine some of its most compelling forms:

> At the center of excommunication is a paradoxical antimessage, a message that cannot be enunciated, a message that is anathema, heretical, and unorthodox, but for this very reason a message that has already been enunciated, asserted, and distributed. Excommunicants become this paradoxical antimessage themselves, their very material existence nothing but a residual indicator of the message. . . . [E]xcommunication is the communication of "no longer communicating," the silence of "nothing more to say." (16)

There are forms of communication that are themselves *rejections* of communication. The people who are rejected become symbols of rejection themselves. Excommunication is *intended* to disrupt, to reject, to push away. It is the fantasy of an absolute end.

If we think about guns as mediation, then we can think of bullets as one-syllable rejections. Each bullet is a big, fat, violent, explosive "No." Excommunication is "a singular communication, both unilateral and unidirectional, a communication which ultimately aims for its own negation. All that remains is the last word, the final utterance, the penultimate gesture" (16). That certainly sounds like a bullet to me. Excommunication renders communication impossible. Excommunication is apocalyptic. The bullet, as excommunication, is "a message for the ending of all messages" (12).

The bullet, we could say, performs a kind of intimate, bracing touch between sender and receiver, at the exact same time as it enacts a violent, radical separation. When a gun is used by one human who shoots another human, it communicates via violent explosion within the body of the recipient, simultaneously beginning and ending an intimate encounter. The bullet is the material residue of a failed encounter—that, paradoxically, succeeds by silencing the other.

The gun as excommunication is an attempt to shut out a world that is too noisy, too complicated, too dangerous. The message delivered is meant to end messaging itself. In a mode that mimics a bunker mentality, the gun becomes a mobile perimeter, a chamber within which one hides, surrounded by the scent of death. In this sense, the gun speaks *without* being fired by promising excommunication. Guns don't need silencers to silence. For the cowboy messiah, every gun is a little god, every bullet a tiny apocalypse.

* * *

The cowboy apocalypse's preoccupation with judgment suggests how some gun owners anchor themselves in American Protestantism. According to the American Calvinist racist mode of predestination, people can't change or reform, because some people are bad from birth. Once you've committed a crime, the reasoning goes, you have revealed yourself for what you *are*, tarnished for life. It's the reason why people can't get jobs after they have been incarcerated, why they can't get social support, why they end up homeless and rejected, why people judge them the moment they meet them—forever. This is one of the most damaging things about this warped version of predestination. It presumes not that people *do* good or bad things, but that people *are* good or bad. Before we were even born, God *already* decided who would be saved or damned. The notion of absolute good and evil is key in both this corruption of Calvinist predestination and in the cowboy apocalypse. Both transfer the right of determining who is good or evil from God to self-appointed human judges.

In racist modes of predestination, some people are born in God's good light, and any wrong they do is an opportunity for learning on the way to God's kingdom. When presumptively good people screw up—no matter how horrendously—they privately tell God (not the victim) they are sorry. When good people err, they assume they are *already* forgiven because they were born *already* chosen. Indeed, their wealth and their whiteness can be viewed as indications of their blessedness. Any mistake is dwarfed by the overwhelming presumptive glory of God's elect. This is why white men from good families with good futures can be excused for appalling crimes. Good isn't a placeholder here or even a mealymouthed expression of potential. It's theological. This is the same fate-driven logic that posits the winner of a duel must have been intended by God to live, while his enemy, presumed guilty, dies.

If a nonprivileged person makes a mistake (say, a Black man), the racist doctrine of predestination says the mistake is proof of what the man *was* all along: damned by God before he was born. It's not hard to see the contemptuous racism here. The good (white) people who judge the Black man for his mistake can pat themselves on the back for outing a spiritual enemy and keeping him away from their children, their neighborhoods, their pretty streets. *That man* doesn't deserve food stamps; he committed a crime. *That man* doesn't deserve a job after serving time—he's bad.

Racism can be so deeply ingrained in predestination that some (usually white) people believe they can—or *should*—presume a Black or Brown person is evil. This is when things like false accusations and preemptive attacks against innocent people like Eric Garner can occur. It's how boys like Trayvon Martin get shot for walking on the street. It's also how would-be immigrants get labeled hoodlums, or criminals, or diseased, simply because they show up at the border homeless. If God loved the poor, says the racist version of predestination, they wouldn't need help from other human beings because God would take care of them. Predestination in racist form gives privileged people the self-authenticated right to determine the worth of others, and to assess them unkindly—then, sometimes, to act violently.

The "stand your ground" gun laws in America establish how someone can defend themselves by shooting another person, even if that other person is unarmed. If the person holding the weapon perceives a threat, he can shoot, no matter where he is—at home, in a parking lot, at a shop, anywhere guns aren't already banned. Twenty-seven states have "stand your ground" laws on the books. These laws are terrifying when read through the lens of racist predestination. Someone in this mindset *already* reads the situation theologically before anyone else even shows up. He *already* sees himself as a good-guy agent of God who—given the chance—will exercise his theological duty against the bad guy. Many American gun owners are not fueled by such odious presumptions of racist theology. But for the glorified "good guy with a gun" fueled by apocalypticism and beliefs in predestination, to shoot is to be righteous.

This mode of warped Calvinism shares an absolutist perspective on good and evil with apocalypticism. To apocalyptically minded people, "there is no 'chance,' no gray zones of suspended meaning" (Landes 2005, 33). Things are carefully measured, grounded in the certainty of unquestioned belief. Apocalypses maintain a focus on the rigidity of "the dualistic struggle between good and evil and on the [expected] destruction of all that is cherished" (Newsom 2016, xi). For those who believe the Constitution (especially the Second Amendment) is sacred writ, Americans have a God-given duty to fight tyranny. But who decides what constitutes tyranny?

In her work on the adaptation of stories, Linda Hutcheon (2012) describes three ways a core story might be adapted and remediated. In the first, the telling mode, a story is written or recited, and the listener can do nothing to change it. In the "showing mode," the viewer is immersed visually and aurally, but again, cannot change the story. In the "participatory mode," the participant engages with a story both "physically and kinesthetically," but nonetheless recognizes the story as a fiction. I want here to add a fourth mode, what I call the "belief mode." For those who believe the cowboy apocalypse, it is richly immersive, to the point of seeming real. To believe is to use one's gun to transform the present world into the future. In this mode of adaptation, stories come to life. The more chaotic the world seems, the more seductive such a story will be. The cowboy apocalypse—and the gun as its central prop—can offer material authentication of a desired white supremacist future. Shooting the gun becomes proof of its intentional design.

We all participate in gun culture whether we play violent videogames or not, whether we watch movies or not, whether we own guns or not. We've been told a lie when people say we have no stake in the gun debate if we don't own weapons. Because guns can do such massive damage, because there are millions of guns strapped to Americans' bodies, and because the story of the cowboy apocalypse has so saturated our media, we all have a stake. Gun culture is *American* culture. I return again to Wallace Stevens's poem, to the apocalyptic undercurrents of the third stanza, which places the blackbird in the context of inevitable change and movements much larger than itself. The gun, like the blackbird, is part of a larger story about who we are and where we are going. To return to Stevens's metaphor for context:

> **The blackbird whirled in the autumn winds.**
> **It was a small part of the pantomime.**
> (STEVENS 1923/1991)

THE BONES

COWBOY APOCALYPSE AS STORY

In fourth grade, I read *Annie Oakley: Little Sure Shot* (Wilson 1958). The rifle in the book was, to me, a symbol of the power Annie took for herself. Like me, Annie performed the women's work of cleaning, then would go get dirty outside. Annie was resourceful, setting quail traps she designed from corn stalks. Nine-year-old Annie had no problem taking the gun down and cleaning it by herself. She took pelts to the local furrier and told the men stories. I wrote my book report in 1981, when Ronald Reagan had defeated Jimmy Carter and the NRA was thrilled. Evangelical Christians were becoming more politically engaged. Racial tensions were high, but not in white Christian Arkansas where the only Black person I met left after two days. I did not know then that the Equal Rights Amendment was being killed. I didn't know who Phyllis Schlafly was. But I knew girls cleaned house and boys mowed grass. My father helped me make an Annie Oakley puppet for school, and I felt no compulsion to make her a toy rifle. It wasn't Annie's gun that thrilled me. I wanted to make Annie *herself* real in me, to make my own decisions and use my voice. By fourth grade, I decided I would leave Arkansas as soon as I was able.

* * *

Storytelling has an apocalyptic whiff to it. Stories narrow the mess of life into *these* characters, *these* events, *these* experiences. And they promise an ending. For those who find the world intolerable, impending catastrophe may be what they need. Novels are apocalyptic because they have beginnings, middles, and ends (Kermode 2000, 138). The material nature of a book implies its completeness. But apocalyptic books are doubly apocalyptic: in the printed format of their storytelling and in their commitment to a world beyond the text.

To engage with a printed book is to touch it, smell it, manipulate it physically. Books are *things*. To access the world of a book, we must engage with paper, ink, or pixels. The materiality of books renders the textual representation of material objects within them subsidiary. You can't shoot a textual gun. But you can read about someone *else* shooting, and you can imagine yourself *as* the shooter. The distance between a real weapon and a textual version may heighten the desire for the real thing. *The Turner Diaries* inspired Timothy McVeigh, who turned textual violence into real violence at the Oklahoma City bombing. As first-century Jewish and Christian apocalyptic writers gave themselves starring roles in their own tales about the end of the world, so today's cowboy messiahs put themselves into the story they want to live for real.

Apocalypses toggle nervously between the present and the hoped-for future. They are "ruptures, pivots, fulcrums separating what came before from what came after" (Berger 1999, 5). Apocalypses leap to aftermaths as storytellers imagine what *could* happen in the future, what they would *like* to be ruptured. We put our world into the plot so current troubles can be imagined as ending. In telling apocalyptic stories, we plot "what we most want and most abhor" (Berger, 11). To tell an apocalyptic story is to perform a ritual of expectation and desire.

In this chapter, I consider a selection of books that *pre*-enact the end times. By tracing key plot elements all the way back to stories told in the horrific years after the Civil War and moving into and beyond the twentieth century, the cowboy apocalypse emerges as a recognizable narrative.

* * *

While the cowboy apocalypse is not fully formed until the twenty-first century, one of its primary predecessors, the Western novel, shows up soon after the rotary steam press was patented in 1845. Within two decades, mass publishing allowed the dime novel to flourish with Westerns as one of its most popular forms (Murdoch 2001, 35). As the Civil War ended, the myth of the heroic cowboy took shape. The cowboy myth taught about a time when: "right and wrong, good and evil, were reduced to elemental simplicities" (3).

In the years after the Civil War, the ideology of the Lost Cause emerged, with its quasi-apocalyptic and resentful refrains grounded in racist appropriations of Christian theology. Using the narrative of the resurrection, Lost Cause proponents hoped white supremacy would, like Jesus, rise in the South again. Lost Cause theology is not overt in mainstream white churches today, but it survives in the individualist theology unconcerned with—and even hostile to—the causes of social justice (Jones 2020, 105). It lives on in underground racist screeds, neo-Confederate culture, and in transmediated forms of the cowboy apocalypse.

Western novelist Owen Wister (1860–1938) wrote about the cowboy as a descendant of Anglo-Saxon knights. Wister blends cowboy nobility with themes of urban unrest, racism, and immigration in an essay called "The Evolution of the Cow Puncher":

> **No rood of modern ground is more debased and mongrel [than America] with its hordes of encroaching alien vermin, that turn our cities to Babels and our citizenship to a hybrid farce, who degrade our Commonwealth from a nation into something half pawn shop, half brokers office. But to survive in the clean cattle country requires spirit of adventure, courage, and self-sufficiency; you will not find many Poles or Huns or Russian Jews in that district. . . . The Frenchman today is seen at his best inside a house. . . . The Italian has forgotten Columbus, and sells fruit. . . . But the Anglo-Saxon is still forever homesick for out-of-doors. (1895, 604)**

To be a cowboy, in Wister's sense, is to own one's place in society as a white man. The explicit racism in Wister's view has been replaced by a sense of mastery, individualism, and manliness that, while depicted as white, does not call attention to that fact. The white cowboy today, in shows like *The Walking Dead* and *Doomsday Preppers*, may expect city dwellers to descend on his rural compound demanding supplies, but his scorn for urban immigrants is couched behind fictional contempt for zombies or condescension toward activism.

In the decades after the Civil War a new kind of Christian apocalypticism appeared. John Nelson Darby (1800–1882), an American Bible teacher, believed time was divided into periods called dispensations. Our current dispensation (the "age of the Church") will end in the

Tribulation, a seven-year period based on Darby's idiosyncratic interpretations of Revelation. The Tribulation will be a time of violence and deprivation, especially for those who have not found Christ. After the Tribulation, Christ will return and defeat the Antichrist. The millennium, the rule of Christ on earth, will ensue.

Whereas post-millennialism is generally optimistic about humanity's future, Darby's premillennialism presumes human depravity. Premillennialism places humanity in a time of sin and despair, dependent on the Second Coming of Christ for justice. Christians wait and pray for individual salvation, seeing the earth as a wasteland. *The Scofield Reference Bible*, published by a Confederate war veteran in 1909, popularized this view, as did later popular Christian novels like Pat Robertson's *The End of the Age* (1995) and the *Left Behind* novels (1994–2007) by Tim LaHaye and Jerry Jenkins. We can see narrative elements of what becomes the cowboy apocalypse in Southern racist literature in the early twentieth century. This presumption of evil informs expectation of ongoing violence by gun rights activists today.

The Clansman (1905)

Thomas Dixon's *The Clansman* was the book on which D. W. Griffith's film *Birth of a Nation* was based. Dixon claims it is a true story about the Ku Klux Klan (KKK), to correct the erroneous stories told by Northerners hostile to the South. Dixon begins by presenting the Klan as playing a messianic role in the apocalypticism of Reconstruction:

> In the darkest hour of the life of the South, when her wounded people lay helpless amid rags and ashes under the beak and talon of the Vulture, suddenly from the mists of the mountains appeared a white cloud the size of a man's hand. It grew until its mantle of mystery enfolded the stricken earth and sky. An "Invisible Empire" had risen from the field of Death and challenged the Visible to mortal combat. (Dixon 1905, iii)

The "Invisible Empire" of the KKK was, for Dixon, a force of light in a dark world. It is an apocalyptic force of judgment as white men meted out justice against their enemies.

The book takes place in the years immediately following the Civil War. It leans on the relationship between Elsie, a Northerner, and Ben, her Confederate love interest. Elsie learns that Ben is a racist but has his reasons. Elsie relaxes her objections to slavery when Ben, grinning, reminds her that her own grandfather was a slave owner—as if the only reason to object to slavery is a sense of moral superiority (106). Ben reminds Elsie that the "cargo of benighted heathen" benefited from slavery by getting to hear the gospel (107).

The South is devastated by war—but blame is placed on mobs of freed slaves who, despite the gentility of their former owners, refuse to live quietly. They burn hotels, rape women, and terrorize the townspeople (160). When a Black man rapes one of the women in the town, she kills herself from shame. Ben and his companions put on white sheets and hunt the man down. Like "Knights of the Middle Ages," they gag him, bind him, take him to a trial in the woods, and execute him (268). Elsie and Ben's relationship flourishes when she learns Ben is a Grand Dragon in the Ku Klux Klan (280).

The racist depictions in the book take my breath away. In language prefiguring contemporary fears about immigration, Black people are described as "an alien, inferior race" (46). Gangs, Dixon says, parade the streets at night firing their guns (132). "Swarms" of dangerous people descend on the Capitol, rioting, with the aim of overthrowing the government (141). A "mob" raises hell in the gallery (146). Freed slaves are described as backward, dangerous, dirty, and malicious. The "Black hordes" are armed with rifles and threaten their former masters (242). The "race of pioneer white freemen" fight back for freedom (244). Frontier mythology meets rank racism in a proto-apocalyptic hue. The depictions anticipate those of zombies in the contemporary cowboy apocalypse.

The Ku Klux Klan or Invisible Empire (1914)

A few years after *The Clansman* was published, the Daughters of the Confederacy published a textbook for children with similar themes. The book claims to be the first written history of the Klan, intended for schools throughout the South.

In the aftermath of the Civil War, the devastation is again described as apocalyptic:

> Business destroyed, farms gone to wreck, homes laid waste, many of the returning soldiers disabled and broken in health. There was a track of desolation and devastation, without a parallel in history, estimated fully five miles wide, from the Tennessee line through Georgia to Savannah, through South Carolina, by Columbia, to North Carolina, and the desolation in the valley of Virginia, if possible, was greater. (Rose 1914, 14)

White landowners had their private property seized by the government. Angry about federal penalties for Confederate soldiers, the author complains that white men of the South "were not allowed to vote or carry firearms, and no indignity was too great to be offered them" (17). Ruled by "brutish despots," they saw no choice but to engage in violence.

The Ku Klux Klan, according to the textbook, kept rambunctious former slaves in line as a public service: "they made the negroes believe that they were the ghosts of their dead masters, and under the conviction that if they did wrong, spirits from the other world would visit them; the negroes became very quiet and subdued" (19). This was done to protect the weak, they claim, especially the women of the South.

> The Ku Klux would visit a negro who had been guilty of wrongdoing, and who had been repeatedly warned to conduct himself in the proper manner, they would carry him out to give him a severe whipping as a punishment, and in order to scare him into behaving himself, and the negro would make an attack on the Ku Klux, who were then forced to kill him in self-defense. (28)

White men in the South have "the purest and best blood of the ages" and want only to "protect the weak, the innocent, and the defenseless, from the indignities, wrongs and outrageous, of the lawless, the violent and the brutal, to relieve the injured and oppressed" (38). White supremacy is front and center in texts like this, blended with a God-sanctioned savior figure. The men of the Klan are proto-cowboy messiahs, a "star of hope" that "gleams again through the dark clouds." They conceal pistols underneath white robes.

The John Franklin Letters (1959)

One of the first books distributed by the conservative John Birch Society was *The John Franklin Letters*. The book is filled with racism and suspicion about government programs that support the poor, who the narrator says are lazy and entitled (10). Most people who get government relief are Black and Puerto Rican and almost all "cause trouble" (18). The narrator considers apocalyptic collapse a solution:

> [I]t's hopeless; we need a fresh start. You can't tell the relatives of an honest man who's been stabbed to death by Negro or Puerto Rican hoodlums, or who has had the life kicked out of him by a juvenile thug too soon released from jail that "social engineering still has problems to solve." It will never solve any problems, because it will never face them. (19)

The author sees himself fomenting revolution. The racism is stunning and prefigures the anti-urbanism and justifications for violence we see in the cowboy apocalypse today:

> Always in all great cities there is at the bottom of society a savage, vile mob which breaks out to rape, murder and loot. . . . [D]uring the civil war draft riots, policemen were literally torn to pieces by subhuman savages on the streets of New York. After the Chicago Fire and the San Francisco earthquake, creatures of this sort came out of their dens to kill and steal. But . . . the collective might of the law-abiding majority soon ended the murderous disorder. That has always been the way of the civilized community with the mob. (20)

Here we see key narrative elements of the cowboy apocalypse in place: denigration of city life, fear of a mob, expectation of looting and mayhem, and the presumption of self-appointed heroes who bring order via righteous violence. The dollar's value plummets and food riots begin, but those in rural areas with chickens, cows, and gardens will do alright. Chaos is unavoidable because:

> [T]he process of eroding American liberties and sovereignty has gone so far that it cannot be reversed. We are going to have to live through a period of what might be called exile in our own land. And so, we are now setting up the underground organization of American patriots which will be the resistance movement to the alien government–miscalled a world government—which almost certainly will take over the United States within a few years. If we can't throw it off we will die fighting it. (86)

Patriots are suspicious of the government. In the fiction of the *Letters*, the world unites under a treaty set up by the United Nations (91). In this racist imaginary, mobs in Harlem break into liquor stores and dance in the streets (93). The author imagines a United States in which justifiably racist people are sent to concentration camps (107). Black and Puerto Rican neighborhoods are ravaged by fire and unrest, as the narrator imagines urban integration as an apocalyptic disaster (120). In a time when the United States was moving toward integration, white supremacists could see apocalypse unfolding.

Frontier imagery crops up. The narrator-protagonist belongs to the Rangers, who are like the "enormously capable mountain men and desert guides of the early 19th century in our land" (87). Though called "bandits," they are heroes. Their hope comes from the National Rifle Association.

> And what a debt we owe to the vigilance of the NRA officers. For when that nationwide registration order was made, most Americans understood its intent: to facilitate the seizure of all guns and of all kinds and thereby render [men] defenseless. (103)

The John Franklin Letters prefigures claims about gun rights we hear fifty years later: because of the NRA, millions of Americans "still have a deadly and trusted weapon" (104).

The Rangers plan an attack on Washington, DC. They easily take over police headquarters, the media, and guard posts. They take out

UN guards and set up a new State Department in which they are in charge (174). The post-apocalyptic world the author imagines is hard won but hopeful: "Now we're back where we started—and this time we know where to go" (176).

Alas, Babylon (1959)

This is one of the first books to imagine life after nuclear war with Russia and was quite popular as early apocalyptic science fiction. The story pivots around Randy Bragg's salvific actions for the small town of Fort Repose, Florida (Frank 1959, 143). The phrase "Alas, Babylon" is a quote from Revelation, part of God's judgment cast down on an evil city "burned off the face of the earth in an hour" (15). Most cities in the novel are burned by nuclear fallout, leaving small towns like Fort Repose to survive on their own. God is absent, and apparently uninterested in human struggle.

Warned of Russia's impending strike, Randy cashes a check twenty-four hours before banks shut down, buys groceries, and stocks up on ammunition. The town survives with little radiation poisoning, but there are disruptions to electricity, water, travel, and communications. The post-apocalyptic context is cause for a new way of being in the world:

> Yesterday was a past period in history, with laws and rules archaic as ancient Rome's. Today the rules had changed, just as Roman law gave way to atavistic barbarism. . . . Today a man saved himself and his family and to hell with everyone else . . . with the use of the hydrogen bomb, the Christian era was dead, and with it must die the tradition of the Good Samaritan. (97)

When the world is radically transformed, one needs guns. Luckily, Randy has assembled an arsenal:

> There was the long, old fashioned 30–40 Krag fitted with sporting sights; the carbine he had carried in Korea, dismantled, and smuggled home; two .22 rifles, one equipped with a scope; a twelve-gauge double-barreled shotgun. In the drawer of his bedside table was a .45 automatic and a .22 target pistol hung in a holster in his

closet. Ammo. He had more than he would ever need for the big rifle, the carbine, and the shotguns. (129)

Randy leads a crew of misfits including his brother's wife and two kids, the Black family who works for him, a love interest and her father, and the annoying woman from across the street. His Black neighbors clean house for him and continue to offer free labor even after the social system collapses. When four men go out to hunt highway robbers, the only Black man puts himself in the line of fire as bait. He is shot and dies. The book is both racist and sexist. The "august world of battle and violence" does not include women (249). Peyton, a twelve-year-old girl who wants to learn to use a gun, is told girls are "fit for sewing, pot washing, and making beds" (289). This chauvinism is a key feature of the cowboy apocalypse.

After the initial blasts, people worry Fort Repose is in danger from "people swarming out of Orlando and Tampa." Escaped convicts hang out on deserted roads. The financial system fails. Food and pharmaceuticals run out. Mail delivery stops. Television shuts down. Highways become jammed with carloads of refugees (117). They arrive in small towns "voracious and all-consuming as army ants" (118). The novel culminates with a rite of passage in which Randy learns to shoot without regret. Even when government forces show up to help, Fort Repose continues to live on its own means with gun-toting Randy in charge.

In the decade following Frank's novel, a storm of pressures converged to threaten white men: the Civil Rights Movement, feminism, gay and lesbian rights, Vietnam, declining incomes (Melzer 2012, 47). The decade of the 1960s was apocalyptic in its critique of American history itself. The Civil Rights Movement called out contemporary racial injustices, but also exposed the history of American slavery and racial oppression. Feminist gains threatened fundamentalist religions, as did the gay liberation movement and the sexual revolution. Conservative Christians began mobilizing to reverse the progress made by these groups. Apocalyptic hope became entangled in white men's aggression, and some authors—like Hal Lindsey—imagined divine intervention.

The Late Great Planet Earth (1970)

Hal Lindsey published *The Late Great Planet Earth* the year I was born. He had recently graduated from Dallas Theological Seminary and served as a preacher for Campus Crusade for Christ. By the end of the 1970s, the novel had sold more than ten million copies. The book depicts the end times in religious terms, predicting the rapture as the first sign of apocalypse. Lindsey's book reflects evangelical anxieties in familiar terms:

> Internal political chaos caused by student rebellions and communists will begin to erode the economy of our nation. Lack of moral principle by citizens and leaders will so weaken law and order that a state of anarchy will finally result. The military capability of the United States . . . has already been neutralized because no one has the courage to use it decisively. When the economy collapses so will the military. . . . Look for the present sociological problems such as crime, riots, lack of employment, poverty, illiteracy, mental illness, illegitimacy, etc., to increase as the population explosion begins to multiply geometrically in the late 70s. (Lindsey 1980, 184–185)

Interpreting Revelation in contemporary terms, Lindsey warns the Antichrist will take over the world to form a "one-world religious system" to bring "all false religions together" (122). The unification of Europe under a common currency is a sign that Satan is hard at work (94). He frets about Communism in China (84). He worries about ballistic missiles that could wipe out a third of the world's population (166). In the 1980s, Ronald Reagan invited Lindsey to the Pentagon to discuss his predictions about the Middle East.

Although the world seems increasingly chaotic, Lindsey thinks Christians can expect God's intervention and he hopes for the same rewards the ancient apocalypticists did, eternal life in an otherworldly paradise.

> Without benefit of science, space suits, or interplanetary rockets, there will be those who will be transported to a glorious place more beautiful, more awesome, than we can possibly comprehend.

> Earth and all its thrills, excitement, and pleasures will be nothing in contrast to this great event. It will be the living end. The ultimate trip. (137)

The hankering for apocalypse is a hunger for retribution. But it is also a need for the world-as-story.

The Turner Diaries (1978)

Neo-Nazi William Pierce's *The Turner Diaries* purports to be a printed copy of a recovered diary written by a white martyr for a terrorist group. The original diary supposedly consisted of five cloth-bound ledgers with loose inserts, recovered in the ruins of Washington, DC, and saved by admirers. What readers get, though, is a paperback filled with racist venom. Black people are called rapists and murderers (Pierce 1978, 28). Jews are described as filth (29). Gangs of "black thugs" wander into schools to rape students for sport (58). LGBTQ folks are ridiculed (58). When non-white people are exiled from Pierce's imaginary white homeland, he describes them as an "unwholesome flood" that creeps, a zombie "swarm" that makes the narrator shudder with revulsion (155).

The terrorists hope to incite a war to take over the government. After they shut down the power supply in cities, "the Black areas" erupt into violence and looting (144). Cities experience disruptions to transportation and communications, bombings, mass food shortages, and assassinations (171). Pierce sees violence as a fulfillment of the religion of white supremacy: "Only by making our beliefs into a living faith which guides us from day to day can we maintain the moral strength to overcome the obstacles and hardships which lie ahead" (9). Guns are essential to the building of this new world, but Pierce imagines the government raiding people's homes to confiscate them. People found with firearms are herded into barbed-wire enclosures (4). To avoid capture, gun owners shoot first.

The book is meant to stir up rage. Reading about a white girl carved up for a Black meal is meant to prompt *real* violence (151). The terrorists drive a truck full of explosives into an FBI building, inspiring Timothy McVeigh's real-life attack years later (33). *The Turner Diaries* is not escapist fiction but a training manual. One survivalist leader told an interviewer, "Everything that's gonna happen is in there" (Coates 1988, 50). Another bought land in the Pacific Northwest with the goal of creating a neo-Nazi homeland, saying the plan was taken from *The Turner Diaries*. In the 1970s, right-wing survivalists complained about Jewish bankers they believed had "spirited all the gold from the vaults at Fort Knox." They hoped God would eradicate "your mongrel, your Jew and your Negro" (Pierce 1978, 7). They wanted to send Black people back to Africa. These influences go all the way back to the Ku Klux Klan and resentment about the Civil War. One of the terrorists explains the duties of a white supremacist:

> We have claimed for ourselves the right to decide the fate of all our people and, eventually, to rule the world in accord with our principles. . . . Each day we make decisions and carry out actions which result in the deaths of white persons, many of them innocent of any offense. . . . We are willing to take the lives of these innocent persons, because a much greater harm will ultimately befall our people if we fail to act now. (98)

The white supremacists in *The Turner Diaries* do not wait for God to intervene. Apocalypse is something that white people *do* in the here and now on God's behalf.

The Stand (1978)

Stephen King's novel exhibits signs of a significant cultural turn toward the cowboy apocalypse and, as one of the most recognizable popular books of the later twentieth century, its impact has been tremendous. *The Stand* is a cowboy novel with guns, frontier imagery, and ample post-apocalyptic violence. But it also reflects 1970s Christian evangelical expectation of divine intervention. When *The Stand* was first published, *The Late Great Planet Earth* and Francis Schaeffer's *How Should We Then Live?* were still on the religious bestseller lists. Billy Graham, Pat Robertson, Jerry Falwell, and Phyllis Schlafly were articulating their places in a new evangelical activism. *The Stand* sits on the cusp between fundamentalist literalist biblical apocalypticism of the sort imagined by

Hal Lindsey and a grittier, earthier cowboy apocalypticism in which guns take God's place as final judge. It would be too much to suggest that *The Stand* supports evangelical apocalyptic views. But it draws freely on Darby's dispensationalism and the panic of conservatives following the Civil Rights Movement.

Nobody would describe King's post-apocalyptic future as feminist-friendly. Women are "slutty bitches" (King 1978, 25). Their breasts swell and threaten to burst out of tight clothing as their nipples point "perkily" (56, 531, 101). We read about a man's "wingwang" hanging out on the beach (47). Another man's penis is a "nine-inch hogleg" (146). We get to smell men's "spunk" and "juices" (604). You can almost hear King hooting at his typewriter.

The main character, Stu Redman, is "one independent son of a bitch" with a "Gary Cooper exterior" (133). He is a "Wild West motherfucker" and a fan of Louis L'Amour (908). He likes Hank Williams and he reads Max Brand novels even after the world has ended (924). Stu is definitely a cowboy, but he can't shoot and he doesn't save anybody.

An elderly Black woman named Abagail Freemantle represents the forces of goodness. Mother Abagail lives in a shack, plays guitar, sings Christian spirituals and Civil War songs, and visits people in their dreams (595). She remembers slavery and is grateful for "what Abraham Lincoln and this country did for me and mine" (596). She reads her Bible. Randall Flagg, the Dark Man, sees people from afar and controls them. Abagail says: "He ain't Satan . . . but he and Satan know of each other and have kept their councils together of old" (634). He is some kind of Antichrist, and sashays about in cowboy boots like he's from a John Wayne movie (729). He has raped women while wearing a white sheet and burned down a "nigger shanty town" (217). Brimstone is in the air.

Nothing much happens, plotwise, in *The Stand*. Guns are everywhere, but they are not effective. In a bungled robbery, a cowboy shoots someone and his intestines spill onto the floor (148). The good guys collect rifles and a rocket launcher, but they don't use them for anything (705). At one point, a gun is used to rape someone (740). Someone else is scalped by a bullet just like a "shoot-out at the O.K. Corral" (1172). Guns are props of horror, not heroics. Mother Abagail tells four people—all men, all white—they must confront the Dark Man. They think they are being sent out like prophets, but they do not accomplish much. Evil does not win in the end, but only because the electric Hand of God appears in the sky and detonates an A-bomb (1354).

One could read *The Stand* as supporting the Christian God, but King's God is a disinterested jerk who detonates a bomb but not to save anybody. It is hard to tell what the point is. *The Stand* could be a violent romp. It could be a critique of the Cold War. There are elements of the emerging cowboy apocalypse: a global catastrophe, societal collapse, survival themes, guns, and cowboys. But they never add up to anything. Although the novel exhibits interest in a new America, nobody talks about problems in the old America. Whiteness is the norm. Men are in charge. Survival is a dubious benefit.

The Stand was recently made into a miniseries (2020–2021); however, the religious elements come off badly despite their faithfulness to the text. Today, we expect Stu Redman to kill the bad guy. Instead, the miniseries gives us an impotent cowboy, a bad guy who survives, and a merciless God. We shouldn't be surprised. But we *are* surprised because today we expect mainstream apocalypticism to be secular. Nobody expects God to reach down from heaven today except Christian fundamentalists.

Essays of a Klansman (1983)

Louis Beam updated the Ku Klux Klan for the 1980s with *Essays of a Klansman*. The Klan had failed during the Civil Rights Movement, says Beam, because they allowed the government to stand even though it was in the "enemy camp." Dissent had been quashed, and the forces of evil had "obtained near-total control of all means of communication" (1983, 10). Beam issued new advice saying that "if America is to be saved" they will need the Klan "for there is and can be no accord between good and evil" (19). Beam believes he is tasked by God to save America. Drawing on apocalyptic imagery, he calls on patriots to "strike at the enemies of our God, our Race, and our Nation." To recover America from the enemy's hands, says Beam, they need "knives, guns, and courage" (23). The new KKK will slit their enemies' throats, "relish[ing] the warmth of tyrant's blood between their fingers" (23). Beam worries patriots like himself will be attacked by "shock troops" carrying automatic weapons while patriots carry only "rocks and bottles." Therefore, "duty demands that both sides have automatic weapons" (68). A new "Revolutionary Majority" has resolved to "die as free men rather than to live as slaves" (91).

Beam draws on the biblical story of Gideon destroying the temple of Baal, applying it to his contemporary work in the KKK. A sword, says Beam, need not be literal. It could be "an M-16, three sticks of dynamite taped together, a twelve-gauge, [or] a can of gas" (30). In the final judgment, entrance to heaven will be guaranteed for the man standing at the gates with "tow-sacks full of the enemies' heads" (30). God is violent, working through his chosen agents to free the United States from Satan's grasp (45). The battle is not about "the proper treatment of others" but "a monumental conflict of the ages, which is to determine the right to life of our race, culture, and posterity" (46).

Beam insists the only way to avoid the "bottomless black abyss" is to make the United States as God intended: a white supremacist state (49). The Reconstructionist Union League is accused of "voodoo" rituals, making Blacks so delirious they riot, burn houses, murder people, and rape women and children (iv). To purify the nation, Beam proclaims, "We will have to kill the bastards" (50). Beam uses language reminiscent of zombies as he points to the "decomposition, decay, and rancid pervasive stench" of a society "teeming in loathsome abundance with things foreign to our nature" (50). To be non-white in America is to be monstrous.

During the 1980s, survivalists listened to Pat Robertson predict Armageddon for the sins of abortion. Some read the antisemitic *Protocols of the Elders of Zion* (1903), a forgery claiming to be a master plan for Jews to seize world power (Coates 1988, 21). They stockpiled machine guns in bunkers, some while reading Hal Lindsey's *The Late Great Planet Earth* and watching *Red Dawn*. As a response to threatening social changes, the survivalist story blends with evangelical and fundamentalist insistence on God's special love for white Christians.

> They reasoned that a nuclear war would cleanse the world of their enemies, leaving them alone to emerge from the irradiated rubble, new Adams and Eves ready to start the human saga over, this time with a single pure white race. . . . The US government has been

taken over by a conspiracy of Jewish bankers and nebulous other dark forces who plan to bleed the country dry, then bring a nuclear attack down upon the withered shell. This final attack is what the Bible calls Armageddon and, the survivalists hold, once the attack has cleansed the earth, their new order of white people will start history over again. (9)

Survivalists in the 1980s gravitated toward small communities where they stockpiled weapons, food, and medicine for the Tribulation (19). Expressing a view also held by many fundamentalists, Ronald Reagan stated, "We may be the generation that sees Armageddon" (cited in Berger 1999, 135). The Soviet Union was the "evil empire" threatening America's power. It is no surprise that the movie *Red Dawn* appeared in 1984. Evil, according to many survivalists, included communism, abortion, gun control, and affirmative action, but also "liberalism, drug addicts, welfare mothers, [and] immigrants" (134). It was around this time Klansmen started patrolling the U.S.-Mexico border to hunt for immigrants (Strickland 2020).

Within an hour of my childhood home in the Ozarks, survivalist groups had built several compounds. I did not know these compounds were there. But I did see rifle racks and confederate flags on display everywhere. As a teen I often drove by Tony Alamo's religious compound. I had been told to never get a ride from a stranger or I might end up as one of his brides. In 1985, there was an FBI standoff at a religious neo-Nazi compound in Three Brothers, Arkansas, a small community about three hours from where I grew up (Coates 1988, 38). As many as two hundred officers approached the compound where the founder prayed. On the property was apparent proof that residents were converting weapons to automatics (Speer 1985). There were also land mines. White resentment was in full swing.

Officers believed the compound's residents were involved in armed robberies to raise funds for war against the U.S. government (King 1985, 12). These 1980s survivalist groups believed that "the world is on the verge of some form of catastrophic renewal, after which the stage will be set for them to eliminate the Jews, blacks, Hispanics, Catholics and others" (Coates 1988, 10). Such claims are not new, though they do provide context for the standoffs at Ruby Ridge and Waco. One line of my ancestors winds its way back through Waco to its establishment as a pioneer town, displacing preexisting Comanche memorials. It's like seeing ghosts I did not know I had.

One of the most well-known leaders of Identity Christianity was Thom Robb, a preacher from a town about two hours from my childhood home (99). He was well-known for organizing racist and antiqueer rallies. Another white supremacist apocalyptic group called The Covenant, the Sword, and the Arm of the Lord (CSA) settled nearby. An FBI report on the organization describes their beliefs, giving a rendition of the cowboy apocalypse in nascent form:

> [T]he United States will suffer a collapse of economy or nuclear war. As a result, there will be chaos, and the panicked masses will roam the country looking for food and protection. Those who are not prepared will be a threat to those who have been preparing. . . . But, if people come to loot, the CSA will kill them. In preparation for this, the group stockpiles food and weapons and trains themselves in military and survival procedures. In addition to training themselves, the group offers survival training to the public, either on the settlement or at various locations throughout the United States. The training includes instruction on organization, survival techniques, and para-military topics. Also taught are firearms and marksmanship, repelling, foraging for food, erection of such obstacles as punji sticks and barbed wire to detour looters, urban warfare, military field craft, national forest survival, home defense, Christian martial arts, Christian military truths, nuclear survival and tax protesting. (Federal Bureau of Investigation 1982)

At least once a year we piled on a school bus to go to high school football games near the CSA compound, where I'd march with the band at halftime. Less than an hour away, at the compound, police found thirty gallons of raw cyanide, enough to poison an entire town (Coates 1988, 140).

The *Left Behind* Series (1994–2007)

The *Left Behind* series is a sixteen-volume collection of fundamentalist action thrillers co-written by Tim LaHaye and Jerry Jenkins. The books lean on potboiler plots, and have been compared to books by John Grisham, Tom Clancy, and Stephen King (McFadden, 2016). LaHaye founded the rightwing Council for National Policy in the 1980s and worked alongside Pat Robertson and Jerry Falwell on the conservative political agenda.

In the opening novel, we hear familiar apocalyptic refrains. Cars are piled up and planes have crashed. Communications systems break down. Looters steal what they can. But in this story, the violence is caused by God's intervention via the rapture of millions of people. The book also draws on an old but active conspiracy theory about an international group of Jewish financiers who control world politics (79). This cabal is in cahoots with the United Nations, who—in fulfillment of predictions in Revelation—will convert the world to one currency and one religion.

The books have been criticized for their violence. For example, in *Glorious Appearing*, Jesus eviscerates the bodies of non-Christians. He blows people up with supernatural heat, so their flesh dissolves and their eyes melt. Jesus *is* a weapon in *Left Behind*, a kind of gun that blasts people he has deemed not worthy of salvation. While *Left Behind* is not a cowboy apocalypse, it does present Jesus as a murdering messiah. The depiction of a "fearsome Jesus" who punishes opposing earthly authorities "corresponds to a widespread sense among many conservative Christians that their values are under assault in a culture war with the secular society around them" (Kirkpatrick 2004). The books present Christians with a means of fighting back, making them God's helpers in violent retribution. The active role invited by LaHaye and Jenkins is made explicit in the affiliated videogame, which requires players to shoot people who reject the message of Christ.

End of the Age (1995)

Christian televangelist Pat Robertson, founder of the *The 700 Club* and the Christian Broadcasting Network, tried his own hand at apocalypse, perhaps inspired by LaHaye. Among Robertson's twenty books, *End of the Age* is the only novel. Robertson tells the story of Carl Throneberry, a "good-looking and charming" gentleman who has taken his faith for granted until a meteor hits the earth (1995, 11). He and his wife Lori escape L.A. mere hours before a meteor hits. They are scooped up by a Lakers basketball player who takes them to his friend's mansion, where they learn that reading the Bible is the best way to cope.

We see the expected social disarray: cars piled up, neighborhoods on fire, people panicking. Looters and gangs rob stores and terrorize people (114). Thousands of people stream out of cities looking for shelter and food (116). The world is awash in refugees (119). The meteor strike has disastrous aftereffects including earthquakes, volcanic eruptions, tsunamis, and floods. Nuclear reactors leak and millions more die. Carl complains Americans act "like God is some kind of big, easygoing teddy bear in the sky who's going to let them get away with trashing all his sacred laws" (84). Instead, God sends destruction while Carl and Lori sip coffee. There are no human cowboys with blazing pistols. We get just Carl, used to comfort and good food. As one Christian says to another, "all we can do now is trust in the Lord" (146). Thank heavens there is a maid at the mansion to cook for them.

Christian survivors set up a camp in the mountains called El Refugio that "had the feeling of a frontier town" (360). The camp is run by Pastor Jack, who dresses like a cowboy and reads the Bible a lot (147). Meanwhile, the Antichrist sets up shop in the government and high-level U.S. officials are killed off. Non-Christians are attacked by invisible demons (166). Satan's rule involves drugs, New Age practices, orgies, pedophilia, incest, and out-of-wedlock pregnancies (317). Pastor Jack blames "gangs of fatherless teenagers," broken families, gay rights, and abortions for God's loss of patience (207). Japan is overwhelmed by a tidal wave (228). Meanwhile, Carl and Lori study the Bible without a "care in the world" (192). Angels hover above the mountain to protect them. The Christians at El Refugio are willing to defend themselves "like the Alamo all over again" (351). As one Christian says: "Jesus Christ is the winner, and I'm on His team" (359).

Guns appear in the novel, but they don't save anybody. The Christian team at El Refugio are saved by prayer, not firepower. In a climactic moment, a gun is turned on the Antichrist. He dies but rises again in demonic imitation of Christ. Even here, the gun is just a prop in a larger drama about God's ultimate power. El Refugio has no guns at all. "We decided at the beginning," says Pastor Jack, "that it would be an exercise in futility to try to resist the forces of evil with the little peashooters we could bring together. So we just asked the Lord for His protection, and He has answered our prayers" (363). With God around, guns are superfluous.

World War Z (2006)

Max Brooks's *World War Z* was published the same year as Stephen King's *The Cell*, also a zombie novel. The film version of *World War Z* appeared in 2013 at the height of zombie fever. This was the same year the Boston Marathon was bombed, and Assad deployed sarin gas against Syrians. One year earlier, James Holmes shot fifty-eight people and killed twelve in Aurora, Colorado, at a screening of *The Dark Knight Rises*. Hurricane Sandy bore down on the East Coast and shut down New York City. Adam Lanza killed twenty-six people in Sandy Hook, Connecticut, most of them children. Real life had more than enough horror, yet fans devoured zombie media. In 2012, a new drug called "bath salts" caused users to consume their victim's flesh. There were a lot of reasons to think about death. Like other forms in the genealogy of the cowboy apocalypse, zombie stories reflect fears about the collapse of civilization.

> The zombie apocalypse is . . . a heady mash-up of horror and survival stories. The themes and motifs feel like they come straight out of westerns that I watched as a kid—justified violence, dangers lurking in nature and in the people you encounter, survival of the fittest, and rugged masculinity—paired with societal breakdown and previously-human-but-now-monsters. (Baker 2020, xxi)

Zombies seem race-less. But the people who survive zombie apocalypses are usually white, and those aware of the dehumanization of Black people in Klan literature recognize the racist tropes. As with most of the books we consider here, readers are expected to accept portions of *World War Z* as fictional but see the rest as predictive—and to know which parts are which.

The expectation that fictional zombie prep could help with real-life threats may seem strange, but others have embraced it. In 2011, the Centers for Disease Control and Prevention issued a comic book inviting readers to prepare for the zombie apocalypse by storing water, food, and basic supplies. In the same year, the U.S. Defense Department produced a zombie survival plan for troops. The plan describes how to protect humans from the zombie horde. The plan is a "completely fictitious scenario" intended for *actual* training.

The novel *World War Z* consists of interviews with people who survived the fictional zombie war. In incident after incident, Brooks depicts a cowboy messiah enacting violent destruction of undead who deserve to be shot, mutilated, decapitated because of their monstrous nature. When viewed alongside other cowboy apocalypses, it becomes easy to see that zombies can serve as a stand-in for other, more obviously racist depictions.

World Made by Hand (2008)

James Howard Kunstler's novel is a post-apocalyptic ode to simplicity cast in the white masculine celebration of frontier values. The main character, Robert, describes life in America "after our world changed" (2008, 1). He mourns the loss of things like electricity, cars, and city sewage management, but celebrates the new times (5). Robert tells a young man in his community that "people are generally better off now" because they "follow the natural cycles" and "eat real food instead of processed crap full of chemicals." They no longer watch television and absorb "sexy advertising all the time" (38). No need to worry about globalization. Everything is local now (15).

We aren't told what caused the cataclysm. There are references to Mexican flu (7, 13), to bombs (8, 15, 28), to oil shortages (15, 245), to radiation sickness (76), and even to an act of jihad (23). Robert hikes past a "raggedy commercial strip" where "pikey mulleins and sumacs" pop through the pavement (11). The suburbs are dangerous (187). Years later, the earth recovers in rural areas. Robert speaks lovingly of flowers and mayflies. Crickets chirp happily. Fish have returned (135). In towns like Union Grove, the population has risen to "pioneer level" (136). People rarely get sick and live peaceful lives farming, smoking meat, and making butter.

Women and uncompensated servants happily cook for men. Kunstler describes "fresh greens, spinach cooked with bacon and green onions, radishes, rocket and lettuce salad, peas with mint" and honey cakes served with cream (56). The men feast at tables "groaning with puddings, new potato salad, sugar snaps, radishes, pickles, sauerkraut, creamed new onions, corn bread . . . cookies and confections, butternut fondants, even a tray of fudge" (209). The "gentleman" Stephen Bullock lives just outside of town where he runs a "plantation" with dozens of unpaid servants whom Kunstler won't call slaves (61, 81). One woman refuses to live as "a damn[ed] serf," but even she must find a man to protect her (122).

Depictions of women are highly sexualized. Robert (in his forties) describes another character, Britney (in her twenties), as "well formed." Her hair smells like "the spice of fresh grass and childbearing" (72). Britney pleads with Robert to take her in because it "isn't a good time for a single woman with a child to live alone" (121). Robert describes Britney's intense desire for him despite his age. He describes the "silkiness of her skin" and the movement of her breasts. Having sex with young Britney is like braving the frontier, "a dangerous wilderness where the animals would never learn to speak and might not be so friendly" (249). The good people in Kunstler's fantasy world are all white, Christian, and heterosexual. Everyone attends the same church, where they sing with gusto and pray without doubt. Nobody seems to care what has become of Muslims, Buddhists, or Hindus. The narrator is embarrassed to be outed as a Jew toward the end of the book, though he attends church anyhow (261).

Urban mobs are racially and ethnically identified. When Washington, DC, is bombed, people form "bandit gangs" who come to rural Pennsylvania seeking to loot: "After a while, it was like cowboys and Indians" (148). Kunstler says it's "poor against whatever rich are left. Black against white" (149). Egalitarian pretenses dissolve and "nobody even debated it anymore" (101). Women who had a career have given it up. Single women survive as prostitutes who are "friendly and available" (144).

Kunstler describes a mobile home park called Karptown near the town dump, "halfway between a frontier outpost and a medieval peasant village" (266). It is filled with "quasi-criminals" loyal to Wayne Karp, the "chieftain of a large clan" (28, 267). Residents are "like the Iroquois who had inhabited the same area four hundred years earlier" (267). Their homes are decorated with totem poles (268). Karp's home is the tribal headquarters where people engage in "wild levees" (267). Karptown is a "nest of rattlesnakes" best avoided (57).

A few of the Union Grove men ride horses to another town in search of missing men. Robert confronts a man there and with "wondrous detachment," draws his gun in "slow motion," and shoots the "fat white target" in self-defense. The man "groan[s] like a steer" as he dies (179). There are no consequences because there are "no real police, courts. No state government. Nothing" (206). Robert learns in this new world his gun makes him "real powerful" (298).

One Second After (2009)

In William Forstchen's *One Second After*, we see close alignment between author and character. Both William Forstchen and his main character, John Matherson, live in Black Mountain, North Carolina. Both teach military history. But whereas real-life Forstchen is a prepper, fictional Matherson is unprepared. Fortunately, over the course of the novel, Matherson learns what it means to be a man in post-apocalyptic America.

Newt Gingrich wrote the foreword for *One Second After*, calling it a work of fiction and "a work of fact" depicting America's "future history" (Forstchen 2009, 11). Gingrich expects an electro-magnetic pulse (EMP) to disable automobiles and disrupt key communications. This fear is not a "wild flight of fantasy" but a real threat (12–13). Americans should prepare now to be ready then (13). To read *One Second After* is to get a glimpse of our real future. Imagining the old world gone, Forstchen replaces it with a cowboy apocalypse starring himself.

Forstchen describes "aging hippies and New Agers, Wiccans, and . . . a lot of drugged-out kids" regretting their own lack of preparedness (125). Bill, one of the town's leaders, explains: "They're used to free clinics, homeless shelters when they need 'em," with people "smiling and giving them a few bucks. That's all finished" (127). In the new world, such weak people will "die like flies." When they run out of food, "anyone with a gun will tell them to kiss off if they come begging" (127). When "the crap hits the fan," men with guns will rule the world.

Forstchen's post-apocalyptic future is, like Kunstler's, reminiscent of frontier America. After the EMP blast, the people of Black Mountain shift back "a hundred and fifty years." They flip through old issues of *Scientific American* so they can rebuild "radios, telegraphs, steam engines, batteries, internal combustion engines" (213). Matherson is asked to lead the town because he understands "patriots' dreams" (214).

A few weeks after the blast, nearby cities burn with "dead people lying in the streets" (108). City dwellers are a "barbarian horde on the march" (190). Millions of people from the cities leave in "a chaotic exodus, like a horde of locusts eating their way across the suburban landscapes" (167). They make a desperate rush for small towns to loot them (110). The interstate swarms with people (109). The men of Black Mountain expect fifty thousand people to storm them (172). Black Mountain's only doctor identifies the refugees as a health threat. He says it "scares the hell" out of him to think about a "recent immigrant from overseas" who could make his way to their town "carrying typhoid, cholera, you name it" (170). Sure enough, weeks into the disaster, refugees camp on the highway in "positively medieval" conditions with "disease breaking out" (189).

This narrative represents white right-wing fears about America's future and attempts to justify racial violence now. The men of Black Mountain can kill refugees because they are "an army as ruthless as anything in history" (248). The college campus in Black Mountain is repurposed into a militia "boot camp" with "every weapon imaginable" in the hands of local young "troops" (203). These "kids" are decked out in camo gear, with piles of weapons at hand (276). Children are taught to make "land mines, satchel chargers, and homemade rocket launchers" (267). Despite the Constitution's being defunct, the Second Amendment call for an armed militia is insisted upon: "every citizen who can carry a gun" must serve in the Black Mountain reserve against the mob about to overrun the town (276).

One group, the Posse, are "gangbangers" and "bad hombres" who get "whatever they want if they have the balls to take it" (270). They are "barbarians" who "gorge and take and inflict pain" (270). Some are even cannibals (280). Matherson coolly shoots at them when they threaten Black Mountain. Matherson gives the ones who survive a visible "mark of Cain" (306).

Forstchen offers plentiful references to Westerns and Civil War films like *The Ox-Bow Incident* (1943) and *Dances with Wolves* (1990). When he shoots people, he feels "like Gary Cooper in *High Noon*" (48–49). Before going to war, the people of Black Mountain sing patriotic songs, recite prayers, and read from the Bible (281). The troops march while singing "Yankee Doodle" (282).

The women of Black Mountain are described in sexist terms. Women serve as nurses, but they would better serve as cooks. Sexist gawking is obligatory. Matherson says: "If you don't check an attractive woman out, even for a second, it's an insult" (76). He watches a woman's dress "riding up to mid-thigh" (83). When caught, the woman tells Matherson "it's normal" for men to ogle (86). Later, Matherson stares at the woman's "sweat soaked" T-shirt as it clings to her body. She interprets his staring as a sign of his returning health (187).

Early in the novel, two men rob a nursing home and are sentenced to death by firing squad. When Matherson executes one of them, he says it feels like he is in "an old western." The crowd was "all but crying 'Lynch 'em!'" (142). The execution is sanctioned by the presence of an open Bible.

> [W]ithout ceremony or flourish, John raised the pistol, centered it on the man's chest . . . [and] squeezed the trigger. He saw the impact; Larry staggered backwards against the concrete wall. . . . He saw his second shot miss, striking above Larry's head as he slid down the wall, leaving a bloody streak. . . . John fought to center his Glock, aimed at Larry's midsection; he was kicking feebly. John could hear screams behind him. He fired again, and then again. (146)

Because this gun exists only in textual form, there is no *bang* and no blood. The printed bullet is silent. This is one of the reasons why, as Walter Ong notes, violence is "less repulsive when described verbally than when presented visually" (1982, 44). Written words are a residue of the things to which they point. However, as we have seen with other forms of white supremacist texts, a book like this can also be read as a ritual invitation to real action. Stories *themselves* cannot kill anybody, but they can perpetuate the kind of hate that makes it easy for a racist to use a real gun for murder.

The Dog Stars (2012)

I was disappointed to hear Jennifer Reese's positive review of Peter Heller's *The Dog Stars* on NPR. Reese finds in main character Hig a "soulful hero" with a "tender (if thin) love story," and sees the book as a "dark, poetic and funny novel." There is an upside to the destruction of civilization, she says. Hig can live in the present and "gaze up at the stars in this purged, rejuvenated universe" (Reese 2012). Is Reese not bothered by the sexism? What does Reese think of Heller's depiction of Hig "screwing" a woman on a "stone bed like an altar" while the woman's father stands over them with a gun (Heller 2012, 211)? Does Reese cringe when Hig finally sees his love interest Cima naked and admires her "mound," her "sweet butt," and her breasts "tight as apples" (248)? It is hard to believe any literary critic with feminist impulses could read this and consider it worthwhile. I can only imagine Reese is unaware of the deep racist and misogynist traditions Heller draws on.

World Made by Hand and *One Second After* lean hard into racist tropes, but the world in *The Dog Stars* isn't populated enough for anyone to think about what happened to non-white people. A mutated superbug escaped from a weapons lab in California (253) and millions die. Due to climate change, waters have warmed and wildlife struggles. When the pandemic first hit, mobs stole supplies off trucks. But now with so many dead, the idea of a mob seems quaint (252). Hig lives in Erie, Colorado, in an old airport hangar. He wakes up in the night crying because "even the carp are gone" (233). Slow to shoot, Hig only wants to fly his airplane around. But this new world is hostile to those without guns. Meeting a surviving group of Mennonites, Hig says it was "like an old Western movie" with a white settler meeting braves in a meadow.

Bangley is a prepper who shows up one day with a pickup full of guns and canned food (53). Bangley will "kill just about anything that moves" (143, 52). Hig, on the other hand, is a reluctant cowboy who must learn to kill. Marauders come to the hangar one night. Bangley shoots them. At first Hig is shocked, but over time when threatened he learns to "murder the fucker and take his woman" (165). The book ends with a group living together at the hangar, spending their evenings on deck chairs "like it was a country store in front of some apocalyptic parody of Norman Rockwell" (318).

Dissolution (2021)

The first book in W. Michael Gear's *The Wyoming Chronicles* series was published by Wolfpack Publishing, an indie print-on-demand outfit that focuses on Western and post-apocalyptic themes. Gear was trained as an anthropologist in the 1970s and has been writing adventure novels since the 1980s, most of them through this specialized press. Wolfpack Publishing is home to dozens of books like Gear's, with angry white men writing themselves into heroic roles of the end times.

Dissolution begins with a cyberattack on the United States' banking system. The electrical grid goes down. Cell towers don't work. People panic. Mobs gather in urban areas. Checkpoints are set up, and people are shot (81). Those who count on the government to restore order learn how mistaken they are. People do "crazy things." They loot and set fires (83). Wyoming halts refugees at the borders (220). People become desperate because they have already eaten all the animals nearby, including their own pets (259)!

Refugee camps house the millions of Americans seeking support (163). Within a short period of time, major cities on the East Coast are hit with nuclear bombs and EMPs (234). Gear's fantasy is vivid: "people burning alive by the millions. Washington DC. The Capitol collapsed into rubble, the Smithsonian buildings and all they contained, incinerated. The Washington Monument blown away. An entire history and heritage vanished in an instant" (235). The characters in the novel are safely holed up, some by sheer luck, in a mountain ranch owned by Bill Tappan.

The author has written himself into Bill Tappan's character. Both Gear and Tappan have a history in anthropology. Both live in the Wyoming wilderness. Gear's home overlooks the Wind River Reservation, like Tappan's in the novel. The Tappans have a "Don't Tread on Me" flag on their front porch (36). The patriarch Bill is a stereotype in cowboy hat, boots, and plaid shirt (37). He is married to a woman twenty years younger in "skin-tight Levi's" who worships him (38). Breeze, one of the Tappan girls, is a rodeo queen and reformed gun-control advocate who keeps a gun in her dorm room. She shoots three men on the highway because they intended to rape her (178). She sees bodies piled up on the interstate and views them with the same concern she would a dead rabbit (147). It all reminds her of the movie *Red Dawn* (298).

Another main character, Sam Delgado, is a "Latino kid from the mean streets of Hempstead" (16). Though he has no Indigenous heritage, Sam is visited by a Shoshoni spirit, a *nynymbi*, who sanctions Sam's killings and affirms his chosen status (387). The book details Sam's rite of passage into manhood as he learns to shoot for vengeance. Shyla Adams, Sam's love interest, has a "sultry long-legged walk" and a "slim waist." She is gorgeous, vivacious, stunning (137). Her breasts constantly swell against her clothes. She happily shifts from sewing Sam's pants to shooting. Shyla and Sam's love story begins when they have shooting lessons together. They bond "over this crazy, taboo instrument of death" (144).

In *Dissolution*, guns are companions, lovers, promises. They are the means of revenge, and a way of expressing devotion. And of course, guns promise order despite the collapse of civilization. Guns are the fetish of Sam and Shyla's love affair. Sam believes the only choice attackers leave you is to kill them because real life is "not like in the movies" (196). Shyla strokes the revolver lovingly while her flannel-shirted breasts swell (197).

An Indigenous spiritual leader spends his time supporting Tappan and his family, leading them on vision quests, and reassuring them their actions are noble. Even though United States law has collapsed, the Shoshone leader supports the white people's ownership of Indigenous ancestral heritage (115). The bad guy in *Dissolution* is Kevin Edgewater, a man compared to a Nazi high official, who has no respect for frontier mythology. He raids the Buffalo Bill Center. He steals Western-style art. He takes guns from the Winchester Museum, and he steals women (223). This is a man who must be shot.

Indigenous researcher Shawn Wilson says the tools we use for analysis are implicated in the worldview we carry, and this in turn determines the knowledge we discern (2008, 13). Eurocentric research has long played a role in the oppression of Indigenous people, as it inherently discounts Indigenous modes of knowing about the world. He cites a story about Coyote, who goes to study Indigenous culture at the university and finds his instructors are all white men who have learned from books by other white men (18). Gear uses his own dominant status to co-opt the voices of Shoshone people in service of a white supremacist plot.

Shanteel is the only Black character. Shanteel had been deeply involved with Black Lives Matter because her mother was shot by police (Gear 2021, 29). She has an "attitude about all things Western, redneck, and rural" (30). She is temperamental, rude, and says *shit* a lot. She thinks she has Cherokee blood (23). Shanteel describes what it was like "growing up black and female in Philadelphia's squalor. About the drug houses, the burned-out buildings and the roaches and rats" (206).

Critical race theorist Derrick Bell has argued that stories are essential for understanding the impact of white supremacy. Some narrative voices are "tacitly deemed legitimate and authoritarian." This voice "exposes, tells and retells, signals resistance and caring, and reiterates what kind of power is feared most—the power of commitment to change" (1995, 907). Gear's easy theft of Shanteel's and the Shoshone leader's voices makes them mouthpieces for Gear's own prejudices. Gear presents Shanteel learning to rely on herself instead of social supports and food stamps (2021, 207). He makes her fall in love with Brandon, a "gun-totin' White man on a horse" (205). Shanteel sits quietly by Brandon's side while he shoots at bad guys. Kelly Brown Douglas says the logic of stand-your-ground culture includes the presumption that someone non-white could be assimilated into white culture and be eliminated as a threat (Douglas 2015, 109). Gear tries to do exactly that.

The End of All Things (2023)

In Mike Kraus's *The End of All Things*, we see the familiar plot of a world collapsed and good guys navigating its horrors with guns. Terrorists infiltrated fuel lines with a flammable bacterium, leading to massive explosions across the United States. Millions die. Ordinary people have turned into thieves and scoundrels (2023, 136). Main characters Alice and James are separated from each other as well as from home and must brave a dangerous world where desperate people attack them.

If they could get there, James and Alice's Michigan have a homestead that is self-sufficient. They have solar panels, supplies, and canned foods. They have chickens, a cow, guard dogs, a fishpond, and a working tractor (229). Ryan, watching the farm for James and Alice, knows the plot already: malicious people will scavenge, and the homestead will be targeted (84). They put extra locks on the barn. They leave their dogs out to guard the house. And they sit by windows, rifles in hand.

James makes his way across a landscape filled with the stench of "flash-bombed flesh" (24). In a grotesque passage, James passes through a hellish landscape of burning parking lots:

> Among the destroyed . . . cars lay a spattering of corpses . . . others were trapped in truck cabins, locked inside like human remains thrown into a barrel fire, the blazing orange tendrils torching them to the bone. . . . Sharp crackles and groans of metal echoed across the parking lots. (61)

James knows the government cannot be trusted (122). The police can't help (140). The world is near collapse, and when things fall apart, survivors put themselves first, viewing everyone else as an enemy. Kraus depicts marauders carrying baseball bats down the street (107). Looters gleefully break into a shop (108). After the marauders leave, James also enters and takes a small sledgehammer, a backpack, and a gun. In another store he takes medicines, snack bars, and a first-aid kit (111). James is not looting, though, because he is a *good* guy. The logic is clear: stealing is acceptable for self-declared good guys, but if others try to steal from *you*, shoot.

There are expected narrative components—what I call the bones of the story—that recur in and across these narratives, linking the cowboy apocalypse to preexisting texts depicting white Christian theology, white supremacist fiction, Reconstructionist resentment, frontier mythology, and apocalyptic expectation. We also see in these narratives, over time, the increasing importance of the gun as God fades from view. Authors imprint themselves onto the narratives, their real-life guns serving as souvenirs for a fantasy of empowerment ritually inscripted into the texts. This forensic study shows how the contemporary myth of the cowboy apocalypse still provides cover for white supremacy, misogyny, and antisemitism. Those who participate in its fandom, then, should know what they are buying into.

3

SHOOTING THE COWBOY APOCALYPSE

A few years ago, the NRA National Firearms Museum had a display called "Hollywood Guns" featuring over a hundred weapons from films like *Dirty Harry*, *Pulp Fiction*, *Die Hard*, and *The Dark Knight*. Curator Phil Schreier invites visitors to admire the "firearms that we've fallen in love with . . . wishing that we too could be like our matinee idols" (Gertz 2013). In an article in the NRA's *American Rifleman*, Stephen Hunter says the museum's gun vault is "like going to Valhalla without . . . having to die first" (Hunter 2010). Hunter picks up a MAC-10 and pretends to shoot a "32-round burst at various enemies of the state and the person." He imagines himself the hero in a movie.

Film presents the world we know but recasts it into a form that is "larger than life, an object of desire" (Turner 2009, 148). In the early twentieth century, filmmakers learned how to use the camera to pan, create angles, manipulate color, and create shadow. They learned to edit, cutting in ways that shaped meaning. By experimenting with visual grammar, storytellers transformed a recording technology into an expressive medium (Murray 1998, 66). Film *transforms the real* as meaning is derived from arrangements of material on film. The reverse can also happen: the real world can be transformed *by* film when viewers accept it as determinative for belief. And this, more than anything, is the focus of this chapter.

Viewing is often presumed to be a passive activity because spectators observe stories but cannot change them. But viewers do participate in meaning-making. Fans looking for deeper engagement with a film acquire props, go to public events, participate in online fan groups, or buy affiliated merchandise. Real guns used as props can invite players to identify with characters played by the likes of John Wayne, Clint Eastwood, Chuck Norris, or Bruce Willis. Those with financial resources might make their own films, making themselves a hero in a story of redemptive violence.

Through a selective history, this chapter tracks films that feed into the cowboy apocalypse before the inflection point of 9/11. It also looks at how films after 9/11 accommodate the trauma of the terrorist attacks by presenting a world in which the cowboy with a gun can save himself simply by shooting the bad guys. Within a few years after 9/11, Hollywood versions of the cowboy apocalypse appear in familiar forms. For those who were already invested in gun culture and right-leaning politics, this shift is easily recognizable. For most people, though, the filmic portrayals of the post-apocalyptic cowboy messiah become an invitation to a soft affiliation with guns as an emblem of control in a time of increasing uncertainty. Eventually overshadowing media about the war on terror, the cowboy apocalypse can be read as a narrative response to global risk—a comforting if imaginary answer to real-life distress.

Early Westerns

Long before apocalyptic films appeared, the Western offered a means of imagining oneself in a world of good against evil. *Cripple Creek Bar Room* (1898) is arguably the first Western movie, but at less than a minute long, it presents a thin narrative about a drunk thrown out of a saloon. *The Life of a Cowboy* (1906) runs about eleven minutes, and features drunks, cowboys shooting guns, and bad guys causing trouble. *The Great Train Robbery* (1903) depicts good guys defeating bad guys in a dramatic shootout. In the classic Western narrative, any problem can be solved by a white man with good aim.

Although not a Western, D. W. Griffith's racist *Birth of a Nation* (1915) presents elements of what would become the cowboy apocalypse: namely, the white supremacist worldview and the experience of social chaos it leans on. The film presents post-apocalyptic disorder in the years after the Civil War, with white people as victims of unruly, violent Black people who are controllable only by guns. A young white woman, Flora, is chased by Gus, a leering Black man with ill intent. Flora jumps to her death. Gus is lynched by the Klan and his body is dumped. Another white woman, Elsie, is wooed by a lecherous Black man and cannot escape. "Crazed negroes" (title card) assemble outside the house where Elsie is held captive. "Helpless whites" look outside at the rioting Black masses. Other white people hiding in an isolated cabin are attacked by Black people. The Klan rides in on horses and fights off the hordes. Elements of this story—especially the angry, violent mob rising up after social collapse—are key components in what becomes the cowboy apocalypse.

Movie cowboys are confident. They know "exactly what to do and when to do it" (Savage 1979, 23). They are good guys who save those in peril; they can "overthrow evil by any of several techniques drawn from their arsenal of cowboy skills." If they lose their gun, they can "outwit and outpunch" their opponent because brains are "the cowboy's most potent weapon" (23). He is a "natural man," who is "schooled" in the "ways of nature." He is "prepared," and could "overcome any adversity and without the benefit of university" (24). These values are celebrated by American cowboys in the movies and beyond.

Western films of the 1940s and 1950s present the frontier as "part of America's legacy of ever-expanding wealth and power, but they ignored the possibility that the conquest could lay destruction in its wake" (Martin 1983, 143). The open frontier couldn't last forever, and it would eventually close, taking the real cowboy with it. The cowboy would largely be confined thenceforth to mediated representations and fantasy reenactments, as the real frontier was filled with homes, shops, malls, freeways, and the very movie theaters in which the cowboy myth survived. The frontier was "chewed up much the way a coyote takes a rabbit—suddenly, frantically, and then it was done" (143). It is no coincidence Western movies were popular, especially during this transition. What better place to preserve the dream of a past that never was? Although the fantasy world of the cowboy can never be fully inhabited, the Western film invites viewers (especially men) into its dusty enclaves, where they can project themselves onto the image of the brave hero with a smoking gun.

Nuclear Nightmares

The first atomic bomb was detonated in 1945, after which films about nuclear destruction began to appear alongside Westerns. There are no marauding hordes in these spare scenes of survival, but guns do show up as symbols of protection. *Five* (1951) is a rich character study of a small group of survivors who fight with one another in nuclear aftermath. A gun appears, but it is not shot. *Panic in Year Zero* (1962) is a classic example of early survivalist drama, depicting a family hiding out on a camping retreat after Los Angeles is destroyed by a nuclear bomb. Here the gun is a necessary means of keeping "law and order" after society has collapsed. In *On the Beach* (1959), no guns are needed as the last humans remaining die miserable, drawn-out deaths as nuclear fallout spreads across the globe.

In the decades following World War II, millions of viewers sought solace in shows like *Gunsmoke*, *Wagon Train*, and *The Rifleman*. Films like *The Gunfighter* (1950) caught the imagination of moviegoers, crafting for them the portrait of a folksy hero who takes justice into his own hands (Winkler 2013, 158). In *High Noon* (1952), Gary Cooper swaggers as the marshal Will Cane who defeats a band of outlaws. In *Shane* (1953), we find a mild-mannered hero who protects homesteaders from wealthy cattle rangers. The basic cabin, small farms, and wide-open plains beneath picturesque mountains are a hard contrast to technological Cold War anxieties. Newsreels shown in theaters not long before *Shane*'s release discuss Britain as the third world power to have the atomic bomb. The "Duck and Cover" reels shown in schools taught children that when a nuclear bomb goes off:

> . . . there is a bright flash, brighter than the sun, brighter than anything you've ever seen. If you were not ready and did not know what to do, it could hurt you in different ways. It could knock you down hard or throw you against a tree or a wall. It is such a big explosion, it can smash in buildings and knock signboards over and break windows all over town! But if you duck and cover—like Bert—you'll be much safer. (Rizzo 1952)

Films transmogrified nuclear energy into a quasi-magical power of mutation. Kids could pay fifty cents for a ticket to watch *The Beast from 20,000 Fathoms* (1953), *Godzilla* (1954), *Them!* (1954), or *Tarantula* (1955). Nuclear themes recur in 1960s films, notably *Dr. Strangelove, or How I Learned to Stop Worrying and Love the Bomb* (1964) and *Fail Safe*

(1964). Cold War anxieties generated invasion movies like *The Thing from Another World* (1951), *Radar Men from the Moon* (1952), *Invaders from Mars* (1953), and *Invasion of the Body Snatchers* (1956).

Cold War Heroes

The 1970s were haunted by the political, racial, and social upheavals of the decade before: the heavy losses of Vietnam, the ongoing Cold War, and the Watergate scandal. These anxieties are depicted in film, in fears of disaster and portrayals of gritty heroes. In *Deliverance* (1972), four men are pursued and assaulted by locals in the woods. *The Texas Chainsaw Massacre* (1974) depicts teens pursued by cannibals. In *The Hills Have Eyes* (1977), cannibals attack a family stranded in the desert. The *Dirty Harry* films (1971–1988) show a disgruntled police officer as an armed vigilante in an evil world. *Earthquake* (1974) predicts looting by survivors and chaotic shooting. *Apocalypse Now* (1979), *A Bridge Too Far* (1977), and *The Deer Hunter* (1978) depict the horrors of war. The 1970s ended with the trauma of the Iranian Revolution and the beginning of the hostage crisis.

The Cold War was too large, too diffuse, for people to imagine that guns could do much good in real life. In films, though, a few men with guns could save their communities. *Red Dawn* (1984) begins with a food shortage in Russia, food riots in Poland, and the fall of El Salvador and Honduras. NATO dissolves and the United States stands alone against Russia. A nuclear strike destroys Washington, DC. Wishing to avoid more nuclear bombs, both sides turn to conventional warfare. The story zooms in on a small town in Colorado. The camera pans over downtown shops, a Chevron station, and a child biking down a quiet street. We watch the town's bucolic peace disrupted when Russian paratroopers land. They shoot people and set off bombs in town. A school bus blows up. The camera pans to a bumper sticker on a stranded pickup, where we see Charlton Heston's famous slogan: "They can have my gun when they pry it from my cold, dead hands." Brothers Jed (Patrick Swayze) and Matt (Charlie Sheen) survive, along with a few others.

The boys stock up on supplies before leaving town to set up a stronghold in the Arapaho National Forest. They grab sleeping bags, canned foods, batteries, guns, and boxes of bullets. The guns range from the AKM to a Tokarev TT-33 pistol and "numerous American classics like the Colt Single Action Army, the Ruger 77, Ruger Mini 14 and the M1911A1" (Rackley 2013). The film hits on a laundry list of gun-related concerns: invasion via the Mexican border; the Communist threat; a government unable to protect its citizens; gun registration logs; and instability that obligates survivors to use violence. A group of kids, previously goofing off, become a crack team of stealth warriors. They learn to hide, shoot, steal, and survive outdoors.

U.S. viewers of *Red Dawn*, who had seen fifty-two Americans taken hostage in Iran, worried about Soviet expansion in Central America and narco-traffickers along the southern borders. The film depicts commercial airliners used for stealth entry across U.S. borders with enemy paratroopers inside, a scenario stoked by recent plane hijackings. The world is precarious, its order liable to be upended at any moment. The phrase *"Red Dawn* scenario" is still used among preppers as shorthand for foreign invasion.

In July 1984, one of the worst mass shootings in U.S. history took place in a McDonald's in San Diego, California. Twenty-two people were killed and another nineteen were wounded. The shooter was a white male prepper who hoarded food and weapons, and believed economic and nuclear collapse were imminent. The victims were nearly all of Mexican descent (Dunbar-Ortiz 2018, 135).

Another favorite film of survivalists is *The Terminator* (1984). The film presents a post-apocalyptic world with a killer robot who is sent back in time to murder Sarah Connor, a woman expected to birth a messiah. Its greatest appeal to gun fans is the display of extreme violence by the film's robotic villain, himself a walking gun. Arnold Schwarzenegger initially auditioned for the hero, Kyle Reese. Reese comes from a future in which humans are on the run from artificial intelligence. James Cameron thought Schwarzenegger would make a better fit for the robotic villain, telling him the movie was not about the hero, but the Terminator. Fans tend to agree, seeing in the villain a model of never giving up the fight.

Even after sustaining massive damage, the Terminator resurrects to continue his murderous pursuit of Sarah Connor. He is reduced to a metallic skeleton with red eyes but keeps on going. He loses his legs but keeps going. He stops only when a compactor crushes his metal frame. The Terminator "can't be bargained with. It can't be reasoned with. It doesn't feel pity or remorse or fear, and it absolutely will not stop—ever—until you are dead" (Rackley 2013). Scores of ordinary people die at the Terminator's hands. Sarah Connor mourns, but she realizes the deaths are collateral damage in a war with bigger stakes. In a demonstration of the exportability of America's gun love, an American-born shooter killed five people in August 2021 in Plymouth, England, after identifying himself as a "Terminator" in a YouTube video released before the murders. Director James Cameron recently said he might not feature as much gun violence if he made *The Terminator* today: "I don't know if I would want to fetishize the gun, like I did on a couple of *Terminator* movies 30 plus years ago, in our current world. . . . What's happening with guns in our society turns my stomach" (Williams 2023).

Cowboys vs. Terrorists

In 1986, a U.S. postal worker killed fourteen people in his local office in Edmond, Oklahoma. More post office shootings took place in 1989, 1991, and 1993, prompting the term "going postal." In 1997, the videogame *Postal* was released, allowing players to control the avatar of a mass murderer on a shooting spree.

The Delta Force, based on the actual 1980 hijacking of TWA Flight 847, was released the same year as the Edmond post office shooting. Early in the film, a terrorist emerges from the lavatory shouting "God be praised!" in Arabic, waving a gun around and announcing his willingness to die as a martyr. Unable to control their hatred, the terrorists reenact a mock Holocaust, segregating Jews in a separate area and smashing their guns against people's heads. They bellow that although millions of Jews died in the Holocaust, it was "not enough!" After they land, Major Scott McCoy (Chuck Norris) acts as a renegade cowboy savior who chases down the terrorists and kills them. With his amalgam motorcycle-rocket-launcher, McCoy becomes a weapon himself.

Die Hard (1988) presents Bruce Willis as disgruntled cowboy police officer John McClane who saves his wife by killing a gang of foreign terrorists at a company Christmas party. Its cowboy appeal lies in its claim that "good can triumph over evil with skill, training, determination and a few well-placed shots." McClane targets the bad guy, but pummels the city itself: the glass, computers, desks, elevators, and all the accouterments of urban life. Cowboy imagery pervades the film's dialogue. The villain snarls at McClane: "You won't hurt me... because you're a policeman. There are rules for policemen" (McTiernan 1988). He accuses McClane of being "another American who saw too many movies as a child, another orphan of a bankrupt culture who thinks he is John Wayne, Rambo, Marshall Dillon." McClane is—at root—a gunslinger: trigger-ready and willing to shoot anyone who crosses him. As a gunslinger, he *makes* the law. In the final moments of the film, McClane is out of ammo. "Still the cowboy, Mr. McClane. Well, this time John Wayne does not walk off into the sunset with Grace Kelly." McClane replies snappily: "It was Gary Cooper, asshole." McClane has an extra gun strapped to his back and whips it out, chirping "Happy trails, Hans." McClane is a redeemer "not from heaven but from earth" (Tompkins 1993, 32). Bang.

Preppers, Survivalists, Terrorists

One of the first films to celebrate the small-town prepper lifestyle, *Tremors* (1990) features characters with massive firearms stocked in their basement. The guns are used to battle enormous, blind snake-like creatures that look like the *Dune* sandworms. The film features Model 70s, AR-15s, and a Desert Eagle rifle. The heroes use rifles, shotguns, and handguns, including a Ruger Redhawk. Part of the fun is spotting all the different kinds of weapons in the film, and seeing the worms explode. Earl (Fred Ward) and Valentine (Kevin Bacon) play heroic roles alongside the prepper couple, Burt Gummer (Michael Gross) and Heather Gummer (Reba McEntire). Together, they fight off the beasts with sharpshooting, homemade bomb tossing, and trickery. The town of Perfection, California, is saved—without the help of their big-town neighbors or law enforcement.

In real life around the same time, similar confrontations were happening in small towns, but the enemy was not a giant sandworm. In 1991, the Bureau of Alcohol, Tobacco, and Firearms (ATF) sent a team to a remote cabin on Ruby Ridge, Idaho, belonging to Randy and Vicki

Weaver, based on rumors that Randy had illegally sold a sawed-off shotgun. After a conflict set off when agents shot the family dog, Vicki Weaver and a young man named Kevin Harris were dead. Bo Gritz, a Vietnam vet whose war stories inspired *Rambo: First Blood Part II* (1985), negotiated an end to the standoff. Also in 1991, a mass shooting took place in a Luby's cafeteria in Killeen, Texas, where 24 people died, 14 of them women. The shooter is reported to have "hated women, as well as gay people, African Americans, and Mexicans" (Dunbar-Ortiz 2018, 136).

In February 1993, the ATF was in another violent standoff about illegal weapons, this time with the Branch Davidian cult compound near Waco, Texas. When agents moved in almost two months later, 76 people were killed in the resulting fire, 25 of them children. After the World Trade Center bombing in 1993, jihadi terrorists figure more prominently in film, setting the stage for public response to the 9/11 attacks (Riegler 2010, 104). Islamic terrorists show up in *True Lies* (1994), where Harry Tasker (Arnold Schwarzenegger) is a spy trying to get nuclear missiles held by an Islamic jihadist. In 1995, Timothy McVeigh, a white man, bombed the FBI building in Oklahoma City: 168 people died, including 19 children. In the first few days after the bombing, news agencies reported it was the work of an Islamic terrorist.

Terrorist themes invoked stereotyped and deeply problematic filmic portrayals of Muslims, as well. *Executive Decision* directly links Islam with terrorism and violence, portraying Palestinian fanatics on an airplane reading the Qur'an to passengers and hiding a bomb. One character shouts "Allahu Akbar" as he brags that his partners are "the true soldiers of Islam" (Baird 1996). In *The Siege* (1999), a white female FBI agent discovers her Muslim lover is a terrorist when she watches him perform a sadistic form of *wudu*, or purification before prayer, as a prelude to killing innocent civilians. These films sowed suspicion and exacerbated Islamophobia after 9/11. *Executive Decision* was reedited to excise the worst references to Islam.

The Matrix (1999) is a favorite for survivalists because it is built around the presumption of secret knowledge, and it presents a hero who acts like a terrorist as he refuses to abide by a corrupt system. The matrix is a machine-generated delusion that fools the humans who are imprisoned in its AI system. The fake world looks like an ordered version of contemporary America, but it is in fact a prison. Humans who escape the matrix live underground where they scurry about in small space vessels hiding from the machines and engage in covert attacks against the system. The film is fiction, of course. But one of its defining features is the question it asks of its prepper viewers: Which world is most real—the world in which survivalists fight the government, or the one in which they follow its laws?

The heroes of the film—unlike us schmucks—have access to higher knowledge. They will save us by using—as the main character Neo puts it—guns, lots of guns. Not surprisingly, "living in the matrix" has become prepper shorthand for people who unwittingly trust the government. Online prepper discussion boards fill with conversations about how to escape the matrix. New preppers are "red-pilled" when they understand the need for violence and arm themselves: "Alt-righters see it as a metaphor for what they consider to be the revelatory power of their ideology" against the mainstream media's lies (Neiwert 2017a, 257).

Again, filmic portrayals and real life are interleaved. Several horrifying copycat murders took place not long after *The Matrix* was released. Josh Cooke, a teenager from Virginia, dressed in clothes like Neo's and shot his parents in their home. Vadim Miesegaes of San Francisco referenced the film before murdering his landlady. Lee Boyd Malvo, one of the "DC snipers," killed multiple people in 2002, then wrote "Free yourself of the Matrix" from his prison cell. The appeal of the film to messianic gunslingers is obvious. They, like Neo, see reality accurately, while the rest of us do not. *The Matrix* was released on March 31, 1999. The Columbine mass shooting happened just a few weeks later, on April 20, 1999.

Islamophobia and themes of inchoate terrorist threat continued during this period. In *Rules of Engagement* (2000), Marines open fire on a Yemeni crowd gathered outside an embassy, killing dozens in a massacre justified by the film's representation of people hiding guns in the crowd and its narrative of Yemeni Muslim brutality. Arab film critic Jack Shaheen says that when he first viewed the film, audience members "rose to their feet, clapped, and cheered" when the Yemenis—including women and children—were gunned down (2012, 15).

September 11, 2001

The September 11 attacks were the most explosive on the U.S. mainland in history, and the first by a foreign power since the War of 1812. The catastrophe led the Bush administration to the "War on Terror" and the invasions of Afghanistan and Iraq, as well as violence between Israel and Hamas and Hezbollah. Terrorist attacks took place all over the world in years to follow, generating fear and insecurity on a global scale (Kellner 2005b). The attacks changed what stories filmmakers told and how they told them.

Witnesses said the attack on the Twin Towers was "like a movie" (Alonso-Collada 2015, 111). Some referred specifically to *Independence Day* (1996), *Deep Impact* (1998), or *Armageddon* (1998). One critic describes how the event looked like an advanced form of computer graphics imagery (CGI) because:

> [T]he fireball of impact was so precisely as it should be, and the breaking waves of dust that barreled down the avenues were so absurdly recognizable—we have tasted them so frequently in other forms, such as water, flame, and Godzilla's foot—that only those close enough to breathe the foulness into their lungs could truly measure the darkening day for what it was. (Lane 2001, 79)

But 9/11 is not the movie we wanted to see. The spectacle was profoundly unsettling, not just for the massive loss of life, but because it communicated the message that "the U.S. was vulnerable to terrorists who could create great harm, and that anyone at any time could be subject to deadly terrorism, even in Fortress America" (Kellner 2005a, 350). Such a story will not do. Another one emerged:

> The master narrative of the cultural trauma of 9/11 was quickly formed within a matter of days of the attacks and saw itself perpetuated in a variety of media forms over the ensuing decade. Its understanding of 9/11 is of a heinous and unprovoked attack on a virtuous and blameless nation. . . . America's responses to 9/11, whatever they may be, were legitimized due to the nature of the crime that had been perpetrated against it. (McSweeney 2014, 10)

In a supersized form of "stand your ground" reasoning, the master narrative took on the logic of the gun lobby. The myth of justified violence must be maintained at all costs. According to the Bush presidency's "don't-think-just-act logic," aggressive military action "offers the only chance for survival, and those who stop to observe, ponder, collect information, or weigh their options end up dead" (King 2005, 128–129). Vulnerability is addressed mythically, narratively. The story of the gun as manly protection against enemies is very old, drawing from Klan narratives, slave patrols, and frontier stories about savage Indians.

Armageddon (1998) was a simple action movie released years before 9/11, but it was to become an interpretive frame in 2001, as the images of a film-blasted Manhattan haunted witnesses of the actual blasts. The film begins with early CGI-crafted images of a terrifying meteor shower causing explosions in New York. Grand Central Station blows up. People run down New York streets from fires and car explosions, smoke billowing between the buildings behind them. A meteor projectile enters a tall building at the same angle as a hijacked airplane two years later. The Chrysler Building collapses. The world stands poised at a moment of reckoning: Will the massive asteroid producing these meteors hit the earth and end human life? Ultimately, renegade oil man Harry Stamper (Bruce Willis) saves the world by drilling into and exploding a bomb inside the enormous asteroid barreling toward earth.

One witness describes the ballooning dirty smoke from the towers on 9/11:

> **Suddenly we understood that it was traveling towards us very quickly. It looked, quite simply, like a huge tidal wave, barreling down the canyons of the financial district to the park we were standing in. . . . It was impossible not to think that were in the scene of Schwarzenegger film, especially at that moment. We were thousands of Hollywood extras, mostly in suits for the office, with handbags and briefcases, just tearing through the streets of the city. (Usborne 2001)**

Lane (2001) describes the exclamations of live witnesses caught on video, "as they see the aircraft slice into the side of the tower: where have you heard those expressions most recently—the wows, the whoohs, the holy shits—if not in movie theatres, and even on your own blaspheming tongue?" (79).

Forty-five film projects were cancelled, altered, or postponed after 9/11 (McSweeney 2014, 105). Forty-eight hours after the airliners hit the World Trade Center, the trailer for *Spider-Man* (2002) was withdrawn because it featured a giant spider's web suspended between the Twin Towers (2). Barry Sonnenfeld's *Big Trouble* (2002) had its release date pushed back because it portrays a nuclear device on a hijacked plane. In *The Sum of All Fears* (2002), Islamic jihadist terrorists were replaced with neo-Nazis. *Bad Company* (2002) was held back because of a scene with a bomb set to explode in Grand Central Station. The release of *The Time Machine* (2002) was delayed because its depiction of a meteor attack on New York was too realistic (3). *Collateral Damage* (2001) was not released right away because it portrays a skyscraper being bombed. *Signs* (2002) does not depict an apocalyptic event or violence in New York. But it did begin filming just days after 9/11. The crew held an emotional vigil before filming, which then set the mood for the scenes they recorded (Leggatt 2012, 13). September 11 has haunted film ever since.

The U.S. invaded Afghanistan in October 2001, with several war films already in production. These films were well received for their clear themes of good versus evil. *Black Hawk Down* (2001) purports to be based on the real events of the Marine intervention in Somalia in 1994, but uncritically blends in fiction to depict unsympathetic Somalis violently attacking downed U.S. helicopters. *Behind Enemy Lines* (2001) is loosely based on events during the Bosnian War, although the soldier who inspired it sued the producers for inaccurate representation.

Fantasy franchises like *The Lord of the Rings*, *Harry Potter*, and *The Chronicles of Narnia* did well in these early years. Fantasy films offered comfort when "reality was too real and painful to be narrated" (Gandasegui 2009, 6). War was winnable. Leadership was clear. Power was predictable. And heroism meant something. Tolkien "gives us the war we wish we were fighting—a struggle with a foe whose face we can see, who fights on the open battlefield, far removed from innocent civilians. In Middle Earth, unlike the Middle East, you can tell an evildoer, because he or she looks evil" (Grossman and DeGaetano

1999, 24–25). America's enemies were hard to understand, so studio executives gambled that audiences would want movies with "identifiable villains and clear, resounding victories, set in distant times or fictional places" (Waxmann 2004).

Superhero movies also performed well, offering viewers the fantasy of "lone" and "all powerful individuals rising up" to defeat bad guys (McSweeney 2014, 106). Joe Queenan has argued "superhero movies are made for a society that has basically given up. The police can't protect us, the government can't protect us, there are no more charismatic loners to protect us and the Euro is defunct. Clint Eastwood has left the building" (Queenan 2013). But there's another option: to *become* Clint Eastwood yourself. The gun can materialize in your hand, escaped from the screen. And you, too, can be a movie hero come to life.

Horror movies have done particularly well since 9/11. This may have to do with the "terror and paranoia" that followed 9/11 when people realized they were "not as safe in their homeland as they once thought" (Alonso-Collada 2015, 112). The gore associated with horror provides an outlet for grief and anxiety after 9/11 and the atrocities of the invasion of Afghanistan and the Iraq War. Arnold Schwarzenegger's election as governor of California in 2003 is not surprising since he represented a "nostalgic desire to return to the heroism and sanctuary of the indestructible America of the 1990s action movie after the very real destruction of such prominent American landmarks" (Leggatt 2015, 8–9). In April 2004, shocking photographs of the torture of prisoners at Abu Ghraib prison came to light. American soldiers were found responsible for assaulting, raping, and even murdering detainees.

It wasn't until 2005 that movies directly depicting 9/11 appeared. *The Guardian* labelled *War of the Worlds* (2005) "the first piece of multiplex fodder ripped straight from the rubble of 9/11" (Preston 2005). Director Stephen Spielberg said of the film: "I think 9/11 reinforced everything I'm putting into *War of the Worlds*. Just how we come together, how this nation unites in every known way to survive a foreign invader and a frontal assault. We now know what it feels like to be terrorized" (Abramowitz and Horn 2005).

On April 20, 2005, Danny Ledonne released *Super Columbine Massacre RPG!*, a videogame in which players reenact the 1999 shootings near Littleton, Colorado. In the documentary *Playing Columbine*, Ledonne (2008) claims the game is meant to provide a means to mourn the victims. In August of the same year, Hurricane Katrina decimated New Orleans and surrounding areas with over fifteen hundred dead and billions in damage.

Zombies

George A. Romero sent the script for *Land of the Dead* (2005) to studios a few days before 9/11. It was "shelved immediately since Hollywood only wanted 'family films' at that time." Interest in the script picked up after the invasion of Iraq in 2003, when people were more primed for gore and violence (Riegler 2010, 25). A radio commentator says of those who have become zombies: "They're not your neighbors and friends. Not anymore" (Romero 2005). The zombies are a ceaseless horde, a mob that never stops pounding outside the door. Terrorism, racial tensions, political antagonism, Islamophobia, and apocalyptic anxieties ramp up to manifest in *Land of the Dead*, which by the time it was made seems to explicitly evoke 9/11:

> The tower of Fiddler's Green evokes the attacks on the twin towers in New York, which is confirmed by Cholo's (John Leguizamo) statement that he will wage "jihad" on Kaufman (and Kaufman's very Bush-like statement that he will not negotiate with "terrorists"). Romero is highlighting here how so-called threats from the "outside" are ultimately linked to the concentration of wealth within the U.S. (DeGiglio-Bellemare 2005, 4)

The radio announces city folk are "raiding small rural towns for supplies like outlaws." This refreshed frontier is dark and terrifying. The humans are not likable. Maybe this is because Romero is "always on the side of his zombies" (4).

I Am Legend (2007) was one of the first films after 9/11 to show massive violence in New York. Robert Neville (Will Smith) is an "ordinary citizen turned hero," one of very few survivors of a plague and the only one with the ability to develop a cure for the virus (Alonso-Collada 2015, 113). We see his gun before we see him. He carries it everywhere.

He has a closet full of guns, and another gun by his bed. When Neville is not shooting at zombies, he works in his lab.

Neville's repeated references to New York as "Ground Zero" are a "none-too-subtle reminder that the apocalyptic fantasy we are watching feeds off post-9/11 anxieties" (Hantke 2011, 172). New York is "doomed, a place of violence and fear, of uncontrollable contagion; it requires constant vigilance and yet may kill you" (168). The symbolic association between terrorism and the zombies is hard to miss. Neville's relative peace is disrupted when he is injured and hordes of zombies follow him home, chasing his scent. Zombies, indicative of forces of chaos, pound at the doors and eventually make their way inside, violently. Neville runs through his burning house, shooting an AR-15 at them:

> **Watching the infected attack in a state of rage in which their bodies become weapons, damaged or destroyed in their assaults, it is difficult not to see in them the right-wing rhetoric of the so-called War on Terror: subhuman enemies, incapable of rational decision making, flinging themselves at us in a grim and never-ending attempt at destruction. (173)**

I Am Legend is an allegory for the "siege mentality of the United States under the Patriot Act." Neville's attempts to protect his home are "evocative of George W. Bush's repeated assertion that the United States must fight the terrorists anywhere but at home" (173). One man with a gun cannot protect us from terrorism. And yet this story—of the hero defeating much more powerful enemies with singular firepower—persists.

The Virginia Tech massacre took place on April 16, 2007. A student armed with semiautomatics entered a dormitory and a classroom building, chaining the latter shut before shooting into four classrooms. Thirty-two people died. Less than a month later, Ryan Lambourn released *V-Tech Rampage*, a Flash-based videogame based on the killings. The player controls an avatar of the killer while reenacting the murders and the shooter's eventual suicide. Lambourn appears to have envisioned the game as a joke, but more startling is the committed desire—as with the Columbine massacre videogame—to adapt real-life murders into playable videogame modules, inviting people to take on the role of a mass shooter.

But representations of mass shooting are an American commodity. *Zombieland* (2009) begins not long after a new virus has contaminated someone via a "burger at a Gas n Gulp" and the virus has spread. The virus gives victims a swollen brain and a fever that makes them violent with "a really, really bad case of the munchies." Law and order have disappeared in a matter of weeks, revealing a new Wild West: "This is now the United States of Zombieland." A voiceover explains:

> As the infection spread and the chaos grew, it wasn't enough to just be fast on your feet; you had to get a gun, and learn how to use it . . . In those moments when you're not sure the undead are really *dead dead*, don't get all stingy with your bullets. I mean, one more clean shot to the head and this woman could have avoided becoming a human happy meal. (Fleischer 2009)

The central characters are nicknamed Columbus (from Ohio) and Tallahassee (from Florida). Columbus is a self-described Sancho Panza character, a bumbling college student unlucky with women who survives because he holed up in his apartment. Tallahassee looks like Yosemite Sam with guns blazing. He is in "the ass-kicking business," dispatching zombies with hedge clippers, a baseball bat, even a banjo. Depicting one's enemies as zombies may make it seem more palatable to hack, explode, or otherwise mutilate their bodies. Tallahassee wears a classic cowboy costume with hat, boots, and gun strapped to his leg. But he will use just about anything handy to dispatch an enemy.

Tallahassee and Columbus are joined by two women, Little Rock and Wichita. The four enter an abandoned souvenir shop filled with ceremonial drums, dreamcatchers, headdresses, beads, and totem poles. The shop is called Kemo Sabe, a reference to the Lone Ranger television series. The four gleefully knock down shelving and topple stacks of tribal ritual objects. The metonymic replay of the destruction of Native American culture is impossible to miss. The film ends with a massive shoot-out between cowboys and zombies. The team of four manage to defeat a horde of killer zombies in a theme park. Wichita helps Columbus realize "some rules are made to be broken" and he too can "be a hero." Columbus saves his friends, learning that to be a man is to be violent. Like Christopher Columbus, he learns to wreck Native American artifacts and shoot up the landscape. Impressed by Columbus's bravery, grit, and willingness to shoot, the girl Wichita gives him the kiss he has been hoping for.

Apocalyptic Dreams

Take Shelter (2011) is a film for preppers, dealing in the expectation of mass collapse. The main character, Curtis (Michael Shannon) is a small-town driller and family man who has apocalyptic visions. Birds swirl unnaturally in the sky. People appear where they shouldn't. His dreams are haunted. He feels compelled to prepare for a coming storm by creating an underground shelter for his family. Curtis is not especially religious, so if the visions are of divine origin, he doesn't know it. His mother has schizophrenia, so he worries his visions might be delusions. He confesses to his wife:

> I've been having dreams . . . They always start with a . . . real powerful storm and . . . this dark thick rain, like fresh motor oil. And then . . . it just makes [people] crazy. They attack me . . . It's not just a dream. It's a feeling. I'm afraid something might be coming, something that's not rain. I cannot describe it. I just need you to believe me . . . (Nickels 2011)

He buries a shipping container and fills it with food and supplies. He plumbs it and installs a toilet. He buys gas masks and an oxygen tank. When he gets in a fight at a town dinner, he shouts at everyone: "You think I'm crazy huh? . . . well, listen up! There is a storm coming like nothing you have ever seen, and not one of you is prepared for it."

Prepper talk about an imminent "storm" was mainstreamed in 2017 after Donald Trump cryptically remarked at a dinner party that we are in "the calm before the storm." The term storm is closely affiliated with the QAnon conspiracy, where it refers to social unrest that presages a societal turning. But *Take Shelter* was made years earlier, suggesting its creators were already tuned in to right-wing circuits. The term may also refer to biblical passages with apocalyptic or prophetic import, predicting God's coming judgment (Prov. 1:22–31; Luke 12:54). Two other references are of note. First, Ellen G. White, co-founder of the Seventh-Day Adventist Church, used the phrase "the storm is coming" to refer to the end times and God's judgment of earth (White 1999). Second, Joseph Goebbels used the metaphor of a coming storm after the Nazi defeat in Stalingrad and massive bombing of German cities, in a speech calling "for total war" and absolute support of Hitler (Goebbels 1943). The NRA and firearms manufacturers used the phrase as early as 2008 during the presidential election campaign, warning in a slogan: "Prepare for the Storm in 2008" (Keller 2009, 9). *Take Shelter*'s awareness of prepper trends runs deep and early, but the film's wide acclaim is indicative of the appeal and mainstreaming of the prepper outlook.

On July 20, 2012, a shooter entered a theater in Aurora, Colorado, and shot dozens of people, killing twelve and injuring seventy. He reportedly was dressed all in black, wearing a ballistic helmet, gloves, and a gas mask, while carrying three guns. On August 5, 2012, a shooter entered a Sikh place of worship in Oak Creek, Wisconsin, armed with a semiautomatic handgun. Fueled by hate carried since 9/11 and thinking he was targeting Muslims, the shooter killed seven people, one of whom was eighty-four years old. It was election season, and anti-Muslim propaganda was rife. On December 14, 2012, a shooter entered Sandy Hook Elementary School and shot and killed twenty-six people, including twenty small children. In response to the shooting, the NRA's Wayne LaPierre condemned "a callous, corrupt and corrupting shadow industry that sells, and sows, violence against its own people" (Lichtblau and Rich 2012). He pointed to "blood-soaked slasher films like *American Psycho* and *Natural Born Killers* that are aired like propaganda loops" (LaPierre 2012).

In April 2014, surrounded by militiamen, Oath Keepers, and self-designated Patriots, Clive Bundy's son described the standoff against federal agents in rural Nevada as "like the movie *Red Dawn*"—presumably meaning the U.S. government was an invading foreign power (Neiwert 2017a, 164). "It was never about grazing fees," Bundy said, "it's about control" (164). A police officer sent to help keep things calm said, "It was like a movie set. It didn't look real" (173). On August 9, 2014, eighteen-year-old Michael Brown was killed by a police officer in Ferguson, Missouri. Protests erupted, and police were deployed in riot gear.

As a blend of post-apocalyptic frontier imagery and gun violence, the cowboy apocalypse offers the promise of justice without the need for divine intervention. It allows for social collapse and promises recovery for the man willing to fight for himself. This hybrid narrative was a comfort in the decades after 9/11 for men who could not fathom an effective response to global terror, but could see themselves surviving on a post-apocalyptic frontier. If the world falls apart, the gunslinger hero will be OK.

The Young Ones (2014) takes place in a gritty post-apocalyptic future. Dusty, gun-wielding men ride horses through a barren desert. The land was green once, but then a drought came and disagreements over water divided "states, then towns, then neighbors." The remaining settlers scrape out a miserable existence. Fertility rates drop. This explains why the villain can sell a stolen child and keep the profit. Men do terrible things in the post-apocalyptic frontier. They get away with it, too, unless they are stopped by *other* men with guns. The film uses the visual trope of a gun in point-of-view shot, much like what one sees when playing a first-person shooter game, with the viewer invited to imagine themselves holding the gun. Ernest shoots, so we do too.

The men wear cowboy hats, deal in dust, drink a lot, and fight with guns. Ernest paralyzed his wife while he was drunk. She is hooked up to an elaborate machine in a facility a day's journey away. Ernest's teenage daughter takes on the chores her mother can no longer do. She prepares food for the men, squeezing out prepackaged gruel onto grubby plates. She does the dishes, scrubbing them with sand. She launders clothes and hangs them on a line. When she is not cleaning, she is locked in her bedroom with the windows nailed closed. Flem says of the bleak world in which they live: "It's easy to think the loneliness and isolation can make a man savage." Flem *does* become savage, although he has as much opportunity to scratch out a life as anyone else.

Flem kills Ernest, impregnates the girl, and takes over the farm. He gets the irrigation system to run through the property and settles in. The men who come to bless the new fertile land engage in a godless prayer, marking this post-apocalyptic landscape as unreliant on divine intervention. Nobody will save anybody else in this world. Jerome's coming-of-age rite is learning to shoot and eventually kill Flem. Jerome embraces his own standard of justice as a gunslinger, which is to say, he becomes a man. There is little glorification of the hero, but his embrace of vindictive violence seems inevitable.

Amerigeddon (2015) was directed by Mike Norris, son of Chuck Norris. It also stars Mike Norris's daughter Greta. Max Norris, Mike Norris's son, is the creative consultant and acts in the film. Internet celebrity Alex Jones shows up too. His show *InfoWars* helped with production. Drawing on his *Curves* fitness club fortune, the film was financed and produced by millionaire Gary Heavin, who wrote the screenplay and plays the leading role. Heavin's wife acts in the film. Heavin lives next door to George Bush, on a prepper ranch in Crawford, Texas, where much of the film was made. This film is a close affair.

Amerigeddon is as much ritual as movie, as much larp (live-action role-play) as visual story. Heavin plays Charlie Gray, the gun-toting hero, acting in the film to authenticate his beliefs. Heavin defends his actual ranch in the film's play-acting as his own vision of the apocalypse unspools onscreen. The fiction of the film is a projection for Heavin's real-life convictions and functions as visual evidence of things to come.

The film begins with news reports about jihadi attacks around the world. The United Nations cooperates with the terrorists, as do some officers in the U.S. military. Government surveillance follows, fed by fears about "global corporations" and "global society." The film uses manipulated footage of Barack Obama to make him say "ordinary men and women are too small minded to govern their own affairs. Order and progress can only come when individuals surrender their rights to an all-powerful sovereign." In the credits, careful readers learn the *InfoWars* crew is responsible for the opening documentary sequence that involves this editing manipulation. The *InfoWars* editors appear to have taken the video from a speech Obama gave in 2014 in Brussels, which had been taken out of context and manipulated (Jacobson 2014).

The UN chairman in Dubai, a George Soros lookalike, says people who live in Africa, India, and China "would be better off dead." To lower the population to a sustainable number, they will murder billions of people using an EMP. They start with America, because "a strong America is the only thing standing in the way of a new world order" (quoting Kissinger, apparently). "When parents see their children starving, families hauled away to FEMA camps or prison or worse, then yes, we expect some resistance at first. These are but the . . . birth pangs of a New World Order." That phrase, New World Order, is antisemitic code for fears about a globalized government and the rule of Satan in the end times. We meet Charlie the cowboy messiah as he confronts a hostile congressional panel.

> I'm here today . . . to encourage the U.S. Congress to take action to protect our country . . . our nation is sustained by a vulnerable and woefully outdated power grid . . . Your peers determined that immediately after the detonation of one of these [EMP] weapons we would lose all sources of power . . . According to your report, 90% of the American population will die in the first 12 months . . . I came here to call you to action. (Norris 2016)

A senator, played by Alex Jones, grows irritated and defensive, but Charlie won't back down.

> You had time to pass the National Defense Authorization Act to give the President the power . . . to arrest any American by simply accusing them of terrorism, [and] imprisoning them indefinitely without charges and no legal counsel . . . I'm an American citizen who's fed up with an out of control dictatorial government . . . I am an American. I am a patriot. You, sir, are nothing but a traitor. (Norris 2016)

The predictable detonation of the EMP by global terrorists results in the immediate loss of the internet, electricity, and computers. Things get dicey fast. One of Charlie's friends on the radio declares FEMA camps have been set up in New York and L.A. The patriots' fears about a New World Order seem to come true. Looters destroy Chicago. A young coed is chased on a college campus by men with axes. She was a feminist but learns her lesson and must be rescued from campus by Charlie in his helicopter. American troops are ordered to "fire on American citizens whether armed or not." Charlie says to his liberal friend: "You were the problem. You can kiss your government goodbye. This is the time when folks run and hide. Or they pull up their bootstraps and they fight" (Norris 2016).

Charlie's neighbors flee to his ranch because he is a manly savior. Charlie's neighbor Betty tells her family that Charlie "will protect you and he will want to." Representatives of the traitorous U.S. government come to Charlie's compound to seize his weapons. At one point, Heavin flies his own helicopter, pretending to defend himself against the U.S. military. Charlie is able, with a small force of select people, to stave them off.

Charlie offers a voiceover after the defeat of the globalists, glorifying himself and inviting viewers to be as paranoid as he is:

> Our story may never be recorded in the annals of history. And our history is now nothing but fond memories of a once great nation, a nation founded by a legion of patriots with a scroll of simple principles. A nation bought and paid for by heroes that were willing to die for her. We are not willing to die for a puppet government run by demonic elite. Jefferson was right: "The tree of liberty must be refreshed from time to time by the blood of tyrants and patriots." It may not have been our choice, but we are the new patriots. (Norris 2016)

Amerigeddon is a vanity film based on Heavin's real-life fears, apocalyptic hopes, and dreams of messianic grandeur. By filming himself as a hero, Heavin uses the film production as a prophetic warning for viewers. The film is a ritualized performance of desire for a time when vigilantes will be justified in killing anyone who gets too close. Heavin desires the downfall of the U.S. government and expects the New World Order will be in league with jihadists. Managing to be racist, antisemitic, Islamophobic, sexist, and ethnocentric all at the same time, *Amerigeddon* is a rich man's fantasy come to life. Heavin takes a preliminary trip to the world to come, and he brings his helicopter and bullets with him.

In real life, confrontations between preppers and government officials were happening as well. In early 2016, there was a violent standoff as far-right extremists led by Ammon Bundy took over the headquarters of the Malheur National Wildlife Refuge in Oregon to protest the imprisonment of two Oregon ranchers. They occupied the building for forty-one days.

At the same time, gun violence permeated American consciousness. On June 12, 2016, a shooter affiliated with ISIS entered Pulse, a gay nightclub in Orlando, Florida. Using a semiautomatic rifle and a nine-millimeter Glock, he killed forty-nine people and wounded fifty-three more. In the fall of 2017, a shooter in Las Vegas killed fifty-nine people and injured nearly five hundred, shooting into a live arena from a window across the street. In his hotel room, he had twenty-two scoped rifles and thousands of rounds of ammunition. He aimed these at a crowd of twenty-two thousand people at a country music festival. All his weapons were legal and registered under his name (Dunbar-Ortiz 2018, 142). On February 14, 2018, a shooter opened fire in Parkland, Florida, at Marjory Stoneman Douglas High School.

In Donald Trump's response to the Parkland mass shooting, he criticized videogames and movies, saying: "You look at some of these videos. I mean, I don't know what this does to a young kid's mind . . . looking at videos where people are just being blown away left and right . . . the level of craziness and viciousness in the movies. I think we have to look at that, too" (Trump 2018). But the problem is subtler and more profound. Guns are reckless props, utilized in all sorts of media as the thing that lives in the *other* of the mediated world and also resides in the material reality of this world. Guns are metaphysical voyagers, an authentication for believers of the screened worlds to which they point.

Guns as Incarnational Props

Consumption of film is about much more than the passive absorption of images. Guns, as props, are incarnational objects. To hold a gun—or a replica of it—is to imagine yourself transported to another world, one you know from film or your own cultivated fantasies. To wield a gun is to imagine yourself like John Wayne as the essential cowboy. Historian Kristin Kobes Du Mez explains in her book *Jesus and John Wayne*:

> John Wayne became an icon of rugged American manhood for generations of conservatives. Pat Buchanan parroted Wayne in his

presidential bid. Newt Gingrich called Wayne's *Sands of Iwo Jima* "the formative movie of my life," and Oliver North echoed slogans from that film in his 1994 Senate campaign. In time, Wayne would also emerge as an icon of Christian masculinity. Evangelicals admired . . . him for his toughness and swagger; he protected the weak, and he wouldn't let anything get in the way of his pursuit of justice and order. . . . He did not live a moral life by the standards of traditional Christian virtue. Yet for many evangelicals, Wayne would come to symbolize a different set of virtues—a nostalgic yearning for a mythical "Christian America," a return to "traditional" gender roles, and the reassertion of (white) patriarchal authority. (2021, 10)

John Wayne is appealing to the gunslinger who hopes that he too might embody these values, live this life. If we think of the cowboy apocalypse as ensconced in a future post-apocalyptic time—imminent though it may be—then it is easier to understand why some fans want ritual authentication. The gun travels symbolically, literally, easily, from the world onscreen to the hands of the gunslinger to the wished for world to come.

Just as Christians wear a cross to remind them of Jesus's death, and as Jews light a menorah to remind them of the ancient Temple, so gun enthusiasts carry a gun as validation of their story of the world. Fans have purchased a prop pulse rifle used in *Aliens* (1986), a shotgun used in *Terminator*, and the pistol used by Agent Smith in *The Matrix*. For those who can't afford props, there are numerous companies providing replica guns. The Beretta 92F used by Bruce Willis in *Die Hard* sold on eBay with bids starting at $20,000 (Sagi 2017). It may seem disturbing to put guns in the same category as crosses and menorahs, but the fundamental relationship of objects to stories in religious practice affirms this approach.

The greatest danger of film is how it can map onto real life ideologically and materially. Of course, not everyone views film this way. But for those who *do*, film can become an invitation to step into the role of a messianic gunslinger, to project themselves into the image of the swaggering hero. The gun is transported back into real life, authenticating the cowboy identity of its wielder. To aim a gun at a bad guy is to lean into a post-apocalyptic future in which one's sense of justice is forcefully enacted. For the gunslinger, to shoot *now* brings us closer to *then*.

The gun has always had a rich tactile appeal for fans of Westerns, action movies, and videogames. The gun can realize—as in, *make real*—a screened experience via imaginative play, fan performance, personalized target shooting, reenactments, cosplay, and gun clubs. Whereas films are fixed narrative streams, the individual viewer's immersive engagement with a film can take more interactive forms offscreen. Films can function as rituals of *pre*-enactment. The screen on which the film plays out becomes a predictive text for a contemporary apocalyptic moment that is authenticated and transcribed through the gun. The gun becomes a sacramental object that authenticates belief in the world to come.

Contemporary cowboy apocalypse films are abundant once you know to look for them. In *The Day* (2012), travelers wander down post-apocalyptic dusty roads in boots and trench coats, guns in hand, searching for supplies while pursued by cannibals. *The Blackout* (2014) depicts a small town after an EMP attack. The local prepper, Jim, asks the other townspeople:

> **What are you going to do when they leave the cities and come pouring in here? . . . When the food runs out, they'll leave . . . their homes and come to ours . . . We're gonna share? We're gonna take them in? What are you gonna do when you have a thousand people coming this way? A hundred thousand? (Mandylor 2014)**

Crowds are hard to depict in low-budget films, so in *The Day* we get a handful of rapists emboldened by the collapse of law and order; weeping women; and men pensively cleaning their guns in poorly lit living rooms. Other films offer similar narratives, though drawing on different causes for collapse. *Global Meltdown* (2017) presumes the disintegration of an Antarctic ice sheet leading to earthquake, tsunami, and lava eruptions from Yellowstone. A small-town mayor and a scientist seek help from a local prepper in fatigues and a cowboy hat. *How It Ends* (2018) involves a symbolic journey west after a destructive event causes social upheaval. Within five days, the United States has collapsed and ruffians block roads, steal supplies, and shoot at will.

The Survivalist (2021) stars John Malkovich in a world of "deranged messiahs." He tries to steal a woman for procreation in a COVID-ridden post-apocalyptic environment. The woman is saved by a man in a vest with a gun. *Once Upon a Time in the Apocalypse* (2021) pits good guys against bad guys in a future bombed wasteland reminiscent of the Civil War in which women are stolen for pleasure and the Wild West has returned. Although it might be tempting to expect all of these films to exhibit a list of key features of the cowboy apocalypse, a more effective read is to see the cowboy apocalypse itself as a core myth that is then transmediated in these different forms, such that the presumption of the storyline draws from the mythic hub.

Films can serve as fan fiction, as actor cosplay, and as fetishized devotion to the gun. Fans who utilize props aren't fulfilling a desire to consume the text; they want to inhabit it. Anthropologist Peter Stromberg calls this "enthrallment": a means of immersion in culturally available fictions (cited in Geraghty 2014, 34). Props, memorabilia, costumes, and other artifacts from the imagined world take on new life in real-life performative activities. Replica objects, especially those crafted by fans, can provide anchors of identity. The gun as prop can work as material evidence of a desired future, held for real in the messianic gunslinger's hands. In a sense, props are sacramental, functioning as material bridges between the world as we know it and the world a fan longs for. Material embodiments of an imagined, otherworldly space and time, guns bring these imaginary spaces to life by bridging here and the beyond. For those who have watched apocalyptic gun violence repeatedly in films, enacting gun violence in real life can seem a kind of ritual confirmation.

On the set of the unfinished film *Rust* in October 2021, actor Alec Baldwin demonstrated how he would lift his character's gun and aim it at the camera: "So, I guess I'm gonna take this out, pull it out and go, 'Bang!'" The gun fired, and for reasons still not satisfactorily explained, it discharged a real bullet. Cinematographer Halyna Hutchins was shot and died not long after. Director Joel Souza was injured. Filmmakers do not need to use functional guns to give the impression of real gunfire, so why were the prop handlers in *Rust* using a real .45 Colt revolver? Baldwin's gun, although technically a prop, was *also* the real thing. Perhaps producers (Baldwin among them) wanted the feel of a real gun so Baldwin could feel like a real cowboy. But Halyna Hutchins's death, while a filming mishap, was also a real death.

The gun generates a sense of presence and force well beyond its mediation. The gun evokes a story, and the story evokes the gun, materializing as a tangible object for substantiating apocalyptic expectation and living out filmic fantasy. For those who view the gun as a sacred object, it cannot be considered outside the context of the narrative that enlivens it. Baldwin's gun functioned within the film even when they were only rehearsing, and although the death was tragic, the gun did what guns do. What does a gun want? A gun wants to shoot.

Shooting

Looking to Colt revolvers and the Gatling gun as inspiration, the French physiologist Étienne-Jules Marey developed the most famous precinematic moving photographic device, a machine to capture the motion of birds. Marey's interest in aerial locomotion of creatures with wings led him to create this recording instrument in 1882 that, like a revolver, shot a bird in its sight. Marey's "photographic gun" could capture images of living things to make study of their movement possible. And this is as valid an origin to the cinema as the shift from still images of photography to moving images.

The idea for the device came from the "astronomical revolver" made by a colleague recording the movement of visible planets (Virilio 1994, 171). But Marey's device looked very much like a rifle, with a lens in the barrel. Pulling the trigger allowed an image to be taken and pulling it in quick succession allowed multiple images. This "motion capture" (172) illuminates the ease with which guns and cameras work using similar technology. The camera captures life, and the gun can extinguish it. Both are movements in time, a series of fragmentary grabs of moments expertly punctuated. Marey's chronophotographic gun was a predecessor to the Lumière brothers' cameras as well as to the machine gun camera used for training in World War I. Cameras and guns are both devoted to "exposing, optimizing, and controlling the forces of life" (174). Today's preoccupation with screened surveillance is an artifact of this relationship between gun and camera.

War today, like film capture, is "fundamentally a game of hide-and-seek" (69). Before there were computers to manage statistical memory of battles, there were camera recordings. War has been shaped by the camera's ability to "reconstitute the fracture lines of the trenches, to fix the infinite fragmentation of a mind landscape alive with endless possibilities" (71). The shift in military perception from conquering space to managing time was facilitated by visual technology of camera and radar, radios and screens (72). The affiliation between bomb and camera horrendously materialized when the first bomb dropped on Hiroshima caused kimono patterns to be tattooed on the flesh of victims (81). With the military drone, "nothing now distinguishes the functions of the weapon and the eye" (83). Drone use to detect illegal refugees on the United States' borders renders these areas a perpetual battle zone.

Today, we set the camera's sights on ourselves in indolent surrender to social media. The camera's eye is always aimed at something, authenticating its existence. Perhaps it is no coincidence that guns feature so heavily in our screened pastimes: our movies, games, and television shows. More than a century ago, the cinema of the Lumière brothers became more reliable than the watchful eye of a "melancholy [battle] look-out who can no longer believe his eyes" (73). Light is the "soul of gun barrels" and the eye of war (83).

To act with self-conviction against a perceived enemy is to tap into the imagined post-apocalyptic world, heralding a future the well-poised gun will instigate. For the cowboy messiah, the gun is not just a totem for Wild West fandom but also a ritual object gesturing toward a desired future. In the cowboy apocalypse, the gun functions as a tool of societal rebuilding in the ideological mold of the believer. The gun is a promise of the power to circumscribe a violent perimeter around the believer's perpetually threatened existence and to kill at will. No wonder this story animates a whole swath of xenophobic believers who wish to return to an American frontier that never really was.

A WHITE MAN'S FRONTIER

THE WALKING DEAD

When I was fifteen, I briefly dated a sixteen-year-old boy who kept a gun rack in the back window of his pickup truck. He lived in a trailer park about ten miles from my hometown. He wore a black cowboy hat and boots, tight Levi's, and a belt with a silver buckle. Like many of the boys I dated, he kept a round tin of Skoal chewing tobacco in his back pocket, and his jeans had a permanent faded ring from the tin. This boy, whose name was Rick or Rob or Ryan, raped me one afternoon in his trailer. He drove me home in his truck with the gun rack against the back of my head. Once home, I told him I didn't want to see him again unless there was no sex involved. He spat back that a relationship without sex was no relationship at all. A few weeks later on a date with a different boy, we were chased down the street by the first boy in his truck while he shouted obscenities. The 1980s were like this for me, filled with anti-feminist fury. Guns were for men—white men—and they were a means to express dominant masculinity.

In its portrayal of the end of civilization as we know it, the television show *The Walking Dead* provides mediated space in which to confront fears about societal collapse through the imagination of the cowboy apocalypse. Religion scholar Mircea Eliade implies that we hunger for apocalypse. He describes what he calls the terror of history, a fear that time will march relentlessly forward despite humanity's miserable search for meaning. Eliade argues that we suffer most when we assume an unceasing unfolding of time:

> [I]n our day, when historical pressure no longer allows any escape, how can man tolerate the catastrophes and horrors of history

from collective deportations and massacres to atomic bombings if beyond them he can glimpse no sign, no transhistorical meaning; if they are only the blind play of economic, social, or political forces, or, even worse, only the result of the "liberties" that a minority takes and exercises directly on the stage of universal history? (1971, 150)

As serialized television, *The Walking Dead* imitates this relentless grind of time, depicting impossibly complicated problems, many of which cannot be solved but only endured. There is no expected conclusion to *The Walking Dead*; after eleven seasons and an apparent end to the original series, multiple spin-offs and an episodic anthology series are already in motion. The show situates itself not at the precipice of tumultuous change, but in the grisly aftermath. It shows the ceaseless horrors of living in a radically transformed environment, where weapons are your only defense against a sea of zombies who want only to consume you. When read from the perspective of the disenfranchised white male, this slog is defined by the relentless presence of those who would disrupt white male leadership: angry feminists, non-white protestors and their allies, class agitators, refugees, and aspiring asylum seekers. Nobody in this post-apocalyptic world rests easily.

Manly Media

The Walking Dead began as a comic book series by Robert Kirkman, Tony Moore, and Charlie Adlard, first issued in 2003 (Kirkman 2003). After NBC and HBO turned the series down, AMC picked it up and it premiered in 2010, with the comics as source material (Darabont 2010). The transmediated components of *The Walking Dead* borrow not only from the comics that inspired the television show, but also from other elements of cowboy apocalyptic culture at large. AMC's website used to offer *The Walking Dead* games tied into Facebook, and apps like the "Dead Yourself" app. In addition to buying *The Walking Dead* action figures and other memorabilia, you could buy *The Walking Dead* toy guns and a fully functional *The Walking Dead* survival kit. For $400 on eBay, you can buy a replica prop gun (a Python) signed by Andrew Lincoln (Lincoln n.d.). There are numerous fan websites, memorabilia, and even an "after show," *The Talking Dead*, which ran until 2022 and invited input from viewers. The host, Chris Hardwick, saw the show as offering "the opportunity to nerd out about the story in a very public forum: what they like, what they don't like, or what questions they may have" (Paul and Wrenn 2014). The NRA's *Noir* show released an episode in 2014 called "The 5 Minute Zombie Apocalypse," in which gun enthusiasts played a shooting game while pursued by zombie actors (Robbins 2014). In *The Walking Dead*, the gun is a visceral evocation of anxiety about a bleak, terrifying future. It is also a manly talisman directed against the endless bombardment of monstrous others disrupting white male privilege.

In their study of evangelical men, *Does God Make the Man?: Media, Religion, and the Crisis of Masculinity*, Stewart Hoover and Curtis Coats discover the overwhelming majority of those interviewed "still cling to an essentialist patriarchy, albeit one that looks different from that of their fathers" (2015, 6). They find that media plays a complex but important role in the persistence of these ideas (6). Media can offer Christian men "salient practical resources for negotiating headship, perhaps even to a greater degree than their faith communities did" (41). But what sorts of media function most effectively in this regard? I propose *The Walking Dead* can be read as a model for white male headship in the twenty-first century, offering the same kinds of values purported to be important to the evangelical men that Hoover and Coats study. Furthermore, the show's post-apocalyptic framework marks it as remarkably similar in function to the biblical texts that still inform many Christian men's views of gender relations today.

An Apocalyptic Edge

The Walking Dead presents itself as a vision of how people are to live in the wake of catastrophe, although it places itself in a secular post-apocalyptic context defined by a desire to return to what those in power see as normal. Apocalypticism is characterized by an interest in boundaries, borders, and thresholds. Eschatology, a phenomenon closely related to apocalypticism, draws its name from the Greek *eschatos*, which means "end" or "edge" or "brink." Apocalypticism defines the edge between *now* and *then*, *here* and *there*, us and them, good and evil. It predicts a definitive ending to struggles for those who see the world as beyond repair. For apocalyptic writers, the world is "poised to end" because it is "so suffused with moral rottenness" that it "should and must end, and it must end because in some crucial sense it has ended." For these writers, "[e]very structure of the world is infected, and only an absolute, purifying cataclysm can make possible an utterly new, perfected world" (Berger 1999, 7).

Apocalypticism opens up a space, an edge, to look beyond the current world and imagine how it might be fixed. The trouble lies in who gets to define the world as broken, and what it means for it to be repaired. Donald Trump's "Make America Great Again" slogan, for example, trucks in white supremacist, sexist, and xenophobic ideals. To fix the world for white supremacy is an apocalyptic desire, but one that is exclusive, bigoted, and easily turns violent. As women's political and social rights have expanded, fundamentalist groups have worked on maintaining "arch-traditional gender norms intentionally and overtly, as a crucial part of the boundary marking that define[s] them as a group" (Brasher 2014, 18). Perhaps it is this tension that has led some fundamentalists to embrace post-apocalyptic media like *The Walking Dead*, where the impending threat of destruction has come and gone, leaving room to rebuild in gender-normative ways. This is the "hot desire of fundamentalism" that "shuts down that opening where the present pulses into its future" (Keller 2005, ix).

Feminist scholar Lee Quinby claims we can easily find apocalyptic views in entertainment media, generating in us a disposition toward "apocalyptic fitfulness" that "heightens gender panic." In these mediated stories, the basic logic of apocalypticism is recognizable, "upholding a hierarchy of male authority and female submission, a demonization of women's independence, and a justification of punishment for activities that are deemed impure" (1999, 111). The panic of apocalypticism provides a cover story for what comes after: when God promises to "wipe away all the tears from their eyes" (Rev. 21:4), he assures only the *male* recipients of his bounty. This rebirth of the world is achieved "without a female body, freed of the obligation to care for others, and relieved of our most profound uncertainty" (Quinby 1999, 112). Gendered order, with its divinely ordained male headship, brings relief, at least for the dominators.

A post-apocalyptic scenario works well in ideologically informed narrative contexts because it removes the advances of technology and unsettles social order (Parrinello-Cason 2012). In this imagined afterworld, "all identities and values are clear" (Berger 1999, 8). This stripping away occurs in *The Walking Dead*, which initially walls off awareness of the world beyond Atlanta, Georgia. The cast members include both white and Black English-speaking characters, one Asian American, and a few Latinx characters. But no Europeans, no Africans, no Chinese characters, and in the early seasons, no Muslims or Jews at all. Queer characters have given up the fight for equality in this new world. Aaron, for example, is gay, and this makes him an outsider. But he's alright with that, because he cares most about making people feel comfortable. Tara, who is lesbian, handles jokes about her preference for women with amiable patience.

Because apocalypticism is an act of imagination, the world to come is "the true object of the apocalyptic writer's concern" (Berger 1999, 6). But *who* gets to determine what is good in the world to come? For white supremacists and misogynists, the past is a time of idealized, unquestioned authority. The present is chaotic and evil. We saw this sort of imagination at work in the brutal quasi-apocalyptic stories told by powerful white men about Black people after the Civil War. For radical feminists and anti-racists, the past *and* the present are defined by oppression.

Feminism is not merely about women's experience. The revolutionary feminist bell hooks links sexism with racism and classism to the feminist fight against patriarchy:

> **Radical visionary feminism encourages all of us to courageously examine our lives from the standpoint of gender, race, and class so that we can accurately understand our position within the imperialist white supremacist capitalist patriarchy. For years many feminist women held to the misguided assumption that gender was the sole factor determining their status. Breaking through this denial was a crucial turning point for feminist politics. (hooks 1997)**

Apocalypticism is never neutral. Its dependence on good and evil marks some groups as essentialized representatives of trouble, and others as sovereign and blessed. Protestors and disruptors open the future into a glorious uncertainty, embracing its messiness and potential for change, moved by the imagination of a world in which all humans are treated with dignity and respect. The very *idea* of a future that is not predetermined, that is driven by love instead of righteousness, is *itself* a threat to self-authenticated white supremacist command. Feminists seek not to conquer men, but to create a world in which white male headship is no longer desired.

In the post-apocalyptic text of *The Walking Dead*, the ideological slate has been wiped clean, carving out a narrow, rigid environment in which—at least in the first two seasons—white men rule without question. By depicting the current world—our world—as a relic visible only in the decomposing bodies of zombies, *The Walking Dead* presents a post-apocalyptic portrait drawn from conservative Christian models of gender norms. These values find their roots in part in the teachings of Paul, the author of several early Christian letters in the New Testament.

The Household Code

The Walking Dead functions as a kind of "household code" for the twenty-first century, especially for evangelical Christian viewers—but also for nonreligious viewers who crave *gender doxa* ("straight" thinking). We can see this by looking at the way the "household code" of the Deutero-Pauline epistles first developed in an apocalyptic context in the ancient world, then see how these values are replicated in *The Walking Dead* and amplified with the introduction of related values, most notably the willing exercise of brutality for the sake of one's family.

The Deutero-Pauline household code constitutes a means of coping with the aftermath of an expected (and delayed) divinely ordained apocalypse. *The Walking Dead* also depicts a world transformed. In both cases, male leaders feel threatened by the potential loss of authorized leadership. Household codes reinscribe gender norms after society has been transformed due to apocalyptic beliefs. Whereas Paul's theology was based on actual historical circumstances and *The Walking Dead* is fictional, the television series nonetheless functions as an effective, if problematic, model for manliness, more than capable of serving as a new household code for viewers who take seriously its vision of ideal gender norms.

Paul wrote self-consciously within an apocalyptic context. Like his Jewish counterparts, Paul's outlook was "dominated by an eager longing for and an earnest expectation of the messianic kingdom." Paul believed he was "living on the boundary between two worlds—one dying and the other being born" (Roetzel 1983, 44). Paul appears to have been more comfortable with the idea of gender equality than most people realize. This is partly because of the common confusion between Paul's authentic letters and later ones written in his name. In his letter to the Galatians, which he certainly wrote himself, Paul famously announces God has appeared in human form: "There is neither Jew nor Greek, there is neither slave nor free, there is neither male nor female; all are one in Christ Jesus" (Paul 3:28). Many scholars think Paul quoted a common baptismal liturgy, one that "proclaimed a fundamental restructuring of the cosmos" as the result of Christ's incarnation, death, and resurrection (Polaski 2005, 67). Paul seems to have accorded new freedoms to women as part of his articulation of changed times (1 Cor. 7:4, 11:8–12).

Feminist biblical scholar Elisabeth Schüssler Fiorenza reads the Galatians liturgy as asserting "there are no longer men and women in Christ, but that patriarchal marriage—and sexual relationships between male and female—is no longer constitutive of the new community in Christ" (1992, 211). Others go even further, asserting the passage announces "a complete erasure of sexual difference" in the early Christian community with an associated "breakdown of hierarchy" (MacDonald 1987). Paul expected he and his contemporaries would still be alive when Christ returned, so fixed social structures were already unwinding.

Paul's letters were shaped by a "heightened awareness of God's impending doom" (Roetzel 1983, 44). His advice about marriage (don't do it if you can avoid it), taxes (pay them), and governmental authority (follow it for now) are all colored by an expectation that time is short (44). So too, his hints about new roles for women are shaped by the sense that things have changed fundamentally *because* the end is near. Accordingly, he viewed women as spiritually equal to men. The passages in Paul's letters referring to women's roles are contested, to be sure. Yet it remains clear there were some women who took Paul's message of "neither male nor female" to heart. Romans 16 mentions no less than ten women engaged in the work of building the church.

A few decades after Paul died, some continued the tradition of Pauline letters, drawing on a longstanding practice of writing under the assumed name of a famous religious leader with credibility. The first set of letters written in Paul's name include Colossians, Ephesians, and 2 Thessalonians. Skeptics point out differences in language, style, and theology when compared to the authentic Pauline corpus (Roetzel 1983, 134), though some people insist these letters were written by Paul after he changed his mind about the time of the end—thus the label "disputed" for these "Deutero-Pauline" letters. In them we see the language of headship expressed in earnest, via what scholars call the household code. Colossians includes what is likely the first iteration of the famous statement of wives' and husbands' duties: "Wives, be subject to your husbands, as is fitting in the Lord. Husbands, love your wives, and do not be harsh with them" (3:18–19). Ephesians exhibits a similar style:

> **Wives, be subject to your husbands, as [you are] to the Lord. For the husband is the head of the wife as Christ is the head of the church, his body, and is himself its Savior. As the church is subject to Christ, so let wives also be subject in everything to their husbands. Husbands, love your wives, as Christ loved the church and gave himself up for her, that he might sanctify her. . . . Even so husbands should love their wives as their own bodies. He who loves his wife loves himself . . . as Christ does the church, because we are members of his body . . . and let the wife see that she respects her husband. (5:22–6:3)**

Here, wives are explicitly told to view their husbands as "head" and savior. These passages are a centerpiece in contemporary evangelical interpretations of male-led households. The code framed in Ephesians, as Hoover and Coats discovered in their work on evangelical men, is key for evangelical men's understanding of their own masculinity.

The household code was a means of coping with the fact that the end didn't come as expected. It offers a new model for family relations in the wake of disappointment. Whereas the authentic Paul had expected the second coming to arrive at any moment, the end is alluded to in Ephesians "only in the most general way," as "the sense of urgency that informs the apostolic mission is gone, and no interest in the Parousia (or Second Coming) is expressed" (Roetzel 1983, 142). The household code worked to reestablish the status quo. Women were to get back in line.

The next layer of Pauline epistles is known as the Pastorals, so called because they offer a pastor-like set of guidelines for new churches. These letters consist of 1 and 2 Timothy, and Titus. The anonymous author of these letters lives on after the expected end, explicitly reestablishing the hierarchy Paul had mostly dismantled, demanding women cease taking on leadership roles for themselves. It seemed Jesus was not returning right away, so the letters sought to undo the social disruption Paul's initial letters had allowed.

The Pastorals are, in a way, post-apocalyptic. They were written in the aftermath of the destruction of the Temple and the disappointment of expectation in Christ's imminent return. A lot of the differences between Paul's authentic letters and the Pastoral letters (by an unknown figure called the Pastor) can be attributed to the difference in historical situation: "For Paul the imminent return of Christ colors all of his thought; for the Pastor the Parousia, or return of Christ, plays little if any role in the order and mission of the church" (154). The Pastoral letters describe a mode of living when the end is no longer imminent. They are also sometimes read as a frustrated, conventional response to the proliferation of proto-gnostic views in early Christianity. The Gnostics believed salvation was "a return to a state of androgynous perfection" in which men and women were spiritually equal, a view most male church leaders could not tolerate (Polaski 2005, 69). As the Pastorals are an indictment of gender freedoms expressed in the second century, so *The Walking Dead* is an indictment of gender freedoms today. Both accomplish this by imagining a world their authors prefer in post-apocalyptic space.

The Pastor insists in his letters that women who receive financial support from the church must be, above all, timid and obedient. They must have been married and had children, presumably to weed out the women who refused to marry. Some women began shaving their heads to pass for men, taking on leadership roles. The apocryphal *Acts of Paul and Thecla* depicts a young woman who pretends to be a man so she can follow Paul and avoid marriage.

The Pastor pushes back against this kind of work. He suggests women should be "sensible, chaste, domestic, kind, and submissive to their husbands, that the word of God may not be discredited" (Titus 2:3–5). He warns about women "upsetting whole households" by taking on roles to which they had no right (Titus 1:10–15). He wouldn't have been so worried about uppity women if some women hadn't been uppity.

In Titus we find some of the harshest expectations for gender structures, including that women should "learn in silence with all submissiveness" and they should have "no authority over men." Forbidding women who refuse to marry from entering into the "order of widows," the Pastor says women will be "saved through childbearing" provided they act with enough modesty (Titus 2:11–15). Lori of *The Walking Dead* fulfills this prescription when she redeems herself by sacrificing her own life, giving birth. The Pastoral letters offer a vision of what the authors think should happen after apocalyptic expectation has waned, using a post-apocalyptic imaginary to urge reinstitution of hegemonic gender norms.

The Walking Dead as Household Code

As I have suggested, gender norms represented in *The Walking Dead* are akin to the early Christian household codes, and the show could well function as a model for contemporary evangelical viewers. Is it possible that the Deutero-Pauline household code has directly influenced the creators of *The Walking Dead*, even if only through the cultural prominence of the Bible in American Christian culture? Yes, of course. In a way, it doesn't matter if the path of influence is direct or indirect; the effect is the same. *The Walking Dead*'s writers could have put anything into the imaginative space of post-apocalypse. They chose to be fundamentalist in the basic sense of the word, and they chose to affirm the conservative values of the Deutero-Pauline household code:

> [T]he survivors are grouped into a hierarchical system of a decidedly male "government." Even though society itself has fallen to the undead, cultural beliefs about gender roles are one of the few shreds of humanity the survivors cling to. A central component of the narrative is two White men struggling for control. It is never called into question whether they have a right to govern the other survivors. It is simply taken for granted that a White man must be in control to protect those who are "Others." (Greene and Meyer 2014, 70)

The show presents us with a world with many of the same values as those celebrated by the Pastoral epistles, where women are subject to their husbands and take their husbands' opinions as seriously as they do their God's.

The Walking Dead is not a progressive vision: "while the writers occasionally take a moment to comment on the state of gender—and of race—in this new world, in the end they leave these issues to die and reconstitute a world in which white men rule" (Berry 2012). The show creates a post-apocalyptic space in which to place conservative gender values—by sweeping away the world as we know it. In the first season, "the old-fashioned ways of domestic harmony" have returned. Men serve as guards for the camp and women "do a seemingly endless supply of laundry." The "domestic sphere has reverted back," to the 1950s, where "women do housework and care for children while men keep the women safe" (Berry 2012). This depiction of women's roles predominates in the first two seasons of the show and remains a standard for most women throughout:

> **Whatever else might be said about *The Walking Dead*, or about zombie narrative in general, its uncritical relationship to a particular pre-feminist narrative about the need to "protect" women and children cannot be glossed over. "Proper" control over wombs, and anxiety that they will somehow be captured, polluted, or compromised, is a kind of Ur-myth for the apocalyptic genre in general and the zombie sub-genre in particular; speaking broadly, the function of women in most apocalyptic narratives is to code the ending as "happy" or "sad" based on**

their continued availability to bear the male protagonist's children when the story is over. (Canavan 2010, 444)

The Walking Dead, especially in these earlier seasons, is a close fit for the ideals that Hoover and Coats (2015) identify as meaningful today to many evangelical Christian men, even if in the show they are punctuated with violence. Hoover and Coats recognize, based on conversations with evangelical men in their study, a kind of "elemental masculinity," that is, "a kind of residual of traditionalism, left over when other, more problematic dimensions of masculinity have been discarded in the process of social progress toward egalitarianism" (23). The man motivated by "elementalism" wants to:

> ... provide for his family, to protect that family, and to engage in purposive action oriented toward the family. The notion of headship is a way of framing gender through a divine order and channeling it through a domestic ideal, where the man's role is particular, focused, and ascendant. (62)

This notion of headship relies on a divine order, but it does not rely heavily on scriptures to support it. Instead, Christian men turn to media for reinforcement of patriarchal beliefs. *The Walking Dead* reflects evangelical values of male provision, protection, and purpose.

The theme of provision runs throughout the show. Teams, consistently composed and mostly led by men, go out on frequent supply runs. These excursions largely drive the plot. Only after the group settles into the prison in Season 3 do they become capable of providing for themselves via gardening and livestock. Such passive means of survival, however, are insufficient, as their pigs catch a disease, and the group is thrust back out to salvage what food and supplies they can from the abandoned homes of the dead.

The theme of protection is also key. The show is filled with fences, boundaries, edges, and closed spaces—because it is only in places with managed borders where one can be safe. Glenn feels a duty to protect Maggie, his girlfriend. Rick, too, feels compelled to protect the women in the camp, and feels personally responsible when his wife dies while he is not nearby. Dale protects Andrea by denying her a gun. An entire storyline takes place at the repurposed prison, where protection looks like walling off dangerous forces. They are safer inside a prison than outside of it. The symbolism here resembles the logic employed by survivalists, who build bunkers in which they imagine the heteronormative, male-led post-apocalyptic future they want. The gun works like a mobile perimeter—wedding independence with greater agency of movement. Zombies in *The Walking Dead* never use guns—it's part of what defines them out of being human.

The male characters in *The Walking Dead* are driven by a need for purpose and seem actualized by a menacing post-apocalyptic environment. Glenn, for example, grows into an important leader of the group, second in command. While battling zombies, Glenn finds comfort by comparing his new life as a powerful, actualized man with his old life: "I'm supposed to be delivering pizzas!" (Season 6, Episode 1). Abraham is driven by the purpose of protecting his family—until he loses them. Then he is animated by the goal of getting Eugene to Washington, DC, since he claims to have a cure for the virus. Rick is, of course, driven by purpose too—especially the protection of his son.

All the women in the early seasons are presented as dependent on men and willing to defer to male leadership. The first season is filled with sexist zingers that undermine women's attempts at independence and control. Andrea, one of the lead women, is called "sugar tits" by Merle, who insinuates he would like to sexually assault her. In Season 2, Glenn confronts Lori about keeping her pregnancy secret from her husband, mopes around Maggie because she won't have sex with him, and asks Dale scathingly, "Are all the women on their period?" (Episode 5). Hershel says to Lori: "Be grateful you didn't have a daughter. If only things were as simple [for them] as wanting to shoot" (Episode 6).

When Andrea, the only woman who does want to learn to shoot, is taught how, her teacher Shane spits at her: "You're too damned emotional ... you shoot like a damned girl" (Season 2, Episode 6). It makes sense that the show's celebration of the cowboy apocalypse wouldn't have much room for a woman to handle guns; the whole point is a rehabilitation of a time when women didn't want that kind of control. Another man, Dale, uses similar reasoning, takes Andrea's gun away from her, and hides it when he deems her too emotional to carry it. Lori, by contrast, fits quite neatly with the Ephesian household code when she insists her job is to support Rick no matter what. Shane asks her to object to Rick's decision to go back into Atlanta, but Lori refuses. "What else would I do? He's my husband."

One of the most damaging scenes in the show isn't even necessary. The Governor, a man leading a survivalist camp, captures Maggie and Glenn. After interrogating Glenn, he makes Maggie take off her shirt and bra, then sexually assaults her, leading her to believe he will rape her (Season 3, Episode 7). The incident is based on a similar event in the comics, but in neither comics nor television series is the sexual assault necessary for plot advancement. Instead, it's a means of demonstrating the appropriate place for women in the cowboy apocalypse household code.

Some might argue that in later episodes, women like Michonne and Andrea are developed more fully, and that Maggie becomes stronger. While that may be true, the skills they develop are manly ones—how to shoot and kill more efficiently. In this respect, the show veers from its biblical model, allowing women the possibility of taking on male characteristics as the way to develop more agency. However, the plot development of these female characters lags far behind the stories about men, and women remain dependent on men for decision-making, deferring without question to Rick's judgment.

In a 2008 interview with Simon Abrams for *Comics Journal*, Robert Kirkman, writer on the series and author of the comics, reveals his own sexist presumptions:

> I don't mean to sound sexist, but as far as women have come over the last 40 years, you don't really see a lot of women hunters. They're still in the minority in the military, and there's not a lot of female construction workers. I hope that's not taken the wrong way. I think women are as smart, resourceful, and capable in most things as any man could be . . . but they are generally physically weaker. That's science. (Abrams 2013)

In this man-centered world, the binary is not disrupted—women are allowed to cross over only temporarily. While female characters "must adopt skills, behaviors, and attitudes typically associated with masculinity. . . . Masculine values and norms still subtly prevail in their post-apocalyptic times" (LeBlanc 2014, 3). Women who make decisions on their own are punished. Carol, for example, goes rogue and decides to burn two people who are near death to prevent spread of their illness. Rick finds out and exiles her from the group, even though he has made those same kinds of decisions many times.

Women in the show can use their sexuality: "any power that women have usually comes to them in the old-fashioned, stereotypical way of manipulating the men in their lives into doing what they want them to do" (Berry 2012). For example, when Andrea finally realizes the Governor is a brute, Carol advises her to "sleep with him" and "give him the greatest night of his life." Then, after he "drops his guard," Andrea is to kill him (Season 3, Episode 11). The story is an obvious echo of the Jewish story of Judith, with a twist. Judith, like Andrea, uses her sexuality to engender desire and enters the bed of the enemy—Holofernes, an Assyrian general who was going to destroy the city of Bethulia. Holofernes gets drunk, passes out, and is decapitated by Judith, who carries his head away in a basket. Andrea, when faced with the same situation, can't go through with the killing. Judith refuses sex but succeeds in killing, Andrea has sex, but fails to kill. The biblical woman successfully uses her wiles to seduce and defeat a man, but Andrea—in the new, post-apocalyptic world the show celebrates—cannot.

Lori and Rick's baby is named Judith by her brother, Carl. The association with the Jewish story of Judith is reinforced by the baby's nickname, "Little Ass-Kicker." Neither of these Judith characters live up to the Jewish textual counterpart, rendering the references ironic. Andrea's death is disappointing. Andrea dies a prisoner of the Governor, seeking absolution from Rick and confessing to him that "I just didn't want anyone to die." The last thing she says to Rick is, pathetically: "I tried." His final words to her: "Yeah. You did."

Even when women act in salvific ways, they defer to men for giving them the power to do it, or they discount what they have done. Maggie, after fighting off a horde of zombies to save Glenn, tells him "I tried to think what you would do if you were here, so I just emptied my clip and hoped for the best" (Season 4, Episode 15). Daryl praises Carol after she saves the entire group by single-handedly taking down the Terminus camp, saying: "You saved us. All by yourself." Carol replies: "We got lucky. We should be dead."

Michonne's character offers the most hope for a feminist model. Michonne is strong, smart, and afraid of nothing. But the show doesn't do her justice, letting her play nanny to Carl (with disturbing racist implications). Michonne follows Carl around deserted towns on errands, and later babysits Judith. As a Black woman, Michonne must earn the trust of the white men in the camp, including the teenager Carl. Indeed, she isn't accepted fully into the group until Carl tells his father she is worthy of his respect. In one pivotal scene, Rick considers "trading" Michonne—against her knowledge and will—with the Governor, in order to get back two group members held hostage (Season 3, Episode 15). The decision is Rick's alone to make, despite his suggestion they vote on it. And when he decides not to sell Michonne out, he decides that independently too. The echoes of the American slave trade are disturbing.

It's true the Pastoral epistles aren't fiction. Perhaps because he believed the apocalypse to have been postponed, the Pastor felt no need to imagine visceral horrors. *The Walking Dead*, by contrast, functions in a time of contemporary apocalypticism. Both offer clear—and remarkably similar—codes for moral conduct driven by gender expectations. Both insert these visions into imaginary space created by seeing their own time as preparatory for a return to patriarchal structures.

It's not hard to see how *The Walking Dead* may function like the Pastoral household code, filtered through the spectacle of media and shaped by the serialized design of the show. But *The Walking Dead* integrates a new and dark element: a call for brutality as the way to prove one's "headship." The willingness to kill without remorse is evidence of men's commitment to provision, protection, and purpose.

Season 4 portrays a long story arc largely focused on the development of Rick Grimes's character as he embraces his role as leader of the group. We can see the centrality of violence in the finale of Season 4 (Episode 16). Rick has killed Lou, one of a group of vicious marauders. Although violent, these men are not driven by ideals of purpose and provision. They want blood from Rick and are driven by an eye-for-an-eye moral code (Season 4, Episode 16). Their leader, Joe, uses apocalyptic language to justify his decision to kill Rick. He calls it a "day of reckoning," a "balancing of the whole damned universe." We see here the first physical display of same-sex sexuality in the entire series—violent and horrific. Carl is attacked as one of the marauders threatens to rape him, giggling maliciously. Rick, meanwhile, finds himself in combat without a gun. Using his body as a weapon, he lunges at the man's neck and bites it. The man dies. Instead of depicting loving same-sex relationships, *The Walking Dead* presents homosexuality in the context of the threat of rape, with the appropriate response being manly, even animalistic, violence. Andrew Lincoln, who plays Rick on the show, describes his character's development in chilling terms:

> [T]his is a man—his journey this season and since the beginning—it goes to the question of can we ever come back to be the people we once were, and certainly the first half of the season was about a man suppressing that and suppressing his brutality for the sake of his son. And now you see a man totally accepting that side of himself, that brutality for the sake of his son. And it's just a really neat play that you get a man who is completely at peace with the fact that he's a man and a monster and he needs to be in this new world and he's probably the most dangerous he's ever been, but also the most capable he's ever been. (Ross 2014b)

The flashback scene after the killing presents a choice. Rick can live passively farming and raising livestock; or he can support the group by going on runs for provisions, guarding fences, and engaging in salvific violence. The scene creates a contrast between two modes of living—one passive, fueled by family, agriculture, and quiet living, and the other inflamed by manly rage. One wonders if there might be more than two options. Rick believes the peaceful way of life has failed, and he must "become a monster, otherwise something terrible is going to happen to Carl, possibly all of them are going to die." Rick is "pushed to his breaking point" and realizes that "this is the world we're in and I have to be in this world, so now I'm going to do whatever I have to do" (Ross 2014a). For those viewers who see our own world as dangerous, this model of manliness appeals.

The Apocalyptic Habit

Brutality can be seen as a form of what feminist Catherine Keller calls the "apocalyptic habit," which manifests as a tendency to "think and feel in polarities of 'good' versus 'evil,'" and to seek to "purge the evil from oneself and one's world once and for all" (2005, 11). This worldview sees "destroying the destroyers" as the only means to cleanse the earth. In choosing violence, Rick embraces the apocalyptic habit. The show encourages this kind of extremism on the part of viewers who look to Rick as a model. If it's true that *The Walking Dead* functions as a kind of contemporary household code, we could argue the code includes a new element—a proof of manliness, exercised through a willingness to commit murder. Rick embodies, in fictional form, the good guy with a gun. He proves he is manly by becoming vicious.

In *The Walking Dead*, the "tools and technologies of empire" are borrowed for priming a "violent colonialist fantasy." We see "swords and guns, tanks and trucks," allusions to the "brutal physical and sexual violence of slavery" and repeated references to frontier imaginary. These are "all employed in a bizarre postmodern pastiche of the history of U.S. imperialism, as different moments of its empire collide into a single simultaneous instant in the face of an essentially inimical and totally implacable racialized threat" (Canavan 2010, 442). The zombie is above all a symbol of how dependent on death this worldview really is.

Counter-apocalypse can offer a "healing ambivalence" by refusing the binaries and absolutes on which apocalypticism depends. Replacing the "for" or "against'" with a "shimmering not-yet-ness" then leaves room for conversation, for growth, for getting to know one another better, for believing a better world is possible (Keller 2005, 220). The opposite of apocalypse is not the reversal of which groups are good and evil. The opposite of apocalypse is a future not yet determined, that has no God-given status. The opposite of apocalypse is a world not yet built. For bell hooks (1997), this world will be built on complexity of identity with the rejection of the interlocking systems of domination that define our reality. Gender, race, and class are all intrinsic to understanding ourselves and the structures of society that elevate some people above others. White supremacy and patriarchy are related. Classism and ableism lean into one another.

Relief to Haiti in 2010 was delayed by a U.S. disaster response that explicitly integrated damaging, racist elements of the cowboy apocalypse narrative as part of its presumptions and plans. *Slate* reports that instead of distributing the aid:

> The U.S. military did what the U.S. military does. Like a slow-witted, fearful giant, it built a wall around itself, commandeering the Port-au-Prince airport and constructing a mini-Green Zone. As thousands of tons of desperately needed food, water, and medical supplies piled up behind the airport fences—and thousands of corpses piled up outside them—Defense Secretary Robert Gates ruled out the possibility of using American aircraft to airdrop supplies: "An airdrop is simply going to lead to riots," he said. . . . Haitians were expected to devour one another and, like wounded dogs, to snap at the hands that fed them. (Ehrenreich 2010)

The same worries were expressed about the aftermath of Hurricane Katrina, as Rebecca Solnit describes in *A Paradise Built in Hell*. After Katrina, rumors spread about "mass rapes, mass murders, and mayhem that turned out later to be untrue, though the national media and New Orleans's police chief believed and perpetuated those rumors. . . . Those rumors led soldiers and others dispatched as rescuers to regard victims as enemies" (2010, 1). Fired up by a story as old as slavery, "racists imagine again and again that without them utter savagery would break out, so that their own homicidal violence is in defense of civilization and the preservation of order" (259). Recognizing the threads linking contemporary racist apocalypticism and America's history of slavery, Solnit notes that the "killing rage of the Klan and lynching parties of the old South were often triggered or fanned into flame by a story, often fictitious or exaggerated, of a crime by an African American man" (259).

Seeing the cowboy apocalypse writ large can become habitual, shaping responses to real-life crises. In her feminist-informed response to apocalypticism, Catherine Keller wants to interrupt the apocalypse habit by refusing its rigidities and reifications, the "history of anti-Jewish, anti-flesh, anti-pagan, anti-female Christian truth claims" (2005, 19).

"EAT LEADEN DEATH, DEMON"

FIRST-PERSON SHOOTER AS END-TIME RITUAL

> Japan is a thermal spring.
> Scotland is a highland fling.
> Oh, better to be anything
> than America as a gun.
> **Brian Bilston, posted on Twitter, February 17, 2016**

> Over the centuries, mankind has tried many ways of combating the forces of evil . . . prayer, fasting, good works and so on. Up until *Doom*, no one seemed to have thought about the double-barrel shotgun. Eat leaden death, demon.
> **Terry Pratchett**

Like apocalyptic performance, videogaming is a ritual in which players are transported to an imaginary space, entering a storyworld that is acted out through user action. This virtual world is not directly touchable, but it *is* real. We *see* it displayed on the screen and we *do* things within it, if from a distance. We walk to a castle. We shoot up a town. We collect resources. We provide input and the game responds by opening a path. We kill bad guys. We are promised the game is winnable. We are promised we can have the weapons we want. A first-person shooter (FPS) videogame is a kind of movable, free-floating ritual of the gun, able to be used in concert with the transmediated world of the cowboy apocalypse.

The FPS game offers a way of acting out desire for domination:

> The "S" in FPS does stand for "shooter," so we shouldn't be surprised that the speech such games enact is usually replete

with violent depictions of fantastic battles of good versus evil. There is a cultural place for such works, just as there is a place for popcorn action films. The FPS game engine was born from the market opportunity to perpetuate the power fantasy among a videogame market almost entirely dominated by young men. (Bogost 2006, 63)

When videogames are part of a larger transmedia world, they are dependent on the narrative and plot depicted in other extensions of that world. An FPS game *does* have a pared-down story, though, repeated across different engines and coded into gamic actions: You are a hero. You shoot bad guys. Your violence saves the world. The FPS game proposes, through its scripted action, that conflict is resolved through gun violence. This story can be read as compatible with the cowboy apocalypse, played out in various FPS contexts.

Game Engines

The FPS game is the most well-known genre of videogames. FPS game engines "construe entire gameplay behaviors, facilitating functional interactions divorced from individual games" (57). The physics of a game can be drawn explicitly from preexisting code. Every bullet is instructed how to shoot. The game's explosions are echoes of explosions in games using the same engine. Game engines mechanically regulate a game designer's options—their "artistic, cultural, and narrative expression," which must function within the preexisting rules of the game engine (56). Game engines exist in the real world "in a way that genres, devices, and cliches do not" (56). Game engines determine what playing feels like, and they script what the player can do. Games designed using the same game engine will have similar properties (58).

Game engines were originally developed by using existing FPS games. Hoping to let hardcore programmers play with the code, parts of *Doom* were released in 1993 and 1994 as shareware, facilitating the creation of new FPS games. By "abstracting and extracting the game's core features, its most salient unit operations," the *Doom* game engine was created. The same company responsible for *Doom*, id Software, created the *Quake* engine (and *Quake II* engine) that has been used for games like *Half-Life* (60). A game's story, insofar as it exists, will be laid *on top* of its engine. Playing different games with the same engine will feel familiar, like a ritual.

This is why some players of FPS games dismiss the fictional elements as "unimportant decoration of the game rules" (Juul 2005, 6). It is the game's underlying structure that is most familiar. For example, the game version of *Star Wars* does not include much narrative. Players are expected to already know the *Star Wars* story. The game offers them the ability to play space battles that slot into the preexisting *Star Wars* world.

Most action shooter games have thin plots, but there are a few that can be read as fully formed cowboy apocalypses. One of the most obvious is *Fallout: New Vegas* (2010). Animating a character called Courier Six, the player wanders a post-apocalyptic wasteland armed with a pistol. Described in frontier imagery, New Vegas is "a town of dreamers and desperados being torn apart by warring factions vying for complete control. . . . It's a place where the right kind of person with the right kind of weaponry can really make a name for themselves and make more than an enemy or two along the way" (Steampowered 2010). Battling human enemies as well as "mutated creatures," the player-character must fight for survival. The game is classified as action RPG (role-play game), but it also has FPS features.

Guns as FPS Props

Videogames are part of the ecology of transmedia storytelling, but "on a level that is often closer to the level of toys and merchandising than to the level of movies or novels" (Juul 2005, 17). The virtual gun is the primary interface for FPS games, but it slides easily from one game to another. A player might choose a virtual replica sniper rifle in any number of FPS games, for example. Photorealistic guns, based on actual weapons, can show up in almost any game. Interactivity, in the case of guns, is "a complex web of user actions and textual affordances" that cycle between producers and consumers, texts and marketing materials, games and other games (Payne 2016, 21). Guns do not belong to specific games; they belong to a larger story of redemptive violence. A dedicated gamer describes his own experience using virtual guns:

In [the film] *John Wick 2*, Keanu Reeves' eponymous assassin meets with an Italian "sommelier" for a "tasting" that involves a detailed rundown of his firearms for an upcoming mission. Wick walks out with a set of Glock-34 and -36 handguns, an AR-15 assault rifle ("compensated with an ion bonded bolt carrier"), and a Benelli M4 tactical shotgun. I nodded with recognition . . . not just because I've read about them or seen them in movies, but because I've used them in videogames. Glock-style pistols, with their squarish shape and silver ejection port, turn up in everything from *Battlefield* to *Half-Life*. I've used AR-15-in-everything-but-name clones in games ranging from *Far Cry 5* to *Grand Theft Auto V*. The first gun you get in *Far Cry 4* looks just like Ordell Robbie's beloved AK-47. And of course, the M4 tactical shotgun is the basis for weapons in just about every shooter I've ever played, from *Max Payne 3* to *Playerunknown's Battlegrounds*. As he talks with his sommelier, John Wick might as well be a videogame character selecting a load-out. (Hamilton 2018)

The gun is a prop for films like *John Wick 2*, and for videogames—especially those games with agreements for product placement of manufacturer's weapons (Meier and Martin 2012). Props—whether religious or secular—become a bridge between this world and another one. Props, relics, and sacred objects promise presence, a tangible link to a desired world.

A videogame controller—whether shaped like a gun or not—invites players to interact with virtual spaces. The deeper the immersion, the more the player identifies with the gun and is "embodied by the shooting mechanic" (Navarro 2012, 65). Videogames utilize graphics, sound, texts, visual cues, haptics, and rules to encourage a sense of immersion. Players collect resources, navigate obstacles, formulate strategies, and engage in conflict. Hand and finger movements signify shooting as the player moves through the digital landscape. The gun is fired via a graspable object *here*, but it expels bullets *there*. There is an in-betweenness to the videogame gun that marks it as a pivot point between real and virtual. It is—and is not—real. It does—and does not—shoot.

The image of a gun can be experienced, to some degree, as part of our body. We are not *really* in the virtual world, and virtual guns do not *really* shoot. But the seduction of the image nurtures a desire to have the gun do what it is supposed to do—shoot for real. For someone who loves guns, to play videogames is to be disappointed and thrilled at the same time (Hamilton 2018). The pleasure of play comes in part through the navigation of onscreen spaces via violent encounter. But as game scholar Bob Rehak argues, the most crucial interaction is "not between avatar and environment or even between protagonist and antagonist, but between the human player and the image of him- or herself encountered onscreen" (2003, 127).

To see oneself onscreen—a hand with a gun—is to feel present, powerful, engaged. To play a videogame is to "toy with subjectivity, play with being" (123). But if we can slide into a game, can the game slide into us? When Eric Klebold and Dylan Harris played *Doom* in the years before the Columbine shooting, they engaged via keyboard, pressing the control key to fire rapidly and the shift key to run.

Games and Rituals

Game engines do not function unless someone plays them. The player feeds inputs into a system that then responds. Ritual too is "rooted in a propensity for order, rhythmic patterning, and play" (Goethals 1996, 258). Ritual "casts us into measures that are outside ordinary time. The flow of everyday existence . . . is suspended and the believer leaps timelessly into creation and . . . eternity" (259). Ritual orients us; it can carry us into another world. To read an FPS videogame as ritual, then, is to see how it affirms a player's place in a larger symbolic order as independent, powerful, and in charge. Rituals, like any social construct, can reinforce hegemony and codify inequity.

Using the lens of ritual helps us understand why games are an essential piece of the transmediated world of the cowboy apocalypse. For those already invested in a narrative of gun-enforced white supremacy, the FPS can work as confirmation of that belief, acted out with a virtual gun. Ritual theorist Catherine Bell insists that ritual is a *doing*, not just a thinking: "Ritual, like action, will act out, express, or perform" a set of "conceptual orientations" (1992, 19). Clifford Geertz maintains that in the performance of ritual, there is a merging between "the world as lived and the world as imagined, fused under the agency of a single set of symbolic forms" (1973, 112–13). Rituals are "enactments, materializations, realizations" of beliefs (114). For those who yearn for a world in which white men with guns can kill their enemies, the FPS videogame is a ritual seeking fulfillment.

Ritual can be about resolving the difference between the real and the ideal, according to ritual theorist Jonathan Z. Smith:

> [A]mong other things, ritual represents the creation of a controlled environment where the variables . . . of ordinary life may be displaced. . . . Ritual is a means of performing the way things ought to be in conscious tension to the way things are in such a way that this ritualized perfection is recollected in the ordinary, uncontrolled, course of things. (1996, 481)

The FPS, in its sparest engine-driven form, offers a ritual enactment of the basic narrative: good-guy-shoots-bad-guy-to-win. For the cowboy messiah (or the man wishing to be one) the ritual of the FPS invokes an experience of how things *ought* to be, who *ought* to be in charge.

Apocalyptic Machines

Through World War I, people tabulated ballistics data by hand (Mead 2013, 12). Computers were too late to help with World War II, but they were used for calculations in the development of the atomic bomb. Some people believed computers, if powerful enough, could solve any logistical and military problems, because enemy tactics would be "anticipated, mapped, and resolved" (Crogan 2011, 48). Videogames are a result of these computer developments in the twentieth century as programmers ran simulations for nuclear deterrence. A look at the historical development of computers shows how videogames emerged from this context of wartime prediction. The first-person shooter descended from computer modeling of apocalyptic disaster, and it retains the vestiges of that fundamental grammar of conflict.

The term "cybernetics" was repurposed by engineer Norbert Wiener in the 1940s to apply to mechanisms with the ability to self-regulate, such as brains and computers. Cybernetics is based on the idea that real-life systems can be translated into manageable information and predictive technologies, leading to the notion that computers could be built to help us think. Perhaps the easiest way to think about cybernetics is as a system that adjusts based on input.

The purpose of cybernetic information is to anticipate the future "so as to render it already past, that is, already under control" (Crogan 2011, 97). Cybernetic thinking has theological implications: "the will to see all, to know all, at every moment, everywhere, the will to universalized illumination" (Virilio 1994, 70). Computers were viewed as "the eye of God which would forever rule out the surprise, the accident, the irruption of the unforeseen" (70). Cybernetics manifests an intense *preoccupation* with the end. One could say it is apocalyptic.

Reflecting on the development of cybernetics, theorist Peter Galison describes three kinds of enemies:

> Enemies are not alike. One version of the enemy, for example the way the Japanese were viewed by the Americans and the British, was the racialized, monstrous, subhuman other. Another distinct Allied vision made the enemy anonymous, the example here being the pilot who bombs a city several tens of thousands of feet below and has no psychological connection through empathy or fellow-feeling. The third category, which is what [Norbert] Wiener was interested in, is an enemy who is much more active than the anonymous invisible inhabitants of a distant city and more rational than the horde-like racialized enemy. This enemy, more complex than either of the other two perspectives, was a cold-blooded mechanized Enemy Other who made at least predictable moves that could be modeled through some kind of black box machinery. (Galison 2011)

Cybernetics presumed this "mechanized Enemy Other," and generated predictions in the computer labs of MIT and other universities (Galison 2011). Calculations determined the likelihood of attack and survival. This celebration of prediction reached massive proportions during the Cold War, when such systems were not just simulations of battle, but of "the total, absolute, and almost unimaginable possible eventuality of large-scale nuclear conflict" (Crogan 2011, 9). Machines simulated events leading to nuclear catastrophe, played out as a means of *avoiding* catastrophe. Reality was translated into data that was simplified, reduced, and calculated as a means of anticipating apocalypse.

The same appeal to prediction, if more crudely executed, has happened in religious apocalyptic thinking. Scripture doesn't offer specific dates for the end times, so interpreters like John Nelson Darby have made predictions based on data they collected from the Bible. This scriptural interpretation lends an "air of deductive certainty" to the theologian's arguments for imminent apocalypse (O'Leary 1998, 80). Computers are, at root, apocalyptic machines.

MIT engineers working on military computer projects developed key elements of what would become gaming technology: the display screen, the light gun, networking, and magnetic core memory (Halter 2006, 150). In 1962, on a whim, the first digital game, *Spacewar!*, was produced by graduate students at MIT in a Pentagon-funded program funded, using a microcomputer about the size of three refrigerators (Mead 2013, 14). The game involves two players using switches to navigate spaceships through a gravity field while firing missiles (15). *Spacewar!* was consistent with military developments: anticipatory management of battle through interactive simulation. From the start, videogames were recognized for their ability to model the real world in a context of scripted—and thus anticipated—conflict.

Kill or Be Killed: Videogame Development

Once computers were available to consumers, game development took off. *Maze War* (1974) and *Spasim* (1974) were shooting games that could be played only on mainframes—large computers with major processing power. But they were also networked, so players could shoot at each other while playing on different computers. They use the "kill or be killed" logic familiar to gamers today (Wolf 2012, 33). In 1977 *Space Wars* was released, with 3D animation and vector graphics (34). Players controlled shooting by punching a key on the keyboard. Arcade games were also released in this decade. Arcade cabinets could be networked together for groups to play.

In 1980, Atari released *Battlezone*, a tank combat simulator game. Its three-dimensional design and first-person perspective invited players to see themselves "peering through their periscopes at the battlefield outside" (Mead 2013, 18). Players could use a joystick and a fire button. The game was modified for military use as *Army Battlezone*, intended to help soldiers learn to navigate an infantry fighting vehicle (Penny 2004, 75). Around the same time, DARPA (Defense Advanced Research Projects Agency) began developing tank simulators that were linked via a network, paving the way for multiplayer game design and cementing the close relationship between entertainment and military development. Networking is the basis of our internet, our streaming television, and our endless Zoom meetings.

Game development went sideways with the 1982 release of American Multiple Industries' videogame *Custer's Revenge* for the Atari 2600 home system. The game depicts a "naked, erect Custer" who dodges arrows with the goal of raping a "naked, bound Native American woman" (Voorhees 2012, 96). The National Organization for Women, the Native American Political Action Committee, and the NAACP protested the game. The president of American Multiple Industries denied the game was about rape. Atari (1982) objected to the game on their systems. *Custer's Revenge* relays nothing about General Custer. Instead, the game is a transmedial add-on to frontier mythology, replicating its racism and misogyny. Agency is reduced to assault. *Custer's Revenge* sparked protests that ended wide availability of videogame porn, at least for a while. It also raised questions about games as violent performances.

One of the best-known early shooter games is *Wolfenstein 3D* (1993), an unofficial sequel to *Castle Wolfenstein*, in which the player fights Nazis and a cyborg Hitler (Voorhees 2012, 101). *Wolfenstein 3D* is 2D but simulates a 3D experience with a gun displayed at the bottom of the screen. The image of gun-in-hand serves as "a sort of imaginary prosthesis" because "it links the player's body into the fictional world . . . emphasizing a continuum between the player's world and that of the game" (Lahti 2003, 161). This convention is integrated into countless games today.

Doom (1993) is lauded as the best example of an early first-person shooter. The 3D environment, rendered in real time, enhances the sense of immersion. *Doom* casts the player as a Marine on Mars after a "teleportation experiment gone wrong that opens a passage to hell." The player is the last surviving Marine and must "fight off the raging hordes of hell in order to save every last human on earth" (Voorhees 2012, 97). This basic story—hero kills bad guy with lots of gore—is the same justification for violence embraced by the cowboy apocalypse, the military, and gun culture. *Doom* has provided a template for every first-person shooter since.

When playing *Doom*, character development depends on "your abilities to obey the directives of the game" and to "satisfy its algorithms" (Halter 2006, 161). Success within the game's constraints make players feel powerful as they act like "one-man vigilante badasses who busted their way through innumerable eighties action flicks ... spurred on by an enemy that deserved death" (162). This is highly scripted badassery; the only way to win is to do exactly what the game's program asks of you. To play *Doom* successfully is to resolve the game's predictive problems. Success is obedience. Despite advances in graphics, speed, and design, contemporary FPS games still demand navigation of a "more or less linear environment from the protagonist's perspective, while dispatching the enemies you encounter with a variety of weapons" (van Zwieten 2011, 1–2). When playing *Doom* and other FPS games, we are as much played as playing.

Duke Nukem 3D (1996) features Duke, a brawny character likened to Clint Eastwood, John Wayne, Bruce Willis, and Arnold Schwarzenegger. Duke is armed with a pistol, a shotgun, a rocket launcher, and pipe bombs. As in other FPS games, the narrative is negligible. In earlier *Duke Nukem* games, the evil Dr. Proton captures L.A., then Duke battles and defeats his evil robots. In *Duke Nukem 3D*, Duke battles aliens attacking earth. The product box describes him as: "Alien butt kicker. Hero of every man. Dream of every woman. When fighting aliens, he's the good and the bad while they're just plain ugly. Politically incorrect and letting nothing stand in his way. Duke is a man of action, with scores of Earth saving adventures, and an even better score with beautiful women." Duke is former military but operates "outside the system with inside government and military data."

Quake (1996) uses similar mechanics as *Doom* and was made by the same team. The narrative is barely present, "leaving only a plot based on the protection and loss of bodily integrity" (Rehak 2003, 117). The game manual recounts the spare narrative context:

> While scouting the neighborhood, you hear shots back at the base. Damn, that Quake bastard works fast! . . . Racing back, you see the place is overrun. You are almost certainly the only survivor. Operation Counterstrike is over. Except for you. You know that the heart of the installation holds a slipgate. Since Quake's killers came through, it is still set to his dimension. You can use it to get loose in his hometown. Maybe you can get to the asshole personally. You pump a round into your shotgun and get moving.

Players fight to get to the slip gate and seek revenge. *Quake* was released as an open-source engine, allowing fans to change out environments, weapons, and enemies in their development of similar games. *Doom* was also released for player modifications (mods). Both games are still played today, as are countless mods.

The natural affinity between the FPS game and frontier themes can be seen in some of the mods based on *Doom*. In *Bastardos*, for example, the player is Boot McKane, "an infamous outlaw" chasing the Bastardos gang. An online introduction to the game explains: "What this means for you is a healthy dose [of] retro run n' gun action in a Wild West setting. The levels are large and packed with secrets and the combat is fast, fun and frantic . . . there's a nice selection of weaponry, from machetes to gatling guns, that make dispatching those pixelated bandits a joy." *High Noon Drifter* (2017) is another contemporary mod with Western themes.

Outlaws (1997) is built on the *Star Wars: Dark Forces* engine (a *Doom*-like model). The player is a U.S. marshal chasing a gang using Old West weapons. Players shoot enemies while moving through tight, themed environments. The core story—shoot to kill—remains the same. *Outlaws* exploits the bad-guy trope to perpetuate racist stereotypes about Indigenous people in America. A game guide tells players what to do when they encounter the boss, Charlie Two-Feathers: "Move close to the door and be ready to fight Charlie. He is a knife thrower, and a good one. . . . Use your scoped rifle and shoot him from long range or get in a bit closer and let him have it." In the "mission debriefing," the player is told that Two-Feathers "like[s] your style, even as he lays dying."

Simulating War

When the Cold War abated, military budgets shrunk (Mead 2013, 22). Strapped for funds, the U.S. Marines licensed *Doom* from id Software and built their own version for soldiers to play. Companies like Sega began designing simulation software for defense contractors, since they could do it more affordably. For a few years, FPS games were all called *Doom* clones since so many of them used *Doom* shareware (Voorhees 2012, 97). Part of the inspiration for the military's collaboration with videogame producers was Orson Scott Card's novel *Ender's Game* (1985), which depicts videogame interfaces for real military battles (Mead 2013, 58).

Doom's world was stripped down and streamlined for *Marine Doom*. Martian dungeons became "sparse, dust-colored plain punctuated by small brick bunkers, foxholes, and barbed-wired barriers" (Halter 2006, 167). Aliens and demons were replaced by "very human-looking opposing forces, clad in simple khaki military uniforms of a vaguely Communist/Nazi cut" (167). The game's new purpose was teaching Marines "how to work together in teams and make split-second decisions in the midst of combat" (Mead 2013, 22). *Doom* served as a basis for further military use of first-person shooters (Stahl 2010, 96). Videogames and military training depended on the same basic logic: "what's good for the Xbox is good for the combat simulator" (Miller 2011, 110). The U.S. military still depends on commercial companies for its training technology.

In 1993, the U.S. Senate convened a joint hearing of the judiciary and government affairs committees to work on a videogame ratings act, responding to complaints about the violence in *Mortal Kombat* (1993) and *Night Trap* (1992). In 1994, the electronic software ratings board was created, making the act unnecessary (Voorhees 2012, 97). In 1997, three students were killed at a high school in Kentucky. In response, activist Jack Thompson filed a lawsuit against the makers of the movie *Basketball Diaries* and against id Software, the makers of *Doom*, *Quake*, and *Castle Wolfenstein* (Voorhees 2012, 99). Thompson asserted videogame violence is causally related to real-life violence. The lawsuit was dismissed, but the concerns were not. Two years later the Columbine massacre happened, and *Doom* was implicated.

In an interview, games critic David Grossman argues FPS games are effective training modules for soldiers and for children:

> [W]hen the children play the violent videogames, they're drilling, drilling, drilling . . . every night, to kill every living creature in front of you, until . . . you run out of bullets. . . . [W]e're reasonably confident that in Pearl, Mississippi, and in Paducah, Kentucky, and in Jonesboro, Arkansas, these juvenile, adolescent killers set out to shoot just one person: usually their girlfriend . . . maybe a teacher. But, then, they kept on going! And, they gunned down every living creature in front of them, until they ran out of targets or ran out of bullets . . . ! (Steinberg 2000)

Grossman is confident *he* knows exactly why shooters target their friends and loved ones: because they had been playing violent videogames.

Some skills do transfer from simulations: "Soldiers shoot at targets shaped like people; this trains them to shoot real people. When pilots work in flight simulators, the skills they develop transfer to the real world" (Penny 2004, 80). Games, like simulations, can "build behaviors" (81). Educators have long recognized the ability of games to shape users. Some studies relate exposure to violent gaming content with "aggressive cognitions, aggressive feelings, and aggressive behaviors" (Gentile 2011, 77). Nonetheless, it becomes difficult to isolate what element of the gaming experience triggered which behaviors afterward (76). More interesting to me is why gun play is so central in the first place.

After training with a military simulation, soldiers go from holding a virtual weapon to holding a real weapon, though their behavior is expected to be the same. A mouse click causes an explosion. Pushing a button shoots a gun: "It requires very little imaginative effort to enter such a world because the sense of agency is so direct" (Murray 2017, 146). Real guns offer a similar sense of agency, with more boom.

The FPS's popularity in the new millennium is not coincidental. As the "perfect platform for post-9/11 military power fantasies," the FPS took an incomprehensible horror and offered an individualized ritual response. In these games, the player enters a war-ravaged world equipped with an arsenal of weapons. The player's mission is to utilize "deadly force repeatedly without fear of moral or legal repercussions." The military shooter is a "ludic antidote" to the shock of 9/11 (Payne 2016, 10). In the FPS fantasy, one soldier can fight back with enough force to make a difference. Videogames, especially FPS games, "promised Manichean moral universes and frontiersman heroes, which could reaffirm our national mythology as the world's lone and righteous military superpower" (27). As forms of *pre*-mediation, military shooters "give players hope that these reimagined 9/11s can have different outcomes than their horrific *ur*-text." Military shooters "give players ways of striking back" (29).

War is often viewed today through games. *Conflict: Desert Storm* (Pivotal Games 2002) reenacts events from the first Gulf War. *Call of Duty 4: Modern Warfare* (Infinity Ward 2007) puts players in spots of real-life military tension in Azerbaijan, Russia, and Ukraine. War is "digitally mediated through computerized targeting, mapping surveillance, and communication systems" revealing how closely aligned game design and military technology are (Dyer-Witheford and de Peuter 2009, 98). A first-person shooter can be distinguished from a "high-end battle simulator" by "the location of one in an adolescent bedroom and the other in a military base" (Penny 2004, 76).

The army developed their own videogame, *America's Army*, released in 2002, with 2.5 million downloads in two months (Mead 2013, 74). For six years it was one of the top online games (71). The game was based on meticulous research: photographs of actual weapons; real sound effects; filming of helicopter rides; realistic animations (like throwing a grenade); and detailed physics (91–93). There were both commercial and Army-only versions of the game (99).

> The U.S. Army hosted a spectacle of military access outside the L.A. Convention Center's South Hall, to promote the new Special Forces edition of their popular title *America's Army*. As part of this spectacle, they offered passersby the opportunity to pose holding a large assault rifle next to a camouflaged Special Forces operative and a Humvee. In a nimble perversion of the tourist trap, the army even offered complimentary Polaroid photos of potential players (and recruits) posed for glorious combat. (Bogost 2011, 134)

The gun is a fully functional prop, an expansion of the *America's Army* world and an invitation into that world. The gun invites accommodation between the real-life world of the military and the game's invitation to gun play.

Full Spectrum Warrior (2004) was also designed for military training before being repackaged and released to the public. The game takes place in a fictional country called Zekistan with characters who look vaguely Middle Eastern. The game teaches soldiers to "defeat any adversary and control any situation, across the 'full spectrum' of possibilities, ranging from nuclear threats to terrorist activities to bands of low-tech tribal warriors" (Halter 2006, 230). The affinity is built in. Every commercial copy has a version of the original Army game hidden within it, accessible via a cheat code (234).

Medal of Honor: Operation Anaconda (2010) identifies the player as a Delta Force sniper and a Navy SEAL in Afghanistan: "running, crouching, jumping and shooting one's way through huts, caves and pastures" (Mirrlees 2014, 96). Players direct missile strikes and drone attacks against ground targets, including Taliban encampments (97). The game promoted war in Afghanistan, attempting to "sell the real military violence of the U.S. state since 9/11" (98). Games like *Medal of Honor* make war seem enjoyable. Far from neutral representations of events, they instigate apocalyptic interpretations of military violence, with good guys fighting bad guys. They use the same logic as FPS games intended for entertainment, and why not? The games are built with similar engines.

The FPS supplements other forms of transmedia storytelling about guns. The gun is a privileged object, a ritual fetish, a prop, a paratext, a souvenir, inscribed within a violent ritual enacted in FPS games. The plot is not irrelevant, but subservient to the experience of shooting. FPS games can be viewed as flexible gun rituals for fans, transmedia extensions for preexisting storyworlds including the cowboy apocalypse.

Cowboy Warriors

A set of action games with distinctive cowboy apocalypse features are *Red Dead Revolver*, *Red Dead Redemption*, and *Red Dead Redemption 2*. All three *Red Dead* games take place in a frontier environment that enables players to act out cowboy fantasies. The *Red Dead* games are built on a proprietary engine also used to make games in the *Grand Theft Auto* franchise. The games incorporate a "Dead Eye" mechanic that lets players slow the action down to aim at different parts of an enemy's body, making shooting aesthetically pleasing. Of *Red Dead Redemption 2*, NPR's Jason Sheehan gushes that the game is:

> ... too big, too sprawling, too *full* for taking on in a piece-by-piece look at the story. Enough, maybe, to say that it tells, over the course of 60-plus hours, an epic, bloody tale of betrayal and obsolescence. It is, in the universe of videogames, our *Godfather*, our *Star Wars* or *Wild Bunch*—the work that transcends its genre and, in this case, its medium. It is a film brought to life, a novel given legs, and to speak about any piece of it is to necessarily reduce it to a bunch of cogs and sprockets—how this piece fits with that one. And that's a disservice, I think. (Sheehan 2019)

Red Dead Redemption 2 undermines presumptions of the cowboy apocalypse when it critiques violence as salvific. As the player's avatar Morgan dies, he is unable to fight. Sheehan explains: "To live by the gun and die by it has a kind of internal poetry that we instinctively accept. . . . But to live by the gun and die on the side of a mountain, coughing your lungs out as everything goes dark? That's harsh judgment in a way that I've rarely seen before. It's brilliant. It's *perfect*" (Sheehan 2019). Unable to escape the illness programmed into the game, the player (as Morgan) comes to question the life of the cowboy hero. Without a noble death or shining triumph, the player is denied a sense of victory. By recognizing features of the cowboy apocalypse story and subverting them, the game can say something new.

Usually, though, the gun represents precision, prediction, and control. Speaking of a gun controller she used in an arcade, media scholar Janet Murray says:

> [T]he six-shooter was an ideal threshold object, a physical device I could hold in my hand that was also an imaginary device in the world of the story. I only had to put my hands around it to enter the immersive trance. Ideally, every object in a digital

narrative—should offer the interactor as clear a sense of agency and as direct a connection to the immersive world as I felt in the arcade holding a six-shooter-shaped laser gun and blasting away at the outlaws. (2017, 180–181)

The virtual gun is a special kind of object; an appendage, a means of expression. We do not see our mouth on the screen, and we rarely (if ever) speak as an avatar in an FPS game. But we *do* make noise:

> We shoot. The gun calls to us because interfaces are discursive, in that their signifying elements are organized around a continuous hailing of the human beings who use them—a beckoning spatial representation marked by the cursor, the startup beep, the avatarial gun. This is the uncanny power of what we might call speaking technologies: the perception, produced even through mundane interaction, that we are the subject of their address, that we have been recognized. (Rehak 2003, 122)

Because the software cannot run without us, it summons us to make it whole. This is the same power held by the unplayed music score, the unperformed drama, and the unacted ritual. In an FPS game, the gun is the star of the show. It is not only used by the player; it *becomes* the player. Or does the player become the gun?

The Cowboy Apocalypse, Transmediated

Storytelling today is increasingly a form of transmedia worldbuilding. Books, novels, props, videogames, live events, and online presence mark fans as devoted while they explore multiple interrelated modes of engaging with their favorite storyworld. Although most of these forms of engagement are with media, fans can also engage with material props as they allow the world of their fandom to leak into their everyday lives. If we situate the FPS game within the context of the transmediated cowboy apocalypse, we find that its ritualized expression via its game engine marks it as a flexible add-on, able to operate effectively within the cowboy apocalypse no matter what thematic content the game draws on. The theme of good-guy-shoots-bad-guy-in-a-violently-disrupted-world allows players to ritually act out themes more pronounced in other extensions of the cowboy apocalypse, like in books, films, and television shows. The material gun can serve as a prop for the FPS ritual of violence, encouraging the most devoted players to experience how the world of apocalyptic resolution might be instantiated in the real world, now. Such a virtual world can, troublingly, serve as a "refuge from the trials and troubles of the world" that some white supremacists, misogynists, and privileged but politically threatened people feel (Wolf 2019, 141).

Transmedia involves fictional extensions that are dispersed but which together comprise a unified entertainment experience (Jenkins 2007). However, transmedia worlds need not provide perfect narrative consistency. What seems to matter most is a *sense* of cohesion and investment. Players care less about the construction of "coherent universes and non-redundant content" and more about compelling experiences (Bertetti 2020, 265). Even though the cowboy apocalypse can be delivered in a multitude of formats with distinctive characters and environments, the core story remains recognizable. The gun is its most vital prop. We could even view the gun as a transmedial hub, with narrative extensions flowing from its ordained place at the center of the good-guy story. The cowboy apocalypse is the center of gravity for all sorts of American media, but it presents a model that is less formal than Hollywood-controlled transmedia.

Hollywood transmedia functions according to the intellectual property (IP) model. Licenses are sold to creators who can then adapt the IP across different platforms (Atkinson 2019, 16). Many of these franchises have film as a central component, like *Star Wars*, *Harry Potter*, or *Transformers*. This "mothership" model presumes a single consistent narrative hub, while acknowledging that different fans may be drawn to different texts. This approach is "inclusive, centripetal, and marked by the need to balance unity and order . . . with users' accessibility" (Boni 2017, 18). *The Matrix*, for example, has films, comic books, a series of short films, computer games, action figures, costumes, and fan-initiated forms of paratexts like sunglasses, boots, and rabbit tattoos. The *Star Wars* franchise has live action films, animated series, comic books, videogames, Lego building kits, toys, and other merchandise.

Likenesses are used in television ads, marketing campaigns, and event appearances (Wolf 2019, 143). Stories across media are compatible.

Thinking of the ways transmedia can be generated in a less systematic form, scholar and writer Paolo Bertetti says we need "a more flexible conception than the one originally described by Jenkins" (2020, 265). Transmedia storytelling is not always planned and strategized, especially when fans are involved in its production. The idea of a unified and coordinated core world is "rarer than one might expect" (375). Fictional worlds do not depend on a fixed set of events or characters (Juul 2005, 173). What is more, a videogame based in a fictional transmedia world (like the cowboy apocalypse) might "only give players access to certain parts of this world and only allow players to act on a certain level" (176). Transmediality has "messy objectives . . . tailored for messy, fragmentary, hard-to-pin-down audiences" (Freeman and Gambarato 2020, 5).

This second kind of transmedia is centrifugal, since it spins outward without a controlling mechanism. It is less rigid and "open to unpredictable results" (Boni 2017, 18). "In older times, proliferation was spontaneous, bottom-up, multi-authored. Stories sprouted branches in many directions, like a rhizome, and storyworlds grew organically. Popular stories inspired transmedia adaptations without having been conceived for this explicit purpose" (43). For example, biblical narratives are transmedia, "dispersed across the world, found in stained glass windows and frescoes, in paintings and performances" (16). Today, they are found in comic books, enacted with action figures, and performed in church plays. Religion has always exhibited a transmedia quality, characterized by fan devotion and creativity.

The cowboy apocalypse is a contemporary example of this rhizomatic model of transmedia. Transmediality "seeks to transform the world into a story and the story into a story world. It is a means of crafting immersion, it seems—and, specifically, offering storytellers creative, pervasive ways to engage audiences emotionally and experientially" (Freeman and Gambarato 2020, 6). Emerging out of frontier-driven and post–Civil War stories, the transmediated cowboy apocalypse succeeds because of fan enthusiasm. In this spontaneous, user-driven mode of transmediation, the storyworld may unfold across many different texts, including the platform of the real world. The cowboy apocalypse is akin to oral culture, grounded in American myths of white supremacy and redemptive violence. Not all oral culture is worth preserving.

Leaky Play

As an expression of white masculine nostalgia, the cowboy apocalypse is tainted with imperialism. The myth appears today as a repeatedly mediated performance of desire for a simpler time when white men defined American values and others knew their place. By positing an imagined world in the future, the cowboy apocalypse is at once a religious expression, a form of fan devotion, and an ideological platform with the potential for violent expression. The FPS shooter is one of the cowboy apocalypse's favorite rituals, valuable for its implicit spillover into real life as people virtually enact violence in a safe space protected as a form of mere play.

Twentieth-century Dutch sociologist Johan Huizinga famously defined play as:

> . . . a free activity standing quite consciously outside ordinary life as being not serious, but at the same time absorbing the player intensely and utterly. It is an activity connected with no material interest, and no profit can be gained by it. It proceeds within its own proper boundaries of time and space according to fixed rules and in an orderly manner. It promotes the formation of social groupings which tend to surround themselves with secrecy and to stress their difference from the common world by disguise or other means. (1955, 13)

Play is "stepping out of 'real' life into a temporary sphere of activity with a disposition all of its own" (8). Huizinga called this place a magic circle and notes its religious and ritual qualities:

> All play moves and has its being within a playground marked off beforehand either materially or ideally, deliberately or as a matter of course. Just as there is no formal difference between play and

ritual, so the "consecrated spot" cannot be formally distinguished from the playground. (10)

Games offer a space in which players are protected from physical consequences of their gaming actions (Bogost 2006, 136). But there is no way to perfectly seal off a game; they leak. The magic circle "is not a metaphysical shield that insulates players from the world." It is a "permeable social barrier that filters out certain elements, while allowing others through." A game is more than the code that governs it because the players "breathe life into it" (Payne 2016, 22). Their real-life commitments are already there: "To play a game is in many ways an act of 'faith' that invests the game with its special meaning—without willing players, the game is a formal system waiting to be inhabited, a piece of sheet music waiting to be played" (Salen and Zimmerman 2003, 98). It is easy to see how gameplay can serve some of the same functions as ritual, which also is set outside ordinary life, proceeds according to generally fixed rules, and encourages commitment that bleeds into real life.

Videogames "cannot help but carry the baggage of ideology" (Bogost 2006, 135). Players enter games with their own opinions and exit the games impacted by scripted, virtual experiences of the game and its rules spill over into life. Players and their presumptions—good or bad—do too. There is a gap in the magic circle through which players move. They carry their own sense of subjectivity in and out of the game: "If the magic circle were really some kind of isolated antithesis to the world, it would never be possible to access it at all" (135). And for FPS players, the gun is central. Although a causal link between videogames and violence is unproven, "the link between videogames and guns is right there in front of us" (Hamilton 2018). David Trend, who is skeptical about the causative influence of media violence on real-life violence, nonetheless claims:

> Many contemporary television shows, movies, and videogames tell a man he needs to be able to use force, to fight, and that fighting is a suitable way to solve problems or get what you want in certain situations. This is one of the areas where media violence really does shape people's thinking in certain ways. It works in the

background, and our unconscious minds, making subtle changes in our attitudes about the world and how we behave. (2007, 63)

Media can "replicate racial profiles and urban stereotypes," and reinforce "inaccurate negative beliefs about immigrants, the poor, people with mental health problems, and anyone who falls outside conceptions of white, middle-class normalcy" (99). Rituals can work this way too, situating us in a larger world in which values (inclusive or exclusive) are reinforced across performative modes of mediation. Worlds do not exist without the people who inhabit them. We choose what we consume, and we choose the worlds with which we will engage. So it is no surprise that someone could participate in gun fandom and express it in a variety of ways. The power of the cowboy apocalypse is that so many people seem to tell it, perform it, consume it, and make it their own.

6

WITNESSING THE FUTURE

DOOMSDAY PREPPERS

Doomsday Preppers is reality TV, marked by the intersection between fake and real. The show is scripted, shaped, and edited. But people featured in the show display actual guns and real supplies for the expected apocalypse. They predict the collapse of governmental supports and the need for manly saviors to protect people from violent marauders. As we will see in this chapter, the notion of belief is central in making sense of performances in reality TV shows like *Doomsday Preppers* (Stone and Andrews 2012). Not only are we compelled to ask questions about the beliefs of the people featured on the show, but the genre of reality TV invites viewers to interrogate our own reactions to the people featured in it. Do *we* believe what they tell us about the world to come? Do we read their intense witness as scripted for dramatic effect, or do we see in their self-proclaimed prophetic status a warning that we ought to adopt as well? Do we turn off the television and joke about the show, or do we go shopping for end-time supplies?

Cowboy apocalypticism is at the heart of *Doomsday Preppers*. The survivalists on the show seem committed to their apocalyptic view and "prep" for it by stockpiling food, resources, and weapons. Some even build elaborate bunkers underground. By showing us the dedicated lives of its participants, *Doomsday Preppers* presents us with a "reality" characterized by its titillating fanaticism and reliance on the larger American cowboy apocalyptic mythos. Indeed, the tension created by the genre of reality TV is resolved by the performative certainty of the people featured on it and the challenge this poses for viewers. *If* viewers take the participants' witness seriously, the participants' witness serves a prophetic function. To authenticate show participants' belief is for viewers to see themselves as part of an elite few who will survive impending doom. Reed Richardson is right that *Doomsday Preppers* "often descends into caricature," but he is also right when he says "dismissing the popularity of *Doomsday Preppers* as mere pop-cultural voyeurism would be a mistake" (Richardson 2013). The show is an invitation to prep, a prophetic call for embracing the larger transmediated cowboy apocalypse myth.

Doomsday Preppers challenges us to sort fact from fiction, to recognize what the preppers in the show claim to already know—American society will soon collapse to make way for a new, darkly refreshed frontier, its chaos to be tamed once again by good guys with guns. Reality TV is a place where discourses "within and outside television culture have temporarily come together in an unstable conjunction" (Bignell 2005, 171). Viewers can read the show as fictional entertainment, and many fans do. But if viewers are *already* inclined to believe in the cowboy apocalypse, they won't let the unstable genre of reality TV undermine their conviction. Indeed, the show utilizes the unstable elements of reality TV to invite viewers into a higher, more stable "reality" embedded in the predictive performances of its participants. To take *Doomsday Preppers* seriously is to believe in the myth of the cowboy apocalypse. To see the participants of the show as offering authentic warnings about the future is to resolve the question about the show's status: the message shared by the real people featured on it is real.

Doomsday Preppers is not the cheap, unrealistic fare of *Keeping Up with the Kardashians* or *Here Comes Honey Boo Boo*. The people featured on *Doomsday Preppers* make grandiose claims about what they expect to happen in an imminent violent future. The people in the show represent extremes. It would be a mistake to presume all preppers are of this sort. Instead, I argue *Doomsday Preppers* is geared toward proponents of the cowboy apocalypse, since so many of its featured participants share versions of its mythos. Even those who do not speak explicitly in the language of the cowboy apocalypse are shifted toward that milieu by producers, who—as we shall see—deliberately edit materials to ramp up the representation of extreme participant belief. We should work to distinguish, then, between the participants featured on *Doomsday Preppers*, the techniques used by the producers, and the response of viewers when they are called to take the witness of the cowboy apocalypse seriously beyond the show itself.

For example, Jerry McMullin of Yellow Jacket, Colorado, calls himself "Jacked Up Jerry." The show presents him first in a darkened room wearing a cowboy hat and leather vest, as he haltingly traces his apocalyptic expectations to childhood fears about the Cuban Missile Crisis. In church, he saw people "on their knees wailing and screaming and crying." Cold war tensions were high because "we were so close to an absolute apocalyptic conclusion." Today, Jerry lives in a fortress of his own design, convinced his manly know-how will save him from terrorists in the apocalypse. Jerry sees his appearance on *Doomsday Preppers* as an opportunity to warn viewers: "It could happen at any moment . . . And there will be chaos. And the best thing to do is prepare for the worst before it ever happens." After the collapse of society, Jerry will use his ham radio to guide brave men in other survivalist households.

Whereas it is perfectly reasonable to see Jerry's childhood fears as impetus for his devoted prepping as an adult, the show presents him as a fanatic, using dramatic lighting and featuring prophetic statements intended to evoke reactions in viewers. For the producers, Jerry's belief can be used to draw in viewers and make money. Will viewers see Jerry's prophetic warning as authentic? If they do, they might buy products featured on the show and tune in for more episodes. Whereas some viewers enjoy *Doomsday Preppers* because they want to ridicule its participants, the most valued viewers are those who take it seriously and purchase the food supplies, weapons, and even real estate advertised through product placement.

Media professor June Deery describes reality TV as having "impact, tenacity, and cultural resonance," even if it lacks "profundity of content" (2015, 1). Deery calls reality TV the crabgrass of television (7). Annette Hill calls it a "feral genre" that is "wildly opportunistic" (2014, 140). Like documentaries, reality TV uses nonactors. Like drama, it provides "detailed exploration of character." Like game shows, it can include competition. Like talk shows, it can portray social issues. Like lifestyle television, it focuses on personal transformation (Bignell 2005, 6). Reality TV exhibits elements familiar to soap operas, sports events, and talent shows (Hill 2014, 9). It begins onscreen but wanders freely to radio, newspapers, magazines, and the internet (13). Fans can buy affiliated apps, music, or games. Shows may even invite viewers to participate through fandom activities like voting, interactive gaming, and live events. In some cases, then, reality TV shows invites viewers to participate in the "reality" the show produces.

Doomsday Preppers didn't offer many sponsored real-life events and there was no voting on contestants. Before the show ended in 2014, there was an anemic online discussion board at the *National Geographic* site and a single app on Google Play, with which players could design a fantasy underground bunker. And yet *Doomsday Preppers* survived with solid viewership for four years. I propose the show had staying power precisely because it functioned as one spoke in a much larger hub of cowboy apocalypse devotion. Fans of *Doomsday Preppers* tap into a preexisting fandom that includes survivalist camps, expo events, and material purchases of things like guns, gear, and food. It is cross-pollinated in countless American films, television shows, and other media.

The earliest forms of reality TV focused on ordinary people and took place in real-world spaces like shops or police stations or hospitals (Hill 2014, 26). Viewers "saw the mundane as strange" when shows like *Big Brother* were new, and "small things" like sleeping and eating "became interesting" (44). Within a few years, the ordinary allure of reality TV gave way to self-conscious performance as it became a "platform for real people to perform an extreme version of themselves" (50). Reality TV became more obviously constructed, and audiences "lost their belief in any playful claims to reality in the genre" (51). Reality TV went "so far down the scripted and structured route" that viewers developed "a hunger once again for the authentic" (23).

Doomsday Preppers can be read as an attempt to recapture that sense of authenticity. By dispensing with the studio and portraying participants in their own homes, *Doomsday Preppers* shows us ordinary people as they enact dramatic visions of the future. The narrative introduction to the first season is an explicit juxtaposition of the ordinary with the extraordinary, the real and the imagined, framed within an apocalyptic context:

> Across the country there is a growing darkness: belief that the end of days is near. Ordinary Americans from all walks of life are

taking whatever measures necessary to prepare and protect themselves from what they perceive is the fast-approaching end of the world as we know it. Next, we go inside the lives of . . . committed preppers who have devised extensive plans, gone to great lengths, and made huge personal sacrifices to ensure their very survival. The experts will assess their extreme preps and decide if they have what it takes to face Armageddon and to survive. This is *Doomsday Preppers*. (Stone and Andrews 2012)

We are meant to see preppers as like us.

For example, we see Jeff Flaningham, who has purchased nineteen acres of land in Kansas. His land includes an abandoned ballistic missile silo where he plans to live after world collapse. Jeff will rehabilitate the command center and install a flamethrower to attack invaders, but the viewer sees only mud and metal. Jeff demonstrates rappelling down the side of the missile storage area, dropping to the bottom to retrieve some of the water there. *Doomsday Preppers* demands future-oriented credulity: to appreciate the show, we must be willing to imagine a world in which Jeff's access to muddy silo water makes him clever.

Another gritty portrayal is of truck driver Martin Colvill (Season 1, Episode 4). He and his wife Sarah live on a semitruck with their two dogs. Martin believes "a very, very terrible time is coming" when China will call in U.S. debt. Within a week, he says, chaos will erupt. Without truck deliveries, there will be no food. Cities will become "deathtraps" and urban refugees will flood the countryside as "marauding bands" of "pirates" seeking supplies. *Now*, Sara stockpiles her cancer medication under the presumption that pharmacies will soon close. But *then*, in the imagined future, Martin will use his truck to help America "become the nation that it should be again." If we believe Martin's predictions about the future, then he and Sarah's current suffering is less real than what is to come.

Robert Earl (Season 2, Episode 2) is a former paramedic who describes himself as "Mad Max meets Rube Goldberg with a little bit of Al Gore thrown in." Robert expects to lead after the apocalypse and fears "everything we know today could go away tomorrow." As he frets, the camera cuts to real-life footage of the aftermath of Hurricane

Katrina and shots of the Los Angeles riots. The producers participate in Robert's predicted future by using *past* footage of actual events—but in a *future*-oriented manner. We watch Robert's family assemble for dinner, and we see his daughter play in the backyard. This is the *now*. But Robert knows things the rest of us don't know. Because he can see through daily life to what lies beyond, Robert will survive while we might not. The producers tend to highlight the most sensationalist aspects of prepping, ramping up the tension between real and fake. The "story person" in a show is the one who whittles footage down to short scenes, adapting it to create a dramatic line (Deery 2015, 41). In reality TV, we witness scripted, predetermined events that are carefully crafted to reinforce dramatic purposes (33).

These events sometimes utilize out-of-context "Frankenbites," which are "reaction shots [used] to construct an interaction that did not actually occur" (41). One *Doomsday Preppers* participant, Lisa, claims producers filmed multiple responses to given prompts about their performance, while intending to use the clips out of context: "Since we had no idea what the critique would be, we were told to give a variety of vocal and facial responses—nodding our head like, 'He's got a point,' to 'I'm not so sure about that' . . . and they did the editing as they saw fit" (SurvivalMom 2011). Another participant, known as "Survivor Jane," reports the crew spent over thirty hours shooting "all for 15 minutes of screen time." She grew exhausted from "saying the same thing a hundred different ways" (Survivor Jane n.d.). Deery (2015) notes this kind of activity is common in reality TV, since producers "anticipate drama, find drama, heighten drama, or induce drama" (35). Producers of reality TV aren't after the truth—they're after ratings and viewers. This is one place where the strange partnership between reality TV producers and preppers comes into focus: both want the audience's eyes and ears, though for radically different reasons.

Selective editing affected Megan Hurwitt (Season 1, Episode 1), who grins on camera while announcing she and her boyfriend would shoot their cats if society collapsed. Megan says: "That comment was taken so terribly out of context that I will NEVER forgive Nat Geo. . . . They conveniently left out a few key points that I discussed before and after that quote." Megan claims she *actually* said that in an emergency situation they would let the cats loose to hunt. They would euthanize them only in the case of a "nuclear wasteland." Megan claims a producer offered her $1,000 to shoot her cat on camera (Griffith 2012). Megan's desire to share her authentic beliefs about the apocalypse runs afoul of the producers' desire to create titillating content.

Nick Klein also complains about producer manipulation on *Doomsday Preppers*. Producers found his "biofuels project" too technical (Season 4, Episode 2). They were more impressed, though, when Nick lit some fuel on fire and "blew a six-foot flame into the air." Nick claims they prompted him to "weaponize rabbit poop" into a flamethrower. He complied but felt exploited: "My hope was to show the BTU value of rabbit manure and make a point that it is a viable fuel source . . . it never made it on the show though it was filmed extensively" (Klein 2012). It's not surprising that Nick and Megan lost control of their narratives. Reality TV producers often use "prefabricated outlines" indicating how they want the drama to unfold (Deery 2015, 34). Such goals are often at odds with what participants themselves wish to convey.

Reality TV challenges our view of reality in what Hill calls a push-pull dynamic (2014, 8). The mere presence of the camera seems like it should be a "guarantee of authenticity" since the "real" has been observed by a machine whose "mechanical operation is an indication of its neutrality" (Bignell 2005, 72). But reality TV is a genre *negotiating* with the truth, so this mechanical witness is constantly undermined. Seeing isn't believing with reality TV, but we feel like it *ought* to be.

Because we *expect* reality TV to toy with our sense of reality, it is—in a way—honest about its dishonesty. For Bignell, this back-and-forth movement between fiction and fact creates an "unstable border between what is considered 'real' and what is a performance of reality" (64). We are kept on edge: fake or authentic, staged or real. Can we believe what participants tell us? By dismissing the clumsily staged elements of the show but affirming the message about imminent doom and transformation, viewers can sort fact from fiction—or at least feel as if they have. For some viewers of *Doomsday Preppers*, satisfaction resides in believing the metanarrative of the cowboy apocalypse while rejecting the fakeness of reality TV. *Doomsday Preppers* illuminates the cowboy apocalypse through four predictable structural elements appearing in each story arc: confession, prophecy, ritual display, and expert assessment. All display elements of the tension between the real and the fake.

Confession

The "confession to camera" is a common trope in reality TV and reflects the intimacy that producers hope to cultivate between viewer and participants (Deery 2015, 67). Anita Biressi and Heather Nunn propose "the desire to be watched, to be witnessed by others uncovering one's intimate identity and even everyday rituals" is also a "craving for an observer to witness the minutiae of one's social performance" (cited in Hill 2014, 65). The self, says Hill, can be experienced as "validated through the media" since we can "show we exist" by allowing "the camera's gaze on our social life" (66). To be seen is to be real. Or in *Doomsday Preppers*, to be seen is to publicly confess one's *beliefs* about the real.

Roger Dougan (Season 3, Episode 1) believes a cyberattack is imminent and "could send our nation back 150 years overnight." The camera focuses on his face, framed by scraggly beard and cowboy hat. He flinches, remembering his house burning down and how "a lifetime of work . . . [can] . . . go up in smoke." As the camera zooms in on Roger's face, he confesses: "And that's why I'm a prepper."

The pattern is predictable. Bryan Smith "confesses" by telling stories of his father's history as a sharecropper. He says the know-how he gained has prepared him for an imminent collapse of the monetary system in the United States. For Jason from Alabama, a frightening experience being lost in the woods in freezing rain causes him to swear his children will never experience something similar (Season 3, Episode 3). Paul Range is a vet who emotionally explains why he never wants to be stuck in chaos again (Season 1, Episode 1). Jason Charles describes his experiences as a first responder in New York on 9/11 and says he can't shake the memory (Season 1, Episode 3). Chuck Vessey of Johnson County, Texas, describes a recent tornado that frightened him because family members were hard to locate afterward.

Even if we question each prepper's predictions, we don't doubt the sincerity of their description of trauma. We *want* to believe, but the placement of the confession in the genre of reality TV destabilizes us. Its "transparency attracts attention but may not guarantee truth" (Deery 2015, 30). Resolution comes through parsing the confession as detached from the genre of reality TV itself. To believe those "confessing" is to find meaning in their message while questioning the reality TV genre. And once we believe their experiences, we're encouraged to also believe their predictions about the future.

Prophecy

The cowboy messiah doesn't need the Bible to tell him the future; he takes the job on *himself*. Nonetheless, the stories participants tell in *Doomsday Preppers* about impending doom are remarkably similar, including key words like "mob," "looting," "rioting," and "chaos." Society, they say, will be upended and angry marauders will roam the countryside demanding supplies. Force (typically guns) will be the only effective means to stop them. In the new frontier, the prepper will be a self-appointed arbiter of justice, since no other law will exist.

Every prepper offers his own prediction of the conditions that will bring about this collapse in society: nuclear fallout, fuel shortages, environmental disaster, terrorism, and so on. *Each* cowboy messiah is convinced *he* alone has the salvific information the world needs. A rumble on a fault line becomes a sign to move out. A rise in fuel prices signals a disruption in food delivery. A super-volcano will cover the world with ash. Solar flares will destroy electronic equipment. Preppers live on a precipice, eyeing the world for hints of doom. Playing the role of prophet and messiah, their desire for certainty becomes its own authentication. Their preparations are proof they know something the rest of us don't. Preppers, like traditional apocalypticists, "acquire an interpretation which they believe to be a fact" (Gutierrez 2005, 56). They read the world like tea leaves and grow agitated, sketching reassuring portraits of what is to come.

> For people who have entered apocalyptic time, everything quickens, everything enlivens, everything coheres. They become semiotically aroused—everything has meaning, patterns. The smallest incident can have immense importance and open the way to an

entirely new vision of the world, one in which forces unseen by other mortals operate. Everything becomes meaningful, even how one brushes one's teeth. The whole world is watching. . . . And all the signs they now can "read" point in one direction: now is the time! (Landes 2005, 21)

We see this kind of apocalyptic confidence expressed in *Doomsday Preppers*. The preppers exercise prophetic expertise by applying their own skills of interpretation.

Some preppers look to the internet as an all-purpose information source in a way not unlike how Christians—ancient and modern—have looked at the Bible. Laura Kunzie, for example, scours the internet using iPad apps and an RSS feed, looking for information suggesting an outbreak of avian flu (Season 1, Episode 10). Braxton Southwick spends time engaging in "research about terrorist attacks" (Season 2, Episode 1). David Sarti uses his computer to try to predict solar flares, even as he also expects computers to be useless after his community is decimated by EMPs (electro-magnetic pulses) (Season 1, Episode 2).

Michiko Kakutani (2018) says the "sheer volume of data on the web allows people to cherry-pick facts or factoids or non-facts that support their own point of view" (121). As with biblical interpretation, apocalyptic belief based on internet research becomes individually centered and self-authenticating. The prepper rakes the internet for signs of political unrest. He charts temperature changes and reads about planetary disturbances. As a result of these labors, he alone has the wisdom needed by the rest of us. Never mind if his version of things ignores the work of experts in the field. Where once biblical prophets relied on divine encounters ("God spoke to me"), today's prophets need only savvy Googling.

For example, Doug Huffman, a retired defense contractor in Northern California, uses his time on the show to enlighten viewers who need the future explained to them:

> In the first nine months of this type of economic collapse, no food, no water, and amazingly, [no] simple sanitation. Without soap and water, boom. Disease everywhere, rampant, unstoppable.

Simulations have been done: up to an eighty percent loss of our population. The government's not going to be able to help you. You are gonna be on your own and that is the reality. (Season 1, Episode 7)

The prophetic warning is also a brag. Huffman has a "four-stage apocalyptic food plan" that includes hunting local game, breeding fish in his lake, a large greenhouse, and farming rabbit meat. Doug details his manly credentials as he tries to impress viewers: "Am I afraid of this economic apocalyptic event? Not really. Bring it on."

Steve H., a contractor living in Washington State, celebrates his own expertise. Steve predicts massive unrest and violence:

I know what's gonna happen. I pray I'm wrong, but I don't think I am. The way I see it, one of two things is gonna happen. Either the government is gonna get their head out of their ass, and they're gonna implement some serious austerity measures, and they're gonna save this economy . . . Or, they're not. (Season 3, Episode 2)

Instead of relying on God—or even other people—Steve relies on himself. He values what he thinks is required for survival: a "bugout location" and a loaded weapon. He fondles his gun ominously: "And when those people that think they're entitled to other people's stuff, don't get the stuff given to them by the government, they're going to come and try and take our stuff. And when they do, this is what they get." The gun is a symbol of desire for a refreshed frontier in the future, although for Steve, its symbolic power is accessible right now. One danger of this thinking is how easily it leads to presumptions about how vulnerable people would act—turning the weak into agents of force before they do anything at all.

The cowboy apocalypse heralds a return to the Wild West, where justice is reinforced via firearms. Beyond the show, prepper Pat Henry connects prepper expectation of violence with frontier nostalgia:

If society is gone and there is no longer any civilization, we will be living in the Wild West. Your neighborhood street might very well become the OK Corral of the future and your only hope of peace will be the [sic] kill those bent on the destruction of you and yours. (Henry 2013)

Husband and wife Ray and Lindsay of Boise, Idaho, appear on *Doomsday Preppers*, where Ray praises frontier skills as the means to survive the coming apocalypse. "Back in the day," he says, "everybody was prepared because they weren't so reliant on other people to make sure their lives work. Preppers today are like how our ancestors used to be: smart." In their off-grid cabin, Ray and Lindsay have three years' worth of food and a stockpile of weapons and ammunition. But Ray's weapons aren't meant to be used now; they're intended for the hereafter, when Ray will put his cowboy credentials to the test.

> **I can totally sleep tomorrow night if I had to use force—deadly force—to prevent people from taking food out of my family's mouth. I have multiple weapons with various calibers. And as a United States marine, I have absolutely no doubt in my ability to hit what I am firing upon. (Season 2, Episode 11)**

The key skill Ray believes he needs in the future is fatal marksmanship. Like a typical cowboy messiah, Ray doesn't intend to save anyone but those closest to him: "I'm constantly told by my friends that if the shit ever hits the fan, we're gonna come looking for you because we know you're prepared. Well, the hard truth is that when the shit hits the fan, I'm not going to be able to support you and your family. You need to have your own preparations."

Many of us won't survive the violent transition—but the cowboy messiah and his guns surely will. Steve, of Washington State, fears the collapse of the U.S. economy and expects riots and looting. Steve, however, is less likely to import his fears into the present. He is so sure he won't need his guns until the apocalypse that he vacuum-sealed them to protect them from moisture. For Steve, the gun resides in the future. Right now, it is a prop in a ritual of expectation, a sacrament of authentication uniting the *now* of expectation with the *then* of apocalyptic fulfillment.

It is hard to underestimate the importance of frontier mythology here as it fuses with apocalyptic expectation. The hope is for a return to gun-enforced values of strength and independence but blended with an expectation among some—even a hope—for society's collapse. To celebrate the gun is to participate in the larger transmediated fandom of the cowboy apocalypse and reside imaginatively in a future space where that gun can—and will—be used to assert reclaimed manly self-reliance.

David Sarti (Season 1, Episode 2), a disabled truck driver from Nashville, Tennessee, jokingly calls himself a fat Tom Cruise. He prophesies that an EMP will soon incapacitate the transportation system in the United States. Trucks won't be able to deliver goods, so resources will be in short supply. Within weeks, he says, there will be massive unrest and rioting. Sarti hoards food and supplies at his house. He reinforces the perimeter of his property, first, by barbed wire; second, by his dogs; and finally, by his gun. Of course, this makes Sarti the symbolic center of the universe. He imagines that, in the post-apocalyptic world, he will be a sought-out authority for those who listen to his ham radio show. In this future world, Sarti will be less lonely and more respected. But the walls around his property will remain to keep the riffraff out.

Bret Maggio of Fruitland, Utah, offers a prophecy about impending economic collapse in the present tense:

> The dollar has no value, and the government is no longer being paid, [and] you will no longer have the way of life that you currently have. Imagine turning on your faucet and the water not coming on. Imagine going to the grocery store and there being no food on the shelves. People don't understand that all of these systems can collapse at any time, leaving people no choice but to fight for survival. (Season 3, Episode 10)

For Bret, post-apocalyptic transformation will be devastating and violent; it will bring about large-scale changes in life that require the cowboy messiah to defend himself, using all those weapons now off-limits for use on other humans. Bret's brother Shane agrees, evoking frontier morality: "There will be no law enforcement to, you know, tell people what they can and can't do. People are going to be murdering other people so they can feed their families." It's hard to tell if Shane is planning how he will hold murderers accountable or excusing his own future murderous behavior.

Few preppers read the expected cataclysm as a result of God's coming judgment—everything that is going to happen results from natural forces (hurricane, earthquake, solar flare, etc.) or human behavior (climate change, nuclear blast, fuel shortages, political chaos). Those who identify as Christians read the Bible primarily to celebrate their *own* expertise as preppers. Jay Blevins, a self-proclaimed Christian, expects an imminent "breakdown of social order caused by an economic collapse" and describes the impending chaos: "You see people rioting and you see people basically destroying things because they're not getting their way." Jay expects a "mob mentality" and a "dangerous" situation. Rather than hoping for divine intervention, Jay thinks every cowboy messiah will be responsible for his own family's safety. Instead of praying for God to defeat his enemies, Jay has seven thousand rounds of ammunition in his bedroom ready to go:

> **If law enforcement cannot respond to protect us from the groups that represent the worst in people during catastrophic situations . . . citizens have the right to protect themselves. This means being prepared to meet an attacker with the legal and proper amount of force. . . . [W]hat if someone shows up with a baseball bat, a knife, or a firearm and they are planning to hurt you or your loved ones? What will you do then? (Season 2, Episode 3)**

The skillful prepper must be ready to meet evil by himself, face-to-face or—better yet—gun-to-face. Jay imagines a "mob assault on his front door," which becomes the "funnel of death" when he shoots the invaders. For Jay, "the moral of the story is: be the good guys, not the bad guys." Of *course* Jay is the good guy.

Lucas Cameron preps for the massive earthquake described in the Book of Revelation. But Lucas doesn't expect God to care for the faithful afterward (Season 2, Episode 10). He believes the coming apocalypse won't have much to do with God, who appreciates human self-reliance. "Scripture's full of preppers," Lucas says. "Noah built an ark, and it saved his family. Joseph made sure to put granaries in Egypt and it saved not only his family but all of Egypt. I intend also to put back so I can save myself and my community." The Bible may be good for predicting the apocalypse, but humans will be expected to care for themselves, with the aid of their guns. Lucas asks his son on camera: "What are guns good for?" His son replies: "Killing people that are trying to kill you." But these guns will be fired at people only *after* society has collapsed, when Lucas and his family (they believe) will be attacked by "marauders" demanding food and supplies. In the new frontier, Lucas and his son will *be* the law. For now, they must embody this hoped-for freedom through prayer and ritual performance.

Lucas's approach is a prepper reconfiguration of Christian apocalypticism, which traditionally celebrated God's intervention in human history for his chosen people. In taking on the role of the cowboy messiah, preppers like Lucas Cameron elevate themselves, as they worry that God might not intervene. There's a powerful slippage at work here. Or perhaps it is simply a realignment, with a recentering on human activity through firepower. Heaven is symbolically replaced with the American frontier as the hoped-for future. Hopes for paradise are replaced by self-reliance and well-tuned violence. To demonstrate how to succeed in this future, *Doomsday Preppers* offers the display of skills, supplies, and firearms.

Ritual Display

Professor of rhetoric and public culture Casey Ryan Kelly argues that "apocalyptic manhood" is deeply intertwined in *Doomsday Preppers* with "mediated performances that confirm the necessity of masculine skills as modern society meets its demise" (2016, 2). We can see this in the rite of passage that Tom Perez of Houston, Texas, performs with his kids on camera. Tom and his family routinely practice escape from the city to their "bugout" home. There, Tom teaches his kids how to kill a goat. The producers placed a goat in a pit on Tom's property, and recorded Tom leading his children to it. Tom helps little Tommy hold the knife to the goat's throat while giving him some stilted advice: "You need to be swift about it, because this animal provides food for many days, OK? And we have respect for animals." The camera zooms in on six-year-old Matthew touching the dead goat's head in a pool of foaming blood. Tom wipes blood onto Tommy's and Matthew's chubby cheeks. "This shows your manhood" (Season 2, Episode 4). One wonders whether Tom would have handled things differently with no cameras rolling.

Michael James Patrick Douglas of Augusta, Maine, has created a "band of heroes"; tweens and teens he trains in foraging and defensive tactics. Unlike many preppers, Michael doesn't use guns but trains in the use of tomahawks and how to trap and kill animals, appealing in another way to frontier ideals. He has a special "rite of passage" for his own children drawing on the same principles. They spend forty nights a year with him living in self-constructed debris huts. Once they prove they can create their own fire and shelter, Michael presents them with their umbilical cords (Season 1, Episode 5).

Jason Johns, from Alabama, wants his teenage son Jacob to spend a year learning wilderness survivalist skills. On the show, Jason and Jacob demonstrate how to use wire to make a choking snare for squirrels. They build a trip-pole trap using nothing but sticks and wire. They build a shelter using three C's: cargo tape, a cutting tool, and cordage. Jason makes Jacob start a fire with flint. If Jacob "passes all the tests and does all the stuff," he will receive a special bullet "as a symbol of his rite of passage." The bullet—also a symbol of the willingness to use force against one's enemies—is meant to give Jacob "the will to survive" in the apocalyptic future. It's a fitting ritual gift for someone who imagines the future as more worth living in than the present, and who sees the gun as the means of surviving in that world (Season 3, Episode 3).

Ritual can be looked at as an "analytical category that helps us deal with the chaos of human experience and put it into a coherent framework" (Kertzer 1988, 8). The kinds of rituals Michael and others engage in place them within such a desirable framework, an imagined future in which survivalist skills indicate superiority over others. No matter how afraid people might feel about what is going on in the world, they can imagine themselves in a future with skills that will enable them to thrive.

Anthropologist Clifford Geertz proposes viewing rituals as realizations of what people *believe*, and thus also what they *want*. Rituals are models of what people believe but also "models for the believing of it" (1973, 114). Ritual allows a fusing of "the world as lived and the world as imagined . . . under the agency of a single set of symbolic forms" (112–113). The way one imagines the world *ought* to be becomes imprinted on the way the world *is* through ritual. It's not hard to see this kind of force in the way preppers speak about their preparations for a new frontier. When Michael and his children leave the woods, they are reassured that unstable global politics won't threaten those with enough guns.

Guns play an important role in these ritual preparations: they provide a mobile perimeter that demarcates the prepper's autonomy in his imagined future. Robert, a prepper in Texas, says: "Firearms are important at any time, but especially after martial law is declared." Robert claims an arsenal that includes several .22 pistols, a .357 Magnum, a Smith & Wesson 500, an M4, and a couple of Uzis. "Once lawlessness takes over, there will be people [who] do whatever it takes to steal, to hurt, to harm. I want to do whatever it takes to prepare so that those individuals cannot harm me or my family" (Season 3, Episode 9). Robert is proud of his Bushmaster 50 caliber, bragging that "[i]f you can't stop 'em with this, you probably need a tank." The gun is a sacrament of authentication, a material prop in the ritual of expectation.

Robert needs guns because violence, he believes, is going to infect America at large:

> We all have examples of what lawlessness can do to cities . . . [like the] Los Angeles riots. Inevitably, Dallas will look like New Orleans after Katrina. Once lawlessness takes over, there will be people that will do whatever it takes to steal, to hurt, to harm. I want to do whatever it takes to prepare so that those individuals cannot harm me or my family. . . . Under martial law, anything can happen. They can reduce our access to fuel. They can reduce our access to power. So it's important that my family is able to survive without the aid or benefit of anyone outside our property. (Season 3, Episode 9)

Robert expects his family to survive in their walled-off compound reinforced with munitions. Robert and his family have installed solar panels and piled up enough buckets of dried food to last for months. Although he looks toward the future, Robert wants to ritually enact separation from the world *right now*. It's one way of denying the shared global fate of humans: simply define yourself out of interdependence and allow the disintegration of society to happen. Then pick up your weapon to protect your own. These are frontier-myth values celebrating manly know-how and cowboy bravery, anchored in a dark apocalyptic hope.

Doomsday Preppers celebrates an apocalyptic future that "recuperates hegemonic masculinity by restaging the plausible real-world conditions under which the performance of manly labor appears instrumental to collective survival" (Kelly 2016, 96). These mediated manhood rituals are cast within the context of a theatric performance of masculinity driven by anticipation of "an apocalyptic event that promises a final resolution to white male alienation" (96). By ritualizing violence in the present, and by imagining a future in which men will perform such violence in a salvific context, *Doomsday Preppers* condones the logic of the cowboy apocalypse.

Physical walls are also a key element in the rituals of the cowboy apocalypse, in that they help the believer imagine himself protected from the chaos and violence of global flows. The construction of walls now is a way of imagining blocking off the world more violently in the future. Jerry McMullin spent $7 million rehabilitating the former AT&T relay station. He's proud of the reinforced glass windows with "Batman shutters" that can withstand a .44 Magnum, and the concrete and steel walls that will protect from nuclear or biological terrorist attack. He has installed twenty security cameras. His wife, Kay, says the only way anybody could get in is with a huge tank to knock the walls down.

Jerry's caretaking is all future oriented. He has multiple means of producing power off-grid for his fortified home: solar, wind, batteries, generators, propane. He runs weekly drills to train his family. Jerry has a "private UHF scrambled system," with which he will "educate the citizens of this country from potential threats." After the collapse, Jerry will be a prophet for prophets, helping men in other survivalist households.

Paul Range of Floresville, Texas, believes a magnetic pole reversal will cause widespread havoc including rapid climate change, disruption of the electric grid, and earthquakes. Paul and his family spend fifty hours a week storing food, practicing defense, and designing gadgets for the post-apocalypse. Paul built The Range, a fortified home with "the layout of a medieval castle." Paul and his family practice shooting at their own house to make sure its defenses will hold (Season 1, Episode 1). After the catastrophe, they expect people from the nearby town to "show up and want food, and you cannot feed the entire world." Preppers like Paul feel overwhelmed by the flow of needy bodies in the world as it is, so they invest in a desired future in which they wall off the bodies they find threatening. While they wait, these self-proclaimed messiahs hoard supplies within those walls. The show's next structural element—the expert assessment—provides the means to encourage preppers in their material investment in this imagined apocalyptic future.

Expert Assessment

In *Doomsday Preppers*, participants buy *now* to feel secure about *then*. This kind of media-affiliated ritual is more than habit; it provides what media scholar Nick Couldry calls a "recognizable pattern, form or shape which gives meaning to that action" that points toward "broad, even transcendent, values" (2013, 3). By integrating the expert assessment with the ritual of consumer acquisition, *Doomsday Preppers* links viewers' desire for the cowboy apocalypse with the promises of the show's participants that this future world is not only possible, but likely, and imminent.

Television is like ritual, since both invite us to experience events "outside ordinary time" and interrupt the "flow of everyday existence." When viewing television or engaging in ritual, the viewer can enter "timelessly into creation and timelessly into eternity" (Goethels 1981, 259). Ritual promises to make life meaningful. Television, under certain conditions, promises the same.

Couldry (2013) believes media can work like ritual because it plays a key role in "ordering our lives, and organizing social space" (1). Media rituals are not about the media texts themselves *per se*; they are about what people *do* with television shows, or movies, or news reports; and how those texts structure people's lives. Media demands not only that we place it at the center of our lives, says Couldry, but also that we believe "there is a social 'center' to be re-presented to us" (45–46). By presenting again the world to us, media can make order from the chaos of ordinary life. Religion has always promised something similar in providing stories and moral instructions that *re*-present the world in a palatable form, taking the messiness of life and ordering it. *Doomsday Preppers* authenticates its authority in part through the cultivation of consumer devotion as reinforced by the show's expert assessment of preppers, who link media's order-making capacity with the consumer's duty to buy more things.

On *Doomsday Preppers*, basements are filled with canned goods, toilet paper, and medical supplies. Dried food is stacked up, hidden under floorboards, even buried in yards. Guns are bragged about, polished, loaded, shot. Underground bunkers are built at great expense and with intense anticipation. As *Doomsday Preppers* indicates, the more preppers are afraid of *this* world, the more they buy to convince themselves they can live in *that* hoped-for world. In order to encourage consumerism, nobody gets voted off *Doomsday Preppers* and nobody wins. Instead, participants are encouraged to be better doomsday consumers.

The slate of expert judges on the show are owners of their own prepping businesses, and they use the show to drum up sales. The experts consider things like how to locate potable water, how to store food, the means to secure one's property, the development of evacuation plans, and accessing energy sources. Regardless of performance, and regardless of how many things they already own, all participants are encouraged to buy more. These are *future*-oriented expectations, implicated in *present*-day consumer practices: go off-grid *now*, so you'll have energy *then*. Buy massive food stores *now*, because there won't be grocery stores *then*. Store as many bullets as possible *now*, because you won't be able to buy them *then*. In prepper logic, the more you buy now, the longer you'll survive when society inevitably collapses. This is an insurance policy in the form of medical masks, ammunition, and canned beans.

On *Doomsday Preppers*, consumerism is sanctified and masculinized. In one episode, Frank Woodworth of Maine blows up dynamite near one of his customized bunkers to prove its strength and drum up buyers (Season 2, Episode 12). In another episode, a volunteer stands behind an advertised brand of bulletproof material while others shoot at him (Season 3, Episode 11). In the same episode, "Johnny Carpet" whoops at the camera from his pickup truck: "You want your flooring to survive the apocalypse? You're not going to get a second chance, so you want to get first quality" (Season 3, Episode 11). For the cowboy apocalypse, the most prized ritualized expenditure is the gun, which offers a material instantiation of frontier values within the apocalyptic hope of reclaimed male hegemony. The end times will recursively repeat the past, as clever men will again live by the bullet.

Purchasing survival supplies marks someone as part of a similarly minded group, as buying the right things "becomes for some a totemistic activity, expressing group identity, loyalty, engagement, a sense of belonging" (Deery 2015, 86). A few weeks after their initial appearance, the participants get a chance to come back and demonstrate how they have increased their stores of food, or acquired new training, or reinforced the walls of their compound, or purchased more ammunition. If we accept the show's expert assessment, we too will buy and belong. Purchase water purification systems and firearms. Stockpile bullets and canned goods. Consumerism is fueled by an imagined future of scarcity, a neo-frontier in which preppers' skills allow them to survive while the rest of us die. The "reality" that *Doomsday Preppers* sells is not the muck of day-to-day struggles, but belief in a radically transformed society.

Doomsday Preppers plays with the relationship between real and fake by encouraging viewers to reject the artifice of reality TV but *accept* the testimony of show participants. Because the cowboy messiah can construct a *possible* narrative from what he sees in the world around him, because the story feels right to him, he believes the narrative must be *true*. To insist on the violent, self-serving narrative of the cowboy apocalypse is to insist that reality itself will bend—already *has* bent—to the story the cowboy tells about the aggrandizing future he desires. The "real" is whatever prevents the cowboy messiah from having to face the reality of shared global risk. Reality TV is, in some ways, the perfect vehicle for a myth that undermines reality itself. What's true for the cowboy messiah is what he *wants* to be true.

* * *

There are two battles for truth today, and it is easy to confuse them. The first battle is about what is *scientifically* true: Are ocean levels rising? Do vaccinations protect children from illness? This battle includes both the defense of objective facts like the temperature at which water boils, as well as "inferences drawn from scientific data" and "conclusions based on statistical analysis" (Kavanaugh and Rich 2018, 21). This battle can be won with time. "Even if you are prepared to deny the facts, they have a way of asserting themselves" (McIntyre 2018, 161). Shorelines shorten and buildings sink. Children die of preventable diseases (161). The truth becomes apparent, whether we like it or not.

The second battle for truth is about *moral* conviction. The cowboy apocalypse is evidence of this battle. The cowboy apocalypse can be viewed as a nationalist retreat, a recursive reference to a violent American past and a dark desire to recreate those conditions. It is not necessarily harmless playacting. For some, it is an expression of a very real desire for violent retribution in the imminent future. The cowboy apocalypse is a story about what some anxious, angry men *wish* were true, what they insist *was* true, what they hope will *be* true again—even if it means the earth itself will be radically transformed. Despite its portrayal of manly force, the cowboy apocalypse reflects what Robert Alter (1966) has called a "failure of nerve, a determination to opt out of the challenges, complexities, and threats of history."

In his book *As If*, philosopher Kwame Anthony Appiah suggests the way to fight small-mindedness is not to pelt people with scientific facts. What matters most is "the truth about what is possible" (2017, 172). Instead of trying to imagine the perfect world in all its complexity—an impossible task—we should "start with the rejection of some current actual practice or structure, which we come to see as wrong" (168). If Appiah is right, then it is possible to work toward a world that supports universal human dignity. Appiah's worldview is fueled by hope instead of fear. If the world runs on belief, why *not* choose beliefs grounded in care? Why *not* craft a vision that is more inclusive and kinder? Belief is not knee-jerk acknowledgment of what someone else says. If we value human dignity, we can *choose* to build a world around values of care.

This kind of constructive storytelling isn't typically performed by governments or political movements. It's enacted by real, impassioned people as they live toward the future they want. "It's only because we can understand what it would be for the world to be different from the way it is . . . that we can build idealizations" (171). Imagining a better future and living into it is neither real nor fake, neither true nor false. But it's the kind of moral truth that gives people the strength to keep on going.

7

THE NRA IN THE GAME

THE MAN BEHIND THE GUN

On June 17, 2014, in Las Vegas, Jerad Miller shot and killed two police officers. Joseph Wilcox shot and killed Jerad Miller. Miller's wife then shot Joseph Wilcox in the back. Because he had killed a killer, Wilcox saw himself as a good guy with a gun. The problem is that Miller *also* saw himself as a good guy with a gun. Miller planned to defend Cliven Bundy against the U.S. government's attempt to remove Bundy's cattle from federal land. Every day in America, good guys with guns fire at bad guys. But it's often impossible to tell who the good guy is. The NRA's version of the cowboy apocalypse draws on American frontier mythology and apocalyptic imagery to produce its own version of the battle between good and evil. In this chapter, I look at the history of the NRA and other gun groups to consider the emergence of the cowboy apocalypse as a form of committed fandom with real-life consequences. Then I consider the role of the NRA's branded videogames in their construction of an apocalyptic worldview. The NRA can be viewed as a gun fandom group, embracing apocalyptic beliefs about the world.

Ghosts

The NRA, established in 1871, initially focused on target shooting and gun safety (Hosley 1996, 54). It was the NRA's mission to deal with the flood of war weapons into everyday life after the Civil War. Easy access to guns combined with frontier themes fueled a belief in America as God's chosen nation: "Guns, technology, and the campaign of western expansion were overlapping layers. . . . Each fed and enabled the other"

(49). The accessibility of rapid-fire guns after the Civil War increased violence and nurtured the development of the Ku Klux Klan (Dunbar-Ortiz 2018, 89).

The ghosts of Civil War battle lines demarcate rough divisions on gun rights even today. The Confederate flag is "unfurled at protests and rallies and at gun shows" in formerly Confederate and racially sensitive areas (289–90). The battered Arkansas history textbook I was issued in 1978 had been first published in 1958. The book is addressed to Southern white children learning about European ancestors and tilts heavily Confederate in its sympathies (Brown 1958, 18). Written by Walter Brown, a University of Arkansas professor, the textbook teaches that Reconstruction was a Northern plan to punish the South by giving freed slaves citizenship (199). The Ku Klux Klan emerged, says Brown, because Southern white men were not protected against "unruly Negroes" (211). As slaves, Black people "had been given food, clothing, and shelter. Now, as free men, such necessities were no longer given to them" (209). In an accusation that anticipates complaints about welfare, Brown says freed Black people expected the government to "take care of their needs" (209). He claims freed slaves were bribed to vote sympathetic to Northern views (211). Black people were framed as criminals, then "run out of the state, hanged, or burned alive as a warning to others" (212). Brown repeats a common story that KKK members were harmless pranksters dressing as ghosts to frighten Black people into "being good" (212). Guns were presumably incidental.

The Man behind the Gun

By the twentieth century, early versions appeared of the NRA's celebration of the good shooter and the innocence of the gun. In 1900, singer S. H. Dudley released a gramophone recording of "The Man behind the Gun." The song claims the soldier and gun cooperate for victory in battle because "guns alone don't win the fray." Guns are "big and mighty" but "we need that modern hero" who is "the man behind the gun" (Dudley 1900). In 1905, Theodore Morse wrote a song with the same title, and sentiment: "On land or on sea, wherever he may be / no matter if a thousand dangers lurk / You'll find him there, to keep our flag in air / It's the man behind the gun who does the work." The song is subtitled "Give the Credit Where It Belongs" (Morse 1905). Writing in 1908, the editors of *Arms and the Man* (later called *American Rifleman*) refer to an inspirational ballad also called "The Man behind the Gun." The refrain identifies the shooter as the essential force, reiterating: "It's the man behind the gun who does the work." The song urges those interested in shooting sports to "adopt the old song refrain as their slogan" ("The Man behind the Gun" 1908, 12).

In 1917, attorney John Warnock Echols gave an address to the Fairfax Historical Society in which he quoted Confederate Georgia chief justice Joseph Henry Lumpkin, a secessionist and supporter of slavery. Lumpkin, perhaps not coincidentally, was the author in 1846 of the first decision in which a court struck down a gun law on the basis of the Second Amendment (Cornell and Rubin 2015). Echols proposes that the "true prosperity of any country" is based on "the man behind the gun" and that "leadership is mostly, if not altogether, indebted" to him (Echols 1917, 6). In these earliest iterations of gun fandom, the separation of gun from shooter was meant to *valorize* the man behind the gun. Later versions will *blame* the man behind the gun when things go wrong.

After World War II, the NRA experienced an increase in membership as returning soldiers wanted to maintain their interest in firearms (Melzer 2012, 36). A hunter education program debuted in 1949. In 1960, the NRA introduced a Police Firearms Instructor certification program that still operates today. In his personal account of the gun culture of the United States, Gerry Souter sees the NRA's primary job during these years as recruiting the "youth of America, to pry them away from those new TV sets infesting American homes, to put a rifle in their hands and teach them discipline and responsibility" (2012, 129). Souter identifies the enemy as Soviet Russia, saying we "need a new generation of hunters and sharpshooters to keep the commies in their place" (129).

In 1960, John F. Kennedy evoked frontier mythology in his acceptance speech for the Democratic nomination:

> I stand tonight on what was once the last frontier. From the lands that stretch 3,000 miles behind me, the pioneers of old gave up their safety . . . to build a new world here in the West. . . . [But] the

problems are not all solved and the battles are not all won, and we stand today on the edge of a new frontier . . . a frontier of unknown opportunities and threats. (Dunbar-Ortiz 2018, 206)

For Kennedy, the choice of frontier mythology was "a complexly resonant symbol," evoking a "set of hero-tales—each a model of successful and morally justifiable action" (Slotkin 1998, 3). Not long after this speech, American troops described Vietnam as "Indian country," with battles between "cowboys and Indians" (3). After Kennedy's assassination in 1963, it was revealed that Lee Harvey Oswald had purchased his gun by mail order through an ad in the NRA magazine *American Rifleman* (Melzer 2012, 37). The transformation of the NRA into a charged political organization ratcheted up when the Vietnam War ended and people began questioning how easily guns could be acquired (Dunbar-Ortiz 2018, 203). Some soldiers brought stolen guns home as souvenirs.

By 1963, the slogan "Guns don't kill" had appeared in "millions of copies of the *American Rifleman* and in other millions of NRA pamphlets, brochures, leaflets, bulletins, and letters, and, in the form of posters and stickers" that were "plastered all over the countryside at gun-club buildings and at firing ranges" (U.S. Congress 1968, 12489). Those who like the slogan are "endlessly amused by carrying it to its illogical conclusion, which is that if one is going to regulate the use of guns because they are sometimes used to kill people, one should then regulate the use of knives, hammers, baseball bats, rope, fireplace pokers, hands, feet, and on and on" (12489). Guns, the argument runs, are no different than any other tool. Despite their violent purposes, guns are innocent.

"Guns Don't Kill People"

In the congressional records of the 1968 debates about gun control, we find full articulation of the now familiar slogan: "Guns don't kill people; people kill people." Gun supporters claimed that "people, and not their guns, must be more strictly regulated" (12489). The Gun Control Act, regulating interstate commerce, passed in 1968, although the NRA did everything they could to stop it. During the debates, one

NRA advocate called for "mandatory penalties for crimes committed with firearms," proposing stricter punishment as the only response to gun crime (12490).

The arguments from the 1968 hearings sound a lot like the arguments we hear today. Gun control proponents pointed out that "more than half of all the murders committed in this country are committed with guns" and "guns have only one use, which is to destroy something, whether a target, a clay pigeon, an animal, or a person" (12489). These arguments, presented to gun rights folks, were "utterly without effect."

> One witness . . . made a favorite NRA point when he testified: "I am perfectly aware that tens of thousands of people are killed in this country every year by automobiles . . . I don't think anyone proposes to make it impossible to buy an automobile because tens of thousands of people are killed." The analogy was very popular in gun circles, even though no one had proposed to make it impossible to buy a gun. Moreover . . . automobiles are essential to modern life, whereas guns aren't, and, in any event, the increasing death toll from automobile accidents has led to increasingly strict regulation. (12489)

The NRA is consistent in its argument for shooters' responsibility while neglecting the weapon's role in violence. On the one hand, the NRA can argue (and it did, even in 1968) that law-abiding citizens should not be punished with gun control legislation (12490). On the other hand, bad people should bear full responsibility for gun violence. In both cases, the gun *itself* is presumed irrelevant, no more harmful than fists or feet—even though the discussion is actually *about* the gun and the harm it can do. The gun is like Schrödinger's cat.

Between 1960 and 1977, there was a dramatic return toward using patriotic language to "justify why mainly white men needed to control what they owned—and why they owned guns" (Burbick 2006, 662). The Gun Owners of America (GOA), formed in 1975, also argued for gun rights but used explicit biblical and apocalyptic language. Today, the GOA is the second-largest pro-gun group in the United States (*No Compromise* 2020). Larry Pratt, who headed the organization for almost forty years, is a pivotal figure in the right-wing militia and Patriot groups and a leading voice, with his son Erich, in the GOA's theological work.

In 1977 at the NRA National Convention in Cincinnati, an ideological conflict erupted between the old guard of the NRA—focused on marksmanship and gun safety—and the hard-liners, who focused on the Second Amendment (Melzer 2012, 37). The hard-liners won, and the NRA has not been the same since. They chose Harlon Carter to lead them. Carter has been described as "Moses, George Washington, and John Wayne rolled into one" (Davidson 1998, 31–32). Carter argues guns are a fundamental right, linked directly to America's frontier past: "Strong men will not shirk or flinch. Free men cannot do so. Ours is a great revolution, which began on this continent 200 years ago" (cited in Burbick 2006, 666).

In an August 1977 article in the *American Rifleman*, the argument for individual gun rights is made explicit: "The guardians of our basic liberties are not formal bodies of police or military. They are not mercenaries hired to preserve and defend the rights of free men and women. The guardians of civil liberty are those, each individual, who would enjoy that liberty" (NRA Institute for Legislative Action Reports 1977). English professor Joan Burbick summarizes the impact of such a claim: "Leeched of morning or weekend musters, training at arms . . . the modern militia member had a right to bear without a duty to provide an essential service to his country" (2006, 666). With this move, a renewed founding narrative "restored the gun owner to his rightful place in the American mythos" (667).

Ronald Reagan's election in 1980 was a watershed moment for the NRA, giving them an enthusiastic president who publicly endorsed their work. Reagan's movie star past associated him with frontier mythology, since he often played the "slow-to-anger-but-willing-to-fight gun-toting pioneer." Reagan was "the perfect person to ride into Washington and clean out the various varmints who were undermining the American way of life" (Davidson 1998, 42). Under Reagan's watch, pro-gun activists put forward the "Firearms Owners' Protection Act," designed to undo restrictions from the Gun Control Act of 1968. This act was signed into law in 1986. Now, guns could be sold at gun shows by hobbyists without oversight. The law eliminated the requirement to keep records of sales and made it easier for felons to legally own firearms.

In his 1987 book *Magnum Force Lobby*, pro-gun spokesman Edward Leddy personifies the NRA's use of flamboyant frontier imagery:

> **If the National Rifle Association were to portray itself as a symbolic person, he would be a pioneer heading west with a rifle. He is self-reliant, morally strong, and competent. He is also peaceful by preference, but ready to defend himself from attack. He believes in personal rather than collective responsibility. He is not against government but sees its role as subordinate and supplementary to individual personal efforts. He opposes arbitrary abuse of government power but is openly patriotic. (Leddy 1987, 29)**

With a shift to Second Amendment defense of individual gun rights, the NRA made a harder appeal to the rugged values of America's mythic frontier origins.

In 1991 Wayne LaPierre, who had been a protégé of Harlon Carter's, was elected executive vice president of the NRA. LaPierre continued the hardline approach to gun control, arguing more stridently every year that without guns to defend ourselves, evil would overrun America. LaPierre led the shift from cowboy symbolism to the cowboy apocalypse in recent decades. The hero of the NRA is the "vigilante-as-citizen, a militia unto himself, under command of his private vision of moral authority stamped with national identity" (Burbick 2006, 668). The lone hero answers only to himself: "The individual becomes the mini-state, the army of one, who dreams of the ultimate in political power, a gun beyond regulation" (669).

Other Gun Groups

The NRA was not the only gun rights group endorsing an apocalyptic mindset. The "Gathering of Christian Men," a white power event, took place in 1992 in Estes Park, Colorado, in response to the confrontation at Ruby Ridge two months earlier. Pete Peters, a Christian Identity preacher, was there. At the Estes meeting were people representing the Ku Klux Klan, Aryan Nations, and early militia groups. Leonard

Zeskind, a researcher of white nationalism, told NPR hosts that "Ruby Ridge was a crisis for them. They believed that Weaver had been targeted over the issue of gun rights and religion . . . They were angry . . . And then the militia movement was born" (*No Compromise* 2020). Also attending the meeting was Larry Pratt of the GOA. The NRA's comfort with white supremacy leaked into public view at the 1997 National Press Club, when NRA vice president Charlton Heston declared his disdain for civil rights, feminism, and the social advances of "cultural warriors" (Dizard et al. 1999, 202). Heston sarcastically complained:

> Heaven help the God-fearing, law-abiding, Caucasian, middle class, Protestant, or even worse evangelical Christian, Midwest or southern or even worse rural, apparently straight or even worse admitted heterosexual, gun-owning or even worse NRA-card-carrying, average working stiff, or even, worst of all, a male working stiff, because then, not only don't you count, you're a downright nuisance, an obstacle to social progress, pal. Your tax dollars may be just as green as you hand them over, but your voice better be quiet, your opinion is less enlightened, your media access is silenced, and frankly mister, you need to wake up, wise up and learn a little something about your new America . . . and meantime, why don't you just sit down and shut up! (Dizard et al. 1999, 201)

After Ruby Ridge and Waco, far-right paramilitary groups began organizing and producing literature like the *Field Manual of the Free Militia* (1994), with members whose work overlapped with that of the NRA and the GOA. The manual engages in biblical interpretation, though without much sophistication. For example, the author uses the Bible to prove the Bible is without error, referring to a passage saying scripture is "God-breathed" (2 Tim. 3:16–17). This is problematic. First, "God-breathed" can mean many different things. Second, a text cannot prove its own veracity. The author follows with a quote from Jesus (Matt. 5:18), saying the "Law" (which he takes to mean the Christian Bible) will not be altered—even though the New Testament did not yet exist in Jesus's time, so Jesus was referring to the Torah.

Why argue for biblical inerrancy in a militia manual? Because the document next argues that Jesus loved guns. Jesus was "not a pacifist" but "approved of the justified use of deadly force" (*Field Manual* 1.1.3). How do we know? Because Jesus told his disciples to get swords. Does he tell them to use them? No. But he does not tell them to get rid of them, either, which the narrator takes as an endorsement of guns. Apparently, a sword and a gun are more or less the same thing. Biblical literalism, in this case, is not required.

Jesus uses "just force" against bad people, according to the manual. In the story about driving merchants out of the Temple (John 2:15), Jesus punishes the guilty with a whip of cords and uses his "divine power against aggressors." Citing Revelation, the manual claims Jesus will bring "deadly punishment" to wrongdoers "on a universal scale." Meanwhile, though, men with guns are needed to do his work on earth:

> **How can we love our enemies and kill them at the same time? Clearly Jesus is saying we should harbor no hatred towards anyone. Our actions should never be motivated by hatred or vengeance but only by justice. . . . God can and does desire a sinner's repentance as he condemns him forever. So also it is possible . . . for us to love our mortal enemies, to pray for their souls and seek to change their minds and behavior, even when we are forced to take up arms against them. (*Field Manual* 1994)**

Interpreting the principles of just war for individual gun use, the guidebook asserts that killing people who deserve to die is not "personal." It's what God would want: "By all means we must seek peaceful resolutions. . . . We are not to get even with an evildoer nor are we to take justice into our own hands. But it is not evil or vengeful for people to individually defend themselves or to collectively exact just punishment" (*Field Manual* 1.1.4). It is the latter that gives the lie to guns as a means of innocent self-defense and exposes them (for this author at least) as a means of enacting God's wrath.

Larry Pratt of the GOA engages in similar modes of stretched biblical interpretation, proposing that "both the Old and New Testaments teach individual self-defense, even if it means taking the assailant's life in certain circumstances" (Pratt 1999). One of the stretchiest of Pratt's claims is his gun-friendly interpretation of Proverbs 25:26: "A righteous man who falters before the wicked is like a murky spring and a polluted well." His argument hinges on the word "falter."

Certainly, we would be faltering before the wicked if we chose to be unarmed and unable to resist an assailant who might be threatening our life. In other words, we have no right to hand over our life, which is a gift from God, to the unrighteous. It is a serious mistake to equate a civilized society with one in which the decent people are doormats for the evil to trample on (Pratt 1999). Despite Pratt's certainty, refusing to falter could mean walking away, remaining silent, keeping one's values when tempted, or something else. It need not involve weapons, and in ancient Israel it certainly did not involve guns. Another stretchy claim takes an obligation to provide for one's family (1 Tim. 5:8) to mean "make adequate provision for their own defense," because to refuse to be armed would be "to defy God" (Pratt 1999). The "righteous" man will be armed.

Good Guy with a Gun

In 1998, *Time* reported one of the first clear instances of the "good guy with a gun" narrative, uttered by a White House staff member after mentally ill shooter Russell Weston entered the offices of Representative Tom DeLay one July afternoon and killed two people, including the "good guy." The staff member said: "Thank God there was a good guy with a gun or there would have been a lot more dead people" (Gibbs 1998).

The NRA's apocalyptic rhetoric took off after 9/11. Jennifer Dawson, a professor at West Point, has studied the use of religious language in the NRA's flagship journal *American Rifleman* and found the use of terms like "God-given right" and "evil" increased dramatically since the September 11 attacks (Dawson 2019). She identifies this tendency as an alignment between the NRA and the new Christian right. But in LaPierre's declarations, we also see the development of cowboy apocalypse mythology, which becomes increasingly strident as time goes on.

In 2003, LaPierre said the world was "increasingly more dangerous," and would soon experience another terrorist attack (LaPierre 2003). In response to three shootings in December 2007 in Colorado Springs, Las

Vegas, and Omaha, LaPierre said: "The only thing that's stopping these bad guys with a gun is a good guy with a gun" (Keen and Stone 2007). Also in 2007, caustic gun-rights pastor Doug Giles published a book in which he wrote about Seung-Hui (Vincent) Cho, the Virginia Tech student who murdered his classmates and professors earlier that year:

> But imagine if at least one Virginia Tech student (with a concealed weapons permit) had his .40 caliber Glock with him, locked and loaded, when this little Charlie Chan chump began his murderous mayhem last Monday on the Hokie campus? . . . I'm a guessin' that this terminal turd might not have dealt out as much death (if any) if the good guy with the gun drew down on him and double-tapped the center mass of this ass with a couple of 165 grain COR-BON jacket hollow points. Yes, if there had been a good guy with a gun, who was licensed and allowed to carry it into class, he could have sent this spawn of Satan to hell where he belongs. (Giles 2007, 87)

Giles moves from this call for an armed campus to rank Islamophobia, suggesting future attacks will come from Muslims:

> I hate to seem pessimistic but given this post-911 era and our current crappy culture, I don't see an atmospheric break in this violent weather pattern. I guarantee that even as I type and our nation weeps, there is, somewhere in the United States of Political Correctness, some Islamic Radical or some other disenfranchised dipstick making plans on how he can trump The Question Mark Kid's quota. Chilling. Until we realize that a trained, licensed and armed civilian is a viable force against these murderous foes on campus, I suggest that both teachers and students learn to capture and kill a murderous puke with whatever is at hand. (88)

In 2008, LaPierre described the "perfect storm gathering on the horizon" and expressed concerns about the strength of U.S. borders with Mexico. By 2009, LaPierre was being credited with the "good guy with a gun" phrase in conservative circles on Twitter (Montopoli 2011). Sarah Palin told a crowd at the 2010 NRA convention: "The only thing that stops a bad guy with a gun is a good guy with a gun" (Palin 2010). In

2011, in response to the shooting of Gabrielle Giffords and eighteen other people in Tucson, LaPierre phrased it almost the same way, saying the "best way to stop a bad guy with a gun is a good guy with a gun" (Montopoli 2011). This time the line stuck. It's a narrative in miniature, an apocalyptic script with three characters: the good guy, the bad guy, and the gun. The other people involved in this narrative—the ones who are shot—are props for the story, non-player characters who could be anybody. The story goes like this: The world is filled with evil. "Good guys" will fight evil with guns because God isn't here to do so. The "bad guys" will be defeated, but the world is tipping toward destruction.

In the NRA's story, mass murder is unavoidable. The best a hero can hope for is to nip it in the bud. New Testament scholar David Aune describes apocalyptic eschatology in a way that would probably make a lot of sense to LaPierre:

> [T]he present world order, regarded as both evil and oppressive, is under the temporary control of Satan and his human accomplices, and . . . this present evil world order will shortly be destroyed by God and replaced by a new and perfect order. . . . During the present evil age, the people of God are an oppressed minority who fervently expect God, or his specially chosen agent the Messiah, to rescue them. The transition between the old and the new ages will be introduced with a final series of battles fought by the people of God against the human allies of Satan. The outcome is never in question, however, for the enemies of God are predestined for defeat and destruction. (1983, 236)

In the end times, the wicked will be judged, the righteous rewarded, and the earth transformed. Until then, good guys with gun will do the job as best they can.

In December 2012, twenty-year-old Adam Lanza opened fire at Sandy Hook Elementary, killing twenty children and six adults. One week after the shooting, LaPierre gave a speech in which he said we have left our children "defenseless, and the monsters and predators of this world know it" (LaPierre 2012). He formulated his now famous slogan in the form it is repeated today: "The only way to stop a bad guy with a gun is a good guy with a gun." In recent years, this slogan has become popular among gun enthusiasts, who emblazon it on T-shirts and mugs, create memes, and slap bumper stickers on their cars. LaPierre's remarks about Adam Lanza reveal dark apocalyptic dreams:

> The truth is that our society is populated by an unknown number of genuine monsters—people so deranged, so evil, so possessed by voices and driven by demons that no sane person can possibly ever comprehend them. They walk among us every day. And does anybody really believe that the next Adam Lanza isn't planning his attack on a school he's already identified at this very moment? (LaPierre 2012)

The language of "demons" and "evil" is not hyperbole. According to Protestant Calvinist reasoning, some people are just bad to the bone, predestined for hell before they were born. Therefore, anyone who enacts a mass murder must have been *always* evil even if he *seemed* to be a good guy. Mass shooters are destined to do harm long *before* they have a gun in their hands. Just as the Antichrist will be exposed as evil only *after* masquerading as the Savior, so the bad guy may seem good before he reveals himself. This is why it is pointless to create laws to keep guns out of the hands of certain people.

Thoughts and Prayers

If guns are like angels, then the proliferation of guns in America ought to make all of us feel safer. There are more good guys with guns than bad guys with guns, so take heart! (Never mind the argument that any good guy could turn bad; this line of theological reasoning is not allowed.) The appeal for "thoughts and prayers" can be read as a theological sleight of hand implying loss of faith in God's imminent intervening power. Despite "thoughts and prayers," God does nothing about gun violence. God needs *help* now, and in the end times. God to His angels: *Could I get a good guy, please? Send him to the mall, Gabriel. Make sure he's armed.* For LaPierre, the world has entered a time in which God is *not* intervening, so the *only* way to defeat the monsters in our midst is for brave men to kill them. This, of course, is why some

NRA proponents advocate for guns in churches and schools. Evil can show up anywhere, anytime.

Apocalypticism is characterized by the conviction that ultimately there will be a divine judgment with rewards for the righteous and punishments for the wicked. LaPierre similarly predicts a judgment, but he sees the cowboy messiah as the one to enact it:

> In this uncertain world, surrounded by lies and corruption, there is no greater freedom than the right to survive, to protect our families with all the rifles, shotguns, and handguns we want. We know, in the world that surrounds us, there are terrorists and home invaders and drug cartels and car-jackers and knock-out gamers and rapers, haters, campus killers, airport killers, shopping mall killers, road-rage killers, and killers who scheme to destroy our country with massive storms of violence against our power grids, or vicious waves of chemicals or disease that could collapse the society that sustains us all. (LaPierre 2014a)

The world is infused with spiritual enemies who *look* like human beings but will do anything to kill. Hoarding weapons and ammunition, then, has serious theological implications. The more guns a good guy has, the more bad guys he can shoot. Bullets are the calculus of the elect. After the Boston Marathon bombing in 2013, LaPierre warned that violent enemies are all around us: "Lying in wait is a terrorist, a deranged school shooter, a kidnapper, a rapist, a murderer—waiting and planning and plotting—in every community across this country" (LaPierre 2013b). The NRA's media campaign took its apocalyptic message to the masses, identifying the members of the NRA as good guys who would make the world right again.

The NRA, LaPierre said in April 2014, is exceptional because it is "so alert and vigilant, so unafraid to take a stand for what is good and right. . . . We are—and, throughout history, have always been—the good guys" (LaPierre 2014b). At the 2015 NRA Convention, LaPierre alluded to insider prepper language about the end of the world as we know it, warning: "National policies built upon lies lead to national collapse, the end of this country as we know it. We wonder what can be done. All of us, we hope and we pray for someone to save America." He then borrows darkly from language associated with the killing of Eric Garner by a police officer in 2014, shifting it to present the NRA's members as victims of suffocation: "the dishonesty in the air, my gosh, it's so thick it's become hard for normal people in this country to breathe." In 2016, LaPierre again described the world as increasingly dangerous:

> The threats are all around us. Russia's advancing. The Islamic State is consolidating power. With beheadings, rapes, murders and atrocities, they're carving a bloody trail that leads to our doorstep. They're already here! How much longer before the horrors we've witnessed in Paris or Copenhagen come to the supposedly "gun-free zone" of the Mall of America? Or for that matter, the mall in your town? It's not "if"—it's just "when." . . . We live in an age when our nation and her freedoms are increasingly vulnerable—from terrorists crossing our borders or embedded within our communities, to the mentally ill who roam our streets, to the criminal class unleashed upon us by those who refuse to protect us. (LaPierre 2016a)

The solution to global violence is more guns: "We individually are in charge of our own security. We are in charge of our own family's safety" (2016a). This is an argument for permanent localized war. When infused with racism, it calls for ongoing violence against people of color and immigrants.

After the 2016 massacre at the Pulse nightclub in Orlando, Florida, LaPierre appeared on *Face the Nation*. Instead of addressing the targeting of LGBTQ people of color, he announced that, without guns, Americans would be overwhelmed by terrorists who would attack churches and malls: "They're coming . . . And they're going to try to kill us, and we need to be prepared . . . Let's get the bad guys off the street. Attack the terrorists and leave the good guys alone" (LaPierre 2016b). After the Las Vegas shooting, he renewed his call for more guns because there are "monsters like this monster out there every day . . . Nobody should be forced to face evil with empty hands" (LaPierre 2016b). The logic is consistent if you think apocalyptically. If "inhuman monsters" like the Pulse shooter and the Las Vegas shooter are around, "you sure as hell want to be able to protect yourself and your community from them" (Anderson et al. 2017, 39). Every new incident of gun violence invigorates the NRA's apocalyptic language, reminding gun owners they are the only thing standing between evil and their loved ones. One gun organization's instructor told participants to:

> [C]oncentrate on the one thing you need to win . . . You want to conquer, destroy . . . Realize the world is a violent place. Understand your opponent, because they are not like you and me. They would cut off your head for your jewelry . . . Visualize. Create movies in your head about you and the bad guy. You have to see yourself winning. (quoted in Anderson et al. 2017, 43)

The NRA will "lead this nation through the dark night to the dawn of an America renewed in truth, justice, opportunity, hope and individual liberty for all" (LaPierre 2014a). The NRA's star has been falling for years now, but the idea that guns are salvific is as potent as ever.

Bad Guys with Guns

How, then, to explain bad guys with guns? How does evil *get* to them? LaPierre exonerates the NRA for the Sandy Hook shootings, instead blaming the "mass media" for producing "vicious, violent videogames" (LaPierre 2012). The videogame industry is "callous, corrupt and corrupting," creating "the filthiest form of pornography." He riffs on his favorite slogan, saying: "Guns don't kill people. Videogames, the media, and Obama's budget kill people." While this might seem a variation on the need for "good guys with guns," the shift to include videogames in the calculus of blame is important, as it is a move to include the *media itself* as an agent of apocalyptic evil, something evangelical Christians (but not the NRA) had done before.

Donald Trump blamed videogames after the shooting at Marjory Stoneman Douglas High School in Parkland in 2018, saying: "[A] lot of bad things are happening to young kids . . . [when] their minds are being formed . . . I'm hearing more and more people say the level of violence on videogames is really shaping young people's thoughts" (Chalk, 2018). After mass shootings in Dayton, Ohio, and El Paso,

Texas, in the same week in 2019, several leading Republican voices blamed videogames too. House Minority Leader Kevin McCarthy complained that videogames "dehumanize" people (Phillips 2019). Texas lieutenant governor Dan Patrick said on *Fox & Friends*: "We've always had guns. We've always had evil. But what's changed where we see this rash of shooting? . . . I see a videogame industry that teaches young people to kill" (Patrick 2019).

Critics were flummoxed, wondering how gun rights folks could target a medium that celebrates guns. Indeed, the NRA produced two videogames with the same visual FPS mechanics as some of the games LaPierre condemns. So *why* does LaPierre see the NRA's games differently? Is he deluding himself? By looking more carefully at the apocalyptic framework that inspires NRA supporters, we can make sense of claims that mainstream shooting games are "vicious" whereas the NRA's games are not.

The videogames named in LaPierre's Newtown speech include *Bulletstorm*, *Grand Theft Auto*, *Mortal Kombat*, *Splatterhouse*, and the online Flash game *Kindergarten Killers*. Most of these games are not first-person shooters, and some of them do not even use a gun as the centerpiece in virtual violence. Apocalypticism is, above all, a moral perspective, shaped by its proponents' conviction in the rightness of their views. For LaPierre, the gun has a sacred quality, and is one means by which owners can express their moral code. The "vicious" mainstream FPS videogames LaPierre targets express a *lack* of morality in his view. Whether we agree with him or not is beside the point; the rhetoric is consistent. The NRA games are viewed as moral because they accord with the larger cowboy apocalyptic worldview. They are geared toward using *real* guns in *real* life, for moral purposes, to reinforce a larger worldview of good guys and bad guys.

A reference to worldbuilding theory may be helpful here. Mark J. P. Wolf borrows from J. R. R. Tolkien in constructing his own notion of engagement between "worlds."

> [Tolkien] extended the idea of Primary and Secondary imagination. . . . He referred to the material, intersubjective world in which we live as the Primary world, and the imaginary world created by authors as secondary worlds. Tolkien's terms carefully sidestepped

the philosophical pitfalls encountered with other terms like reality and fantasy, while also indicating the hierarchical relationship between the types of worlds, since secondary worlds rely on the Primary World and exist within it. (Wolf 2012, 25)

Wolf explains how a secondary world is connected to the Primary World (even sharing certain rules of space and time with it) but is also "set apart from it enough to be a 'world' unto itself" (26). Videogames can be viewed as secondary worlds with avatars that embody a character distinct from, though closely affiliated with, the player. The NRA's shooting games, though, are more like simulations than secondary worlds. They are meant to be read as situated within the Primary World, teaching gun skills in a way that is meaningfully like learning to shoot a real gun, at least in some ways.

This claim of continuity is dangerous because it allows that gaming can teach people how to be violent in real life. Indeed, this accusation is made every time the NRA produces evidence that a mass shooter was also a videogame player. But the claim of continuity also explains why the NRA does not see its target-shooting games as dangerous. If one learns how to handle a gun safely in virtual space, one can learn how to handle one safely in embodied space. For the NRA, virtual target shooting, real-life target shooting, and real-life defensive shooting all take place in the Primary World. If *NRA High Power Competition* has simulation qualities to it, then so does *Mortal Kombat*. Nothing escapes an impact in the Primary World in this line of reasoning. There is no such thing as neutral gun play, though the NRA's games are (its members believe) *moral* game play.

Bulletstorm, for example, invites players to imagine themselves in the twenty-sixth century in a complex plot that involves space pirates and murder. The game includes a "skillshot" system that rewards the player with extra points for creative kills. *Grand Theft Auto* appeared in 1997, with eleven variations released over two decades, the most recent in 2013. The game allows the player to steal, drive drunk, and assassinate enemies. *Mortal Kombat*, which first appeared in 1992 as an arcade game, was eventually released for home gaming systems with multiple iterative versions. The game is iconic for its introduction of a system of extended button-pushing sequences, resulting in vivid kills. The ESRB videogame rating system was, in part, a reaction to the disturbing and violent visuals developed for *Mortal Kombat*, the first game to receive a "mature" rating. *Splatterhouse* is a 1988 arcade game rebooted in 2010 for home gaming systems. *Splatterhouse* presents the player as Rick, a masked, chainsaw-wielding brute who destroys his enemies amid "buckets of gore" (Murphy 2018). The games LaPierre criticizes require the player to engage in immoral acts excused by the cover of gaming. None of them present a heroic figure using guns for salvific purposes.

Killing children is at the heart of the final game criticized by LaPierre, *Kindergarten Killers*. LaPierre appears to evoke this game to shock listeners and imply a connection between Adam Lanza's actions and the actions of players-as-shooters. For LaPierre, it seems that the main problem with games like *Bulletstorm* and *Kindergarten Killers* isn't guns. Rather, the problem is guns *without* the appropriate moral and apocalyptic values in place. Games like *Kindergarten Killers* train *players* to see killing as fun rather than serious business.

The videogames endorsed by the NRA have much less graphic violence, relying on the trope of target practice. Even their names—*NRA Gun Club* and *Practice Range*—reveal that these games do not present free-standing narrative worlds; rather, they are meant to reference the real world of gun culture. Three other games, all lent the NRA branding in 2008, have similar purposes: *NRA Varmint Hunter*, *NRA High Power Competition*, and *NRA Xtreme Accuracy Shooting*. *NRA Gun Club* was first approved for ages four and up, although after complaints that was raised to twelve and up.

At first glance, it's easy to see why the NRA was accused of hypocrisy. Not only do the games mimic the procedural rhetoric of violent shooting games, they also utilize the same visual mechanics as more violent games. Particularly striking is the visual portrayal of a gun nestled at the bottom of the screen in first-person perspective, a core feature of FPS games. In *NRA Gun Club*, players choose from more than a hundred faithfully recreated firearms with which they shoot realistic targets, including clay pigeons, bull's-eyes, and watermelons.

The production description says "the traditional 1st person shooter now has a different perspective—*NRA Gun Club* is void of violence or blood." There is no story to *NRA Gun Club* because the storyworld isn't nested within the game—it's lived every day by NRA gun members who walk around the streets as potential heroes. The cowboy apocalypse is a created world so tightly integrated into the Primary World that it is not recognized as fiction by the people who love it. Belief is performance. The apocalyptic context is *true*. To play *NRA Gun Club* is to participate in the larger fandom of the cowboy apocalypse, virtually training for a real-life encounter with bad guys.

Practice Range was released in January 2013, one month after the Newtown shootings. Criticism was immediate and severe. Lori Haas, whose daughter survived the Virginia Tech shooting, said: "How two-faced of the NRA to introduce a violent videogame on the heels of their blame game" (Fantz and Griggs 2013). When asked about *Practice Range*'s release following Newtown, game designer Ian Bogost said that the NRA "blamed violent media instead of gun ownership for the tragedy, singling out videogames in particular" (Fantz and Griggs 2013). Bogost recognizes that *Practice Range* is not violent: "The player discharges firearms at paper and clay targets. For the NRA, it offers a model of responsible gun use" (Fantz and Griggs 2013). *Practice Range* disappeared from the Apple Store in March 2018, possibly due to backlash in the wake of the mass shooting at Marjory Stoneman Douglas High School.

The NRA videogames are intended to teach kids how to shoot, so they can eventually perform *real* violence with *real* guns in the *real* world against *real* bad guys in an apocalyptic, deadly serious real-life context. These NRA-trained kids will grow up to become armed citizens enacting the "good guy with a gun" rhetoric not on American *screens*, but on American *streets*. The NRA's games inform a *larger* apocalyptic worldview with real teeth. The gun is how the righteous will survive the coming scourge: "Hurricanes. Tornadoes. Riots. Terrorists. Gangs. Lone criminals. These are perils we are sure to face—not just maybe. It's not paranoia to buy a gun. It's survival" (LaPierre 2013a).

NRA mythology functions more like pervasive gaming than digital gaming, since the movement is always toward infusion of gaming elements into real life. A pervasive game is a game that "has one or more salient features that expand the contractual magic circle of play spatially, temporally, or socially" into real life (Montola 2010, 12). The world of a pervasive game spills over, shaping ordinary experiences with predetermined purpose and rules. The NRA sees *all the world* as a vast (and very real) apocalyptic game.

Pervasive Gunning

In *Pervasive Games: Theory and Design*, game scholars Markus Montola and Jaakko Stenros describe a longstanding pervasive game called *Killer: The Game of Assassination*, which was codified in written form by Steve Jackson Games in the 1980s (2009, 3). The game is played in ordinary life space—on buses, outside your home, and in parks or public areas. Each player is assigned a person to "assassinate" with harmless tools like pouring vinegar in their drinks or shooting them with water pistols. At the same time, a separate player tries to kill the killer. Those playing the game must "stay alert at all times, watching [for] signs of danger" (Montola 2009, 12).

The *NRA Guide to the Basics of Personal Protection Outside the Home* similarly advises people to be alert at all times for signs of danger. The gun owner should constantly be looking for threats. For example, they shouldn't wear headphones while jogging because someone might attack from behind (*NRA Guide* 2000, 30). They should watch bushes, alleys, and areas that may "conceal a violent assailant" (31). Games like *Killer* incorporate real spaces and objects into a gaming environment with purpose. Montola and Stenros propose that *Killer* "takes the tangibility and realness of everyday life into the game. Whatever you want to do in *Killer*, you have to do it for real" (2009, 5). The *NRA Guide* does something similar, telling gun owners to transfer its rules into real-life spaces. Pervasive games "pervade, bend, and blur the traditional boundaries of game, bleeding from the domain of the game to the domain of the ordinary" (Montola 2009, 12).

Playing a game involves the formulation of a fixed location in which special acts, dictated by rules, occur. However, those playing *Killer* or the *NRA Guide* can follow the rules of the game wherever they happen to be. Both urge players to keep their weapons nearby. Both invite a mindset of vigilance.

While playing *Killer*, you might be sipping coffee at the corner shop, but anyone seated around you could be an assassin. The NRA's *Guide* urges vigilance too, but *real* enemies lurk in dark alleys; *real* criminals lie in wait outside your door. *Any* stranger who knocks must be looked at with suspicion. Evil men concoct evil plans to attack schools, movie theaters, and malls. If the world is filled with evil forces that can be stopped only by vigilante violence, then *of course* you want your gun nearby. If enemies lie in waiting to harm you, then *of course* you must be armed. And while *Killer* also functions under a premise of presumed threat, the suspicion you have of others is playful. After all, you're armed with a water pistol and not an AR-15. And of course, when the game of *Killer* ends eventually, all the players will still be alive.

Game designer Jane McGonigal (2023) coins the term "Pinocchio effect" to describe the mindset engaged in during pervasive games. The "Pinocchio effect" is the strong desire for a game to become real life or for everyday life to become a game. We so badly want game play to be real that, like Geppetto, we *wish* it into being. For McGonigal, the transformation into the real never quite materializes in pervasive games like *Killer*. She points to "the essential and stubborn distinction between an intentional *performance* of belief and belief itself" (McGonigal 2003). McGonigal claims players always know, deep down, they're playing a game, and this makes pervasive games safe. In *Killer*, players don't worry that the vinegar is really arsenic. In the NRA's game of "good guys versus bad guys," though, belief is expected. For some gun owners, the apocalyptic gun fandom takes permanent hold and determines how they move through the world. Belief becomes how-things-are.

To internalize the algorithm of the *NRA Guide* is to be aware, suspicious, and fully armed. It is to be prepared to "win" against an enemy who is not *pretending* to be evil, but who *is* evil. "The single most crucial factor in prevailing in a life-threatening encounter is the determination to persevere and win" (*NRA Guide* 2000, 36). If we view the NRA's apocalyptic rhetoric as evidence of an imaginary world into which fans enter, then the real-life gun can be viewed as a threshold prop that invites fans to believe themselves in that world.

To play the cowboy apocalypse game is to believe the world is at war. The chaos that looms is inevitable. To shoot one's weapon is not just to shoot it here, in the mundane moments of daily life. If one performs the role of a "good guy," to shoot is to play a role in a cosmic story in which action is the same as belief. The gun moves from the narrative spaces of the cowboy apocalypse to lived reality, where shooting becomes the authentication of the "good guy with a gun."

The deaths of the children at Sandy Hook Elementary become stories of martyrdom that inflame the faith. These stories are not embarrassments for the NRA but a hagiography of loss. With every new mass shooting event in America, the mythology of apocalypticism is reinvigorated and the call to arms refreshed. To try to disarm the good guys is to leave children defenseless against evil. The NRA is frequently misunderstood because outsiders doubt the sincerity of their belief in evil and their investment in apocalypse. This is a mistake.

In the years since the NRA's videogames were released, Donald Trump has been elected, left office, been re-elected, and the world has grown more unstable, with millions of refugees seeking asylum wherever they can, foreign governments interfering in U.S. politics, and calls for violent responses to immigration growing louder. Americans of all political leanings are angry about the instability of our country and worried about its future.

In an interview on *Face the Nation* after the Las Vegas shooting, LaPierre described the perfect world as one in which everyone is armed—not as one in which there is no evil, but one in which good guys are not prevented from shooting bad guys. He tells a halting story of the "good guy with a gun," trying to fit it into the actual events of multiple failed attempts to interrupt the shooter:

> **Finally, good guys with guns got there. I mean, the guy killed himself first, but thank God there were good guys with guns on the way. I mean, Dianne Feinstein wants this utopian world without guns . . . But the fact is in that utopian world every time bad happens, evil happens, it's good guys with guns that stop it. (LaPierre 2016b)**

The real-life game some NRA fans play is a powerful antidote for ennui. And it does suggest that humans can handle evil whether God shows up or not. But the NRA's apocalyptic mythology is dangerous because the price is the reduction of victims to symbols in an apocalyptic story, and a refusal to consider how limiting access might keep more guns out of the hands of evil men. For the NRA, the only way to prevent *more* violence is for *more* people to shoot *more* guns at *more* people. There is no end to it. It begets a world of ceaseless violence. Shooting is reactive; it does not solve anything. The bullet may be a performance of conviction, but every utterance of this creed requires that somebody pull the trigger, and that somebody else must die.

8

SOUVENIRS OF APOCALYPSE

Some of my ancestors were ruffians. Dirt farmers, men with hot tempers who doubtless participated in the theft of land from Native Americans. Hotheads and builders, preachers, and wanderers. One of my relatives beat his wife so badly the case ended up in the Alabama Supreme Court, where she was granted a divorce at a time when women weren't allowed to ask for such things. But I am also descended from Squirrel King and Mary Thawkila Vann of the Chickasaw and their daughter Vashti Vann, of the Vann family in South Carolina. This family shows up in *The 1619 Project* in the description of James Vann, a half-Scotch, half-Cherokee man who established a plantation in the early 1800s on which he owned and worked seventy men, women, and children of African descent (Miles 2021, 147). Vashti Vann married Benjamin Jernigan, who was a friend of Andrew Jackson's. Benjamin took Vashti down to Escambia, Florida, where she died in 1821 of yellow fever. The other Vanns, including "Rich Joe" Vann, were sent to Oklahoma by federal troops during the Trail of Tears. Many of my ancestors, though, come from Germany and Prussia, landing in Texas around the turn of the twentieth century after abolition, before World War I, and without much money.

Some of my ancestors had slaves, but many did not. Some of my Indigenous ancestors cooperated with European settlers, and some married them. Others came from England and Wales, with stories I don't know. I cannot claim Native American ancestry despite this history. I'm adrift in a story that implicates and disorients me. By living in America and benefitting from the way whiteness works, I am complicit in the stories that inform America's heritage, and I am responsible for my ancestors, even if I never learn how many slaves they might have owned. America's traumas are my traumas. Or at least, I play a role in the perpetuation of others' trauma if I fail to acknowledge how history shapes the present. We are indicted by ignorance. In this chapter, I look at the phenomenon of absence and loss by turning in my hands the relationship between apocalypse and trauma, flip sides of the same story of America's origins and evidence of the entanglement of suffering and violence in American history.

Apocalypticism and trauma both deal with disaster. Consider this description of events that can produce trauma:

> Earthquakes strike, buildings fall, and people die; bodies are devastated by bullets and bombs; famine, drought, and genocide decimate entire populations; planes crash (and disappear), trains derail, and cars smash into each other, twisting metal and limbs; loved ones become sick and die, or they are brutally murdered; sexual assault is pandemic; tornados and hurricanes rip houses off their foundations and children from their parents' arms; wars shred lives, communities, and landscapes and send soldiers home in body bags. (Wertheimer and Casper 2016, 3)

Apocalypse and trauma both refer to the "shattering of existing structures of identity and language" (Berger 1999, 19). The difference may be primarily one of perspective. Whose story is it? Who is assaulted, raped, shot, or murdered? Who *does* the assaulting, raping, shooting and murdering? Who starts a war with whom, and why? Apocalyptic stories have been told by both the powerless and the powerful for different purposes. Trauma is experienced differently depending on whether you are the perpetrator or the victim. One person's apocalyptic fantasy is another person's trauma. Both trauma and apocalypse instigate "erasures from memory," though for different reasons (19).

Apocalypse looks to the future to obliterate the present. Trauma looks to the past as obliteration. In apocalypse, time is structured, linear, predictable. In trauma, time itself crumbles. In apocalypse, enemies are erased. In trauma, one's loved ones, one's home, or one's reasons to live are erased. Apocalypticism is a story about what happens when good guys win, and bad guys lose. But what if the good guys aren't good? What if the bad guys aren't bad?

Old Wounds

The word "trauma" comes from the Greek word for wound. To experience trauma is "to be slashed or struck down by a hostile external force that threatens to destroy you," says theologian Serene Jones (2009, 12). Trauma is distinguished from other sorts of distressing events by a debilitating "threat of annihilation" (13). And yet, most theories about trauma "assume a racially unmarked citizen-subject" and are silent about how intersectionality shapes trauma (Stevens 2016, 21). This is a mistake, especially in America where the cowboy apocalypse supports white supremacy. To ignore others' trauma is to orient oneself nostalgically—to center whiteness, dominance, and exclusive forms of patriotism. It is to deny responsibility. Taking responsibility for America's history comes not in claiming one's white ancestors' actions as one's own, but in recognizing the harm they did, and the impacts those wrongs have today. It is to tell a true story of abuse, murder, and brutality in America's past and acknowledge its ongoing impact. To acknowledge trauma is to expose the silence around settler colonial histories and to expose settler forgetfulness. It is to forgo apocalypse.

Traumatic experience is "not a story but a cascade of experiences, eruptions, crevasses, a sliding of tectonic plates that undergird the self" (Kirmayer 1996, 14). Trauma consists of inarticulable events that disable and disturb. Traumatic events "emaciate language and, at times, the body." They "explode discourse and materiality" (Stevens 2016, 25). Trauma is a *disruption* of the order that gives shape to life. Being unable to represent your experience of trauma can eat at your sense of belonging and purpose. One rape survivor says: "If I live in a world in which my experience is not reflected back to me, then maybe I'm not real enough; maybe I'm not real at all" (Allison 2016, 246). Trauma impoverishes: "Can't say that, can't say that. Look who the world would think I am if they knew I lived through that. There are some things you are sure should have killed you and if you are alive, if it didn't kill you, well then you must not have been good enough to have died" (248).

But storytelling, imperfect as it is, can be a salve. Trauma calls for "technical mediation in order to make it knowable" (Pinchevksi 2019, 23). The purpose of trauma writing is to shape pain into a story, to turn an absence of meaning into something else. It allows victims to construct a "witness where there was none before" (Kaplan 2005, 20). Trauma survivors can craft a "heroic narrative" or "whatever the fuck serves your purpose to get through it alive" (Allison 2016, 250). In writing about impossible things: "You're going for redemption. You're going for meaning. You're going for a cure" (253). The purpose of trauma writing is "to organize pain into a narrative that gives it shape for the purposes of self-understanding" (Kaplan 2005, 20). To write is to be seen. The trauma story imagines when things were *not like this* in the past, and it looks toward the future. The trauma story exerts agency. It resists absence, replaces silence, gives voice to the voiceless. It renders the uncontrollable at last controlled within a story of redemption, recovery or, at least survival. Trauma storytelling can take an apocalyptic arc, mimicking the narrative biblical sweep from paradise, to fall, to redemption.

The trauma story serves to rehabilitate the myth of individuality, to reassure ourselves that we can, in fact, make it on our own as a "seamless self" with agency, that the "everyday precariousness" of life will not stop us from being independent and self-sufficient (Stevens 2016, 27). In this view, the self can avoid trauma by "technologies of self-protection" like gas masks, security systems, and guns (31). Survivors can tell stories about how things may have turned out otherwise had they recourse to such tools. Suzanna Hupp, for example, whose parents were both killed in a shooting at Luby's in Killeen, Texas, in 1991, was at the restaurant with her parents when it happened. She had a gun in her purse, but she had left her purse in her car. Imagining she could have saved her parents by shooting the shooter, today she advocates for concealed weapons (Hupp 2022). The trauma story demands an imagination of relief, of the declaration of how things will be different. In its insistence on self-sufficiency outside of community, the trauma story is haunted by the threat of new isolation.

Dark Tourism

If trauma storytelling is the attempt to describe what one has lost, then nostalgia is the sickening need to talk about what one *imagines* one has lost. To be nostalgic is to drown in a "seemingly ineffable homesickness" (Boym 2001, 41). Nostalgia directs its attention "beyond the present space of experience, somewhere in the twilight of the past or on the island of utopia where time has happily stopped" (13). Nostalgia is "a mourning for the impossibility of mythical return, for the loss of an enchanted world with clear borders and values" (8). Nostalgia has no room for trauma, as it speaks from a position of authority and comfort. And yet nostalgia, like the trauma story, envisions an original paradise.

Nostalgia is longing that is inauthentic because "it does not take part in lived experience," says Susan Stewart (1993, 23). Nostalgia is a story told from a position of wistfulness, not grief. "Hostile to history and its invisible origins, and yet longing for an impossibly pure context of lived experience at a place of origin, nostalgia wears a distinctly utopian face, a face that turns toward a future-past, a past which has only ideological reality" (23). Nostalgia is the imagination of things otherwise, fueled by a sense of displacement and an assuredness of one's own righteousness.

Apocalyptic longing is never far behind nostalgia. "A mythical belief in a past-we-have-lost may be combined with an apocalyptic often blind utopian quest to regain that lost wholeness or totality in a desired future, at times through violence directed against outsiders who have purportedly destroyed or contaminated that wholeness" (LaCapra 2001, 195). One thinks of the "Make America Great Again" slogan about an America that never was. "From the moment we heard Donald Trump say, 'Make America great again,' black people and other people of color instinctively knew what most white people couldn't get . . . people of color were fearful" (Jones 2009, 172). Nostalgia is fundamentalist in its imagination of a past in which one's own desires were met, and so they should be again. It is patriotism run amuck, white supremacy in full bloom, and patriarchal demands for service on blast. Nostalgia can manufacture a "phantom homeland, for the sake of which one is ready to die or kill" (Boym 2001, xvi). It is the "disease of an afflicted imagination" (4).

In a visit during 2016, performance professor Patrick Duggan considers the city of New Orleans the site of a "particular kind of staging" that obscures the physical, social, and political wreckage of Katrina (2019, 44). After visiting areas that were rebuilt and thriving, he is driven around the Lower Ninth Ward to see enduring damage thirteen years after the flood. He interrogates his own position as a white man touring wreckage and poverty in predominantly Black neighborhoods, as someone seeing trauma from the outside: a voyeur. When a local resident engages in conversation with his driver, Duggan becomes painfully aware of his white status and outsider privilege (49). Whereas wealthier (white) people in New Orleans proclaim themselves "done with Katrina," there is a "new form of race and class wreckage" because the storm's legacy is no longer relevant for those with the resources to leave it behind (46). Katrina's ongoing devastation is visible in less wealthy neighborhoods in the overgrown, empty plots where houses once stood. Absence witnesses to the disparity between "those who can make it back to the area to work on their plot and those who cannot." The empty plots are "traces of lives not (yet) recovered" (50). Duggan, of course, can still go home.

Can we consider this trip to New Orleans a form of dark tourism? Dark tourism is "the act of travel to sites associated with death, suffering and the seemingly macabre" (Stone 2006, 146). The term was coined in a study of tourist interest in the John F. Kennedy assassination (Foley and Lennon 1996, 195). You can still visit the Sixth Floor Museum in Dallas and see the spot from which the president was shot. At the gift shop, you can buy a mug with crosshair gunsights (Barton 2001). The phenomenon of dark tourism is much older, though. It includes ancient visits to the ruins at Pompeii, Roman gladiatorial events, medieval religious pilgrimages, witch trials, lynchings, public torture, and war. During the Victorian period in England, people could tour morgues. In prisons of the nineteenth century, visitors could pay a fee to see people flogged (Stone 2006, 147). The Capuchin Catacombs of Palermo, Italy, have drawn tourists for centuries interested in seeing the hundreds of dehydrated bodies hanging on the walls. Though it does not tend to show up as dark tourism in scholarly literature, we could also include tourism to Jerusalem to see where Jesus died and trace his final walk to Golgotha.

Because it is a form of recreation, dark tourism is enjoyed by those furthest from the trauma exhibited. Tourists wanting a safe thrill can engage in a border crossing at El Alberto, Hidalgo. In a four-hour nighttime hike, they can pretend to be illegal immigrants and splash about in mud, hide from fake border patrols, and flee from fake gunshots as they try to cross into the United States from Mexico (Healy 2007). Others may be drawn to a *Titanic* cruise on which they can eat the same meals provided to the ill-fated passengers, as they make their way to the exact spot where those passengers died (King 2012). In June 2023, a submersible carrying billionaire passengers on their way to see the *Titanic* wreckage imploded, fatally ending one of the most expensive dark tourism packages in history.

In Colombia, tourists can take a "narco-tour" to see places affiliated with the life of Pablo Escobar, and if they wish, engage in a paintball battle emulating a fight between police and drug traffickers (Beauvais 2022, 27). Andrew Drury seeks out situations of ongoing violence for regular adventures:

> The [tourist] flame was lit on a safari trip to Uganda, which took a strange turn when Drury accidentally crossed a border into war-ravaged Democratic Republic of Congo and was forced to flee a machete-wielding farmer. Since then, the builder's travels have taken in downtown Mogadishu and the insurgent heartlands of Afghanistan. He says he's dodged Russian soldiers in the bombed-out ruins of Chechnya, infiltrated a Ku Klux Klan militia, played golf in Pyongyang and stayed with a former headhunting tribe in Myanmar. (Monks 2016)

Those tourists less willing to risk their lives can camp out on old battlefields in Vietnam (Clark 2009, 164). They can crawl through the Cu Chi Tunnels near Ho Chi Minh City and fire replica AK-47 rifles (Sharpley 2009, 18). Alec Baldwin's horrifying mishap with the gun prop in the 2021 filming of *Rust* is not dark tourism, but it is a nostalgia-laced performance of a mythic past, when cowboys aimed guns at people with cool confidence that killing is OK. Baldwin gets to play out the Wild West, pretending to be a hero who kills without regret; except he kills a real person by accident. Dark games and dark tourism are close cousins, and both are only a small step away from dark larps (live-action role-plays).

Material objects at dark tourism sites can evoke the trauma experienced there, like the hair left from victims of the Holocaust, or the bones littering memorials in Rwanda, or the melted coins recovered from the rubble at the World Trade Center. There are mounds of shoes at the Holocaust Museum, a tangible sign of victim accounts that will never be heard. The particularity of the objects and the *loss* of the particularity of their owners creates an unresolvable breach and impossible sorrow. What such material objects mediate most poignantly is *absence*.

Proxy objects placed at sites of trauma—flowers, candles, photos, notes—suggest how the site of suffering can work as a portal into a world beyond. These are attempts at communication, indicative of sights and sounds, messages sent to the beyond. Two hundred thousand objects were left at the spontaneous shrine for Columbine's losses (Doss 2006, 298). An estimated million objects were left at the memorial for the Oklahoma City bombing in 1995 (298).

Dark tourism is often punctuated by the collection of resonant objects, items that evoke suffering via absence, as in the scrap of barbed wire that one man took from Auschwitz (Butnick 2014). Rocks from Stoneman Douglas High sold for eighty-five dollars apiece as a form of murderbilia (Christensen 2018). Balbir Singh Sodhi's Sikh turban was recovered after a gunman shot him four days after 9/11 in Mesa, Arizona, outside his gas station where he was planting flowers. The Smithsonian display of the turban sits atop a faceless mannequin head.

Dark tourism is ghoulish and sometimes barbaric. In April 1899, a crowd of two thousand in Georgia attended the lynching of Sam Hose, and they carried away parts of his body as souvenirs, chopping off some body parts before the man had even died (Young 2005, 639). These souvenirs, the stuff of nightmares, were indicative of the dehumanization of Black men. A souvenir "makes tangible what was otherwise only an intangible state. Its physical presence helps locate, define, and freeze in time a fleeting, transitory experience, and bring back into ordinary experience something of the quality of the extraordinary" (Gordon 1986, 135). The ghastly souvenirs—including cars, fingers, pieces of liver, and genitals—would certainly not have been souvenirs to Sam Hose's family. What were the crowd commemorating? What did they hope to remember?

Sam Hose's severed toes become props for a mythic imagination of an America that thrives on white supremacy. When considering horrific souvenirs like his dismembered body, the presumptive optimism of most scholarly considerations of souvenirs becomes painfully apparent. Susan Stewart says in *On Longing* that the souvenir evokes an "imagined prelapsarian experience" drenched in nostalgia (1993, 139). The white onlookers who ripped apart Sam Hose's body were also activated by nostalgia, but one that ignited their sense of violent domination. But what marks Sam Hose's shredded body as a collection of souvenirs? What makes his murder festive?

The word "souvenir" comes from the Latin word *subvenire*, which means "occurs to" or "aids with." Souvenirs remind us of things. Usually associated with the past, they serve as traces of experience (135). They take us back to a lost experience, evoking a time and place no longer accessible. We need souvenirs because we want evidence of

> . . . material [that] has escaped us, events that thereby exist only through the invention of narrative. . . . The souvenir speaks to a context of origin through a language of longing, for it is not an object arising out of need or use value; it is an object arising out of the necessary insatiable demands of nostalgia. The souvenir generates a narrative which reaches only "behind," . . . rather than outward toward the future. (135)

Souvenirs are nostalgic. To make Sam Hose into a party game is to exercise domination over his body, yes. But it is also to wish for a time when Black people's humanity was more easily denied, when they were slaves and nothing more. To exercise a ritual of dismemberment and to take these relics home is to place a sign of longing for white supremacy on one's bedside table, a finger, perhaps. The souvenir remains gestural, but it "articulates the play of desire" (136). Guns can work the same way.

During World War II, GIs collected souvenirs. Although War Department rules forbade soldiers from bringing home items stolen from prisoners of war, they took them anyway (Van Ells 2019, 132). Officers collected hunting rifles, shotguns, rugs, oil paintings, fur coats (131). Weapons were a top choice. One officer describes how his soldiers looted defeated enemy property and brought him an Italian carbine, Italian goggles, and an Italian gas mask (125). Others collected the German luger pistol, the German .25 caliber Walther pistol, or the

MP 40 submachine gun. Even grenades were collected, with expected surprise detonations (126). They brought home Japanese swords. They hacked up enemy aircraft and brought home the pieces, with the metal sometimes pressed into crosses or hearts (127). These items were furtively carried back to the United States.

Some Marines used pliers to extract gold teeth from dead Japanese soldiers (132). Some GIs "went so far as to fashion necklaces of teeth, collect ears, or decapitate corpses, boil away the flesh, and keep the skulls as souvenirs. . . . The bones of dead Japanese were even occasionally carved into rings, letter openers and other kinds of trench art" (132). Stay with me, now. Did you know after the Battle of Horseshoe Bend in 1814, Jackson's troops made reins for their horses from the skin of Muskogee people's bodies? (Dunbar-Ortiz 2014, 99). In 1864, captive Cheyenne and Arapahos were attacked on a reservation and butchered. They scalped people and mutilated their corpses, including babies. Then they "decorated their weapons and caps with body parts—fetuses, penises, breasts, and vulvas—and, in the words of Acoma poet Simon Ortiz, 'Stuck them / on their hats to dry / Their fingers greasy / and slick'" (137). We are a brutal people. Some of us want to prove it, again and again.

The aftermath of atomic detonation in Hiroshima can be witnessed in preserved objects that manifest the absence of the people who died, including: "melted housewares, permanent shadow imprints . . . [and] iconic clocks and [a] watch [that] is stopped at the moment of detonation" (Clark 2009, 170). Dark souvenirs are acquired from sites like Ground Zero or Chernobyl. The force of such objects is the recognition, through trembling material presence, that there *is* no story that will make sense of the loss. But for those who *enact* such horrors, resonant objects evoke not trauma, but the thrill of the victor: apocalyptic vindication by a self-proclaimed god.

Today there are the remains of over a hundred thousand Indigenous people still held in storage at museums, institutes, universities, state historical societies, warehouses, and shops against the will of their descendants (Dunbar-Ortiz 2014, 231; Small 2021).

From the very birth of the nation, the United States government truly had carried out a vigorous operation of extermination and

removal. Decades before Jackson took office, during the administration of Thomas Jefferson, it was already cruelly apparent to many Native American leaders that any hope for tribal autonomy was cursed. So were any thoughts of peaceful coexistence with white citizens. (Cherokee chief Wilma Mankiller, quoted in Dunbar-Ortiz 2014, 108)

One anthropologist argues bodies are "a marker of value. . . . It is my claim that Indian identity, and its material form, the dead Native body, has functioned for a very long time, and with increasing power, as a fetish marking the possession of land by those who have conquered it already" (quoted in Dunbar-Ortiz 2014, 232). We might not initially consider the retention of corpses by museums a form of dark tourism, but we can certainly view this practice as a performance of power, an objectification of humans, and an exercise in white supremacy.

White Nostalgia

Tourism has become vital in maintaining nostalgia for the Lost Cause. The Lost Cause glorifies an "escape into constructed memories of a more glamorous, heroic past where slavery plays only a minor or no role at all" (Adamkiewicz 2016, 17). Such storytelling, false though it is, offers comfort to those who would rather forget America's past. White nostalgia can be understood as a "mode of remembrance celebrating a specific time and place in history by erasing narratives of racism and by whitewashing memories" (17). Lost Cause tourism involves supposedly "unproblematic, glorified, and 'noble' depictions of the antebellum South" (21). These depictions, though, are anything but unproblematic.

The cowboy apocalypse intersects with racist dark tourism vital in maintaining nostalgia for the Lost Cause. Is visiting plantation sites a form of dark tourism? Plantations are sites of trauma, but they are also sites of the *erasure* of trauma, as most now have little if anything to say about slavery. Toni Morrison said in 1989:

> There is no place you or I can go, to think about, or not think about, to summon the presences of, or recollect the absences of

> slaves; nothing that reminds us of the ones who made the journey and of those who did not make it. There is no suitable memorial or plaque or wreath or wall or park or skyscraper lobby. There's no 300-foot tower. There's no small bench by the road. There is not even a tree scored, an initial I can visit, or you can visit in Charleston or Savannah or New York or Providence, or better still on the banks of the Mississippi. (Morrison 1989, 4)

Although some memorials to recognize what slaves endured have been erected since Toni Morrison penned her lament, slavery remains a highly neglected element of U.S. history. There are over 350 plantations museums in the United States, but most teach visitors little about slavery. The enslaved people from plantations are "absent presences" because there is so little left of their lives to "affix them to these spaces" (Modlin et al. 2018, 342).

The Whitney Plantation Museum, in Louisiana, is an exception. Here visitors learn about the capture of Africans, their forced migration, and what life was like at a typical plantation. Visitors see full-sized sculptures of enslaved people on the property, inviting the imagination of lived embodiment, and they hear stories about their lives. The Whitney Plantation is a "memoryscape" more than a museum, because it makes the "unseen visible by reembodying the traces of the men, women, and children" who lived there (8). North Carolina's Stagville Plantation and Louisiana's Laura Plantation also acknowledge the dignity of the people who were enslaved. In most plantation museums, though, the presence of slaves is "an invisible afterthought" (Raymen 2017, 19).

The consignment of slavery to "another space-time and alternative political economy" is a form of what Slavoj Žižek calls "fetishistic disavowal" (Raymen 2017, 18). Žižek's disavowal imagines how people cope with witnessing brutality without doing anything about it. They say something like: I know it, but I don't want to know that I know, so I don't know. This means also: "I know it, but I refuse to fully assume the consequences of this knowledge, so that I can continue acting as if I don't know it" (Žižek 2008, 53). Visiting plantation sites as emblems of a long distant past, tourists can refuse awareness of how "modern day forms of slavery and human rights abuses continue" (Raymen 2017, 18).

In her book *Tales from the Haunted South: Dark Tourism and Memories of Slavery from the Civil War Era*, Black writer Tiya Miles describes her experience visiting the Myrtles Plantation in St. Francisville, Louisiana. She witnesses the titillation of white visitors as tales of ghosts of mistreated slaves are repeated, with the hope the ghosts might appear. Miles is kept at a distance by white guests, one of whom nearly mistakes her for a ghost. Dolls of a dead slave are sold in the gift shop, along with postcards, T-shirts, recipe mixes, and pendants. Kitsch objects like these are meant to soothe troubling emotions at sites of suffering or atrocity, making death and disaster seem more palatable (Miles 2015, 107). They cater to "modern racist depictions of the past but also to post-racial attitudes that assume that while racism was problematic in the past—acknowledging the terrors of slavery to a certain degree—racism no longer exists" (Adamkiewicz 2016, 24). Speaking of white visitors to plantation sites, scholar Perry Labron Carter observes:

> They know. They all know. How could they not? No matter the level of acknowledgment or obscuration of enslavement at plantation museums, visitors know at some level of consciousness that the enslaved habited these spaces and that their traces still exist in these rooms and across these landscapes. To see them, all they need to do is be willing to look. Visitors understand, at some level, that unnamed black men, women, and children haunt these spaces. They know this because slavery haunts the Americas and, more broadly, the transatlantic world. It is a past that Americans willfully seek to forget, to move past, in their attempt to escape past and present culpability. (Modlin et al. 2018, 341)

For those who refuse to consider the impact of past slavery on America's present, plantation sites become "comfortable spaces of refuge and longing for an uncritical and colorblind—yet unrealistic—past" (Adamkiewicz 2016, 13). Plantation sites *are* sites of trauma, and the stories of those who suffered there can never be fully known. This ought to invoke grief.

Other forms of tourist culture are similarly brushed with white nostalgia. Silver Dollar City in Branson, Missouri, presents a "faux heritage space" that imitates a nineteenth century mining town (Morris and Arford 2019, 426). Silver Dollar City constructs a space with "simulated authenticity" believable for its white visitors precisely *because* it "erases racialized violence and naturalizes whiteness" (427). Silver Dollar City, like plantation sites, whitewashes, reimagines, and sells to consumers a collective amnesia to erase slavery, convict leasing, and imprisonment from the scene (427). Visitors can enjoy the "Great Shootout," a play event in the Flooded Mine Ride, and shoot laser light guns at animatronic convicts trying to escape (423). The ride is a site of "penal spectatorship" that invites viewers to ignore the realities of imprisonment while claiming to bring them closer to it (Mussell et al. 2021, 4).

The "Bald Knobbers," a vigilante group from the nineteenth century, show up in reenactments at Silver Dollar City where they are presented as "mischievous, masked characters who engage in playful antics." Silver Dollar City is stuck in an "alternate history in which Indigenous genocide, slavery, Jim Crow laws, and other forms of racialized violence do not exist" (Morris and Arford, 440). Shooting guns at people is presented as a source of pleasure and fun. The park celebrates a world of easy white nostalgia.

Slave Patrols

The traumas of slavery and attempted Indigenous genocide remain within us, even if they are whitewashed in popular culture. One way the trauma of slavery lives on is in the modern police force, which grew out of the horrors of slave patrols. The first slave patrol was authorized in 1702 in South Carolina. Serving on slave patrols was required of all white men (Lepore 2020). Slaves had to show passes to authorize their movements and subject to questioning and punishment. Slave patrols drew from the militias, who were tasked with fighting Native Americans (Dunbar-Ortiz 2018, 60). Professor of gender studies Tanya Shields traces Dylann Roof's murder of parishioners at the Emanuel African Methodist Episcopal Church to the logics of slave patrols, seeing in him a self-declared agent of the white militia intending to teach a brutal lesson to any Black people he could find:

The slave patrol evolved from any white South Carolinian's ability to "apprehend or chastise" enslaved people with the formation of the first policing entity in 1704. In the Carolinas, the patrols' primary function was to (1) recapture runaways; (2) to maintain plantation discipline, often through terror tactics; and (3) deterrence—prevent trouble from starting or escalating, also a function of modern policing. (Shields 2017, 10)

Slave patrols had powers of search and seizure and the right to administer twenty lashes: "One result of the 'patroller for hire' process was patrols consisting of boys or idle men whose primary ambition . . . seemed the harassment of slaves" (Reichel 1992, 4).

After abolition, surveillance of Black people continued, and many of them were forced to return to work on the plantations (Dunbar-Ortiz 2018, 66). This form of organized terrorism drew on the Ku Klux Klan, which served as a kind of self-regulated slave patrol to "control black labor when slavery ended" (67). White Southerners formed rifle clubs so they might mobilize quickly. These early preppers "burned homes, confiscated the guns of Freedmen, and, of course, inflicted punishment similar to slave patrols' beatings, but had far more freedom to torture and murder" once former slaves were no longer seen as valuable property (69). Even though the Thirteenth Amendment abolished slavery, it provides an exception for people convicted of a crime. Free Black people could be arrested for supposed loitering, being unemployed, or walking at night after curfew. Black Codes made it easy to arrest free Black people and imprison them, then use them for convict labor. Some plantations were even converted to prisons (Morris and Arford 2019, 435).

This terrifying past still thrums in the constant deaths of young Black men in America today. In a study from 2015, researchers found less than 19% of white deaths in the U.S. were homicides. In the Black population, 82% were homicides (Reeves and Holmes 2015). Most victims are teenagers and young Black men. Although Black men and boys from fifteen to thirty-four are only 2% of the U.S. population, they were 37% of the gun homicide victims in 2019 (Hassanein 2021). The devaluation of Black lives by white people can be measured in the bullets aimed at young Black men today by jumpy white people in gated neighborhoods and other predominantly white spaces. White supremacy is a deadly habit. The cowboy apocalypse, as a contemporary justification for gun violence, experienced largely as entertainment, offers cover for the history of slave patrols and their deadliness. The past is still with us:

> Unaddressed, unnamed, and unprocessed, enslavement and its consequences resurface at critical and seemingly unexpected moments. I do not equate the racism experienced now with the violence of enslavement, nor am I saying that trauma is genetically encoded. Rather, I argue that the trauma of enslavement remains with us (and connects us) in a palimpsestic way to the past. Narratives of slavery, denial, reconstruction, and beyond seep through daily life and bleed through to the surface. (Shields 2017, 14)

Writer Ta-Nehisi Coates points to slave patrols, lynchings, mass incarceration, and a failing criminal justice system as the primary tools today for "managing the divide between black and white. We've done this for so long that we are now almost on autopilot. Tamir Rice, Walter Scott, and Freddie Gray keep happening because they have to keep happening" (Coates 2015b). The other alternative is eliminating cultural amnesia. We don't know because we don't want to know.

In Our Bones

At the end of the nineteenth century, Wilmington, North Carolina, was a busy port city with a thriving majority Black population. One night in November 1898, armed white men entered the Black neighborhoods where they chased Black citizens, shot at them, burned buildings, and ran people out of town. Their goal was to disenfranchise Black voters (Tyson 2006, 1). This story, told in an insert in the 2006 *News and Observer*, is an attempt to set history right. But some asked why dredge this up since you can't change the past. Because "the past holds our future in its grip, especially when it remains unacknowledged" (3). In a settler society that "has not come to terms with its past," trauma lives on, in the "assumptions and behavior of living generations" (Dunbar-Ortiz 2014, 229).

When white people claim they aren't responsible for the actions of their ancestors, theologian Serene Jones says we all carry those events in our bodies, and in the way we move through the world (2009, 170). We cannot escape the habits of behavior and thought so basic to our culture unless we acknowledge they are there:

> And there's something in white people's bodies that sees a Confederate flag and it either means nothing to them, which is a privilege, or it makes them feel at home. Oh, this is my country. It is amazing how many white people, even progressive, liberal, white people, can sing folk ballads about Dixie as though they're not about slavery, or about the Civil War, and they're bemoaning the loss of the South, as if slavery wasn't one of the most cruel, torturous, inhuman systems in the history of human beings. Because this silent history gets passed down through this entitlement of silence and the protection of silence, we white people continue to protect ourselves and not deal with this. We don't want to deal with it because we would have to admit that our current privilege comes out of this bloody history and that slavery is not a story just about black people. It's a story about white people who enslaved black people.... It's a white story—because it was white greed and hatred that created and sustained slavery from the very beginning. (172)

Jones calls for an imagination "shaped by grace" that enables something different. She invites people into community with one another, because "you need to find a community for this new story to be told, and you need to be able to tell the story in order to imagine a new way" (181).

But something else is needed too: a recognition that we are knit together in deepest history. The legacy of settler colonialism in the United States is as imminent as a heartbeat, evident today in:

> ... endless wars of aggression and occupations; the trillions spent on war machinery, military bases, and personnel instead of social services and quality public education; the gross profits

of corporations ... the incarceration of the poor, particularly descendants of enslaved Africans; the individualism ... that on the one hand produces self-blame for personal failure and on the other exalts ruthless dog-eat-dog competition ... and high rates of suicide, drug abuse, alcoholism, sexual violence against women and children, homelessness, dropping out of school, and gun violence. (Dunbar-Ortiz 2014, 229–230)

Guns are emblems of the cowboy apocalypse for some Americans. They signify freedom and patriotism. They offer safety and protection. They are a means for the good guy to beat the bad guy and restore equilibrium. What if the guy holding the gun isn't a good guy, but is flustered by old hate in his bones from the legacy of the Lost Cause? What if the young Black man on the other side of the barrel is a teenager eating Skittles? The cowboy apocalypse has force because it grew from a mean history yet to be discarded. For George Zimmerman, the gun was a souvenir, to be auctioned to the highest bidder. To Trayvon and his family, the gun was a bomb exploding sense, sickeningly familiar trauma with no language to hold it.

To be white in America is to carry this shameful legacy; to be Black in America is to breathe this pain. Race is a construct, but history lives in our blood, shaping the way we greet one another, the presumptions we make, the things we neglect. If the cowboy apocalypse is an expression of white supremacy, then the presumption of good versus evil, us versus them, is sewn right into the way we treat each other. And trauma, the product of apocalyptic violence, is in our bones. We are a damaged nation, built on death and purported ignorance. To be something else requires the replacement of narratives of death with some kind of authentic recognition, deep sorrow, and some way of learning how, finally, to love one another. We must *want* to know.

LIVE-ACTION ROLE-PLAY

REAL PLAYERS, REAL BULLETS

We have considered what happens when the cowboy apocalypse is delivered through television, films, videogames, and other forms. We have analyzed the propaganda of the NRA and seen how preppers engage in activations of the narrative as they imprint their apocalyptic expectations onto the physical spaces around them. Here I consider a platform of play that is not visually or digitally mediated—instead it is lived out on the platform of real life, with actual objects and humans on which the narrative unfolds. On January 6, 2021, in the raid on the U.S. Capitol in Washington, DC, fans of the cowboy apocalypse united with closely related alt-right fandoms, including those committed to overt bigotry and racism. Protestors acted as if they were part of a "giant live action role playing (LARP) game, and not real-world people who would be held accountable" (D'Antonio 2021). Fandom is expressed not only through consumption of preexisting stories, but also through active, embodied immersion within those stories in costumed role-play, in the acting out of favorite narratives, and in the placement of those narratives onto the stuff of everyday life. In a violent parody of fan convergence, the protestors enacted an apocalyptic larp so desired that the distinction between play and reality dissolved.

The costuming of insurgents ranged from "sinister white supremacist, extremist paramilitary garb to the familiar 1776 get up of Tea Partiers, but also vaguely frontiersman-like furs and pelts, and of course the pseudo-tribal cosplay of Jacob Chansley, the notorious QAnon shaman" (Lockett 2022). Protestors donned war paint and utility vests. There were visual references to Pepe the Frog and people flew the green-and-white flag of Kekistan. Activities included slogan slinging and wall climbing. There were confederate flags and Trump flags, Hawaiian shirts, Crusader crosses, Norse imagery, QAnon iconography, and clothing in red, white, and blue. Participants likely had "Hollywood on their mind" as they "pillaged and took selfies" (Kornhaber 2021). Unruly crowds donned logos, capes, caps, spears, flags, helmets, masks, bandanas, and banners denoting political identities, though all seemed to profess a loyalty to Donald Trump. Some, like Oath Keepers founder Stewart Rhodes, showed up in cowboy hats (Giglio 2022).

Alt-Right Larping

Jennica Falk and Glorianna Davenport define "larp" in a way that could easily apply to the apocalyptic narrative unfolding behind the scenes at the Capitol. A larp is:

> . . . a dramatic and narrative game form that takes place in a physical environment. It is a storytelling system in which players assume character roles that they portray in person, through action and interaction. The game world is . . . governed by a set of rules—some of which must be formal and quantifiable. . . . Like other games, [larps] have a system of rules, context for advancement and goals, as well as obstacles and threats to those goals. (2004, 128)

The violent larp of January 6 can be read as an extension of the cowboy apocalypse. While personal human agency remains critical in this mythology, God remains largely uninvolved. Many of the rioters seem to have been motivated mainly by rage—borrowing apocalyptic imagery of a people under siege, presenting themselves as victims of a system set against them. The lineage of association with the cowboy apocalypse seems clear: "The alt-righter's 'nation' is a hero-narrative about how the freedom of the individual (masculine) self can be secured, in part by adopting the toxic rhetoric of overt white supremacy" (Burton 2016, 4). And since for many this hero narrative involves an expectation of transformative, apocalyptic violence, what we see is less a replacement of the cowboy apocalypse than a new rendition of the same old narrative.

One rioter, Paul Hodgkins, appears in footage on the Senate floor "with the staff of his red Trump flag resting on his shoulder," goggles dangling from his neck, and arms "protected by leathery cuffs like those sold with *Game of Thrones* costumes" (D'Antonio 2021). Another man in gladiator costume is seen amid the popular camo gear. There were MAGA trucker hats and several iterations of the Punisher from Marvel comics in full costume. There were people wearing "emblems from the Zombie Outbreak Response Team" (O'Kane 2021, 13). Mações (2021) notes in the outfits of January 6 an "almost complete replacement of serious politics by subterranean fantasy and role playing [that] induces a sense of vertigo." This gaudy pageantry is consistent with Parham's claim that Trump's rise to power has been "anchored by an acutely corrosive variety of fandom."

Alt-right versions of history were also on display. One protestor wore a Templar cross (Fahey 2021). Others wore T-shirts with "Civil War, January 6, 2021" printed on them (Mações 2021). There were "men in body paint and plastic Viking hats screaming in the faces of cops, a lone fanatic in a beanie making a Roman salute in the speaker's chair" and "a congressman in some kind of space suit fleeing goodness knows where" (Walther 2021). People dressed in pioneer costumes, superhero costumes, lots of camouflage, as well as Uncle Sam, Lady Liberty, and Abraham Lincoln (Sheppard 2021). At least one person wore a sweatshirt with "Camp Auschwitz" on the front and "staff" on the back. The so-called history evoked by the alt-right is "a mishmash of tropes, telescoping different historical moments" with little concern for accuracy, context, or taste (Sheppard 2021). It reveals less about America's past than about its fraught present:

> Americans across the political spectrum are currently waging war over the right to control the country's story. The sides of this battle disagree about more than chronological accounts of the events that have shaped the country; in the characteristics of their heroes and villains, and their choices about what to remember and what to forget, their narratives reveal different visions of Americanness itself. (Braunstein 2021, 18)

Indeed, debates rage about critical race theory in public schools, the defense of racist textbooks, and disagreements about who or what a patriot is. These debates are visible in our videogames, our television shows, our movies, our live-action role-plays, and in the larp-like events on January 6. But whether we view the attack on the Capitol as a larp or not, it was no joke. It revealed harsh white apocalyptic fears "stoked and converted into populist rage" even as they are performed in the seemingly innocuous language of fandom (Ioanide 2021, 325). As a kind of deadly larp denying its seriousness, January 6 was playful and violent, an expression of fandom and also of war.

The "far right" is sometimes called the "alternative right," a term coined in 2010 by white nationalist Richard Spencer. The far right is a spectrum of individuals and groups who share "exclusionary and dehumanizing beliefs, anti-government and anti-democratic practices and ideals, existential threats and conspiracy theories, and apocalyptic fantasies" (Miller-Idriss 2021). They have, in recent years, united in their appreciation of Donald Trump. The alt-right is a diffuse network which shares the belief that whites are under attack in a multicultural and globalized world. Like the Klan, they "claim to be the victims of culture wars, struggling to defend whiteness" (Baker 2016). They oppose immigration, refugees, feminism, Black Lives Matter, and identity politics in general. They see themselves aligned against so-called social justice warriors. This perspective underlines the us-versus-them of their apocalyptic views and shapes the way they see their future unfolding: through intentional violence.

The rioters on January 6 acted as one might in a videogame: busting through fences, eluding capture, swinging hockey sticks and crutches at the faces of Capitol police, and fighting for control of enemy territory. This embodied action surely felt *more* real than a videogame. Things moved from virtual to real, from online to offline, from trolling and shitposting to real-life violence with the body as the medium and the Capitol as a marked-out space of play. When fandom moves beyond the "fictionalized territories of TV or gaming" it is "more fraught with real-world risk" (Parham 2018). Immersion is "a subjective experience of being a *part* of an imagined reality instead of being only in a *relation* to the imaged [sic] reality" (Lappi 2007, 75).

A spatial narrative "requires a physical presence. It employs the complete array of our corporeal senses," says scholar of cultural studies Meyrav Koren-Kuik (2013, 151). We engage not only with our thoughts but with our bodies, our will power, and our weapons. The interaction is "no longer limited to the realm of action within narrative" because individuals bring their own "desire into the physical space" (151). This movement is a sort of incarnation: the materialization of nonmaterial entities within the everyday world. The protestors' traipsed and shuffled within the forbidden rooms of the Capitol, where they imprinted the sacred space with embodied transgressive play: shouting, sitting in the Speaker's chair, climbing atop the seats and tables, and scribbling threatening notes. Half a dozen people smoked joints under the Capitol rotunda (Roberts 2021). Pervasive games can function as an excuse for violating social norms. For example, in the pervasive larp *Isle of Saints*, one player "behaved really badly in posh restaurants," where he combed his hair with a fork and "messed up the whole table" (Montola 2007, 182). While the ability to circumvent social norms can be harmless, it can also invite more serious transgressions.

Pervasive Play

If we had to decide what *kind* of larp January 6 was, it would be urban pervasive. Urban pervasive larps are embedded in a city's landscape where actual landmarks, buildings, or even crowds of people can be integrated into game play. Interacting with the material world around you can make for "visceral, tangible experiences" and the "illusion of being there" in another world (Montola, Stenros, and Waern 2009, 201). Pervasive games are "the dream of the virtual to be real" and "the dream of the players for the real to be virtual" (McGonigal 2003). In the case of January 6, the movement across boundaries of play was not as much about transport *to* another world as it was about imposing *another reality* onto the Capitol building, imprinting the area inside and around it with Trump-determined bodies and the distinctive paraphernalia of his supporters.

Games can make us feel a part of something bigger. The desire for life to "become a real little game" is also "the desire for the formal call to action, direction, and the sense that others are working toward the same goal," says larp designer Jane McGonigal. For those who embrace the TINAG principle ("this is not a game"), the shared excitement can be thrilling: What if the election *really was* stolen? What if there *really is* a secret cabal of global villains kidnapping children for sex trafficking? What if a white ethnostate *is* the only way that America can be saved? When we larp, we "project a fictional story" onto the canvas of everyday life and allow this new story to replace our personal history (Lappi 2007, 75). Role-playing "removes the participant to a different temporary reality," and in this sense resembles religious ritual. Both rituals and role-play experiences take place "in a state continuous with mundane reality but separate from it" (Harviainen 2009, 70). To be part of the larp on January 6, though, was not to project a story onto the canvas of everyday reality, but to let that projection *replace reality itself*, and to show one's firm commitment by refusing to distinguish between what is the game and what is not.

Larps involve the intentional projection of a fictional view of reality and "acting in accordance with the projected representation while being aware of its counterfactual nature" (Rognli 2008, 200). When larping, we "map our mental representation of a fictitious state of affairs [on]to our concrete surroundings." We transform a cardboard box to a car or a "rubber sword to a deadly weapon." But we don't *really* transform the cardboard box into a car. We just *pretend* to. We suspend *disbelief*, but we do not *believe*. On January 6, the protest larpers seem to have gone a step further, as pretense gave way to full-on belief.

The insider experience depended on adopting a new set of rules for reality itself—including the claim that Trump had *explicitly asked* his supporters to enter. They were to enter the "magic circle" of play and act *as if* their beliefs defined the *actual* state of things. Games—especially pervasive games—require a similar kind of buy-in:

> **[T]o play a game is in many ways an act of "faith" that invests the game with its special meaning. . . . To decide to play a game is to create out of thin air an arbitrary authority that serves to guide and direct the play of the game. The moment of that decision can be quite magical. . . . The magic circle can define a powerful space, investing its authority in the actions of players and creating new and complex meanings that are only possible in the space of play.**

But it is also remarkably fragile as well, requiring constant maintenance to keep it intact. (Salen and Zimmerman 2003, 1998)

An apocalyptic videogame is a magic circle. A bunker is a magic circle. Movies are a magic circle. So is the violent larp at the Capitol. Protestors entered it in a spirit of transgressive play, convinced of their own starring role in a predetermined plot. In a pervasive game, the players' experience spills over, integrating real-life environments: "The whole world becomes a playground" (Stenros and Montola 2008, 8). Random bystanders are injected into the game's story, "making them unaware participants" (8).

An effective pervasive game "allows players to use reality as the all-encompassing sourcebook for the game world" (Montola, Stenros, and Waern 2009, 212). Bystanders might experience harassment or abuse without realizing it is "play." People who happen to show up in the vicinity of a hardcore pervasive game may become "part of the environment" (Harviainen 2008, 227). Pervasive larps "break the usual boundaries of games" (Montola, Stenros, and Waern 2009, 198). They invite the thrill of violation. Pervasive larps allow forbidden actions while granting immunity. Players can push against social constraints and experience what feels like "empowerment" (214). To play a larp is to pretend the manufactured world of the larp is *real*. The January 6 larp pushes this process so players pretend the *real* world is *less real* than the larp. It may seem a subtle shift, but this move into a gamelike mindset means Trump's rules become—through sheer insistence—the same rules that govern everyday life. These rules become *how things are*—because he said so. Belief becomes determination to *make* the world what one wants by sheer fiat.

Social media platforms can be used to reinforce beliefs that drive the larp. Platforms like BitChute, Gab, Parler, Rumble, and Telegram were created because of conservative grievances about mainstream platforms like Twitter (X), YouTube, Facebook, and Instagram (Walther and McCoy 2021, 100). Neo-Nazi groups prefer online services like Wire, Rocket Chat, Telegram, and Discord to encrypt conversations (Loadenthal et al. 2022, 96). In these online communities, users can produce isolated arenas of "hate speech and violent extremist dialogue" that boil over into more public forms of media (Walther and

McCoy 2021, 101). Anonymity leads fans to see themselves as a faceless mass. There is "gleeful trolling . . . disembodied behind a digital screen." Sometimes there is "real-world violence" (Burton 2019). 4chan and other alt-right meeting spaces cultivate a "mask culture" in which one's individual identity is effaced (Tuters 2019, 40).

To repost a meme is to join an asynchronous trolling chorus. "Meme magic" is when "something espoused and affirmed in the digital realm also becomes true beyond it" (Burton 2016, 2). People who don't follow the insider language are "normies" or NPCs (non-player characters), no different than the NPCs who are non-human artifacts of programming (Tuters 2021, 65). Memes convey ideological narratives, draw new supporters, and make extremist thought appear mainstream (Askanius and Keller 2021, 2523).

The Kekistan Myth

The raid on the Capitol is a larp-like enactment of the mythical land of Kekistan. The Kekistan myth took shape on chat boards in 4chan devoted to *World of Warcraft* (WoW) games in which:

> . . . participants can chat only with members of their own faction in the "war" (either Alliance or Horde fighters), while opposing players' chats are rendered in a cryptic form based on Korean; thus, the common chat phrase "LOL" (laugh out loud) was read by opposing players as "KEK." The phrase caught on as a variation on "LOL" in game chat rooms, as well as at open forums dedicated to gaming, animation, and popular culture, such as 4chan and Reddit—also dens of the alt-right, where the Pepe the Frog meme also has its origins, and similarly hijacked as a symbol of white nationalism. (Neiwert 2017)

Kek became an inside joke. An Egyptian god who brings chaos and darkness, Kek seemed a perfect fit for "the alt-right's self-image as being primarily devoted to destroying the existing world" but in a half serious, trolling sort of way (Neiwert 2017). Mark Furie originally created Pepe the Frog in 2005 for the comic *Boy's Club*. By 2009, Pepe had become a hate symbol appropriated for far-right groups, who deployed it ironically to laugh at the liberals who would see a cartoon frog as dangerous. Most of the people posting about Kek "don't actually believe that Pepe the Frog is an avatar of an ancient Egyptian chaos god," or that 4chan posters predicted Donald Trump's presidential win. But they pretend that they do: "It's a joke, of course—but also not a joke" (Burton 2016, 2). Kek is:

> ... the apotheosis of the bizarre alternative reality of the alt-right: at once absurdly juvenile, transgressive, and racist, as well as reflecting a deeper, pseudoo-intellectual purpose that lends it an appeal to young ideologues who fancy themselves deep thinkers. It dwells in that murky area they often occupy, between satire, irony, mockery, and serious ideology; Kek can be both a big joke to pull on liberals and a reflection of the alt-right's own self-image as serious agents of chaos in modern society. (Neiwert 2017)

Other religious tropes followed—including a sacred text and common prayers. One Kek prayer celebrates the ability to infuriate: "for thine is the mimetic Kingdom, and the shitposting, and the winning, forever and ever. Praise Kek." Kek is "the god of *lulz*—the sly, universal internet indicator of a humorous put-on" (Burton 2019). The symbolism around Kek has been "taken up by some white nationalists and alt-right personalities as a way to mock political correctness and praise Donald Trump, whom many in this milieu see as an avatar of Kek, disrupting social norms and spreading chaos" (Sheedy 2021). Kek is the deity of an "ironic religion" whose primary ritual is to "shock and troll liberals and 'self-righteous' conservatives alike" (Sheedy 2021). Kekistan, the land of Kek, is a fictional space defined by the feckless behavior of its citizens, who celebrate ridicule, racism, misogyny, and contempt. Devotion to Kek offers something else too: a sense of community. The shitposter is:

> ... not a Lone Ranger but rather part of a group whose stated fascination with cowboy individualism is at odds with the intense collectivism of internet culture—a culture where likes, reposts, upvotes, hearts, and other expressions of communal acceptance take on outsize importance. There is something intensely collectivist

about even the most outrageously social-contract-breaking denizens of the internet. (Burton 2016)

A shitposter's nasty behavior is "secondary to his understanding of himself as free, an Alamo-style resister . . . a masculine agent not subject to such feminized niceties as politeness and compassion" (4). Freedom here means freedom to "say and do anything, beholden to nothing and to nobody—a freedom that finds expression through transgression," as in saying racist or sexist or homophobic things that nobody else will say (3). The shitposter shares with the cowboy messiah a sense that he is (or *deserves* to be) beyond the rules of society. Kek trolls are individual heroes even as they participate in something larger than themselves: "No one shitposts alone. But shitposting nonetheless imbues a powerful sense of individual significance" (4). The larp at the Capitol could be seen as the physical incarnation of transgressive online play, a substantiation of Kekistan-as-larp. To act on January 6 was to shift the *online* rules of trolling in Kekistan to the offline world. It was an attempt to make the trolling an embodied activity, pervasive and *real*. It was trolling incarnate. Increasingly Kekistan came to be viewed as an "imaginary homeland for trolls" (Tuters 2019, 41). It was a place that did not exist except in the minds of the people who claimed residency. It was an identity, but not a material location. It was virtual, but also real.

Contrasted to Kekistan is Normistan, what the devotees of Kek would call "normal, mainstream culture" (Sheedy 2021). In a series of YouTube videos in 2017, the Kekistan meme "developed the mythology of an imaginary country with its own flag in history, a kind of 'ethno state' in the language of the European New Right, whose people imagine themselves to be engaged in a civilizational conflict against the forces of 'political correctness'" (Tuters 2019, 41). To wear the Kekistani flag as a dramatic cape at the U.S. Capitol on January 6 is to perform the desire, ironic or not, that a white ethnostate might be imposed on America—*ha, just kidding.*

The Kekistani flag is modeled on the Nazi flag, an echo intended to trigger: "while the ironic use of Nazi iconography may appear baffling, the logic deployed is that, as memes, even the most taboo symbols can be disconnected from their fixed historical meaning and made to function as floating signifiers for those who understand the rules of memes" (42). The Kekistani flag has a dual purpose: to upset outsiders and signal insiders. Despite the ideological innocence claimed by those who display the flag, its transgressive appeal comes from the possibility that its display *just might be* serious (42). It draws power from the confounding of online versus offline experience, real versus pretend.

The pervasive larp *Momentum* invites a similar slippage between reality and fiction, though without the political views. *Momentum* offers a "seamless merger of life and game" (Stenros et al. 2011, 121). The game takes place in the streets, office buildings, and homes of daily life. *Momentum*'s rules infuse everything players do for weeks, implicating unknowing coworkers and friends in the game.

> **The seamless merge of ordinary life and game reality enables the participants to avoid treating the game as a game. . . . Anything in the surroundings can be a part of the game so the players will see and interpret things in the everyday environment that they might not have noticed before. The world is changed by altering the way the players see and experience it. (124)**

A pervasive larp makes the world itself seem designed for the players, who look at everything—and everyone—with an eye to integrating them. In *Momentum*, "it is only the knowledge that the game is a game that differentiates it from reality" (124).

Momentum is based on the fiction that the player can be possessed by a ghost. In this way, players are given freedom to slip in and out of character as they move through their everyday, non-game lives. When they need to act out-of-game, the ghost departs. When they are ready to play in-character again, the ghost returns. In this respect, *Momentum* is a pervasive experience, knit into everyday life, enchanting it. Looking at the "good guy with a gun" plot as a subset of the cowboy apocalypse larp helps to make sense of how real people can be forced into a game they are not playing. Young men like Trayvon Martin are NPCs, characters there for the enacting of a story the good guy has predetermined. Or worse, they are obstacles in a plot line existing for the enjoyment of the first-person shooter. As NPCs, victims are treated more like props than people. The game pivots around the shooter instead.

Bleed

The cowboy apocalypse can be read as an alternate reality game (ARG), a close relative of pervasive larps:

> What if reality were different? What if you suddenly discovered not just different customs but different rules, different rewards, wholly different aspirations—a reality in which everyday occurrences were not exactly what you thought, in which certain activities suddenly took on a rich and newly meaningful sense of possibility? Alternate Reality Games take the substance of everyday life and weave it into narratives that layer additional meaning, depth, and interaction upon the real world. The contents of these narratives constantly intersect with actuality, but play fast and loose with fact, sometimes departing entirely from the actual or grossly warping it—yet remain inescapably interwoven. (Martin 2006, 6)

Conspiracy theories share features with ARGs, inviting people to weave conspiracy narratives into the stuff of actual life, warping the actual to fit into the plot of the game. Because the actual world can be seen as part of the game, the most immersive gaming experience is "not being able to see the difference between the game and the rest of the world" (Nordgren 2010, 246). Players can "throw themselves fully into playing as if the game was real," and "the real world can completely melt away" (246). Such a belief-driven approach is consistent with what we would expect in conspiracy-oriented groups.

Theorists of pervasive games use the term bleed to refer to the degree of influence a game can have on the non-game lives of players. A Nordic collective of game designers describes bleed this way:

> Bleed is experienced by the player when her thoughts and feelings are influenced by those of her character, or vice versa. With increasing bleed, the border between player and character becomes more and more transparent. . . . A classic example of bleed is when a player's affection for another player carries over into the game or influences her character's perception of the other's character. (Montola 2010)

The problem of bleed cropped up for larper Shoshanna Kessock when she played *Dystopia Rising*. In the game, three teams compete to escape from a post-apocalyptic war scenario. Amid props like barbed wire and tarps, there is an electric fireplace called the Furnace. Extras wander about moaning, dressed "something like concentration-camp inmates." The allusions to the Holocaust are not accidental. Players must throw other players into the Furnace to escape and win the game. Kessock, who is Jewish, ultimately found the game intolerable. Half of her teammates, though, had no problem with the Furnace. To Kessock, the bleed was too great—and the game was too real (Simone 2014).

If we can read the events on January 6 as an alternative reality game or a pervasive larp, then we might ask what bleed there looks like. During a larp, play can become an alibi for troubling in-game actions. Perhaps it was this kind of mechanism that fueled the surprise of some when faced with legal repercussions for their actions on January 6. If the raid were just a playful form of trolling, then there *ought* to be no real-life consequences. This tension might also explain why Rep. Josh Hawley could raise his fist in solidarity with the protestors *before* they breached the Capitol but run and hide *after*. The bleed of the game was too real for him in the end.

In another post-apocalyptic larp, *Ground Zero*, players are locked into a basement bunker together. The game is set in the time of the Cuban Missile Crisis, in a world decimated by nuclear blast. There is no audience, and the gamemaster sits among the players. The place is filled with objects that function in both the larp and the real world at the same time: "Every object represents itself, [so] disbelief needs [sic] not be suspended.... The goal is to create a feeling of truly being there" (Stenros and Montola 2008, 7). Because people play *as* themselves, there is spillover of character traits between character and player (Harding 2007, 32). Holter uses religious language to describe how a player abandons his ego much as Christians say Christ performed *kenosis* (emptying of the divine self) in order to incarnate as a human being (2007, 20). Like those answering an altar call, players of pervasive larps *choose* to enter the imagined environment, *choose* to sink their identities into the characters they play, and *choose* to believe the world works as the game demands.

Another game with significant bleed is the intentionally repulsive *Gang Rape*. This freeform game is designed to maximize bleed effects without pressing players to the point of actual rape. Characters are paper-thin to force players to engage mostly as themselves. Players act out the events leading up to the rape (Montola 2010). Then they sit to narrate the parts they can't act out. Players must look into one another's eyes while describing sexual violence.

Gang Rape constitutes a near erasure of the magic circle by driving players into behavior considered disgusting, strange, or unnatural and forcing them to feel as if they are (nearly) performing those acts themselves (Montola 2010). The larp-generated world is not the same world in which players live, but the two worlds are in such close proximity the player is left uneasy. A similar set of uncomfortable feelings was evoked in the larp *The Journey*, based on Cormac McCarthy's *The Road*. There, players enacted scenes involving murder, cannibalism, sexual manipulation, and abandonment. The designer "wanted people to feel a little bit dirty," and to "have a bad feeling in their stomachs. . . . I wanted the potential for some really raw, really rough, really scary role-playing" (quoted in Montola 2010).

My interest here is the line—perhaps imperceptible—between extreme larping and the political action of today's alt-right groups. Larps are typically framed as bounded experiences, with a beginning and an end, involving deep immersion but also at least *intended* to be distinct from everyday life. And yet some larps press at this distinction purposefully, like *Gang Rape* and *Ground Zero*. And some real-life actions, like the "Unite the Right" rally in Charlottesville and the storming of the Capitol on January 6, seem fueled by a set of rules and narratives that are encountered in game-like ways. Indeed, participants seem to thrive in acting as if their most offensive activities are both very serious and not serious at all.

QAnon, the Game

Game designer Adrian Hon has recognized this kind of bleed in QAnon, saying that although people take QAnon very seriously, it looks like an ARG (Thompson 2020). QAnon is based on a hodgepodge of bizarre beliefs, including that the 2020 presidential election was stolen and that Donald Trump was "thwarted from saving the world from a Satan-worshipping pedophilia ring run by Democrats, Jews, and other agents of the deep state" (Thompson 2020). "Q drops" are clues left periodically on anonymous discussion boards by a presumed insider in the Trump milieu, but the Q drops are vague and notoriously hard to interpret. As soon as they appear, enthusiastic readers "begin Googling the phrases, then energetically share their own exegesis online" (Thompson 2020).

QAnon is a "massive crowdsourcing project that sees itself cracking a mystery" (Thompson 2020). It is also a quasi-religious activity, based on habits of scriptural interpretation hard baked into the American Christian experience. Q's followers "behave like religious devotees who pore over their faith's central texts, crafting interpretations that become part of the official creed" (Thompson 2020). Some, like the Omega Kingdom Ministry, blend their Q interpretation and their biblical interpretation, seeing both as sacred activity. Some have begun parsing Trump's speeches using *gematria*, a Jewish interpretive practice that involves coded transitions between numbers and letters to reveal secret messages (Fox 2022). QAnon is evidence of a "new kind of post-digital far-right activism" that has spread to mainstream social media and to Republican Party politics. QAnon is a "real-world game" and "addictively participatory" (Tuters 2021, 63).

QAnon can be read as a kind of serious pervasive game. Game designer Jane McGonigal recognizes the tendency of pervasive games to make players more suspicious and more inquisitive. Players detect "game patterns in non-game places" and the "more a player chooses to believe, the more (and more interesting) opportunities are revealed" (McGonigal 2003). The physical world becomes an "endless source of information that is interpreted into the imaginary world" (Montola 2007, 180). The primary frame of real life is implicated in play.

> **Larping is an extraordinary example of how close to the primary frame a game can become. Because larp is a version of RPG that is acted out rather than described, players interact in a manner that could easily be miskeyed as the primary frame—instead of saying "I scream at him," players *actually do* scream at other players. Larp participants have to be aware that the line between the performance frame and the primary frame is extremely thin,**

and actions done in-character could be downkeyed and taken seriously instead. (Choy 2004, 60)

Like other pervasive games, QAnon invites players to see the world as shaped by secret forces that are discoverable only by the determined, the clever, and those with special insider information. QAnon devotees are driven by apocalyptic expectation of a sort, looking to a time called "The Storm," "when mass violence will topple the elite cabal of pedophiles who they imagine to be running the government" (Taub and Bennhold 2021). The Pew Research Center conducted a survey in 2022 that found 39% of adults believe we are living in the end times (Diamant 2022). Whether we read QAnon as a larp or not, it has many of the same features as pervasive games. To embrace QAnon is to see the world as a game, and to see online research as an essential activity. QAnon is a game that seems real, inviting players to see what is real as very gamelike.

Bring It On: Accelerationism

Another alt-right phenomenon with pervasive apocalyptic longing is accelerationism. The goal of alt-right accelerationism is "to foment divisiveness" and "induce the collapse of the existing order and spark a second civil war" (Hoffman 2022). Accelerationists hope for "chaos, collapse, and revolutionary change that promotes white power" (Walther and McCoy 2021, 105). They look to a time when government, society, and the economy "will be wiped out in a wave of catastrophic violence, clearing the way for a utopia that will supposedly follow" (Taub and Bennhold 2021). Like preppers, they expect extreme disruption. The Oath Keepers and other accelerationist organizations like Atomwaffen Division "seek to catalyze and spread systemic breakdown, inflame racial, ethnic, and religious tensions already present in society, and prepare to fill a prophesied future power vacuum with revolutionary, white supremacist violence" (Loadenthal et al. 2022, 89). They believe "civil war is inevitable and that individuals should train, arm themselves, and prepare to incite violence" (Walther and McCoy 2021, 105).

Accelerationists are driven by a racist narrative of victimization they call the "Great Replacement." Influenced by Jean Raspail's

1973 anti-immigrant fantasy novel, *The Camp of the Saints*, the "Great Replacement" is the belief white people are "being replaced in their countries by non-white immigrants . . . and the end result will be the extinction of the white race" (Anti-Defamation League 2021). There is a bizarre scene in Raspail's novel of "a mob of Indian mothers swarming the gates of a European embassy, desperately pressing their children through the bars, and onto the good graces of white society" (Allen 2019). It's hard not to see this as inspiration for the opening visuals of *The Walking Dead*, with its iconic image of hospital cafeteria doors bursting at the seams with gruesome, grasping zombie arms reaching out.

The Boogaloo Bois are among America's newest accelerationists. They are anti-government, anti–law enforcement extremists who eagerly anticipate transformational violence (Institute for Strategic Dialogue 2022, 3). The name is drawn from a 1984 dance movie, *Breakin' 2: Electric Boogaloo*. Because the movie is a sequel, the term "boogaloo" is insider code for a sequel Civil War. Many Boogaloo Bois are also preppers "fantasizing about the Boogaloo" and engaging in apocalyptic ideation about what could happen when SHTF. Boogalooers prepare for an "armed battle against law enforcement and anyone else they perceive as threatening their rights, particularly their right to bear arms" (Bertelsmann Foundation 2020). Boogalooers frequently reference Ruby Ridge and Waco, even though those events occurred before many Boogalooers were born. Boogaloo memes on Facebook embraced larping and used "videogame language of 'quests' and 'achievement points' to describe acts of real-world violence" (Tuters 2021, 66).

In 2020, Boogalooers became "increasingly engaged in real world activities . . . showing up at protests and rallies around gun rights, pandemic restrictions, and police-related killings" (Anti-Defamation League 2021). Their costume consists of Hawaiian shirts and symbols of igloos, based on a riff: Big Luau and Big Igloo. Drawn to symbols like the "Don't Tread on Me" Gadsden flag, they overlap with other accelerationists, preppers, and survivalists who look forward to apocalyptic collapse (Kriner and Clarke 2020). And like other fans at the riot on January 6, they created props to display at the Capitol, including "symbols, flags, patches, clothing, and stickers" (Anti-Defamation League 2021). They are easy to spot in the footage of the events on January 6; some wear full face masks or carry igloo-themed flags.

The Hawaiian shirts are a cosplay outfit that allows Boogalooers to "present themselves as merely LARPers—thereby self-consciously obfuscating sincere political commitments under a veil of self-deflating irony" (Tuters 2021, 66).

The cowboy apocalypse can be viewed as an accelerationist pervasive larp. The game space—the magic circle of cowboy apocalypse imagination—is extended into real life as the good guy plays out a plotline to which he is already committed. The world is overwhelmed with evil and in need of a savior figure. To play the cowboy apocalypse as a larp is to view other people as props in the service of one's own performance. It is to invest deeply in a vision of the future that celebrates one's dominance, reinforced by the mythical celebration of white male hegemony in America's past. The cowboy apocalypse can even be larped in retrospect—as it is imposed onto events that do not fit as they should.

The "Good Guy" Larp

In 2017 in Sutherland Springs, Texas, twenty-six churchgoers were killed and twenty-two more wounded by shooter Devin Patrick Kelley, wielding a Ruger AR-556 semiautomatic weapon. Kelly eventually fled, chased by Stephen Willeford, who had shown up to confront Kelley with his AR-15. In *Fox News* coverage of the event, Andrew O'Reilly called Willeford a hero and a good guy with a gun and played up his affiliation with the NRA (O'Reilly 2017). O'Reilly then lists a series of other shooting incidents that seem to fit the narrative of the armed civilian who becomes a hero. O'Reilly says that as horrific as Kelley's rampage was, it could have been much worse if it wasn't for Willeford. But the narrative of the good guy larp overwhelms facts that don't fit, such as the twenty-six people in the Sutherland Springs church who died before the hero arrived, or the fact that the good guy injured the bad guy, then the bad guy escaped and killed himself. The "good guy with a gun" is a larp imposed on real-life shootings whether the people involved enact it or not. It is a story gun rights activists *want* to be true because it makes them feel noble and powerful.

Active players of larps can immerse deeply within a story. They make take on a double life, such that "on a surface level players seem ordinary ... but they have a secret identity ... [as] the player becomes a character in the diegesis of the game" (Montola, Stenros, and Waern 2009, 208). When a game lasts for a long time, "there is a risk of the game world getting in conflict with the real world." In the case of Willeford, identification as a "good guy" means that one must always be armed. The larp could crop up at any time—and the plot requires a shooting be met with more shooting. The story is authenticated by its own expectations.

> [T]he role-taking in larps not only provides a means for immersion but the character also enables another level of experientiality. Through the possibility (and the obligation) to embody an element of the narrative, past and present experience of a player merge [to], become a momentum in several realities during a larp. (Kamm and Becker 2016, 45)

Success in a pervasive larp requires players develop what McGonigal calls "stereoscopic vision," which "simultaneously perceive[s] the everyday reality and the game structure in order to generate a single, but layered and dynamic worldview" (McGonigal 2003). Players perceive a merged terrain of the game's play and the real world. The effect can linger as players continue to see games where games don't exist (McGonigal 2003). The player may achieve a "subjective, immersive state where they feel in a more or less pronounced way that they *are* the character in the game world" (Lukka 2014, 81, emphasis added). An immersed player may "lock their perspective to that of the character and attempt to uphold the diegetic reality" (85). To larp as a good guy is to have *already* committed oneself to that story regardless of actual events. The story is more important than the victims, who are objects in a preexisting plot.

The gun is integrated into the pervasive play of the "good guy" in the same way that landscapes, unsuspecting people, and city streets are integrated—as they *really are*. In most larps, a gun would be represented by a plastic toy gun or a cardboard prop. An indexical prop is an object that represents *itself* in the game. In an indexically propped larp, a *real gun* would represent a *real gun*. To bring a real gun into a pretend experience is to authenticate that fake experience with real consequences. The whole experience then seems real in a way that suggests it was wrong to ever assume it fake. The gun spills its authenticity, like contagion, onto what would otherwise be mere play. Just as religious sacraments can authenticate religious experience ("This *is* the body and blood of Jesus Christ"), so the gun can authenticate the fantasy of entry into another world, another way of being, another way of seeing *this* world. To shoot at a bad guy is to force the belief of one's own messianic identity into reality, to layer it so firmly atop the real world that it is simply so.

Alt-right activities are so firmly entrenched online that the cowboy mythology may seem too ephemeral most of the time:

> **The narrative of the Lone Ranger, conducted like a drone strike from behind a keyboard, thus becomes both cause and effect of the alt-right's mythos. They participate in the "meme wars" in search of a narrative of self-determination that the incorporeality of their chosen battlefield will always deny them. (Burton 2016, 5)**

But this incorporeality *did* become real on January 6 when protestors placed their bodies within the sacred space of the Capitol with the potential for real violence. Just as belief is authenticated for Christians through sacraments like communion, so alt-right beliefs can be authenticated by embodied presence in the Capitol, or perhaps by a toke under the rotunda.

Even though few shots were fired on January 6, 121 people have been charged with using or carrying dangerous weapons at the rally, and one woman, Ashli Babbitt, is dead. Trump supporters were found with Molotov cocktails, pistols, handguns, rifles, crossbows, machetes, smoke bombs, chemical spray, bear spray, stun guns, and clubs. Although the rioters did not get to use the weapons they brought, the hope was they *would*. One texted his family that he was going to collect "traitors' heads." Another, wearing a Trump 2020 cowboy hat, shot pepper spray in the face of a DC Metropolitan police officer (Klasfeld 2022). Trump himself reportedly *wanted* the rioters to carry their guns past the metal detectors, and he knew some of them were wearing body armor. Cassidy Hutchinson, a former aide, reported Trump said: "I don't fucking care that they have weapons, they're not here to hurt me . . . They can march to the Capitol from here, let the people in and take the mags away" (Stahl 2022). In a crowd with people wearing Civil War T-shirts dated January 6, 2021, it is hard to grasp why more violence did *not* occur.

The ability of guns to authenticate a sense of self-righteousness is explained by reporter Rachel Monroe, who borrowed an AR-15 for a two-day tactical training event where participants would learn to shoot "as if we were engaged in small-unit armed combat" (Monroe 2021). People drawn to these events include "gun bros and gamers, preppers and adrenaline junkies, larpers who want to spend their weekends cosplaying as commandos, and crime victims seeking a particular flavor of empowerment." Some of these people imagine themselves heroes, and others just feel threatened. She visits Arizona's Gunsite Academy, which she calls Disneyland for gun lovers—thirty-two hundred acres, with "simulators where students are trained in how to stop a home invasion or engage an assailant in a parking lot." The Academy has classes for church defense and tactical tracking. Its clients are mostly "white, male, and middle aged, with an air of moderate affluence." Fandom elements include "digital camouflage, wrap-around Oakleys, Black Rifle coffee . . . and the AR 15" (Monroe 2021).

In one scenario, Monroe was asked to deal with some presumed drug addicts who had kidnapped a family member. "[W]e had to track them through the field, moving as a unit, then enter a wooded area and react to what we found there" (Monroe 2021). They shot at photorealistic targets, including one depicting a pregnant woman. In a larp, this kind of activity could be viewed as part of play. Here it is intended to "inoculate yourself to trauma" so that "it's not such a drastic departure from your reality" to shoot people. As Monroe remarks, "by rehearsing for a situation, we were, in a small way, calling it into being." The scenarios were fake, but the bullets were real. Training for combat implies an enemy. Militarized civilians and law enforcement "increasingly identify that enemy among their fellow Americans." One shooter, upon hitting a cardboard person "right in the ocular cavity," said: "It was hugely satisfying, and it felt—I don't know how else to describe it—like being right" (Monroe 2021).

Perhaps it was with similar satisfaction on January 6 that the crowd dragged a police officer out of the building and began to beat and taser him, nearly killing him. As Monroe learned, people may act violently *in order to* authenticate their story. And just because the rioters were called off the Capitol grounds, there is reason to believe they still await the violence that will authenticate their cause. What happened on January 6 was not a game, despite its association with fandom practices. In tilting beyond the magic circle of play, participants borrowed the conventions of gaming to justify real violence. They imposed game rules onto the stuff of life, making their bodies and the very structures of Congress into the platform on which the game was played. Such activities remind us games are not by definition harmless.

When the world is viewed as an apocalyptic game, it can *become* one. When people want to believe the end is near, they will try to bring it on. When their world is disrupted, when they begin to lose power, they will view events through a cosmic lens. The center of this cosmos is not God, or even Trump—but themselves. Just as in first-person-shooter videogames, the January 6 apocalyptic larpers are the center of their own immersive experience. For apocalyptic larpers, the guns, the pellets, and even the bullets, are real. This is the materialization—the incarnation—of belief, the proof of one's place at the center. The body proves it, as it is pummeled by police, trampled by protestors, as whiteness is visually assaulted all around. The gun proves its rightness when it is fired at a determined enemy. Being a victim of siege is made real, and the experience must be intoxicating.

CONCLUSION

OTHERWISE

Nostalgia is longing that neglects lived experience. Instead, it depends on an imagined past. *If only* we could live the way we used to. *If only* there were just one story to tell. *If only* we could be at ease. We are experiencing a white apocalypse, an end to the world as white people in America have known it. The shit has hit the fan, and those of us who are white cannot continue unchallenged for theft, indifference, greed, and harm. But what follows the-world-as-we-know-it need not be a barren, bullet-riddled wasteland. What would it mean to survive together with those we have heretofore ignored? What, besides the imagination of gun-driven paroxysm, is possible? In her collection *Holy Moly Carry Me*, poet Erika Meitner describes the sacred quality stories cast when we let them be loose, open, undone. She says: "There are holes in all of these stories—our stories—open-mouthed gaps in the fence, a singing presence. Holy moly, *please can we just keep driving*." In this conclusion, I look at some of these unfinished stories as told by those who, in the cowboy apocalypse, would be erased, demonized, or otherwise left out. What would it mean to see the holes in our stories and, untethered, "keep driving" toward something new?

In today's media, "pastiche and nostalgia are central modes of image production and reception" as Americans immerse themselves in a "social *imaginaire* built largely around reruns" (Appadurai 1998, 30). This mediated memory has qualities we will recognize in the cowboy apocalypse:

> The drug wars in Colombia recapitulate the tropical sweat of Vietnam, with Ollie North and his succession of masks—Jimmy Stewart concealing John Wayne concealing Spiro Agnew and all

of them transmogrifying into Sylvester Stallone, who wins in Afghanistan—thus simultaneously fulfilling the secret American envy of Soviet imperialism and the rerun (this time with a happy ending) of the Vietnam War. (30)

Our new wars are reruns of our old wars. Our cowboy heroes and our military heroes look a lot alike. The past "has become a synchronic warehouse of cultural scenarios, a kind of temporal central casting" intended to reinforce the idea that all our problems can be solved by violence (30). This casting has, until recently, been mostly white—and obsessed with guns. Nostalgia breeds apocalypse. Gun nostalgia breeds the cowboy apocalypse.

Racialized Apocalypse

In his recent collection of essays, *We Gon' Be Alright*, Jeff Chang indicates a recognition of the cowboy apocalypse, though he gives it a different name:

> Racial apocalypse is the recurring white American narrative in which the civilizers, the chosen people meant to fulfill their destiny, are overrun by the savages, the barbarians who embody chaos and ruin. It's in the stories told about the Alamo, General Custer, Reconstruction, the sixties. It's even there in the fixation on the Civil War, Lincoln's life and assassination, and the common disappearance of slavery from that story. The racial apocalypse is part of the DNA of American pop culture—Buffalo Bill Cody's cowboys-and-Indians show, D. W. Griffith's *The Birth of a Nation*—but instead of bloodshed and death, we got happy endings. The end of whiteness is one of the oldest, most common stories Americans tell to scare ourselves (even though we don't all scare equally). (2016, 14)

This repetitive story is not just an exercise of the imagination. It is insisted on by its faithful followers through real guns and real bullets, as self-declared white heroes level their aim at living Black people, Indigenous people, and—through America's wars—people around the globe. The gun is a symbol of settler colonialism, of America's self-determined role as world savior. It is an ideological tool and a weapon for murder.

Scholars Philip Gorski and Samuel Perry see such mythic American stories working like a "barebones movie script":

> They include a cast of heroes and villains, and well-worn and familiar plots that events are supposed to follow. And, like many classic scripts, they are made and remade, with tweaked storylines and new leading men. . . . Like any story, this one has its heroes: white conservative Christians, usually native-born men. It also has its villains: racial, religious, and cultural outsiders. . . . Sometimes, the conflicts culminate in violence—violence that restores white Christians to what they believe is their rightful place atop America's racial and religious hierarchy. (2022, 4)

The story is familiar enough now that we are beginning to pick it out of our own history, a sign of increasing critical maturity.

Black feminist theologian Kelly Brown Douglas attests that myths like manifest destiny exonerate white people "from taking moral responsibility for certain immoral, dehumanizing, and even deadly actions they might perpetrate against non-white bodies" (2015, 107). Claiming divine justification for the appropriation of space itself, manifest destiny is the logic of white supremacy reinforced by violence. The narrative of manifest destiny is a "declaration of war" against Black and brown bodies (107). This war is enacted today on front lawns, in public parks, and in supermarkets across America. The castle doctrine supports it. This law allows shooters to fire anytime they feel threatened. It allows for defense of one's space as well as one's home, and in many states this right is extended to public space. "Stand your ground" purportedly applies to any American, but in reality, it allows for "the protection of white space, which is whatever space white bodies inhabit. The white body becomes essentially a mobile castle" with the gun as its protector (115). This inherently violent culture is a means of reinforcing white supremacy, as almost always the people standing their ground are white men with guns.

In 2014, the police who rolled down Ferguson's streets in armored vehicles with gun ports believed they were confronting an enemy. Or at least, the armored props they were riding in let them *make* Black protestors into an enemy. The protestors *must* be terrifying because *look at the weapons we use to confront them*! Jeff Chang describes the scene in Ferguson on August 9, a few hours after Michael Brown was shot:

> At dusk, a full moon was rising, and three of the four lanes on West Florissant had become a parking lot of police vehicles bearing the names of more than twenty-nine departments from across the county. BearCat tanks moved up the fourth lane toward Canfield. Police in MARPAT camo battle dress awaited instructions in the parking lot of Original Red's BBQ next to the QuikTrip. Sirens lit the street in oscillations of blue and red. Helicopters buzzed above. Hundreds of Ferguson residents who had come down from their houses took in the scene with horror. (2016, 91)

Two days later in Ferguson, there were snipers on armored vehicles and paramilitary police with tear gas launchers and knives. "Ferguson looked like occupied territory, a zone of civil war," Chang says (102). Ferguson's Black residents were exiled from the very idea of America, and the guns aimed at them seemed proof of their unbelonging. The guns were a means of excommunication, the refusal to communicate. Guns unmake the world. They push people out, define borders, and reify white supremacy.

In her study of the American Right, Arlie Russell Hochschild uses the metaphor of waiting in a long line for the American Dream. White, older, Christian men are in the middle of the line, irritated at those people (*not* white, older, Christian men) cutting in front of them (2016, 137). She imagines the men describing it this way: Black people push in front through affirmative action; women are taking jobs; immigrants are getting special benefits; refugees are "young men, possibly ISIS terrorists," who want to "your tax money" (138). There is even a brown pelican covered in oil. "Blacks, women, immigrants, refugees, brown pelicans—all have cut ahead of you in line. But it's people like you who have made this country great" (139). This "deep story" of aggravated whiteness winds through Hochschild's study. But the story is based on rank inaccuracies, prejudice, and worst of all, a presumption that there *is* such a thing as the American Dream waiting beyond the next hill, accessible only if we wait our turn and keep the cheaters away.

Shared risk has made denial of interdependence impossible, even for otherwise comfortable people. Increasingly, we are "living in a direct and universal proximity with everyone else" (Beck 2009, 6). The most jarring apocalyptic fears—nuclear destruction, war, social unrest, shortages of food and fuel, natural disasters, and terrorism—are risks for everyone, no matter our wealth or privilege. Climate refugees are *already* being forced to move. Wars *already* displace people across the globe. We are *already* running short on fresh water and fuel. Climate change, while not as frequently cited due to its slower burn, *already* changes the way people live, heaving apocalyptic storms, floods, and heat waves on exhausted communities. Millions of people in America are homeless and hungry, unable to access basic support. There is something disappointing about the image of a line of white men complaining that refugees are cutting in front of them, as if life itself were a queue for a newly released videogame, as if the only way to interact were ranking order.

Biblical scholar Adela Yarbro Collins says the apocalyptic division of the world into us-versus-them is an oversimplification that eliminates the "complexities of life in which there are always shades of gray" (1984, 170). One's enemies are "denied their full humanity" (170). But this is only a small part of the story. The division of people into good and evil can hide a million sins. Call Native Americans evil, and you can decide you own the land on which they live. Call Black people inhuman, and you can justify owning them, killing them, ignoring them. Call poor people evil and you can walk right by when they are hungry. Call yourself good and you can justify shooting a young Black man pretty much anywhere in America, if you are white.

America's actions toward Native Americans have parallels in the Holocaust:

> [W]ere the will there we could learn much about ourselves from the Nazi experience. Manifest Destiny anticipated nearly all the ideological and programmatic elements of Hitler's Lebensraum policy. In fact, Hitler modeled his conquest of the East on the American

conquest of the West . . . it was the Nazi holocaust that discredited the scientific racism so pervasive a feature of American intellectual life before World War II. (Finkelstein 2000, 145)

Ta-Nehisi Coates describes how whiteness was achieved "through the pillaging of life, liberty, labor, and land; through the flaying of backs; the chaining of limbs; the strangling of dissidents; the destruction of families; the rape of mothers; the sale of children" and other acts meant to deny Black people "the right to secure and govern" their own bodies (2015a, 8). Racism is visceral and material. It "dislodges brains, blocks airways, rips muscle, extracts organs, cracks bones, breaks teeth" (10). It also justifies the bullets that steal the lives of young Black people every day. The American Dream was built with stolen labor, on land that was not available, and on the blood of others. Coates indicts those who will not see:

> The forgetting is a habit, is yet another necessary component of the Dream. They have forgotten the scale of theft that enriched them in slavery; The terror that allowed them, for a century, to pilfer the vote; the segregationist policy that gave them their suburbs. They have forgotten, because to remember would tumble them out of the beautiful Dream and force them to live down here with us, down here in the world . . . In the dream they are Buck Rogers, Prince Aragorn, an entire race of Skywalkers. To awaken them is to reveal that they are an empire of humans and, like all empires of humans, are built on the destruction of the body. It is to stain their nobility, to make them vulnerable, fallible, breakable humans. (143)

The apocalyptic worldview is a position entered into from desperation by the powerless (as in the case of the ancient Jews in Rome) but also from spite by the powerful (in the endless flow of self-published post-apocalyptic novels by white men today). Apocalypticism, like other forms of worldbuilding, is an imaginative attempt to "reconcile life's inherent contradictions in an explanatory story whose effect is to promote social order" (Daniels 2014, 11). Apocalypse claims to "force the world to make sense, to moralize and convert it, and at least some of its human inhabitants, to the holy realm it was originally supposed to be" (11). But such a claim is intrinsically ideological. Social order for some can be slavery to others. The reconciliation of contradictions can happen through stamping out other people's beliefs. The world may make sense only when you are in charge. Perhaps apocalypse has been able to present itself as neutral by being so foundational in Judaism, Christianity, and Islam, where for many it functions as a demand for justice. But the cowboy apocalypse is anything but neutral. Indigenous writer George Tinker describes how white supremacy has dulled people's ability to imagine other perspectives:

> What Euro-Americans do not yet have is a story that accounts for their history of systemic violence in the world and their easy proclivity for rationalizing any act of military or economic colonization and conquest as somehow good. Instead, Euro-Americans and their elected officials seem to engage in a behavior pattern well-known in alcohol and drug addiction therapy: denial . . . like ostriches with their heads in the sand . . . living in the protected zones of American society. (1997, 101)

Feminist Catherine Keller identifies our preoccupation with apocalypticism as a violent compulsion. This presumptive binary impacts all aspects of life when it is rallied for misogynistic, racist, ethnocentric, or fascist ends. Apocalypticism often signals suffering because it "rests upon an either/or morality: a proclivity to think and feel in polarities of 'good' versus 'evil'; to identify with the good and to purge the evil from oneself and one's world once and for all" (2005, 11).

Alt-right accelerationism is built on a version of white-supremacist apocalypticism. Current society is "doomed to failure" and must "crash down around us" (soon) so a "white utopia" can be built. Accordingly, accelerationists seek to "hasten the end through terroristic guerilla war" (Burley 2021, 13). Their post-apocalypticism is the means to imagine things otherwise, to envision a paradise that is only a paradise for the select few. White nationalist groups like the one that idolized Dylann Roof promised to "deliver their people to the promised land only after the horrors (started by multiculturalism and ended by their bombs) were wiped away" (14). Seeing themselves as oppressed, they sought a salvation of their own making.

The millennialism embraced by the far right has a prophetic framework that reinterprets social forces "through a story that sits well with their gut instincts of bigotry and rage" (27). The alt-right views itself as "beset on all sides by tyranny, about to be destroyed unless someone chooses to act" (118). The lesson for those of us who do *not* want to be white supremacists is how easily we too can be swept up in an apocalyptic story that promises relief without calling us to account for the suffering of anyone else. Apocalypticism need not be supernatural for its impact to be real. Instead of being the end of the world, apocalypticism is:

> . . . the end of our world, the one we have today. We are experiencing an apocalyptic event by any measure, but that means the end of the structures and systems that define everything from our governments to our commodities to our social relationships. They will not exist as we know them in the future, they lack the permanence we ascribed to them. Global capitalism, carbon fuel sources, infinite growth, destructive forms of mass production, and liberal democracies were all built on quicksand. When we discovered what we had done we were already sinking. To create a real fight we have to become post-apocalyptic, to think about how we build something new that protects people now and can give us the tools to find that sustainability. (171)

My quibble with this assessment is its unacknowledged presumption of white privilege. Lots of people *already* deal with the collapse of structures and systems, or maybe they never benefited in the first place. Black people in America have *already* lived through apocalypse. Native Americans have also. We have trashed our waterways, exiled wild animals from their habitats, and poisoned our atmosphere. The structures and systems in decay now are those that have been engineered to benefit white people most. The-end-of-the-world-as-we-know-it is most troubling for those who have most enjoyed themselves in the-world-as-we-know-it-so-far.

The cowboy apocalypse is a lie propped up by denial of change. Individualism, the sacredness of the family, borders and boundaries are "arcane relics, bargains of survival in a world with expired rules" (178). Gun-infused cowboy apocalypticism is a kind of protective fundamentalism and thus subject to the same kinds of mistakes that fundamentalism makes. Martin E. Marty and R. Scott Appleby define fundamentalism as a "tendency, a habit of mind" that "manifests itself as a strategy, or set of strategies, by which beleaguered believers attempt to preserve their distinctive identity as a group or people." Fundamentalism is an effort to restore "threatened certainty" (1993, 3). Although the term is frequently applied to religious groups, there are also secular fundamentalisms. Indeed, "just about any idea or practice can become the foundation of a fundamentalist project" that looks to a "(real or imagined) certainty in the past" that would tell the believer: "you will know who you are, and you will know how to live" (Berger 2014, 9). For cowboy messiahs, the way to live is in charge, drinking deeply from privilege and resources presumed gifted by divine right.

To justify their own blessedness, fundamentalists see the world as "divided into unambiguous realms of light and darkness peopled by the elect and reprobate, the pure and impure, the orthodox and infidel" (Appleby 2000, 88). Fundamentalism is "a pattern of religious militance in which self-styled true believers attempt to arrest the erosion of religious identity by outsiders, fortify the borders of the religious community, and create viable alternatives to secular structures and processes" (Almond et al. 2003, 5). Fundamentalists turn selectively to the past, celebrating a previous golden age. Fundamentalisms, with their "nostalgia for a mythical uncorrupted past," are becoming "rearguard attempts to stem a more sweeping tidal change" (Cox 2009, 2). Nostalgia is a heady brew. For cowboy apocalypticists, white supremacy serves it up.

One of the most distinctive traits of apocalyptic discourse is its interest in alternative worlds, places where the world is more in line with what people wish were so. Ancient Jewish and Christian apocalyptic writers were powerless, facing the threat of their own dissolution, so they told stories about the future, about paradise and a new earth. Today's apocalyptic narratives are more often told by those *already* in power, though they may feel threatened. What a thrill to be both judge of the present world and self-designated creator of the world to come. How exciting to see this story repeated in books, television shows, movies, and videogames, as if it were self-evidently true. "No rhetoric is more powerful than apocalyptic rhetoric, no greater motivation exists in the human repertoire than the belief that one's every action is crucial to the final destiny of the human race" (Landes 2005, 39). Such impulses reflect a "desire for stability and order" amid the "turbulence and upheaval of global transformation." Contemporary storytellers, "having tossed out God from the apocalyptic scenario," have "replaced his immense destructive powers with [their] own" (39). God has left the wasteland. The good guy with a gun has arrived.

Media can offer scripts for "possible lives," offering "fantastic film plots" that provide "resources for self-imagining as an everyday social project" (Appadurai 1998, 4). The mediated imagination is a "staging ground for action" (7). The media offer symbolic resources for the "construction of imagined selves and imagined worlds" (3). But not all these worlds are desirable. Absorbing apocalyptic stories on a regular basis can make us think the world is hopelessly riven, unrecoverably depleted, and irreparably saturated with violence. If the world is unfixable, then we are relieved of the slog of improving it. There is a "coldly glittering appeal" to imagining everything swept away, leaving behind only those with whom we agree (Alter 1966). And for some, there is a thrill in imagining themselves as saviors destroying the bad guys.

In the rest of this conclusion, I outline other ways of imagining the future and other stories drawn from the voices and traditions of people who are poorly represented props in the cowboy apocalypse. Here you will find Indigenous voices, Black voices, and feminist voices. You will hear from literary theorists, novelists, musicians, theologians, and other visionaries. By listening to what they have to say about storytelling and the future, we will be able to "poke openings" into the dangerous habit of apocalyptic storytelling (Keller 2005, 14).

Feminist Dis/closure

Feminist Catherine Keller claims apocalyptic dualism reflects the "hot desire of fundamentalism" that "shuts down that opening where the present pulses into its future" (2005, ix). Closing down conversations about what is possible, apocalypticism offers a "regime of truth" that has been "especially oppressive toward women and racial and sexual minorities" (Quinby 1999, 10). The logic of biblical apocalypticism upholds "a hierarchy of male authority and female submission," claiming it to be timeless and divinely ordained (111). For Keller, the apocalypse is not an external event about to happen. It is a way of seeing the world that shuts down our options, demonizes others, and makes us (especially powerful white men) into rigid, self-celebratory jerks. As Americans live with seemingly endless insecurity, our apocalypticism is characterized by "infantile cravings for gratification and rescue" (Keller 2005, 56). When God promises to "wipe away all the tears from their eyes" (in Rev. 21:4), he promises this to men only (80).

Approaching the idea of apocalypse from a feminist perspective, we can imagine something different, what Keller calls "dis/closing" apocalypse (289). We can *refuse* the authoritarian closure that apocalypticism demands. We can embrace the gap between what is and what could be. We can be open, curious, looking for what is possible. We do not *have* to see the world teetering on the brink of collapse. The slash in dis/closure indicates a resistance to apocalyptic closure and certainty. Dis/closure doesn't require violence, and transformation need not be an ending. This is *disclosure* in the general sense of the word: a message we need to hear.

Keller proposes a radical embrace of *now* as a way of "conceiving a sustainable, just, and lovable future by living it already." Instead of looking to future violent transition, she advises sitting where we are: "There is no *there* but *here* and now." Dis/closure is "an opening of the present as the only site of memory and hope" (30). If we focus on the "moment-to-moment" we can "evade the grand narratives of dread, hope, and closure" (84). She gestures toward a "healing ambivalence" that evokes possibility, conversation, rich imagination, and hope (220).

For Black feminist Toni Morrison, the salve for such lopsided storytelling is dialogue:

> Listening, assuming sometimes that I have a history, a language, a view, an idea, a specificity. Assuming that what I know may be useful . . . My memory is as necessary to yours as your memory is to mine . . . we ought to know all of the past . . . we ought to know exactly what that legacy is—all of it and where it came from. (2019, 71)

When the future seems difficult, we "turn to sorcery: summoning up a brew of aliens, pseudo-enemies, demons, false 'causes' that deflect and soothe anxieties about gates through which barbarians saunter" (118). The distance between people is sometimes called racism, or classism, or sexism. But it all has a common root:

> ... a deplorable inability to project, to become the "other," to imagine her or him. It is an intellectual flaw, a shortening of the imagination, and reveals an ignorance of gothic proportion as well as a truly laughable lack of curiosity.... If education is about anything other than being able to earn money (and it may not be about any other thing), that other thing is intelligent problem-solving and humans relating to one another in mutually constructive ways. (43)

The redemptive future is "race-inflected, gendered, colonialized, displaced, hunted." It will be shaped by those "pressed to the margins," and "dismissed as irrelevant surplus" because "the current disequilibria is a stirring, not an erasure" (126). America's history is rife with what it ignores. A "journey into the cellar of time is a rescue of sorts, an excavation for the purposes of building, discovering, envisioning a future" (123). Dreaming allows entrance into "someone else's situation, sphere" (69). It is a kind of projection that "permits intimacy with the Other without the risk of being the other." This kind of intimate interaction is the only thing, she says, that can save us (69).

Ecological feminist Donna Harroway argues that instead of obsessing over apocalypse, we ought to settle down as "mortal critters entwined in myriad unfinished configurations of places, times, matters, meanings" (2016, 1). The goal ought to be a "common livable world" that is "composed bit by bit, or not at all" (40). Our job—especially as feminists—is to imagine things otherwise. Stories are templates that tell us where we might go: "It matters what worlds world worlds. It matters what stories tell stories" (35). She means: "It matters what worlds we use as the basis for imagining new worlds." If we assume too much is normative and fixed, we won't imagine enough possibility for transformation. Instead of accepting the apocalyptic imagination, we can "[d]ream the world as it ought to be" (70).

Counterstory/Critical Race Theory

Scholar Aja Martinez describes her Huichol grandfather's passage through the borderlands of Mexico into a new life in the United States in the early twentieth century (2020, xxvi). She was inspired by the ways her grandfather's stories exist in tension with the grand narratives of the United States. This led to an interest in rhetoric, specifically the ways that counterstory can push against received narratives of American identity. She considers the controlling narratives that still shape border legislation, insisting that established law is not "disconnected from the lived realities of its subjects" (97). Rather, law tells its own stories about who belongs.

Her grandfather's stories were a balm for Martinez growing up in the United States. She developed resistance to the "historically crafted master narratives" that cast her among "those who have been conquered—as those who should shoulder a sense of shame at our indigenous status" (xxviii). All stories reflect perspective (16). "Stock stories" are master narratives, "repeated until canonized or normalized, as those who tell them insist that their version of events is indeed reality" (34). The cowboy apocalypse is one of the most repeated and least questioned of these master narratives.

Critical race theory exposes "majoritarian" stories that silence the experiences of people of color (71). Martinez calls for a critical race methodology that can challenge these stories of white privilege (3). This approach, dubbed "counterstory," works through the formation of new stories that disrupt majoritarian erasures. She draws on the work of Richard Delgado, Derrick A. Bell, and Patricia J. Williams especially, as foundational critical race theorists interested in how stories can work as methodology (2). For example, she critiques the "racial progress narrative" of the Civil Rights Movement. Instead of eliminating racism, "systemic and institutional prejudice" remain as lived realities for people of color in the United States (6). Counterstory invites people impacted by stock stories to tell their own version of things.

White people, when "self-reflective of their whiteness," can also tell counterstories (23). Martinez imagines a conversation with Frankie Condon, a white scholar who engages in critical race methods. Martinez has Condon say white people must release the conviction that our stories "confer transcendence of our whiteness upon us." We should excavate so-called "history" for narratives that have been suppressed (90). Counterstories respond to asserted neutrality by offering "embodied knowledge of people of color" as "legitimate and critical," disrupting stories that are "disguised in the rhetoric of normalized structural values and practices" (22). Counterstory is a special kind of story, intended to respond to racial, class, gender, or ableist oppression. Counterstories express a commitment to challenging dominant ideology through lived experience (17). What would a counterstory to the cowboy apocalypse look like? It might look like the traumatized witness of mothers whose beloved sons lost their lives to good guys with guns.

Queer Theology

Marcella Maria Althaus-Reid attests that she doesn't mean to shock readers when she calls theology "the art of putting your hands under the skirts of God" (2004, 99). Instead, she means to make public the "closeted affairs between theology and sexual ideology." She means to expose the heteronormativity of most theological approaches. Appealing to the binary of gender (male/female), some people use Christianity as a mode of oppression. Pointing to the Bible and insisting on rigid interpretations of gender and sex, some Christians reject the intrinsic queerness of our relationship with God. Colonialist ideology is reinforced by the heteronormativity of mainstream theology, as God becomes the Man-in-Charge reassuring the men-in-charge of their authority.

Althaus-Reid disrupts simplistic presumptions about God (that God is a man); about theology (that it must be about a disembodied entity); and about sexuality (that God prefers heteronormativity). Theology itself, she claims, *is* sexual because it is about an intimate (queer) relationship between God and us. This indecent realization can "destabilize the decent order" that has been "ideologically sacralized" (101). When we destabilize our view of God as a judging man, we make room for new ways of reading apocalypse. Destabilizing the notion of the sacred itself is a means to destabilizing judgment. The queer God doesn't judge.

The responsibility for damning apocalyptic theology lies with its authors and nobody else: "When it is said that theological practices do not come from heaven, I agree. In fact, I think they come from the theologian's own bedrooms, which also means from the theologians' own closets" (106). Queer theology promises salvation as we seek redemption for "all the strangers who are entombed in us" (108). In this view, we are all queer, and always have been. To love our queerness is to be redeemed. There is no use for self-righteousness in a world where everyone is unfinished business, always figuring themselves out. Using a queer hermeneutic, we find that judgment—in the sense of rejecting others—is undermined by queerness. Rightly read, Revelation *itself* resists divisions into good and evil. Alluding to Christ appearing with a sharp sword in his mouth (Rev. 19:15) at the final judgment, radical theologian Jeff Hood says queerness itself "promises to bring a sword from the mouth" as it indicts "all who seek to remain in normative spaces" (Hood 2018). Queerness saves by deconstructing. It judges judgment, refusing the banal effects of boxing, labeling, rejecting, exiling. Queerness bursts from the theological closet, proudly.

Apokalypsis is an unveiling, an opening to the truth of how things *are*. This unveiling is the ownership of one's queerness and the queer incompleteness of the world. God is queer by definition: unfathomable, unquantifiable, glorious, and unable to be confined to fixed categories. God's queerness is revealed to John, whose heavenly vision provokes a recognition of queerness within us all:

> **John is transported away from all normativity and into the queerest heavens to see the Queer on the throne of all queerness. . . . The Queer has been, is and will always be queer and we get to embrace the totality of it all if we are willing to go to, with and into the Queer. . . . Make no mistake. There is a war raging in the hearts of humanity. God is fighting for our queerness and Satan is battling for us to be just like everyone else. (Hood 2018)**

Queerness constitutes "a world set to rights or a world made right" by *letting* it be unfathomable, unquantifiable, beyond fixed categories of good and evil, in or out (Hood 2018).

Queerness disrupts our relationship with time, so we stop looking for legitimization in the past "nor for a memory of a harmonious trajectory" (Althaus-Reid 2004, 109). There is no grand narrative to turn to. Instead, we let things—and people—be complicated. We let God be more than we can imagine. We let ourselves open. To be queer is to be undone. To queer theology is to let loose its certainties. To queer the cowboy apocalypse is to drop the gaping gun barrel and stand, gape-mouthed and in love with the person we might otherwise have killed.

Globalization

In the past couple of centuries, human communities have "gradually been drawn into a single web of trade and a global network of information," to the point that "each of us can realistically imagine contacting any other of our six billion conspecifics." The challenge is to "live together as the global tribe we have become" (Appiah 2016, xii–xiii). The world is populated with people in motion: "tourists, immigrants, refugees, exiles, guest workers, and other moving groups" exist in complicated, rhizomatic networks of identity (Appadurai 1998, 33). We live in a world of intertwined fates. A gun won't do anything to purify water or save us from disease.

The term "cosmopolitan" has a complicated past, including its pejorative use by Nazis, who used it to describe Jews as wanderers. Despite its misuse, the term can be reconsidered through association with Voltaire's case for our "obligation to understand those with whom we share the planet" (Appiah 2006, xv). Cosmopolitanism is an "everyday, historically alert, reflexive awareness of ambivalences in a milieu of blurring differentiations and cultural contradictions" (Beck 2006, 3). In its sense of defining a *cosmos* (world) that is also a *polis* (city) in which everyone lives, I use the term here with caution and care.

Apocalypticism and cosmopolitanism are opposite sides of the same global coin. Apocalypticism shuts down global flows by demanding a future of perimeters. Cosmopolitanism opens them up, by a willingness to live with uncertainty, impermanence, and risk, as these make room for care. Nationalism and cosmopolitanism are in tension with one another. Nationalists seek refuge in a "strategic 'as-if' essentialism of ethnicity in an attempt to fix the blurred and shifting boundaries between internal and external, us and them" (Beck 2006, 4). They fortify borders, exclude people, and make globalization a thing to fear. The either/or, insider/outsider categories of nationalism mirror the us/them, good/evil categories of apocalypticism, and they blend well with the mindset of the cowboy apocalypse and its resistance against transnational awareness. Nationalism, as a form of "closed cosmopolitanism, is 'premised on impenetrability'" (Ong 2009, 454). It trucks in "borders, barriers and boundaries, walls and firewalls, fences and fortresses." It wants "gated societies, ghettoes, camps" as it retreats to "tropes of the tribe" (454).

Cosmopolitanism, by contrast, invites a consideration of what the world *should* be, and could be. Instead of building walls, we could develop "habits of coexistence: conversation in its older meaning, of living together" (Appiah 2016, xix). Conversation is not just the dialogue we have with one another, though it includes that. It is the give and take of everyday life, the ways we share space with one another, how we greet each other in the street. It is getting to know each other. Conversations across differences can be fraught, but a world in which people are "neatly hived off from one another seems no longer a serious option, if it ever was" (xx). Cosmopolitanism signals a "condition of self-confrontation [and] incompleteness" (Delanty 2006, 38). Instead of viewing people as insiders or outsiders, we owe *all* people respect. Cosmopolitanism, unlike apocalypticism, invites complexity, curiosity, and openings. In this way, it echoes the dreaming evident in the other perspectives we consider here.

Religious Pluralism

With increasing globalization, people of different religions will encounter each other more and more. Conversations already happen all around us, at coffee shops, in grocery stores, on playgrounds, and in doctors' offices. Already we live in "deep interdependence" with one another (Eck 2003, ix). Channels of interfaith dialogue move across cultures and the world becomes "marbled with the colors and currents of the whole" (x). The whole planet is an "enormous city," shaped by engagement (3). Observing the dangers of fundamentalism, world religions scholar Diana Eck asserts that "[e]specially among exclusivist Christians there has been an unprecedented tantrum of theological pronouncements" (xiv). People make claims about other people's beliefs, claiming God as their own and constructing a self-authenticating "fortress of 'only-ness'" (87). Eck warns: "Our possessive ideas of God may become graven images of ourselves as we raise the sacred canopy of our religion over the most self-serving of worldviews" (xv).

By contrast, religious pluralists focus on "questions rather than answers." They let God be "more mysterious than everything we think we mean" (xv). Eck speaks of her friend J. Krishnamurti, who draws from multiple religions but claims no single one. Religious labels function as "a buffer zone of security" for those overwhelmed by difference (8). But religions are "more like rivers than stones" (2). Interfaith dialogue has the potential to spur mutual transformation and make room for ideas we didn't know were possible. Everyone may not agree, but we will understand each other more clearly as we "begin to replace ignorance, stereotype, even prejudice, with relationship" (19). Robert Orsi says he has often felt a "sense of intrusion" entering the religious spaces of others. He addresses this disorientation by inviting curiosity and openness:

> To study a world of meaning and practice other than one's own . . . means making one's arduous way from an initial experience of difference that may be deeply disorienting or even alienating toward understanding . . . by means of a careful, thoughtful, self-reflective engagement with the ways of these other worlds and a deep and disciplined attentiveness to language, practice, history, and geography. Slowly people and practices that had seemed quite alien no longer do. . . . Difference is not otherness, in other words. (2016, 161–162)

America needs new myths, new narratives, that make room for multiple religious identities (Patton 2018, 152). These new narratives should offer antidotes to narrow, rigid, white supremacist narratives like the cowboy apocalypse.

Pluralism is a situation in which "people with different ethnicities, worldviews, and moralities live together peacefully and interact with each other amicably" (Berger 2014, 1). Pluralism is developed through "sustained conversation" and time spent in the company of others (1). Such engagement results in "cognitive contamination" as an "ongoing condition." This is a *good* thing because if people continue talking, "they will influence each other" and discover new ways to live (2). Pluralism infects us with hope.

Pluralism "undermines religious certainty" and opens "cognitive and normative choices" (20). Today, people have little choice but to engage with others around issues of belief. Life "becomes an interminable process of redefining who the individual is in the context of the seemingly endless possibilities" (5). Even if one buys into a preexisting religious tradition, "the believing individual will face doubt" (31). This state of choice and identity formation can make people feel as if "nothing is certain, and there are no more reliable guides to how one ought to live" (8). The goal of religious pluralism, as with cosmopolitanism, is association and curiosity (Appiah 2016, 78):

> Conversations, across boundaries of identity—whether national, religious, or something else—begin with the sort of imaginative engagement you get when you read a novel or watch a movie or attend to a work of art that speaks from some place other than your own. . . . And I stress the role of the imagination here because the encounters, properly conducted, are valuable in themselves. Conversation doesn't have to lead to consensus about anything, especially not values; it's enough that it helps people get used to one another. (85)

Pluralism is practical. It consists of getting to know the people already around us, those we might otherwise brush past. It is driven by curiosity and care, not control.

Afrofuturism

Afrofuturism is speculative fiction that addresses African American concerns "in the context of twentieth century technoculture—and . . . appropriates images of technology and a prosthetically enhanced future" (Dery 1994, 180). It is "an intersection of imagination, technology, the future, and liberation" (Womack 2013, 9). Afrofuturism blends elements of science fiction, fantasy, historical fiction, and Afrocentricity. It "stretches the imagination far beyond the conventions of our time . . . and kicks the box of . . . preconceived ideas of blackness out of the solar system" (16). Using themes of alien abduction and time travel, Afrofuturists "unearth the missing history of people of African descent and their roles in science, technology, and science fiction" (17). For Afrofuturists, the desire to be free of society's restrictions is "like pixie dust sprinkled throughout the tracks" (57). The imagination is steered toward dreaming as an instigation of the possible.

Afrofuturism's biggest star is Janelle Monáe, a singer, dancer, producer, arranger, songwriter, painter, futurist, and world builder (Hassler-Forest 2017, 378). Monáe is a "contemporary griot, conjuring significant figures of black history" and linking the past to the present and future (Smith 2019, 38). This is a form of "hopeful worldbuilding" that sees the "revolutionary power of love"—especially self-love—as "the antidote to violent oppression" (39). In Afrofuturist science fiction, readers will find time travel, reincarnation, and even parallel universes to "supersede limitations of history while restoring power to both the narrative and its readers" (Womack 2013, 155). The "historical hot potato" of slavery is not erased or ignored but faced squarely as a source of profound loss and a desire for regeneration (157). Monáe's work is "sonic fiction" that "reimagines black life into the future" (Smith 2019, 31). For Monáe, music and sound can "counter the violence of the contemporary moment" (42).

Monáe's expression of Afrofuturism embraces elements of cosplay with her "coiffed 1950s pompadour and snug tuxedo" (Womack 2013, 74). In live performances, Monáe presents herself as a time traveler whose DNA was stolen for the creation of her "android alter-ego," Cindi Mayweather. Monáe has arrived by time machine while her android clone resides in a "post-apocalyptic dystopian future" (Hassler-Forest 2017, 384–385). Mayweather represents an oppressed "class of 'othered' bodies" and thus is an obvious reference to the experience of Black people in America (385). Monáe obscures the distinction between this world and the future to destabilize "subject and object, history and myth" (380).

Monáe's imagined world, Wondaland, has its own mythology, enacted via her songs, videos, album art, and public performances. In the futuristic performances of this mythology, Monáe's android alter ego is a "silver metallic-dipped android" working to free the city of Metropolis from its overlords (Womack 2013, 74). The year is 2719:

Mayweather's story begins with what Monáe calls her "geno-rape," a practice that links her to the history of the medical mistreatment of African Americans as demonstrated in the cases of the Tuskegee syphilis experiment and of Henrietta Lacks. . . . Yet black women have [nonetheless] staked claim to their bodies in a number of ways. . . . Monáe's Mayweather [is] a figure of fiction based in the social reality of black women's lived experience in a manner that highlights black women's embodiment as more than ephemeral material or disposable, excess flesh devoid of value. . . . As much as Mayweather taps into a future, her story consistently reminds us of its past. It is at this critical juncture between present and future that [Monáe as] the ArchAndroid emerges as a rogue rebel destined to preserve the representation of black women's humanity. (Smith 2019, 36)

Wondaland is "a refuge from the fictive city of Metropolis, a futuristic, dystopian place characterized by class division, oppression, and the delimiting of love as a forbidden emotion." Wondaland is real but can only be seen by closing your eyes because this blocks out "the world as it is . . . to invite a vision of future possibilities, especially amid a seemingly unbearable present" (35).

Monáe's Afrofuturism is shaped by the history of Black struggle: "the brutality of generations of enslavement, the violence of reconstruction and the Jim Crow South, to the ongoing crises of mass incarceration, over-policing, and police killings in the twentieth and twenty-first centuries" (35). Afrofuturism as an art form calls on the Black past to visualize a better future:

Faced with the historical brutality that has sought to dispossess and destroy black life through colonization and transatlantic slavery, black intellectuals, artists, and activists have been met with the exhausting task of overcoming material and intellectual challenges. . . . Like the rest of black expressive culture, Afrofuturism is informed by its conditions of imagination. Rather than providing escapism through idyllic fantasy, Monáe's vision of Wondaland offers strategies for persisting through the seemingly unlivable state of modern black life. (36)

The Afrofuturism of Monáe is a challenge to "white-centric traditions of worldbuilding" like the cowboy apocalypse. Her approach resists the logic of white supremacist patriarchy in favor of a different future (Hassler-Forest 2017, 378). Monáe's work is not just fictional; it *manifests* what it imagines. As a kind of faith, it is an "insistence that black life is possible in spite of anti-blackness, past and present" (Smith 2019, 31). Faith is not "a hoping for but a believing that the future imagined will come" (32). Worldbuilding has immense political implications, imagining how things *might* be, rather than how they are. To appreciate the "critical potential of imaginary worlds," we must look beyond transmedia forms neatly separated from our everyday world and look instead to worldbuilding as a radical practice (Hassler-Forest 2017, 382). By reimagining the history of slavery as well as the future of Black people in America, Monáe and other Afrofuturists "fracture the metaphysical model that has privileged one form of identity over another" (383). The whiteness (and maleness) of mainstream worldbuilding contrasts with Monáe's Black-centered creation. The story Monáe weaves in her music is "elliptical and endlessly ambiguous, evading straightforward storytelling" (384). By reimagining the past and invoking a new future, Afrofuturism destabilizes white supremacy in the present.

Otherwise

In 2015 at UC Riverside, the *Otherwise Worlds* conference was held to promote intellectual and political exchange between Black studies and Native studies. The participants recognized a kind of "stuckness" that was also an invitation to relationship (King, Navarro, and Smith 2020, 1). The relationship between Indigenous people and Black people in America is "not fixed and easily knowable" (2). They asked hard questions about the complexities of their relationship. Choosing conversation instead of argument, they engaged across differences without "the pretense of knowing" (6). The insights developed there are ones that non-Black, non-Native people can also consider, as we engage with our own whiteness.

Theologian J. Kameron Carter was there. In his writing for the conference, he identifies the world of white supremacy as a faulty human construct. He points to other, better worlds anterior to this one, prior, always underneath and beyond it. In Carter's view, worldbuilding is a flawed settler colonial concept. Visionaries can reject "that violent imposition of the [white supremacist, settler colonialist] World on top of the earth, the imposition of boundaried ownable place on top of open space" (2020, 164). The idea of the world *itself* is a construct. White supremacist patriarchy can claim ownership, but this is no less imaginary than any other form of worldbuilding.

By questioning the very notion of how we define the world, Carter invites a reconsideration of what it means to live in it and determine the value of others:

> I'm interested in how the notion of the sacred as it comes to be attached to the settler concept of World bespeaks a violent and general horror that, rather than disavowing malpractice, in fact calls for it, a relationship to the earth that exceeds and that is at the end of the (settler's) World and that refuses the very notion of World as an organizing and ordering concept. To dwell in the World's nullification gets close to what I am trying to get at with the idea of malpractice—the malpractice of the sacred or sacred malpractice. What if the malpractice of the sacred, the sacred as released or in flight from the World's enclosure, opens us to the question of otherwise worlds, otherworldly im/possibilities beyond the myth of the World, the mythos of politicality and of racial capitalism? What if malpractice takes us (to) nowhere? (163)

To go "nowhere" is a *good* thing. It takes us out of the world of white supremacy and into another. It is "malpractice" in the sense that it disrupts the practice of white supremacy. It is to embrace the sacred as something more than can be integrated into settler colonialism. It is the "excessive, ecstatic, or rapturous" that is "nonpossessable, a nonsubjective zone irreducible to property and thus irreducible to propertied subjectivity" (165). The "otherwise world" of Carter's "malpracticed" imagination cannot be stomped out by borders, boundaries, and walls.

He contrasts white supremacy with a liberated, liminal, dynamic view of Blackness. "This cosmicizing or would-be worlding of the earth into ownable, bordered territory entails the production and thus the imposition of spatial order" (172). The cure is "dark energy or promiscuous intensities." These energies are "out of this world" and constitute an "otherwise totality" drawn from the Black radical tradition (172). That which refuses to be contained offers a hope for the future that is not limited, not linear, not colonial, not sexist, not racist, not classist. That which has been dubbed monstrous by white supremacy is freed when it steps outside of the world that white supremacy has built.

Carter chucks the cowboy apocalypse like he chucks white supremacy, marking these institutional modes of violent control as a delusional spell. Carter also critiques capitalism, which is part of the white supremacy complex. Capitalism is a story we tell, with material consequences, that attempts to nullify Native rights to land and resources, Black people's rights to their own bodies, and women's right to independence. Carter's approach is haunted by zombies, though he doesn't use that language. White supremacists routinely pronounce Black culture and Indigenous culture dead, zombifying them. Carter's theoretical implosion of white supremacy offers an apt counterstory to the white male glorification of the cowboy apocalypse.

To think about "otherwise worlds" is more than an intellectual exercise. Carter plays with language to imagine a world that defies the limitations of language itself. He invokes a nowhere that is "anterior to interpellation" by white supremacy. This nowhere calls forth an "alternative imagination of matter everywhere" (158–159). By using the imagination to cancel out the imprint of white supremacy, Carter invites consideration of *another* way of being that—rather than coming *after* apocalypse—*already* lies beneath white patriarchy and its gobbling of life and land from others. This *nowhere* already exists. "Nullifying this world, blackness as numinous nod takes us to *Other Worlds*. Or perhaps even more rigorously put, it takes us *Nowhere*, to the sacred otherwise" (160). Blackness as Carter imagines it is an explosion of creativity that exposes white supremacy as the real zombie. Feminism offers a similar invitation to the bloom of possibility.

Carter considers the violent events of Charlottesville, Virginia, in August 2017. Drawing on a sermon by Reverend Bill Lamar about those shameful events, Carter borrows the term "malpractice," but invites his readers to question the state (162). To presume the state's authority is to presume the legitimacy of the social order, to presume it is valid and authoritative, that things *ought* to be this way. In imagining another way of being, Carter's "malpractice" is a critical diaspora that "animates Blackness precisely in its would-be corpsing" (164).

I am no longer sure who the zombies are—those imagined to be dangerous because they stand outside the walls and weep, or those who are so dead inside they choose not to hear them? Instead of offering a new way to be in community, the cowboy apocalypse perpetuates the same old saws. To be dehumanized at the end of a white man's gun is to be deemed a monster, and then to be killed for being one. Carter rejects such "corpsing" by rejecting the built world that defines such murder as righteous.

This is why Carter's use of the language of death is so powerful here. To commit "malpractice" is to voluntarily *make* oneself a corpse, a monster in the eyes of those who are losing their hold on power. The Black radical is a "monstrous" manifestation of the sacred, exuberant and unstoppable (164). Using language easily applied to zombies, Carter points to the "ceaseless volatility, in restless rupture and rapture" that is "harbinger of a sociality or congregationality . . . without limit or completion" (167). The cowboy messiah seeks to eliminate chaos. But those engaging in "malpractice" *seek out chaos* to undermine racist, settler presumptions. The settler state results from "efforts to arrest that antinomian something, that anoriginal chaos of foundations, by converting it into property" (168). And yet, even if stolen, Indigenous land *remains* Indigenous land. Even if corpsed, humans *remain* human. In Carter's approach, it is the settlers and murderers who are zombies: predatory and inhuman.

Carter asks: "What if we do not presume the World?" That is, what if we object to the world as given? The Charlottesville Black Lives Matter protestors are a "monstrous sign" but not monsters. Carter offers an alternative imaginary that releases the sacred from "settler logics of sovereignty," inducting a new "habit of otherworld assembling" (181). Worldbuilding can be a form of salvation. If the world we live in is driven by racism, misogyny, and colonial logic, then we ought to build a different world.

Conversation is the opposite of excommunication. Excommunication is erasure and silencing. It is a bullet, a border, a perimeter, barbed wire, a wall. It is a bunker. It is also broken treaties and refusing to teach critical race theory or Black history in schools. It is the erection of statues to Confederate heroes and the erasure of non-Christians. Excommunication, in whatever form, is a ritual of settler colonialism and white supremacy, the violent denial of conversation and the *refusal* to open possibilities. The approach evoked by the Otherwise Worlds conference is quite different:

> . . . to have the difficult conversations and to hear things from each other that may sound very critical of the presumptions we deem essential to our intellectual and political projects of survival. The only way for these conflicts to not have the last word is to go through them rather than to avoid them so that otherwise relationalities can emerge. (King et al. 2020, 8)

A conversation grounded in "otherwise relationalities" has no "presupposed endpoint" (9). Whereas traditional Christian communities focus on heaven as a means of imagining a beyond, the Otherwise Worlds conference conjured new "visualities and relations . . . outside of settler colonialism and the afterlife of slavery" (12). What would it mean to step outside the majoritarian stock story of a world claimed on the basis of racist myths? What does it mean to live an "otherwise life"? (13). And for readers like me who were raised in white culture, what would it look like to step outside of a world built on whiteness and settler colonialism? What would it mean to listen, be changed, and imagine things otherwise?

An otherwise ontology would reject the desecration of Michael Brown's impromptu memorial by the ruthless police officers who drove over it repeatedly. An otherwise approach would ask what it would look like to honor Native sovereignty. It would invite consideration of God's queerness and ask how this view challenges religious violence against LGBTQ people. The gun is a palpable relic of white supremacy, heteronormativity, and patriarchy. It is a one-man local tyranny and a tantrum not yet spent. The gun, by design and purpose, is a ritual refusal to engage in conversation. It has no curiosity.

To live an otherwise life is to imagine other stories for America, even those that dismantle the idea of America itself. White readers can ask, alongside Native and Black communities: "How do we guarantee an otherwise world for our children and their children?" (14). In an interview with the *Good Life Project*, Sikh author and activist Valarie Kaur talks about how wonder leads her actions in the world. She says:

> If I choose to see the world through the eyes of wonder, and if I choose to see you as a part of me I do not yet know . . . I must be open to hearing your story, to letting your grief in my heart, to fighting for you if you are in harm's way. That kind of love has always been disruptive, has always challenged the oppression of any era. What if we saw George Floyd as our brother and Brianna Taylor, a sister? A migrant child caged at the border as your own daughter? You know, what would we risk? How would we show up differently if even a fraction of that kind of energy we could bring to our labors in the world? (Kaur 2021)

An otherwise world enlists the imagination in the telling of a story with no predetermined ending.

Guns are no solution to unrest. They are just a shutting down. In her book *Emergent Strategy*, adrienne maree brown teaches us how to listen without recoil, backfire, and kick:

> [T]he whole universe might exist just to teach me more about love. I listen to strangers, I listen to random invitations, I listen to criticisms, I listen to my body, I listen to my creativity and to the artists who inspire me, I listen to elders, I listen to my dreams and the books I am reading. I notice that the more I pay attention, the more I see order, clear messages, patterns, and invitations in the small or seemingly random things that happen in my life. (2017, 8–9)

I am a white woman in the second half of her life. I do not own a gun, though I grew up around them in a world of white men with little use for me. I have no answers, but I am listening. I have only grief and two arms to carry what I can. I tell the story of the cowboy apocalypse here to expose and unravel it, using the tools at my disposal. I cannot say what will take its place. I only know that something must. With poet Erika Meitner, I say: "Holy moly, *please can we just keep driving.*"

EPILOGUE

ON "MADMEN"

Blaming people with mental illnesses for mass shootings is a form of scapegoating that valorizes "good guys with guns" by drawing on apocalyptic beliefs about good and evil. When we let religious belief shape policy, vulnerable people become props for other people's fantasies. The "good guy with a gun" shoots the "bad guy with a gun"—and Brandon Lynch is killed in the hallway of his own home while in desperate need of psychiatric care. Guillermo Medina is shot in the back while in a mental health crisis. Raul de la Cruz is shot less than a minute from when police arrive to help him and his family. Because people with mental illness are *already* defined as "evil" in the cowboy apocalypse script, their needs are often not taken seriously. The story of the "good guy with a gun" is a story of battle. It has no room for love and care, except perhaps for one's nearest and dearest. Everyone else is a potential enemy, a scavenger, a demon.

Instead of noting that *some* shooters *may* have a diagnosis of mental illness, we are supposed to believe that *all* people with mental illnesses could *all* become mass shooters. People suffering from mental illness are the "monsters" and "lunatics" Wayne LaPierre fears. The cowboy apocalypse targets the weakest people among us, those with the least ability to get appropriate healthcare, and stigmatizes them in the worst possible way. It is despicable. Even more so, since people with mental illnesses may have a harder time telling their own stories or—when they do tell them—being believed.

The few mass shootings conducted by people with mental illnesses are a boon for the gun lobby, who without them would have no "evil" enemy to blame. If shootings did not begin and end with apocalyptic storytelling and madmen, we could have conversations instead about rage, masculinity, domestic violence, background checks, and white supremacy. We could talk about poverty, homelessness, racism, police violence, and a militarized state. We could think about child abuse, school safety, equity in education, and social supports. We could talk about healthcare, including who gets it, who needs it, and why it costs too much. We could talk about social justice in real terms. We could talk about how many lives would be saved if guns weren't so easy to get. If *any* gun violence is caused by failing mental healthcare in the United States, then *anyone* opposed to gun violence should be fighting for universal, affordable healthcare for all. Mental healthcare is healthcare.

Nearly 4% of people in the world will experience some sort of psychotic episode in their lives. With a U.S. population of 330 million, that's over 13 million people—about the population of Pennsylvania. At any given time, over 3 million people in the United States are living with a diagnosis of schizophrenia and almost 6 million with bipolar disorder ("serious mental illness"). It is remarkably common. People with serious mental illnesses are more likely to be victims of violence (including police violence) than *cause* violence. And with a powerful gun lobby using struggling people as "proof" for their apocalyptic religious beliefs, we are unlikely to see meaningful changes in healthcare anytime soon. It is easier to blame a group that is already stigmatized, already suffering, already afraid than think about the troubling symbolic role that guns play in American society. Serious mental illness is one of the few disabilities left that we actively demonize. Guns are part of the reason why.

Ron Powers tells the gripping story of his sons' experiences with mental illness in *No One Cares about Crazy People*:

> To begin consciously searching into the world of mental illness is to see it snap into focus before your eyes. It is everywhere. It has been hiding in plain sight, awaiting notice. Its camouflage is little more than the human instinct to reject engagement with the pitiable, the fearsome, the unspeakable—and to close our eyes to the moral obligations that those states of being demand of us. To focus one's heart and consciousness on the mental illness is to see abstractions transmute to flesh and blood. (11)

People with mental illnesses are *people*, and they do not deserve to be scapegoated for the gun industry. What if gun violence is more complicated than "good guys" versus "bad guys"? What if we need more nuanced solutions than just killing the "bad guys"? There is a difference between a hard-nosed killer and someone suffering from an untreated brain disease. Why should good, law-abiding people who happen to live with mental illnesses be treated like criminals because a handful of people with mental illness (and many more people *without* mental illnesses) commit crimes?

Scholars of psychiatry who specialize in gun violence say that we "must abandon the starting assumption that acts of mass violence are driven primarily by diagnosable psychopathology in isolated 'lone wolf' individuals. The destructive motivations must be situated, instead, within larger social structures and cultural scripts" (Metzl et al., 2021). I agree, and I have set out here to expose one of the most powerful of those "cultural scripts," the cowboy apocalypse.

ACKNOWLEDGMENTS

This book was ten years in the making. Writing it is one of the hardest things I have ever done. Thank you to my partner, John Lasseter, for believing in me and for washing all those extra dishes. Huge thanks to Isaac Wagner for cooking so many delicious meals while I sat scribbling or typing through dinner. Thank you to Ithaca's robust folk music community for giving me a reason to put down my work and come play music every now and then. Thank you to Alder for your big smiles and infectious giggles. Thank you for the incredible kindness of friends who helped our family survive the hard times this past decade. You know who you are.

Thank you to the following students for reading and talking through early drafts with me, and for offering useful suggestions that were incorporated into the final copy: Cecil Decker, Olivia Acuna, Newt Andia, Hino Hinojosa, Vincent Kang, Zoe Williams, Colin Kelley, Gabrielle Santiago, Achille Ricca, Indiana Ward, Madeleine Martinez, Colin Cody, Luke Foley, Gianna Nigro, Cole Smith, Paul Winter, Patrick Kuehl, Kendall Martin, Dylan Haraden, Yair Assayag, Owen Dunn-Hindle, Shannon King, Matt Knutsen, Brennan Carney, and Michelle Pei. It would not be as good without you!

Mark Steen kindly read through a first whole draft and helped with organization and proofing. John Lasseter read so many drafts, and even helped with formatting. Colleagues and friends at conferences throughout the last decade have listened to me, read sections, and offered insights as this argument slowly took shape. I appreciate all of you. Thank you also to my anonymous reviewers for offering so many helpful suggestions! Thank you to Ithaca College for supporting my writing through the Robert Ryan Professorship, and for offsetting the cost of editing with a provost's mini-grant. Thank you to NYU Press for taking me on and being such a pleasure to work with. Thank you to Jill Swenson, who helped me with editing and assembling, fully believing in my project and giving so much of herself to make it happen.

And look, the work is far from finished. This is a book about big pain and about how America has failed too many people. I did not write this book for praise, recognition, forgiveness, or out of guilt, but to try to play a part—however small—in changing the story about America and guns. For anyone who has had their life radically changed by gun violence, I see you and I love you.

BIBLIOGRAPHY

Abramowitz, Rachel, and John Horn. "Post-9/11 Anxieties Influence Spate of Films." *Los Angeles Times*, January 29, 2005. Accessed July 7, 2023. www.latimes.com.

Abrams, Simon. "The Robert Kirkman Interview." *Comics Journal* no. 289 (2008): 41–96.

———. "Think *The Walking Dead* Has a Woman Problem? Here's the Source." *Houston Press*, April 4, 2013. Accessed July 26, 2023. www.houstonpress.com.

Adamkiewicz, Ewa A. "White Nostalgia: The Absence of Slavery and the Commodification of White Plantation Nostalgia." *aspeers: emerging voices in american studies* 9 (2016): 13–31. Accessed July 11, 2023. DOI: 10.54465/aspeers.09-03.

Allen, Ian. "The Far Right's Apocalyptic Literary Canon." *New Republic*, October 1, 2019. Accessed July 5, 2023. https://newrepublic.com.

Allison, Dorothy. "A Cure for Bitterness." In *Critical Trauma Studies: Understanding Violence, Conflict and Memory in Everyday Life*, edited by Monica J. Casper and Eric Wertheimer, 244–256. New York: New York University Press, 2016.

Almond, Gabriel A., R. Scott Appleby, and Emmanuel Sivan. *Strong Religion: The Rise of Fundamentalisms around the World*. Chicago: University of Chicago Press. 2003.

Alonso-Collada, Inés Ordiz. "Apocalyptic Visions of the Present: The Zombie Invasion in Post 9/11 American Cinema." *L'Atalante* 19 (January–June 2015): 111–117.

Alter, Robert. "The Apocalyptic Temper." *Commentary Magazine*, June 1, 1966. Accessed June 25, 2023. www.commentary.org.

Althaus-Reid, Marcella Maria. "Queer I Stand: Lifting the Skirts of God." In *Sexual Theologian: Essays on Sex, God and Politics*, edited by Marcella Maria Althaus-Reid and Lisa Isherwood, 99–109. New York: Bloomsbury, 2004.

Anderson, Joe, Deborah Durham, Niklas Hultin, Hugh Gusterson, and Charles Fruehling Springwood. "Debate." *Journal of Ethnographic Theory* 7, no. 3 (2017).

Anti-Defamation League. "The Great Replacement: An Explainer." April 19, 2021. Accessed July 5, 2023. www.adl.org.

Appadurai, Arjun. "Introduction: Commodities and the Politics of Value." In *The Social Life of Things: Commodities in Cultural Perspective*, edited by Arjun Appadurai, 3–63. Cambridge: Cambridge University Press, 1986.

———. *Modernity at Large: Cultural Dimensions of Globalization*. Reprint edition. Minneapolis: University of Minnesota Press, 1998.

Appiah, Kwame Anthony. *Cosmopolitanism: Ethics in a World of Strangers*. New York: Picador, 2016.

———. *As If: Idealization and Ideals*. Cambridge, MA: Harvard University Press, 2017.

Appleby, R. Scott. *The Ambivalence of the Sacred. Religion, Violence, and Reconciliation*. Lanham, MD: Rowman & Littlefield, 2000.

Askanius, Tina, and Nadine Keller. "Murder Fantasies in Memes: Fascist Aesthetics of Death Threats and the Banalization of White Supremacist Violence." *Information, Communication & Society* 24, no. 16 (2021): 2522–2539.

"Atari Trying to Halt X-Rated Video Games." *Ocala Star-Banner* (Ocala, FL), October 17, 1982, 8B.

Atkinson, Sarah. "Transmedia Film: From Embedded Engagement to Embodied Experience." In *The Routledge Companion to Transmedia Studies*, edited by Matthew Freeman and Renira Rampazzo Gambarato, 15–24. New York: Routledge, 2020.

Aune, David. *Prophecy in Early Christianity and the Ancient Mediterranean World*. Grand Rapids, MI: William B. Eerdman Publishing, 1983.

Baird, Stuart, dir. *Executive Decision*. Burbank, CA: Warner Brothers, 1996.

Baker, Kelly J. "The New White Nationalists?" *Religion and Politics*, October 20, 2016. Accessed July 5, 2023. https://religionandpolitics.org.

———. *The Zombies Are Coming: The Realities of the Zombie Apocalypse in American Culture*. Chapel Hill, NC: Blue Crow Books, 2020.

Barton, Robin. "Atrocity Sites Draw Crowds of Tourists." *New Zealand Herald*, June 2, 2001. Accessed July 11, 2023. www.nzherald.co.nz.

Bastardos. Videogame. Accessed July 8, 2023. www.freegameplanet.com.

Baudrillard, Jean. *The System of Objects*. Translated by James Benedict. New York: Verso Books, 1996.

Beam, Louis. *Essays of Klansman*. Hayden Lake, ID: A.K.I.A. Publications, 1983.

Beauvais, Camille. "Dark Tourism, 'Netflix Tourism': Stakes and Conflicts of Actors in Medellin." *Via Tourism Review* 22 (2022). Accessed July 11, 2023. https://journals.openedition.org.

Beck, Ulrich. *Cosmopolitan Vision*. Cambridge, UK: Polity Press, 2006.

———. "Critical Theory of World Risk Society: A Cosmopolitan Vision." *Constellations* 16, no. 1 (2009): 3–22.

Bell, Catherine. *Ritual Theory, Ritual Practice*. Oxford: Oxford University Press, 1992.

Bell, Derrick. "Who's Afraid of Critical Race Theory?" *University of Illinois Law Review* 1995, no. 4 (1995): 893–910.

Berger, James. *After the End: Representations of Post-Apocalypse*. Minneapolis: University of Minnesota Press, 1999.

Berger, Peter. *The Many Altars of Modernity: Toward a Paradigm for Religion in a Pluralist Age*. Berlin: De Gruyter, 2014.

Berry, Lorraine. "'The Walking Dead' Has Become a White Patriarchy." *Salon*, November 11, 2012. Accessed June 25, 2023. www.salon.com.

Bertelsmann Foundation. "The Boogaloo Ballad of Henry Graves." Polarization and Extremism Research and Innovation Lab. Center for University Excellence. American University, September 21, 2020. Accessed July 5, 2023. https://assets.ctfassets.net/9vgcz0fppkl3/6bXsq9LYP3zAO5t6fZ0sSf/f24d-7810b085abe37d220f602d7feb54/Boogaloo_Ballad_Education_Guide.pdf.

Bertetti, Paolo. "Transmedia Archaeology: Narrative Expansions across Media before the Age of Convergence." In *The Routledge Companion to Transmedia Studies*, edited by Matthew Freeman and Renira Rampazzo Gambarato, 263–271. New York: Routledge, 2020.

Bignell, Jonathan. *Big Brother: Reality TV in the Twenty-First Century*. Basingstoke, UK: Palgrave Macmillan, 2005.

Bilston, Brian. "America Is a Gun." Twitter post. February 17, 2016, 11:40 a.m. Accessed July 15, 2023. https://twitter.com/brian_bilston/status/700011838415704064.

Bogost, Ian. *Unit Operations: An Approach to Videogame Criticism*. Cambridge, MA: MIT Press, 2006.

———. *How to Do Things with Video Games*. Minneapolis: University of Minnesota Press, 2011.

Boni, Marta. *World Building: Transmedia, Fans, Industries*. Amsterdam: Amsterdam University Press, 2017.

Boym, Svetlana. *The Future of Nostalgia*. New York: Basic Books, 2001.

Brasher, Brenda E., and Lee Quinby. *Gender and Apocalyptic Desire*. New York: Routledge, 2014.

Braunstein, Ruth. "The 'Right' History: Religion, Race, and Nostalgic Stories of Christian America." *Religions* 12, no. 2 (2021): art. 95.

Brooks, Max. *World War Z: An Oral History of the Zombie War*. New York: Crown, 2006.

brown, adrienne maree. *Emergent Strategy: Shaping Change, Changing Worlds*. Chico, CA: AK Press, 2017.

Brown, Walter L. *Our Arkansas*. Austin, TX: Steck Company, 1958.

Burbick, Joan. "Cultural Anatomy of a Gun Show." *Stanford Law & Policy Review* 17, no. 3 (2006): 657–669.

Burley, Shane. *Why We Fight: Essays on Fascism, Resistance, and Surviving the Apocalypse*. Chico, CA: AK Press, 2021.

Burton, Tara Isabella. "Apocalypse Whatever: The Making of a Racist, Sexist Religion of Nihilism on 4Chan." *Real Life Mag*, December 13, 2016. Accessed July 8, 2023. https://reallifemag.com.

———. "How 'Joke Religion' Turns Deadly Serious When the Online Alt-Right Comes to Life." *Religion News*, May 14, 2019. Accessed July 5, 2023. https://religionnews.com.

Butnick, Stephanie. "Tourist Steals Barbed Wire from Auschwitz." *Tablet*, April 1, 2014. Accessed July 11, 2023. www.tabletmag.com.

Canavan, Gerry. "'We *Are* the Walking Dead': Race, Time, and Survival in Zombie Narrative." *Extrapolation* 51, no. 3 (2010): 431–453.

Carey, Greg. *Ultimate Things: An Introduction to Jewish and Christian Apocalyptic Literature*. St. Louis: Chalice Press, 2005.
Carlson, Jennifer. *Citizen-Protectors: The Everyday Politics of Guns in an Age of Decline*. Oxford: Oxford University Press, 2015.
Carter, J. Kameron. "Other Worlds, Nowhere (or the Sacred Otherwise)." In *Otherwise Worlds: Against Settler Colonialism and Anti-Blackness*, edited by Tiffany Lethabo King, Jenell Navarro, and Andrea Smith, 158–210. Durham, NC: Duke University Press, 2020.
Cave, J., and D. Buda. "Souvenirs in Dark Tourism: Emotions and Symbols." In *Handbook of Dark Tourism*, edited by P. Stone, R. Hartmann, T. Seaton, R. Sharpley, and L. White, 707–726. Basingstoke, UK: Palgrave Macmillan, 2016.
Centers for Disease Control and Prevention, Office of Public Health Preparedness and Response. *Preparedness 101: Zombie Pandemic*. Washington, DC: U.S. Government, 2011. https://stacks.cdc.gov/view/cdc/6023.
Chalk, Andy. "Trump: 'Violence on Videogames Is Really Shaping Young People's Thoughts'" (updated). *PC Gamer*, March 1, 2018. Accessed July 22, 2023. www.pcgamer.com.
Chang, Jeff. *We Gon' Be Alright: Notes on Race and Resegregation*. New York: Picador, 2016.
Choy, Edward. "Tilting at Windmills: The Theatricality of Role-Playing Games." In *Beyond Role and Play: Tools, Toys and Theory for Harnessing the Imagination*, edited by Markus Montola and Jaakko Stenros, 53–64. Helsinki: Ropecon, 2004.
Christensen, Doreen, and Skyler Swisher. "Selling Rocks from Stoneman Douglas Campus for $85? How 'Sick and Perverted' Souvenir Sellers Make 'Blood Money' Online." *Sun Sentinel* (South Florida), June 25, 2018. Accessed July 11, 2023. www.sun-sentinel.com.
Clark, Laurie Beth. "Coming to Terms with Trauma Tourism." *Performance Paradigm* 5, no. 2 (2009): 162–184.
Coates, James. *Armed and Dangerous: The Rise of the Survivalist Right*. New York: Farrar, Straus and Giroux, 1988.
Coates, Ta-Nehisi. *Between the World and Me*. New York: Spiegel & Grau, 2015a.
———. "There Is No Post-racial America." *The Atlantic*, July/August 2015b. Accessed July 20, 2023. www.theatlantic.com.
Collins, John J. *The Apocalyptic Imagination: An Introduction to Jewish Apocalyptic Literature*. Grand Rapids, MI: William B. Eerdmans Publishing, 1998.
Cornell, Saul, and Eric M. Rubin. "The Slave-State Origins of Modern Gun Rights." *The Atlantic*, September 30, 2015. Accessed June 23, 2023. www.theatlantic.com.
Couldry, Nick. *Media, Society, World: Social Theory and Digital Media Practice*. Oxford: Polity Press, 2013.
Courtwright, David T. *Violent Land: Single Men and Social Disorder from the Frontier to the Inner City*. Cambridge, MA: Harvard University Press, 2009.
Cox, Harvey. *The Future of Faith*. New York: HarperCollins, 2009.

Crogan, Patrick. *Gameplay Mode: War, Simulation, and Technoculture*. Minneapolis: University of Minnesota Press, 2011.
Daniels, Ted. "Charters of Righteousness: Politics, Prophets, and the Drama of Conversion." In *War in Heaven/Heaven on Earth: Theories of the Apocalyptic*, edited by Glen S. McGhee and Stephen D. O'Leary, 3–17. New York: Routledge, 2014.
D'Antonio, Michael. "Trumpland's Dangerous Role Playing Games." *CNN Opinion*, July 21, 2021. Accessed July 5, 2023. www.cnn.com.
Darabont, Frank, dir. *The Walking Dead*. New York: AMC Networks, 2010.
Dawson, Jennifer. "Shall Not Be Infringed: How the NRA Used Religious Language to Transform the Meaning of the Second Amendment." *Palgrave Communications* 5, no. 58 (2019). https://doi.org/10.1057/s41599-019-0276-z.
Davidson, Osha Gray. *Under Fire: The NRA and the Battle for Gun Control*. Iowa City: University of Iowa Press, 1998.
Deery, June. *Reality TV*. Oxford: Polity Press, 2015.
DeGiglio-Bellemare, Mario. "Land of the Dead." *Journal of Religion & Film* 9, no. 2 (2005): art. 10. Available at https://digitalcommons.unomaha.edu/jrf/vol9/iss2/10.
Delanty, Gerard. "The Cosmopolitan Imagination: Critical Cosmopolitanism and Social Theory." *British Journal of Sociology* 57, no. 1 (2006): 25–47.
Dery, Mark. "Black to the Future: Interviews with Samuel R. Delany, Greg Tate, and Tricia Rose." In *Flame Wars: The Discourse of Cyberculture*, edited by Mark Dery, 179–222. Durham, NC: Duke University Press, 1994.
Diamant, Jeff. "About Four-in-Ten U.S. Adults Believe Humanity Is 'Living in the End Times.'" Pew Research Center, December 8, 2022. Accessed July 21, 2023. www.pewresearch.org.
Dixon, Thomas. *The Clansman*. New York: Doubleday, Page & Co, 1905.
Dizard, Jan E., Robert Muth, and Stephen P. Andrews. *Guns in America: A Historical Reader*. New York: New York University Press, 1999.
Doss, Erika. "Spontaneous Memorials and Contemporary Modes of Mourning in America." *Material Religion* 2, no. 3 (2006): 294–318. https://doi.org/10.1080/17432200.2006.11423053.
Douglas, Kelly Brown. *Stand Your Ground: Black Bodies and the Justice of God*. Maryknoll, NY: Orbis Books, 2015.
Dudley, S. H., prf. "The Man behind the Gun." United States: E. Berliner's Gramophone, 1900. Audio. Accessed July 1, 2023. https://www.loc.gov/item/00580059.
Duggan, Patrick. "Rethinking Tourism: On the Politics and Practices of 'Staging' New Orleans," *Performance Research* 24, no. 5 (2019): 44–56.
Dunbar-Ortiz, Roxanne. *An Indigenous Peoples' History of the United States*. Boston: Beacon Press, 2014.
———. *Loaded: A Disarming History of the Second Amendment*. San Francisco: City Lights Books, 2018.

Durkheim, Émile. *Elementary Forms of Religious Life*. New York: Oxford University Press, 2001(1915).

Dyer-Witheford, Nick, and Greig de Peuter. *Games of Empire: Global Capitalism and Video Games*. Minneapolis: University of Minnesota Press, 2009.

Echols, John Warnock. "The Man behind the Gun: An Address by John Warnock Echols. Before the Historical Society of Fairfax County at Fairfax, Virginia on the Anniversary of Washington's Birthday." February 22, 1917. Washington, DC: Press of Judd & Detweiler, 1917. Accessed June 25, 2023. https://archive.org/details/themanbehindgun00echo/page/n3.

Eck, Diana. *Encountering God: A Spiritual Journey from Bozeman to Banaras*. Boston: Beacon Press, 2003.

Ehrenreich, Ben. "Why Did We Focus on Securing Haiti Rather than Helping Haitians?" *Slate*, January 21, 2010. Accessed June 23, 2023. https://slate.com.

Eliade, Mircea. *The Myth of the Eternal Return: Cosmos and History*. Princeton, NJ: Princeton University Press, 1971.

Fahey, Richard. "Marauders in the US Capitol: Alt-Right Viking Wannabes & Weaponized Medievalism." *Medieval Studies Research Blog*. University of Notre Dame, January 15, 2021. Accessed July 5, 2023. https://sites.nd.edu.

Falk, Jennica, and Glorianna Davenport. "Live Role-Playing Games: Implications for Ubiquitous Computer Game Interfaces." *Interactive Cinema: Media Fabrics*. MIT Conference Proceedings. ICEC September 1–4, 2004: International Conference on Entertainment Computing No. 3, Eindhoven. Accessed July 5, 2023. https://mf.media.mit.edu.

Fantz, Ashley, and Brandon Griggs. "NRA Draws Heat over Its New Shooting Game." *CNN*, January 16, 2013. Accessed July 22, 2023. www.cnn.com.

Federal Bureau of Investigation. "The Covenant, the Sword, the Arm of the Lord CSA." File 100-HQ-487200. Kansas City, MO: Department of Justice, Federal Bureau of Investigation. July 2, 1982. Accessed July 18, 2023. https://vault.fbi.gov/The%20Covenant%20The%20Sword%20The%20Arm%20of%20the%20Lord%20/The%20Covenant%20The%20Sword%20The%20Arm%20of%20the%20Lord%20Part%201%20of%202.

Finkelstein, Norman G. *The Holocaust Industry: Reflections on the Exploitation of Jewish Suffering*. New York: Verso Books, 2000.

Fleischer, Ruben, dir. *Zombieland*. Culver City, CA: Columbia Pictures, 2009.

Foley, Malcolm, and J. John Lennon. "Editorial: Heart of Darkness." *International Journal of Heritage Studies* 2, no. 4 (1996): 195–197.

Forstchen, William R. *One Second After*. New York: Forge Books, 2009.

Fox, Mira. "Why Conspiracy Theorists Keep Turning to Jewish Mysticism—From Early Nazis to Modern-Day MAGA." *Forward*, August 15, 2022. Accessed July 5, 2023. https://forward.com.

Frank, Pat. *Alas, Babylon*. New York: J. B. Lippincott, 1959.

Field Manual of the Free Militia. Foreword by Skipp Porteus. Great Barrington, MA: Riverwalk Press, 1994.

Freeman, Matthew, and Renira Rampazzo Gambarato. "Introduction: Transmedia Studies—Where Now?" In *The Routledge Companion to Transmedia Studies*, edited by Matthew Freeman and Renira Rampazzo Gambarato, 1–12. New York: Routledge, 2020.

Galison, Peter. "The Ontology of the Enemy: Norbert Wiener and the Cybernetic Vision." In *The Search for a Theory of Cognition*, edited by Stefano Franchi and Francesco Bianchini, 53–87. Leiden, Netherlands: Brill Academic, 2011.

Galloway, Alexander R., Eugene Thacker, and McKenzie Wark. *Excommunication: Three Inquiries in Media and Mediation*. Chicago: University of Chicago Press, 2013.

Gandasegui, Vicente Diaz. "Spectators after 9/11: This Is (Not) Like a Hollywood Film." Paper presented at the conference Representing the War on Terror: Post 9/11 Television Drama and Documentary, at the ATRiuM, CCI, University of Glamorgan, Cardiff. Saturday November 21, 2009. Open Access. University of Madrid. http://hdl.handle.net/10016/11279.

Gear, W. Michael. *Dissolution*. Book 1 in *The Wyoming Chronicles* series. Las Vegas: Wolfpack Publishing, 2021.

Geertz, Clifford. *Interpretation of Cultures*. New York: Basic Books, 1973.

Gentile, Douglas A. "The Multiple Dimensions of Video Game Effects: Video Game Effects." *Child Development Perspectives* 5, no. 2 (2011): 75–81.

Geraghty, Lincoln. *Cult Collectors: Nostalgia, Fandom and Collecting Popular Culture*. New York: Routledge, 2014.

Gertz, Matt. "NRA Blames Violent Films for Mass Shootings, but Their Museum Features 'Hollywood Guns.'" *Media Matters*, January 2, 2013. Accessed June 28, 2023. www.mediamatters.org.

Gibbs, Nancy. "Murder in the House: Shots, Screams and Heroism as a Gunman Invades the Capitol." *Time*, August 3, 1998.

Giglio, Mike. "The Lonely Revolutionary: Oath Keepers Stewart Rhodes Has Made His Worst Fears Come True." *The Intercept*, March 8, 2022. Accessed July 5, 2023. https://theintercept.com.

Giles, Doug. *A Time to Clash: Papers from a Provocative Paster*. Irving, TX: Town Hall Press, 2007.

Goebbels, Joseph. "Nun, Volk steh auf, und Sturm brich los! Rede im Berliner Sportpalast." *Der steile Aufstieg* (Munich: Zentralverlag der NSDAP), 1944, 167–204. Accessed July 8, 2023. https://research.calvin.edu.

George, Robert. "Author's Call to Arms Gets Answer." In *Guns in America: A Historical Reader*, edited by Jan E. Dizard, Robert Muth, and Stephen P. Andrews, 441–443. New York: New York University Press, 1999.

Goethels, Gregor. *The TV Ritual: Worship at the Video Altar*. Boston: Beacon Press, 1981.

———. "Ritual: Ceremony and Super-Sunday." From Goethals, *The TV Ritual*, reprinted in *Readings in Ritual Studies*, edited by Ronald L. Grimes, 257–268. Hoboken, NJ: Prentice Hall, 1995.

Golan, Menahem, dir. *The Delta Force*. Beverly Hills, CA: Metro-Goldwyn-Mayer, 1986.

Gordon, Beverly. "The Souvenir: Messenger of the Extraordinary." *Journal of Popular Culture* 20, no. 3 (1986): 135–146.

Gorski, Philip S., and Samuel L. Perry. *The Flag and the Cross: White Christian Nationalism and the Threat to American Democracy*. New York: Oxford University Press, 2022.

Greeley, Horace. *An Overland Journey, from New York to San Francisco in the Summer of 1859*. Michigan Historical Reprint Series. Scholarly Publishing Office, University of Michigan Library, 2006.

Green, John, and Michaela D. E. Meyer. "The Walking (Gendered) Dead: A Feminist Rhetorical Critique of Zombie Apocalypse Television Narrative." *Ohio Communication Journal* 52 (2014): 64–74.

Gregersen, Andreas, and Torben Grodal. "Embodiment and Interface." In *The Video Game Theory Reader 2*, edited by Bernard Perron and Mark J. P. Wolf, 65–83. New York: Routledge, 2009.

Griffith, Justin. "How Nat Geo Misrepresented the Foxhole Atheist 'Doomsday Prepper,' Megan Hurwitt." Interview with Megan Hurwitt, February 8, 2012. Accessed through the Internet Archive Wayback Machine July 26, 2023. http://freethoughtblogs.com.

Grossman, Dave, and Gloria DeGaetano. *Stop Teaching Our Kids to Kill: A Call to Action against TV, Movie & Video Game Violence*. New York: Crown, 1999.

Gun Violence Archive. "Past Summary Ledgers." Accessed January 23, 2024. https://www.gunviolencearchive.org/past-tolls.

Gutierrez, Cathy. "The Millennium and Narrative Closure." In *War in Heaven/Heaven on Earth: Theories of the Apocalyptic*, edited by Stephen O'Leary and Glenn McGhee, 47–60. Millennialism and Society Series, Vol. 2. New York: Routledge, 2005.

Halter, Ed. *From Sun Tzu to Xbox: War and Video Games*. New York: Thunder's Mouth Press, 2006.

Hamilton, Kirk. "Real Guns, Virtual Guns, and Me." *Kotaku*, March 29, 2018. Accessed July 8, 2023. https://kotaku.com.

Hantke, Steffen. "Historicizing the Bush Years: Politics, Horror Film, and Francis Lawrence's I Am Legend." In *Horror after 9/11: World of Fear, Cinema of Terror*, edited by Aviva Briefel and Sam J. Miller, 165–185. Austin: University of Texas Press, 2011.

Harding, Tobias. "Immersion Revisited: Role-Playing as Interpretation and Narrative." In *Lifelike*, edited by Jesper Donnis, Morten Gade, and Line Thorup, 25–33. Copenhagen: Projektgruppen KP07, 2007. In conjunction with the Knudepunkt 2007 conference.

Harjo, Joy. "Everybody Has a Heartache: A Blues." *Poetry*, March 2014. Accessed July 11, 2023. www.poetryfoundation.org.

Harroway, Donna. *Staying with the Trouble: Making Kin in the Chthulucene*. Durham, NC: Duke University Press, 2016.

Harviainen, J. Tuomas. "Kaprow's Scions." In *Playground Worlds: Research and Theory*, edited by Markus Montola and Jaake Stenros, 216–231. Helsinki: Ropecon, 2008.

———. "A Hermeneutical Approach to Role-Playing Analysis." *International Journal of Role-Playing* 1 (2009): 66–78. doi:10.33063/ijrp.vi1.188.

Hassanein, Nada. "Young Black Men and Teens Are Killed by Guns 20 Times More than Their White Counterparts, CDC Data Shows." *USA Today*, February 23, 2021. Accessed July 11, 2023. www.usatoday.com.

Hassler-Forest, Dan. "The Politics of World Building: Heteroglossia in Janelle Monae's Afrofuturist WondaLand." In *World Building: Transmedia, Fans, Industries*, edited by Marta Boni, 377–391. Amsterdam: Amsterdam University Press, 2017.

Healy, Patrick O'Gilfoil. "Run! Hide! The Illegal Border Crossing Experience." *New York Times*, February 4, 2007. Accessed July 28, 2023. www.nytimes.com.

Heller, Peter. *The Dog Stars*. New York: Vintage Books, 2012.

Henry, Pat. "Doomsday Preppers Shows the Dark Side of Survival." *Prepper Journal*, November 14, 2013. Accessed June 20, 2023. https://theprepperjournal.com.

Hill, Annette. *Reality TV*. New York: Routledge, 2014.

Hills, Matt. "From Dalek Half Balls to Daft Punk Helmets: Mimetic Fandom and the Crafting of Replicas." In "Materiality and Object-Oriented Fandom," edited by Bob Rehak. Special issue, *Transformative Works and Cultures* 16 (2014). Accessed July 5, 2023. https://doi.org/10.3983/twc.2014.0531.

Hochschild, Arlie Russell. *Strangers in Their Own Land*. New York: New Press, 2016.

Hoffman, Bruce. "A Year after January 6, Is Accelerationism the New Terrorist Threat?" *Council on Foreign Relations*, January 5, 2022. Accessed July 5, 2023. www.cfr.org.

Holter, Matthijs. "Stop Saying 'Immersion!'" In *Lifelike*, edited by Jesper Donnis, Morten Gade, and Line Thorup, 19–24. Copenhagen: Projektgruppen KP07, 2007. In conjunction with the Knudepunkt 2007 conference.

Hood, Jeff. "Praying for the Apocalypse: The Queerness of Revelation." *Patheos*, December 31, 2018. Accessed July 3, 2023. www.patheos.com.

hooks, bell. "bell hooks: Cultural Criticism & Transformation." Interview with bell hooks. Media Education Foundation. Transcript. Produced and directed by Sut Jhally, edited by Mary Patierno, Sut Jhally and Harriet Hirshorn, editing and production assistance by Sanjay Talreja, 1997. Accessed July 9, 2023. https://www.mediaed.org/transcripts/Bell-Hooks-Transcript.pdf.

Hoover, Stewart M., and Curtis D. Coats. *Does God Make the Man?: Media, Religion, and the Crisis of Masculinity*. New York: New York University Press, 2015.

Hosley, William. *Colt: The Making of an American Legend*. Amherst: University of Massachusetts Press, 1996.

Huizinga, Johan. *Homo Ludens: A Study of the Play Element in Culture*. Boston: Beacon Press, 1955.

Hunter, Stephen. "Hollywood Guns: Behind the Curtain." *American Rifleman*, 2010. Accessed May 26, 2023. www.americanrifleman.org.

Hupp, Suzanna. "30 Years Ago, She Survived a Mass Shooting. Now, She Advocates for Concealed Carry." *Weekend Edition Saturday*, Scott Simon, host, National Public Radio. May 28, 2022. Accessed July 21, 2023. www.npr.org.

Hutcheon, Linda. *A Theory of Adaptation*, 2nd ed. New York: Routledge, 2012.
Indiana State Teachers Association. Twitter post. March 20, 2019, 4:13 p.m. https://twitter.com/ISTAmembers/status/1108461641400807424.
Infinity Ward. *Call of Duty 4: Modern Warfare*. Videogame, 2007.
Institute for Strategic Dialogue. "The Boogaloo Movement." London: Institute for Strategic Dialogue, 2020. Accessed July 21, 2023. www.isdglobal.org.
Ioanide, Paula. "Apocalyptic Fears in a Time of Dying (of) Whiteness." *Journal of Speculative Philosophy* 35, no. 4 (2021): 323–348.
Isaac, Rami K. "Every Utopia Turns into Dystopia." *Tourism Management* 51 (2015): 329–330.
Jacobson, Louis. "Video of Barack Obama Speech Circulating on the Internet Was Edited to Change His Meaning." Politifact: Poynter Institute, June 23, 2014. Accessed July 27, 203. www.politifact.com.
Jenkins, Henry. "Transmedia Storytelling 101." *Henry Jenkins Confessions of an Aca-Fan* (blog). March 21, 2007. http://henryjenkins.org.
The John Franklin Letters. Belmont, MA: John Birch Society, 1959.
Jones, Robert P. *White Too Long: The Legacy of White Supremacy in American Christianity*. New York: Simon & Schuster, 2020.
Jones, Serene. *Trauma and Grace: Theology in a Ruptured World*. Louisville, KY: Westminster John Knox, 2009.
Joustra, Robert, and Alissa Wilkinson. *How to Survive the Apocalypse: Zombies, Cylons, Faith, and Politics at the End of the World*. Grand Rapids, MI: William B. Eerdmans Publishing, 2016.
Juul, Jesper. *Half-Real: Video Games Between Real Rules and Fictional Worlds*. Cambridge, MA: MIT Press, 2005.
Kahler, Kathryn. "Americans Love Their Guns but Fear Violence." In *Guns in America: A Historical Reader*, edited by Jan E. Dizard, Robert Muth, and Stephen P. Andrews, 158–161. New York: New York University Press, 1999.
Kakutani, Michiko. *The Death of Truth: Notes on Falsehood in the Age of Trump*. New York: Tim Duggan Books, 2018.
Kamm, Björn-Ole, and Julia Becker. "Live-Action Roleplay; or the Performance of Realities." In *Simulation and Gaming in the Network Society*, edited by Toshiyuki Kanada, Hidehiko Kanegae, and Yusuke Toyoda, 35–51. Translational Systems Sciences 9. New York: Springer, 2016.
Kaplan, Ann E. *Trauma Culture: The Politics of Terror and Loss in Media and Literature*. New Brunswick, NJ: Rutgers University Press, 2005.
Kaur, Valarie. "Valarie Kaur: A Revolutionary Love." Interview. Good Life Project. September 13, 2021. Accessed July 5, 2023. www.goodlifeproject.com.
Kavanaugh, Jennifer, and Michael D. Rich. *Truth Decay: An Initial Exploration of the Diminishing Role of Facts and Analysis in American Public Life*. Santa Monica, CA: Rand Corporation, 2018.
Keen, Judy, and Andrea Stone. "This Month's Mass Killings a Reminder of Vulnerability." *USA Today*, December 20, 2007. Accessed July 18, 2023. http://usatoday30.usatoday.com.

Keller, Catherine. *God and Power: Counter Apocalyptic Journeys*. Minneapolis, MN: Augsburg Fortress, 2005.

Keller, Larry. "The Second Wave." In *The Second Wave: Return of the Militias*, 5–10. Montgomery, AL: Southern Poverty Law Center, 2009. Accessed July 1, 2023. www.splcenter.org.

Kellner, Douglas. "Social Memory and the Representation of 9/11 in Contemporary Hollywood Film." *Spiel* 24, no. 2 (2005a): 349–362.

———. "Media, Culture and the Triumph of the Spectacle." In *The Spectacle of the Real: From Hollywood to "Reality" TV and Beyond*, edited by Geoff King, 25–36. Bristol, UK: Intellect, 2005b.

Kelly, Casey Ryan. "The Man-Pocalpyse: Doomsday Preppers and the Rituals of Apocalyptic Manhood." *Text and Performance Quarterly* 36, no. 2–3 (2016): 95–114.

Kermode, Frank. *The Sense of an Ending: Studies in the Theory of Fiction*, 2nd ed. New York: Oxford University Press, 2000 (1967).

Kertzer, David I. *Ritual, Politics, and Power*. New Haven, CT: Yale University Press, 1988.

King, Geoff. *The Spectacle of the Real: From Hollywood to Reality TV and Beyond*. Bristol, UK: Intellect, 2005.

King, Robin Levinson. "100 Years Later, Extravagant Cruise Recreates the Titanic's Voyage." *National Post*, April 10, 2012. Accessed July 11, 2023. https://nationalpost.com.

King, Stephen. *The Stand*, complete and uncut ed. New York: Doubleday, 1978.

King, Tiffany Lethabo, Jenell Navarro, and Andrea Smith. "Beyond Incommensurability: Toward an Otherwise Stance on Black and Indigenous Relationality." In *Otherwise Worlds: Against Settler Colonialism and Anti-Blackness*, edited by Tiffany Lethabo King, Jenell Navarro, and Andrea Smith, 1–23. Durham, NC: Duke University Press, 2020.

King, Wayne. "Officers Searching Sections of Survivalists' Compound." *New York Times*, April 22, 1985, A12.

Kirkman, Robert. *The Walking Dead*. 1. Portland, OR: Image Comics, 2003.

Kirkman, Robert, Tony Moore, and Charlie Adlard. *The Walking Dead*. Developed by Frank Darabont. New York: AMC, October 31, 2010–November 20, 2022; 11 seasons, 177 episodes.

Kirkpatrick, David D. "Wrath and Mercy; The Return of the Warrior Jesus." *New York Times*, April 4, 2004. Accessed July 17, 2023. www.nytimes.com.

Kirmayer, Laurence J. "Landscapes of Memory." In *Tense Past: Cultural Essays in Trauma and Memory*, edited by Paul Anze and Michael Lambek, 172–198. New York: Routledge, 1996.

Klasfeld, Adam. "Virginia Man in 'TEAM TRUMP' Cowboy Hat Charged with Assaulting Police with Chemical Spray at the U.S. Capitol on Jan. 6." *Law and Crime*, January 26, 2022. Accessed July 5, 2023. https://lawandcrime.com.

Klein, Nick. "The 'Reality' of Reality TV: Doomsday Preppers." *Hostile Hare*, August 5, 2012. Accessed July 27, 2023. www.hostilehare.com.

Kobes Du Mez, Kristin. *Jesus and John Wayne*. New York: Liveright Publishing, 2021.
Koren-Kuik, Meyrav. "Desiring the Tangible: Disneyland, Fandom and Spatial Immersion." In *Fan Culture: Essays on Participatory Fandom in the 21st Century*, edited by K. M. Barton and J. M. Lampley, 146–158. Jefferson, NC: McFarland & Co., 2013.
Kornhaber, Spencer. "The Superhero Fantasies of Trump's Mob." *The Atlantic*, January 8, 2021. www.theatlantic.com.
Kraus, Mike. *The End of All Things*. Independently published, 2023.
Kriner, Matthew, and Colin P. Clarke. "Eclectic Boogaloo: The Anti-government Extremist Movement's Loose Structure and Adaptability Is the Key to Its Growth." *Slate*, August 19, 2020. Accessed July 5, 2023. https://slate.com.
Kunstler, James Howard. *World Made by Hand*. New York: Grove Press/Atlantic Monthly Press, 2008.
LaCapra Dominick. *Writing History, Writing Trauma*. Baltimore: Johns Hopkins University Press, 2001.
Lahti, Martti. "As We Become Machines: Corporealized Pleasures in Video Games." In *The Video Game Theory Reader*, edited by Mark J. P. Wolf and Bernard Perron, 157–170. New York: Routledge, 2003.
LaHaye, Tim, and Jerry B. Jenkins. *The Left Behind Collection*. Carol Stream, IL: Tyndale House, 2014 (1995).
Landes, Richard. "Roosters Crow, Owls Hoot: On the Dynamics of Apocalyptic Millennialism." In *War in Heaven/Heaven on Earth: Theories of the Apocalyptic*, edited by Stephen D. O'Leary and Geln S. McGhee. 19–46. Sheffield, UK: Equinox Publishing, 2005.
Lane, Anthony. "This Is Not a Movie." *New Yorker*, September 16, 2001, 79.
LaPierre, Wayne. *Safe: The Responsible American's Guide to Home and Family Security*. Washington, DC: WND Books, 2010.
———. "Transcript of NRA Press Conference." December 21, 2012. Accessed July 17, 2023. https://whnt.com/news/transcript-of-nra-press-conference.
———. "Stand and Fight." *Daily Caller*. February 13, 2013a. Accessed July 22, 2023. https://dailycaller.com.
———. Annual Members Meeting, NRA, Houston: May 2–5, 2013b. Accessed July 22, 2023. https://www.youtube.com/watch?v=iJQqr8PpG98.
———. 2014 American Conservative Union: Conservative Political Action Committee Conference. Address. March 6, 2014a. Accessed July 22, 2023. https://www.youtube.com/watch?v=z87ehuPU22I.
———. 2014 NRA Members Meeting. Videorecording. Fairfax, VA: NRA, 2014b. Accessed July 19, 2023. https://www.youtube.com/watch?v=BCFB0N_jzMk.
———. 2016 American Conservative Union: Conservative Political Action Committee. Address. 2016a. Accessed July 22, 2023. https://www.c-span.org/video/?c4598939/nra.
———. *Face the Nation*. Interview broadcast June 19, 2016b. Accessed July 19, 2023. https://www.cbsnews.com/news/transcript-wayne-lapierre-on-face-the-nation-oct-8-2017.

———. Annual Members Meeting. NRA, Orlando, FL: April 24–27, 2003. Accessed July 22, 2023. https://www.c-span.org/video/?176428-3/national-rifle-association-annual-meeting.

Lappi, Ari-Pekka. "Playing Beyond Facts: Immersion as a Transformation of Everydayness." In *Lifelike*, edited by Jesper Donnis, Morten Gade, and Line Thorup, 75–82. Copenhagen: Projektgruppen KP07, 2007. In conjunction with the Knudepunkt 2007 conference.

Latour, Bruno. "On Technical Mediation: Philosophy, Sociology, Genealogy." *Common Knowledge* 3, no. 2 (1994): 29–64.

———. "A Collective of Humans and Non-humans Following Daedalus' Labyrinth." In *Pandora's Hope: Essays on the Reality of Science Studies*, 174–215. Cambridge, MA: Harvard University Press, 1999.

———. "The Berlin Key or How to Do Words with Things." In *Matter, Materiality and Modern Culture*, edited by Paul Graves-Brown, 10–21. New York: Routledge, 2000.

LeBlanc, Amanda K. 2014. "The Future Looks Awfully Familiar: Gendered Representations in Popular Dystopian Television." Master's thesis, University of Colorado at Boulder, 2014.

Leddy, Edward. *Magnum Force Lobby*. Lanham, MD: University Press of America, 1987.

Ledonne, Danny, dir. *Playing Columbine: A True Story of Video Game Controversy*. Washington, DC: Emberwilde Productions, 2008.

Leggatt, Matthew. "Melancholic and Hungry Games: Post-9/11 Cinema and the Culture of Apocalypse." In *Popping Culture*, 7th ed., edited by Murray Pomerance and John Sakeris, 325–333. Carmel, IN: Pearson Learning, 2012.

———. "You Gotta Keep the Faith: Making Sense of Disaster in Post 9/11 Apocalyptic Cinema." *Journal of Religion and Film* 19, no. 2 (2015): art. 6.

Lepore, Jill. "The Long Blue Line: Inventing the Police." *New Yorker*, July 20, 2020. Accessed July 11, 2023. www.newyorker.com.

Lichtblau, Eric, and Motoko Rich. "N.R.A. Envisions 'a Good Guy with a Gun' in Every School." *New York Times*, December 21, 2012. Accessed July 17, 2023. www.nytimes.com.

Lincoln, Andrew. "'The Walking Dead' Signed Replica Prop Python Revolver JSA Cert." eBay listing. Accessed June 25, 2023. www.ebay.com.

Lindsey, Hal. *The Late Great Planet Earth*. Grand Rapids, MI: Zondervan, 1970.

Loadenthal, Michael, Samantha Hausserman, and Matthew Thierry. "Accelerating Hate: Atomwaffen Division, Contemporary Digital Fascism, and Insurrectionary Accelerationism." In *Cyber Hate: Examining the Functions and Impact of White Supremacy in Cyberspace*, edited by Robin Maria Valeri and Kevin Borgeson, 87–118. Lanham, MD: Lexington Books, 2022.

Lockett, Christopher. "Why It's Grim, but Unsurprising, That the U.S. Capitol Attack Looked Like It Was Out of a 'Zombie Movie.'" *The Conversation*, January 4, 2022. Accessed July 5, 2023. https://theconversation.com.

Lukka, Lauri. "The Psychology of Immersion." In *The Cutting Edge of Nordic Larp*, edited by Jon Back, 81–92. Halmstad, Sweden: Knutpunkt, 2014.

MacDonald, Dennis Ronald. *There Is No Male and Female: The Fate of a Dominical Saying in Paul and Gnosticism*. Harvard Dissertations in Religion. Philadelphia: Fortress Press, 1987.

Maçães, Bruno. "The Role Playing Coup." *City Journal*, January 7, 2021. Accessed July 5, 2023. www.city-journal.org.

"The Man behind the Gun." *Arms and the Man* 69, no. 1 (1908): 12.

Mandylor, Louis, dir. *The Blackout*. Beverly Hills, CA: Charlemont Pictures, 98 Films, and EchoWolf Productions, 2014.

Martin, Adam, ed. "Alternate Reality Games White Paper." International Game Developers Association. IGDA Alternate Reality Games Scientific Interest Group, 2006. Accessed July 5, 2023. www.christydena.com.

Martin, Russell. *Cowboy: The Enduring Myth of the Wild West*. New York: Stewart, Tabori and Chang, 1983.

Martinez, Aja. "Counterstory: The Rhetoric and Writing of Critical Race Theory." Conference on College Composition and Communication, National Council of Teachers of English, Champaign, IL, 2020.

Marty, Martin E., and R. Scott Appleby. "Introduction." In *Fundamentalisms and Society: Reclaiming the Sciences, the Family, and Education*, edited by Martin E. Marty and R. Scott Appleby, 1–19. Chicago: University of Chicago Press, 1993.

McFadden, Robert. "Tim LaHaye Dies at 90; Fundamentalist Leader's Grisly Novels Sold Millions." *New York Times*, July 25, 2016. Accessed January 23, 2024. www.nytimes.com.

McGonigal, Jane. "A Real Little Game: The Performance of Belief in Pervasive Play." Conference Paper. Digital Games Research Association Conference Proceedings, Utrecht, Netherlands, November 2003. Accessed July 5, 2023. www.avantgame.com.

McIntyre, Lee. *Post-Truth*. Cambridge, MA: MIT Press, 2018.

McSweeney, Terence. "Decade of the Dead: Zombie Films as Allegory of National Trauma." *The War on Terror and American Film: 9/11 Frames per Second*. Edinburgh: Edinburgh University Press, 2014.

McTiernan, John, dir. *Die Hard*. Los Angeles: 20th Century Fox, 1988.

Mead, Corey. *War Play: Video Games and the Future of Armed Conflict*. New York: Eamon Dolan/Houghton, Mifflin, Harcourt, 2013.

Mechling, Jay. "Gun Play." *American Journal of Play* 1, no. 2 (2008): 192–209.

Meier, Barry, and Andrew Martin. "Real and Virtual Firearms Nurture a Marketing Link." *New York Times*, December 24, 2012.

Meitner, Erika. *Holy Moly Carry Me*. Rochester, NY: BOA Editions, Ltd., 2018.

Melzer, Scott. *Gun Crusaders: The NRA's Culture War*. New York: New York University Press, 2012.

Metzl, Jonathan M., Jennifer Piemonte, and Tara McKay. *Harvard Review of Psychiatry* 29, no. 1 (2021): 81–89. https://pubmed.ncbi.nlm.nih.gov/33417376.

Meyer, Birgit. "Picturing the Invisible." *Method and Theory in the Study of Religion* 27, no. 4–5 (2015): 333–360.

———. "Religion as Mediation." *Entangled Religions* 11, no. 3 (2020). Accessed July 11, 2023. https://doi.org/10.13154/er.11.2020.8444.

Miles, Tiya. *Tales from the Haunted South: Dark Tourism and Memories of Slavery from the Civil War Era*. Chapel Hill: University of North Carolina Press, 2015.

Miller, Toby. "The Media-Military Industrial Complex." In *The Global Industrial Complex: Systems of Domination*, edited by Steven Gest, Richard Kahn, Anthony J. Nocella II, and Peter McClaren, 97–115. Lanham, MD: Lexington Books, 2011.

Miller-Idriss, Cynthia. "White Supremacist Extremism and the Far Right in the U.S." *Political Extremism and Radicalism: Far-Right Groups in America*, Boston: Cengage Learning EMEA, 2021. Accessed July 5, 2023. www.gale.com.

Mirrlees, Tanner. "*Medal of Honor: Operation Anaconda*: Playing the War in Afghanistan," *Democratic Communiqué* 26, no. 2 (2014): art. 6.

Mitchell, Richard G. "Secrecy and Disclosure in Fieldwork." In *Experiencing Fieldwork: An Inside View of Qualitative Research*, edited by W. B. Shaffir, and R. A. Stebbins, 97–108. Newbury Park, CA: Sage, 1991.

Modern War Institute at West Point. "Max Brooks." West Point, NY: United States Military Academy, April 4, 2016. Accessed July 27, 2023. https://mwi.westpoint.edu.

Modlin, E. Arnold, Stephen P. Hanna, Perry L. Carter, Amy E. Potter, Candace Forbes Bright, and Derek H. Alderman. "Can Plantation Museums Do Full Justice to the Story of the Enslaved? A Discussion of the Problems, Possibilities, and the Place of Memory." *GeoHumanities* 4, no. 2 (2018): 335–359.

Monks, Kieron. "Andrew Drury Vacations in War Zones—Iraq, Afghanistan, Somalia." *CNN Travel*, January 12, 2016. Accessed July 11, 2023. www.cnn.com.

Monroe, Rachel. "I Am Not a Soldier, but I Have Been Trained to Kill." *Wired*, January 15, 2021. Accessed July 26, 2023. www.wired.com.

Montola, Markus. "Tangible Pleasures of Pervasive Role-Playing." In *Proceedings of DiGRA 2007 Situated Play Conference*, edited by Akira Baba, 178–185. University of Tokyo, September 24–28, 2007.

———. "Games and Pervasive Games." In *Pervasive Games: Theory and Design*, edited by Markus Montola, Jaakko Stenros, and Annika Waern, 7–24. Boca Raton, FL: CRC Press, 2009.

———. "The Positive Negative Experience in Extreme Role-Playing." In *Proceedings of the 2010 International DiGRA Nordic Conference*, Stockholm. Experiencing Games: Games, Play, and Players, August 16–17, 2010. www.digra.org.

Montola, Markus, and Jaakko Stenros. "Killer: The Game of Assassination." In *Pervasive Games: Theory and Design*, edited by Markus Montola, Jaakko Stenros, and Annika Waern, 3–6. Boca Raton, FL: CRC Press, 2009.

Montola, Markus, Jaakko Stenros, and Annika Waern. "Philosophies and Strategies of Pervasive Larp Design." In *Larp, the Universe, and Everything*, edited by Matthijs Holter, Eirik Fatland, and Even Tømte, 197–222. Copenhagen: Projektgruppen KP07. In conjunction with the Knudepunkt 2009 conference.

Montopoli, Brian. "NRA's Wayne LaPierre: 'Government Policies Are Getting Us Killed.'" *CBSNews.com*, February 10, 2011. Accessed July 19, 2023. www.cbsnews.com.

Morris, Patricia, and Tammi Arford. 2019. "'Sweat a Little Water, Sweat a Little Blood': A Spectacle of Convict Labor at an American Amusement Park." *Crime, Media, Culture: An International Journal* 15, no. 3 (2019): 423–446. Accessed July 27, 2023. https://doi.org/10.1177/1741659018780201.

Morrison, Toni. "A Bench by the Road." *World: Journal of the Unitarian Universalist Association* 3, no. 1 (1989): 4–5, 37–41. Accessed July 11, 2023. www.uuworld.org.

———. *The Source of Self-Regard. Selected Essays, Speeches, and Meditations*. New York: Alfred A. Knopf, 2019.

Morse, Theodore. "The Man behind the Gun." Toronto: W.H. Hodgins, undated sheet music. Accessed July 22, 2023. https://archive.org/details/CSM_01418.

Mullally, William. "The Avatar Franchise Is the Moral Quest of James Cameron's Life." *Esquire Middle East*. No date. Accessed January 23, 2024. www.esquireme.com.

Murdoch, David Hamilton. *The American West: The Invention of a Myth*. Lincoln: University of Nebraska Press, 2001.

Murphy, Eoghan. "The House That Rick Built—The Rise and Fall of Splatterhouse." *DualShockers*, October 30, 2018. Accessed July 22, 2023. www.dualshockers.com.

Murray, Janet H. "From Additive to Expressive Form." In *Hamlet on the Holodeck*, 1st ed. Cambridge, MA: MIT Press, 1998.

———. *Hamlet on the Holodeck: The Future of Narrative in Cyberspace*, updated ed. Cambridge, MA: MIT Press, 2017.

Mussell, Linda, Kevin Walby, and Justin Piché. "'Can You Make It Out Alive?' Investigating Penal Imaginaries at Forts, Sanitaria, Asylums, and Segregated Schools." *Journal of Qualitative Criminal Justice & Criminology* 10, no. 3 (2021). Accessed July 11, 2023. https://doi.org/10.21428/88de04a1.d3d18f84.

Navarro, Victor. "I Am a Gun: The Avatar and Avatarness in the FPS." In *Guns, Grenades, and Grunts: First-Person Shooter Games*, edited by Gerald A. Voorhees, Josh Call, and Katie Whitlock, 63–88. London: Bloomsbury, 2012.

Neiwart, David. *Alt-America: The Rise of the Radical Right in the Age of Trump*. New York: Verso, 2017a.

———. "What the Kek: Explaining the Alt-Right 'Deity' behind their 'Meme Magic.'" *Southern Poverty Law Center*. May 9, 2017b. Accessed July 5, 2023. www.splcenter.org.

Newsom, Carol. "Foreword." In *Apocalypses in Context: Apocalyptic Currents through History*, edited by Kelly J. Murphy and Justin Jeffcoat Schedtler, ix. Minneapolis: Fortress Press, 2016.

No Compromise. "The Original No Compromisers." Season 1, Episode 5. National Public Radio. R. Lisa Hagen, host. October 13, 2020. Accessed July 18, 2023. www.npr.org.

Nordgren, Andie. "Prosopopeia Bardo 2: Momentum." In *Nordic Larp*, edited by Jaakko Stenros and Markus Montola, 242–253. Stockholm: Fëa Livia, 2010.

Norris, Mike, dir. *Amerigeddon*. Culver City, CA: Sony Pictures Home Entertainment, 2016.

NRA Guide to the Basics of Personal Protection in the Home. Fairfax, VA: NRA, 2000.

NRA Institute for Legislative Action. "The Right to Keep and Bear Arms: An Analysis of the Second Amendment." *American Rifleman* 125, no. 38 (1977).

O'Leary, Stephen D. *Arguing the Apocalypse: A Theory of Millennial Rhetoric.* New York: Oxford University Press, 1998.
Ong, Jonathan Corpus. "The Cosmopolitan Continuum: Locating Cosmopolitanism in Media and Cultural Studies." *Media Culture & Society* 31, no. 3 (2009): 449–466.
Ong, Walter J. *Orality and Literacy: The Technologizing of the Word.* London: Methuen Young Books, 1982.
Orsi, Robert A. *Between Heaven and Earth: The Religious Worlds People Make and the Scholars Who Study Them.* Princeton, NJ: Princeton University Press, 2005.
———. *History and Presence.* Cambridge, MA: Harvard University Press, 2016.
O'Kane, John. "Insurrection, or Menacing Mashup of Misrecognition?" *AMASS Magazine* 25, no. 3 (2021): 12–16.
O'Reilly, Andrew. "Texas Church Shooting Not the First Time a Good Guy with Gun Takes Down Mass Shooter." *Fox News*, November 8, 2017. Accessed July 5, 2023. www.foxnews.com.
Palin, Sarah. "Sarah Palin at the 2010 Celebration of American Values." National Rifle Association-Institute of Legislative Action, May 27, 2010. Accessed July 19, 2023. www.nraila.org.
Parham, Jason. "The Ultimate Toxic Fandom Lives in Trumpworld." *Wired*, July 23, 2018. Accessed July 8, 2023. www.wired.com.
Parker, Kim, Juliana Horowitz, Ruth Igielnik, Baxter Oliphant, and Anna Brown. "America's Complex Relationship with Guns." Washington, DC: Pew Research Center, 2017. Accessed July 24, 2023. www.pewresearch.org.
Parrinello-Cason, Michelle. "Sex and Laundry: The Role of Women in Post-apocalyptic Landscapes." *Balancing Jane*, March 9, 2012. Accessed July 27, 2023. www.balancingjane.com.
Patton, Laurie. "Plural America Needs Myths: An Essay in Foundational Narratives in Response to Eboo Patel." In *Out of Many Faiths: Religious Diversity and the American Promise*, edited by Eboo Patel, 151–180. Princeton, NJ: Princeton University Press, 2018.
Patrick, Dan. *Fox & Friends.* Fox News, August 4, 2019. Accessed July 19, 2023. www.foxnews.com.
Paul, Lorna, and Susan Wrenn. "The Walking Dead Aftershow." *The Walking Dead.* TheStream.tv, 2014.
Payne, Matthew Thomas. *Playing War: Military Video Games after 9/11.* New York: New York University Press, 2016.
Penny, Simon. "Representation, Enaction, and the Ethics of Simulation." In *First Person: New Media as Story, Performance, and Game*, edited by Noah Wardrip-Fruin and Pat Harrigan, 73–84. Cambridge, MA: MIT Press, 2004.
Peters, Ian. "Peril-Sensitive Sunglasses, Superheroes in Miniature, and Pink Polka-Dot Boxers: Artifact and Collectible Video Game Feelies, Play, and the Paratextual Gaming Experience." In "Materiality and Object-Oriented Fandom," edited by Bob Rehak. Special issue, *Transformative Works and Cultures* 16 (2014). Accessed July 5, 2023. https://doi.org/10.3983/twc.2014.0509.

Phillips, Amber. "Videogames. Homelessness. Social Media. After Shootings, Republicans Have Avoided Talking about Trump and White Nationalism." *Washington Post*, August 5, 2019. Accessed July 22, 2023. www.washingtonpost.com.

Pierce, William. *The Turner Diaries*. Hillsboro, WV: National Vanguard Books, 1978.

Pinchevski, Amit. *Transmitted Wounds: Media and the Mediation of Trauma*. New York: Oxford University Press, 2019.

Plate, S. Brent. *A History of Religion in 5 1/2 Objects: Bringing the Spiritual to Its Senses*. Boston: Beacon Press, 2014.

Podoshen, Jeffrey S., Vivek Venkatesh, Jason Wallin, Susan A. Andrzejewski, and Zheng Jin. "Dystopian Dark Tourism: An Exploratory Examination." *Tourism Management* 51 (2015): 316–328.

Polaski, Sandra Hack. *A Feminist Introduction to Paul*. St. Louis: Chalice Press, 2005.

Pratchett, Terry (aka "Pterry"). "Over the Centuries." Comment on alt.fan.pratchett usenet group. June 1, 1998. Archived at https://groups.google.com/g/alt.fan.pratchett/c/FvOcPGokWW4/m/RTYB9Lu4qGsJ.

Pratt, Larry. "What Does the Bible Say about Gun Control?" Gun Owners Foundation, August 1, 1999. Accessed July 18, 2023. www.gunowners.org.

Preston, Peter. "Popcorn from the 9/11 Rubble." *The Guardian*, July 4, 2005. Accessed July 10, 2023. www.theguardian.com.

Queenan, Joe. "Man of Steel: Does Hollywood Need Saving from Superheroes?" *The Guardian*, June 12, 2013. Accessed July 19, 2023.

Quinby, Lee. *Millennial Seduction: A Skeptic Confronts Apocalyptic Culture*. Ithaca, NY: Cornell University Press, 1999.

Rackley, Paul. "Coolest Gun Movies." *American Rifleman* 161, no. 5 (2013).

Raymen, Thomas. "Slavery, Dark Tourism and Deviant Leisure at the American Society of Criminology in New Orleans." *Plymouth Law and Criminal Justice Review* (2017): 15–26.

Reese, Jennifer. "'Dog Stars' Dwells on the Upside of Apocalypse." *National Public Radio*, August 7, 2012. Accessed July 7, 2023. www.npr.org.

Reeves, Richard V., and Sarah E. Holmes. "Guns and Race: The Different Worlds of Black and White Americans." Washington, DC: Brookings Institute, December 15, 2015.

Rehak, Bob. "Playing at Being: Psychoanalysis and the Avatar." In *The Video Game Theory Reader*, edited by Mark J. P. Wolf and Bernard Perron, 103–127. New York: Routledge, 2003.

Reich, J. J. "Why We Name Our Guns." *American Hunter*, June 14, 2011. Accessed July 5, 2023. www.americanhunter.org.

Reichel, Philip L. "The Misplaced Emphasis on Urbanization in Police Development." *Policing and Society* 3, no. 1 (1992): 1–12.

Richardson, Reed. "The *Doomsday Prepper* Caucus." *The Nation*, April 2, 2013. Accessed June 26, 2023. www.thenation.com.

Riegler, Thomas. "We're All Dirty Harry Now: Violent Movies for Violent Times." In *The Domination of Fear*, edited by Mikko Canini, 17–41. Leiden, Netherlands: Brill Academic, 2010. Accessed July 18, 2023. https://doi.org/10.1163/9789042030855_003.

Rizzo, Anthony, dir. *Duck and Cover*. New York: Archer Productions, 1952.
Roberts, Jamie, dir. *Four Hours at the Capitol*. New York: HBO Documentary Films, 2021.
Robertson, Pat. *The End of the Age*. Nashville: Thomas Nelson, 1995.
Robbins, Amy. "The 5-Minute Zombie Apocalypse." *Noir*. NRA News. October 2, 2014. Accessed July 26, 2023. https://www.youtube.com/watch?v=-YsB2jQe8tg.
Roetzel, Calvin J. *The Letters of Paul: Conversations in Context*. London: SCM Press, 1983.
Rognli, Erling. "We Are the Great Pretenders: Larp Is Adult Pretend Play." In *Playground Worlds: Creating and Evaluating Experiences of Role-Playing Games*, edited by Markus Montola and Jaako Stenros, 199–205. Helsinki: Ropecon, 2008.
Romero, George, dir. *The Land of the Dead*. Pittsburgh: Universal Pictures, 2005.
Rose, Frank. *The Art of Immersion: How the Digital Generation Is Remaking Hollywood, Madison Avenue, and the Way We Tell Stories*. New York: W. W. Norton, Reprint Edition, 2012.
Rose, Laura Martin. *The Ku Klux Klan or Invisible Empire*. New Orleans: L. Graham Co., Ltd, 1914.
Rosen, Elizabeth K. *Apocalyptic Transformation: Apocalypse and the Postmodern Imagination*. Lanham, MD: Lexington Books, 2008.
Ross, Dalton. "'The Walking Dead': Robert Kirkman Previews 'Big' Episode." *EW.Com*, March 14, 2014a. Accessed July 7, 2023. https://ew.com.
———. "'The Walking Dead': Andrew Lincoln Promises 'We Will Rain Hell upon These Termites!'" *EW.Com*, March 31, 2014b. Accessed July 9, 2023. https://ew.com.
Ryan, Marie-Laure. "Story/Worlds/Media: Tuning the Instruments of a Media-Conscious Narratology." In *Storyworlds across Media: Toward a Media-Conscious Narratology*, edited by Marie-Laure Ryan and Jan-Noël Thon, 25–49. Lincoln: University of Nebraska Press, 2014.
Sagi, Guy J. "Beretta 92FS Used in 'Die Hard' Sold Online." *NRA Shooting Illustrated*, July 3, 2017. Accessed July 17, 2023. www.shootingillustrated.com.
Salen, Katie, and Eric Zimmerman. *Rules of Play: Game Design Fundamentals*. Cambridge, MA: MIT Press, 2003.
Savage, William W. *Cowboy Hero: His Image in American History and Culture*. Norman: University of Oklahoma Press, 1979.
Schaefer, Jack. *Shane*. Boston: Houghton Mifflin, 1949.
Schaeffer, Katherine. "Key Facts about Americans and Guns." *Pew Research Center*. September 13, 2023. Accessed January 23, 2024. www.pewresearch.org.
Schechner, Richard. *Performance Studies: An Introduction*. New York: Routledge, 2002.
Schreier, Philip. "Gun Show Fever." *American Hunter* 40, no. 4 (2012): 32.
Schüssler Fiorenza, Elisabeth. *In Memory of Her: Feminist Theological Reconstruction of Christian Origins*, 2nd ed. London: SCM Press, 1996.
The Scofield Reference Bible. Edited and annotated by Cyrus I. Scofield. Oxford: Oxford University Press, 1909.
Shaheen, Jack. *Reel Bad Arabs: How Hollywood Vilifies a People*. Revised and updated edition. New York: Olive Branch Press, 2012 (2001).

Sharpley, Richard. "Shedding Light on Dark Tourism: An Introduction." In *The Darker Side of Travel*, edited by Richard Sharpley and Philip Stone, 3–22. Bristol, UK: Channel View Publications, 2009.

Sheedy, Matt. "Kek Smoke Show." *Uncivil Religion*, January 6, 2021. Accessed July 5, 2023. https://uncivilreligion.org.

Sheehan, Jason. "Reading the Game: *Red Dead Redemption 2*." *NPR*, January 1, 2019. Accessed July 1, 2023. www.npr.org.

Sheppard, Elena. "Pro-Trump Capitol Rioters Like the 'QAnon Shaman' Looked Ridiculous—by Design." *NBCNews*, January 13, 2021. www.nbcnews.com.

Shields, Tanya. "Magnolia Longing: The Plantation Tour as Palimpsest." *Souls: A Critical Journal of Black Politics, Culture, and Society* 19, no. 1 (2017): 6–23.

Simone, Olivia. "LARP-ing at the Crematorium (in a Suburban Hyatt Hotel)." *Tablet Magazine*, September 2, 2014. Accessed July 5, 2023. www.tabletmag.com.

Slotkin, Richard. *Gunfighter Nation: The Myth of the Frontier in Twentieth-Century America*. Oxford: Oxford University Press, 1998.

Small, Zachary. "Push to Return 116,000 Native American Remains Is Long-Awaited." *New York Times*, August 6, 2021. Accessed July 11, 2023. www.nytimes.com.

Smith, Jonathan Z. "The Bare Facts of Ritual." From Smith, *Religion: From Babylon to Jonestown* (1982), reprinted in *Readings in Ritual Studies*, edited by Ronald Grimes, 473–494. Hoboken, NJ: Prentice Hall, 1996.

Smith, Marquita R. "Visions of Wondaland: On Janelle Monáe's Afrofuturistic Vision." In *Popular Music and the Politics of Hope: Queer and Feminist Interventions*, edited by Susan Fast and Craig Jennex, 31–48. New York: Routledge, 2019.

Solnit, Rebecca. *A Paradise Built in Hell*. New York: Viking. 2010.

Souter, Gerry. *American Shooter: A Personal History of Gun Culture in the United States*. Sterling, VA: Potomac Books, 2012.

Speer, David. "Police, White Supremacists in Standoff at Mountain Compound." *AP News*, April 20, 1985. Accessed June 25, 2023. https://apnews.com.

Stahl, Jeremy. "The Genuinely Shocking Bombshells from Cassidy Hutchinson's Jan. 6 Testimony." *Slate*, June 28, 2022. Accessed July 9, 2023. https://slate.com.

Stahl, Roger. *Militainment, Inc: War, Media, and Popular Culture*. New York: Routledge, 2010.

Steampowered. "Fallout: New Vegas." Accessed July 24, 2023. https://store.steampowered.com.

Steinberg, Jeffrey. "Interview with David Grossman: Giving Children the Skill and the Will to Kill." *Executive Intelligence Review*, March 17, 2000. Accessed July 23, 2023. http://members.tripod.com/~american_almanac/grossint.htm.

Stenros, Jaakko, and Markus Montola. "Introduction." In *Playground Worlds: Creating and Evaluating Experiences of Role-Playing Games*, edited by Markus Montola and Jaako Stenros, 5–11. Helsinki: Ropecon, 2008.

Stenros, Jaakko, Markus Montola, Annika Waern, and Staffan Jonsson. "Play It for Real: Sustained Seamless Life/Game Merger in *Momentum*." In *Proceedings of*

DiGRA 2007 Situated Play Conference, edited by Akira Baba, 121–129. University of Tokyo, September 24–28, 2007.

Stevens, Maurice E. "Trauma Is as Trauma Does: The Politics of Affect in Catastrophic Times." In *Critical Trauma Studies: Understanding Violence, Conflict and Memory in Everyday Life*, edited by Monica J. Casper and Eric Wertheimer, 19–36. New York: New York University Press, 2016.

Stevens, Wallace. "Thirteen Ways of Looking at a Blackbird" (1923). In *Collected Poems*. New York: Random House, 1991.

Stewart, Susan. *On Longing: Narratives of the Miniature, the Gigantic, the Souvenir, the Collection*. Durham, NC: Duke University Press, 1993.

Stone, Dominique, and Brian Andrews, prods. *Doomsday Preppers*. Washington, DC: National Geographic Studios, 2012. Accessed July 1, 2023. www.nationalgeographic.com.

Stone, Philip. "A Dark Tourism Spectrum: Towards a Typology of Death and Macabre Related Tourist Sites, Attractions and Exhibitions." *Tourism: An Interdisciplinary Journal* 54, no. 2 (2006): 145–160.

Strickland, Patrick. "The U.S.-Mexico Border Has Long Been a Magnet for Far-Right Vigilantes." *Time*, February 17, 2022. Accessed July 19, 2023. https://time.com.

Stroud, Angela. *Good Guys with Guns: The Appeal and Consequences of Concealed Carry*. Chapel Hill: University of North Carolina Press, 2016.

SurvivalMom. *Survivalist Boards*. June 28, 2011. Accessed July 1, 2023. http://www.survivalistboards.com/showthread.php?t=211048&page=4.

Survivor Jane. "Why I Decided to Appear on Doomsday Preppers." Accessed July 1, 2023. www.survivorjane.com.

Taub, Amanda, and Katrin Bennhold. "From Doomsday Preppers to Doomsday Plotters." *New York Times*, June 7, 2021. Accessed July 21, 2023. www.nytimes.com.

Taylor, J. D. *American Gun Culture: Collectors, Shows, and the Story of the Gun*. El Paso, TX: LFB Scholarly Publishing, 2009.

Thacker, Eugene. "Dark Matter." In *Excommunication: Three Inquiries in Media and Mediation*, edited by Alexander R. Galloway, Eugene Thacker, and McKenzie Wark, 77–150. Chicago: University of Chicago Press, 2014.

Thompson, Clive. "QAnon Is Like a Game–a Most Dangerous Game." *Wired*, September 22, 2020. Accessed July 5, 2023. www.wired.com.

Tinker, George. "An American Indian Theological Response to Ecojustice." *Journal for the Study of Religion, Nature and Culture* 2, no. 1 (1997): 85–109. https://doi.org/10.1558/ecotheology.v2i1.85.

Tompkins, Jane. *West of Everything: The Inner Life of Westerns*. Oxford: Oxford University Press, 1993.

Treatment Advocacy Center. "Serious Mental Illness and Treatment Prevalence." Background paper from the Office of Research & Public Affairs. January 2022. www.treatmentadvocacycenter.org.

Trend, David. *The Myth of Media Violence: A Critical Introduction*. Malden, MA: Blackwell Publishing, 2007.

Trevor, S. Twitter post. May 31, 2015, 8:55 p.m. https://twitter.com/trevso_electric/status/605175896648089600.

Trump, Donald. "President Trump Meeting with Governors on Gun Violence." C-SPAN, February 26, 2018. Accessed July 27, 2023. https://www.c-span.org/video/?441769-1/president-trump-meeting-governors.

Turner, Frederick Jackson. *The Frontier in American History*. New York: Henry Holt, 1920.

Turner, Graeme. *Film as Social Practice IV*. New York: Routledge, 2009.

Tuters, Marc. "LARPing & Liberal Tears. Irony, Belief and Idiocy in the Deep Vernacular Web." In *Post-digital Cultures of the Far Right: Online Actions and Offline Consequences in Europe and the US*, edited by Maik Fielitz and Nick Thurston, 37–48. Bielefeld, Germany: Transcript Publishing, 2019.

———. "A Prelude to Insurrection: How a 4chan Refrain Anticipated the Capitol Riot." *Fast Capitalism* 18, no. 1 (2021): 63–71.

Tyson, Timothy B. "The Ghosts of 1898: Wilmington's Race Riot and the Rise of White Supremacy." *News Observer*, November 17, 2006. Accessed July 11, 2023. http://media2.newsobserver.com.

Usborne, David. "It Took Minutes to Grasp Horror of What I Saw." *Belfast Telegraph*, September 12, 2001. Accessed July 27, 2023. www.belfasttelegraph.co.uk.

U.S. Congress. Senate Proceedings of 90th Congress, Second Session. "Omnibus Crime Control and Safe Streets Act of 1967." *Congressional Record* 114 (May 9, 1968): 12437–12528. Accessed July 15, 2023. https://www.congress.gov/bound-congressional-record/1968/05/09/114/senate-section/article/12437-12528.

USS Constitution Museum. "A Gun by Any Other Name." *Ussconstitutionmuseum.Org*, March 7, 2014. https://ussconstitutionmuseum.org.

Van Ells, Mark D. "An Amazing Collection: American GIs and Their Souvenirs of World War II." In *War and Memorials: The Second World War and Beyond*, edited by Frank Jacob and Kenneth Pearl, 105–148. Leiden, Netherlands: Brill, 2019.

van Zwieten, Martijn. "Danger Close: Contesting Ideologies and Contemporary Military Conflict in First-Person Shooters." *Proceedings of DiGRA 2011 International Conference: Think Design Play*. Hilversum, Netherlands, September 14–17, 2011. Digital Games Research Association.

Varandani, Suman. "George Zimmerman Lists Gun Used to Kill Trayvon Martin for Auction, Calls It 'an American Firearm Icon.'" *Ibtimes.Com*, May 12, 2016. Accessed July 2, 2023. www.ibtimes.com.

Vasilogambros, Matt. "The Gun That Killed Trayvon Martin Finds a Buyer." *Atlantic Monthly*, May 18, 2016. Accessed July 1, 2023. www.theatlantic.com.

Violence Policy Center. "Gun Shows in America: Tupperware® Parties for Criminals." Washington, DC: Violence Policy Center, July 1996. Accessed June 28, 2023. https://www.vpc.org/studies/tupintr.htm.

Virilio, Paul. *The Vision Machine*. Translated by Julie Rose. Bloomington: Indiana University Press, 1994.

Voorhees, Gerald. "Monsters, Nazis, and Tangos: The Normalization of the First-Person Shooter." In *Guns, Grenades, and Grunts: First-Person Shooter Games*, edited by Gerald Voorhees, Joshua Call, and Katie Whitlock, 89–111. London: Bloomsbury Academic, 2012.

Wachowski, Lana, and Lilly Wachowski, dirs. *The Matrix*. Burbank, CA: Warner Brothers, 1999.

Walther, Matthew. "The Limits of LARPing: America's Play-Acting of Civil War Briefly Turns Real." *The Week*, January 7, 2021. Accessed July 5, 2023. https://theweek.com.

Walther, Samantha, and Andrew McCoy. "US Extremism on Telegram: Fueling Disinformation, Conspiracy Theories, and Accelerationism." *Perspectives on Terrorism* 15, no. 2 (2021): 100–124.

Waxmann, S. "At the Movies, at Least, Good Vanquishes Evil." *New York Times*, May 10, 2004. Accessed July 9, 2023. www.nytimes.com.

Wertheimer, Eric, and Monica J. Casper. "Within Trauma: An Introduction." In *Critical Trauma Studies: Understanding Violence, Conflict and Memory in Everyday Life*, edited by Monica J. Casper and Eric Wertheimer, 1–18. New York: New York University Press, 2016.

West, Elliott. *The Essential West: Collected Essays*. Norman: University of Oklahoma Press, 2012.

White, Ellen G. *The Ellen G. White Writings*. Silver Spring, MD: Ellen G. White Estate, 1999.

White, Richard, and Patricia Nelson Limerick. *The Frontier in American Culture*. Edited by James R. Grossman. Berkeley: University of California Press, 1994.

Wilson, Ellen. *Annie Oakley: Little Sure Shot*. Indianapolis, IN: Bobbs-Merrill, 1958.

Wilson, Shawn. *Research Is Ceremony: Indigenous Research Methods*. Black Point, NS: Fernwood, 2008.

Winkler, Adam. *Gunfight: The Battle over the Right to Bear Arms in America*. New York: W.W. Norton, 2013.

Wister, Owen. "The Evolution of the Cow Puncher." *Harper's* 91, no. 544 (1895): 602–617.

Wolf, Mark J. P. *Building Imaginary Worlds*. New York: Routledge, 2012.

———. "Transmedia World-Building: History, Conception, and Construction." In *The Routledge Companion to Transmedia Studies*, edited by Matthew Freeman and Renira Rampazzo Gambarato, 141–147. New York: Routledge, 2019.

Womack, Ytasha. *Afrofuturism: The World of Black Sci-Fi and Fantasy Culture*. Chicago: Lawrence Hill Books, 2013.

Yarbro Collins, Adela. *Crisis and Catharsis: The Power of the Apocalypse*. Louisville, KY: Westminster/John Knox Press, 1984.

Young, Harvey. "The Black Body as Souvenir in American Lynching." *Theatre Journal* 57, no. 4 (2005): 639–657. doi:10.1353/tj.2006.0054.

Žižek, Slavoj. *Violence*. New York: Picador, 2008.

INDEX

abortion, 64–65, 68
accelerationism, 230–32, 243
action movies, 106
active shooter drills, 36
Adlard, Charlie, 111
Afrofuturism, 255–58
Alamo, Tony, 65
Alas, Babylon (Frank), 57
alt-right, 217–18, 228, 230, 234, 243–44; alt-righters, 90, 222–23; larping, 216
American culture: the Bible as center of, 26, 119; mass shootings center of, 26
American exceptionalism, 18
American justice, 24
American Rifleman, 81, 176–77, 179, 183. See also National Rifle Association
Amerigeddon, 101–3
ancient apocalypse, 11, 14, 59
Antichrist, 52, 59, 62, 68–69, 186
anti-racist future, 22, 114, 260–61, 266
antisemitism, 64–65, 67, 71, 87, 102–3, 114, 128; globalization and, 252; in Kekistan myth, 227–28; in *The Turner Diaries*, 60–61
apocalypse: ancient, 11, 14, 59; counter-, 127; cowboy, 13, 15–17, 19, 215; discourse, 12–13, 245; dispensations, 51, 62; future, 3, 13–14, 50, 172, 198; habit, 128, 243; hunger for, 110, 247; imagery, 19, 63, 174, 216; mythology of, 196; Native American, 244; organizing principle, 12; passivity, 11; post-, 119, 169; protective fundamentalism, 245; racist, 128, 238–39, 243–44; relationship to trauma, 198; Revelation, 12, 52, 57, 59, 67, 113, 164, 182, 251; rhetorical pleasures of, 11; white, 52, 61, 235; worldbuilding, 242; zombie, 69–70, 112

Apocalypse Now, 85
apocalyptic dualism, 246
apocalypticism, 3, 11, 18, 47, 51–52, 113–14, 125; cosmopolitanism as opposite of, 252–53; mass shootings mythology of, 196; post-, 243–44; secular, 63; terrorists and, 187–88; traditional, 112, 165, 247
apocalypticists, 14–15, 26, 159, 245
apocalyptic longing, pervasive, 230
apocalyptic mindset, 47, 58, 137, 164, 190, 247
apocalyptic videogames, 16–18, 67, 221
ARGs (Alternate Reality Games), 21, 226, 228. See also LARP
Armageddon, 64–65
Armageddon (movie), 91–92
Army Battlezone (videogame), 137
Aurora, Colorado mass shootings, 69
avatar, 40, 87, 96, 133, 144–45, 191, 223

Bad Company, 93
bad guy with a gun trope, 184–86, 189–214, 232, 234, 265. *See also* good guy with a gun trope
Baldwin, Alec, 203
Bastardos (FPS videogame), 139
Battlefield (FPS videogame), 132
Battlezone (videogame), 136
Beam, Louis, 63–64
Beast from 20,000 Fathoms, The, 84
Behind Enemy Lines, 93
the Bible: biblical inerrancy, 181; as center of American culture, 26, 119; cowboy messiah doesn't need, 159, 165; depictions of moral characters with Bibles, 62, 65, 68, 74; as moral authority connected to guns, 29, 37; New Testament, 115, 181, 185; Revelation, 12, 52, 57, 59, 67, 113, 164, 182, 251; Scofield Reference Bible, 52; scriptural interpretations of, 136, 160, 164, 182, 250
Big Trouble, 93
Birth of a Nation, 52, 82, 238
Black cowboy, 10
Black Hawk Down, 93
Blackout, The, 106
bleed, 149, 194, 212, 226–28
bombs, nuclear, 76, 84, 93, 164, 168
Boogaloo Bois, 231
Boston Marathon bombing, 69, 181
boundaries, between real and play, 121, 148, 194–219, 221. *See also* make belief/make believe
Brady Act, 31
Branch Davidians, 89
Bridge Too Far, A, 85
Brooks, Max, 69–70
buckaroo, cowboy, 10
Buffalo Bill's Wild West Show, 6–9, 77, 238
Bulletstorm (videogame), 190–92
Bundy, Ammon, 103
Bundy, Cliven, 99, 103, 174
Bush, George W., 96, 101

calm before the storm, 98
Calvinism, 29, 45–47, 186. *See also* Protestantism
Camp of the Saints, The (Raspail), 23
Carter, Harlon, 179–80
Charlottesville, Virginia, 228, 260–61. *See also* Unite the Right
Christian. *See also* Apocalypticism: broadcasting, 67; conservative, 58, 67, 239; early Christianity, 118–19, 243; evangelical, 49, 61, 115, 181, 189; functional model for world-bridging with guns, 43; fundamentalism, 61, 63–64; fundamentalists, 63, 253; martial arts, 66; masculinity, 105, 112, 115, 121, 180; military truths, 66; mode of oppression, 250; Nazi, 180; new Christian right, 183; novels, 52, 59, 61, 67–68, 71; QAnon, 229; spirituals, 62; theology, 51; white, 49, 64, 239–40; white Christian theology, 79
Chronicles of Narnia, The, 93
chronophotographic gun, 108
civil rights, 181
civil rights movement, 10, 58, 62–63, 249
Civil War, 74, 82, 107, 114, 147, 209, 213, 217, 235, 238; ghosts of, 174–75; reenactments, 42; songs in *The Stand*, 61–62; storytelling of, 49–55
Clansman, The (Dixon), 52–53
Cold War, 63, 84–87, 135, 149, 153; movies, 85
Collateral Damage, 93
Colt Manufacturing Company, 33, 37; firearms, 8, 29, 86, 107–8
Columbine mass shootings, 90, 95–96, 133, 140, 204
concealed weapons, 9, 30–31, 55, 184, 200
Confederacy, 51–54, 65, 175–76, 213, 216, 262
confession to camera trope, 158–59
conspiracy: -oriented groups, 226; theories, 65, 67, 218, 226; theorists, 10, 98

Cooke, Josh, 90
cosmopolitanism, 252–53, 255. *See also* globalization
cosplay, 106–7, 232, 235, 256
costumes, 27, 107, 146, 217
counter-apocalypse, 127
counterstory, 249–50, 260
Covenant, the Sword, and the Arm of the Lord, 66
cowboy: Black, 10; buckaroo, 10; cattle driver, 10; gaucho, 10; history, 4; messiahs, 3, 11–12, 14–15, 18–19, 22, 45, 50, 70, 82, 102, 109, 134, 159, 162–65, 171, 187, 224, 245, 261; movies, 9, 83; myth, 4, 6, 8, 10, 19, 50, 83, 234; myth enacted in videogames, 2, 15; vaquero, 7, 10; as white man, 51
cowboy apocalypse. *See specific topics*
cowboys: Indians and, 5, 9, 71, 92, 177, 238
criminal justice system, 212
Cripple Creek Bar Room, 92
critical race theory, 22, 78, 218, 249, 262
Custer's Revenge (videogame), 137
cybernetics, 134–35

Dances with Wolves, 74
Darby, John Nelson, 62, 136, 151–52
Dark Forces (game engine), 139
Dark Knight, The, 81
Dark Knight Rises, The, 69
dark tourism, 35, 200–207, 209
DARPA (Defense Advanced Research Projects Agency), 137
Daughters of the Confederacy, 53
Day, The, 106
Dayton, Ohio mass shooting, 189
Deep Impact, 91
Deer Hunter, The, 85
defense of civilization, racist, 128
delayed justice, 13–15, 24
Deliverance, 85
Delta Force, The, 87

depictions: of moral characters with Bibles, 62, 65, 68, 74; racist, 8, 53, 55, 58, 70, 82, 125, 209
Die Hard, 81, 87, 105
Dirty Harry, 81, 85
dispensations, apocalypse, 51, 62
Dissolution (The Wyoming Chronicles) (Gear), 76–77
Dixon, Thomas, 52–53
Dog Stars, The (Heller), 75
Doom (FPS videogame), 137
Doom (game engine), 130, 133, 137–38, 140
Doomsday Preppers (TV show), 2, 15, 20, 51, 151–73
drones, 40, 109, 143, 234
Dr. Strangelove, 84
Dudley, S. H., 175
Duke Nukem 3D (FPS videogame), 138
dystopian, 3, 15, 33, 256–57
Dystopia Rising (LARP), 227

early Christianity, 118–19, 243
Earthquake, 85
Eastwood, Clint, 19, 82, 94, 138
El Paso, Texas mass shooting, 189–90
EMPs (electro-magnetic pulses), 76, 160
End of All Things, The (Kraus), 78–80
End of the Age, The (Robertson), 52
end times, 14, 50, 59, 76, 99, 102, 136, 171, 185–86, 230
Entertainment Software Rating Board (ESRB), 191–92
enthrallment, 107
eschatology, 13, 112, 185
ESRB videogame rating system. *See* Entertainment Software Rating Board
Eucharist, 43
evangelical Christian, 49, 61, 115, 181, 189
excommunication, 44–45, 240, 261–62
Executive Decision, 89
expert assessment, 155, 158, 160–64, 169–73

Failsafe, 84
Fallout: New Vegas (FPS videogame), 131
Fallwell, Jerry, 61, 67
fans: anonymity behind masks, 222; cowboy apocalypse, 13, 15–17, 19, 215; gun fandom, 13, 31, 42, 86; January 6, 213; live events, 154; merchandise, 81, 154; NRA, 196; prediction and confirmation of beliefs about future, 12; prop fandom, 19, 42, 81, 105, 107, 145, 195; transmediated fandom, 146–47, 154; Western, 106; zombie, 69
Far Cry 5 (FPS videogame), 132
FBI, 60, 65–66, 89
feelies, 42
feminism, 1, 3, 5, 8, 114, 181, 218, 260
feminist, 58, 62, 75, 102, 110–16, 120, 125, 127–28, 239, 243, 246–48
Ferguson, Missouri, 100, 239–40
fetishistic disavowal, 208
fetishizing the gun, 16, 33, 77, 87, 107, 143
film, 15–19, 42–43, 52, 69, 74, 81–109, 130–32, 142, 144, 146, 203, 215. See also movies; *specific movies*
firearmsm Colt, 8, 29, 86, 107–8
first-person shooter (FPS), 20, 41, 100, 129–43, 146, 148–49, 190, 192, 225
first-person shooter videogames: *Bastardos*, 139; *Battlefield*, 132; *Doom*, 137; *Duke Nukem 3D*, 138; *Fallout: New Vegas*, 131; *Far Cry 5*, 132; *Grand Theft Auto V*, 132, 144, 190–91; *Half-Life*, 131; *High Noon Drifter*, 139; *Max Payne 3*, 132; *Outlaws*, 139; *Playerunknown's Battlegrounds*, 132; *Wolfenstein 3D*, 137
Five, 84
Forstchen, William, 72
FPS. *See* first person shooter
Frank, Pat, 57
freedom to be racist, 224
frontier: environment, 19, 83, 143; ideals, 2, 22, 42, 166; imagery, 56, 61, 100, 131, 180; masculinity, 30; midpoint between savagery and civilization, 4, 71; morality, 163; mythology, 2–3, 5–6, 11, 53, 77, 79–80, 131, 137, 162, 172, 174, 176–79; nostalgia, 161; post-apocalyptic, 100; reenactments, 6, 42; replacement for heaven, 165; story, 2, 5, 92; themes, 139; towns, 8–9, 68; values, 70, 168, 171; white man's frontier, 2, 110–28
fundamentalism, 58, 65, 67, 113, 119, 201, 246, 253; Christian, 61, 63–64, 253; secular, 245
future apocalypse, 3, 13–14, 50, 172, 198

game engines: *Dark Forces*, 139; *Doom*, 130, 133, 137–38, 140; *Marine Doom*, 140; *Quake*, 130, 138–40; *Star Wars: Dark Forces*, 131, 139, 144, 146
Gatling gun, 108
gaucho cowboy, 10
Gear, W. Michael, 76–77
Gender: binary, 250; equality, 116; expectations, 125; freedoms, 118; *gender doxa*, 115; norms, 113, 115–16, 119; panic, 113; relations, 112; roles, 105, 120; status, 114; structures, 119, 127; values, 120
Giles, Doug, 184
Gingrich, Newt, 72
Globalization, 3, 22, 70, 252–53. *See also* cosmopolitanism
Global Meltdown, 106
Godzilla, 84, 91
good guy with a gun trope, 3–4, 5, 47, 127, 174, 183–86, 193, 195–96, 225, 232. *See also* bad guy with a gun trope
Graham, Billy, 61
Grand Theft Auto (videogame), 132, 144, 190–91
Grand Theft Auto V (FPS videogame), 132, 144, 190–91
Great Replacement narrative, 230–31
Great Train Robbery, The, 82
Greeley, Horace, 5
Ground Zero (LARP), 96, 227–28

gun fandom, 13, 31, 42, 86
Gunfighter, The, 84
Gun Owners of America, 178
gun(s), 194–95; *See also* Colt Manufacturing Company; stand your ground; the Bible as moral authority connected to, 29, 37; collectors of, 31; as computer program, 39–41; culture, 23, 32, 48, 82, 138, 176, 192; as deadly antagonist against Native American, 29; as deterrent, 29–30; fetish, 87, 189; handgun, 28, 31, 35, 41, 88, 99, 132, 187, 234; justice reinforced with, 161; laws, 8, 47; as media, 44–45; network, 38–39; nostalgia, 238; as person, 37–38; phantom limb, 23; props, 41–42, 62, 81, 104–8, 131, 240; rifles, 33–34, 37–38, 53, 57, 62, 79, 88, 104, 187, 203, 205, 234; as ritual object, 22–23, 26–27, 33–34, 37, 80, 129, 143, 146, 167, 171; as sacrament, 26, 43–44, 106, 107, 167, 234; semiautomatic weapons, 27, 38, 41, 96, 99, 104, 232; shows, 18, 31, 175, 179; slavery and man behind the, 176; as souvenir, 34–36; as symbol, 30; 3D-printable, 41; as tool, 27–28; as totem, 31–32; toy, 36–37; videogames and, 16, 40, 106, 132–33, 189–90, 193; virtual, 39–41, 131–32
"Guns Don't Kill People," 38, 177–80, 189
Gunsmoke (TV show), 84

Half-Life (FPS videogame), 131
Hardwick, Chris, 112
Harry Potter, 93, 146
Hawley, Josh, 227
Headship, 112–21, 125. *See also* masculinity
Heller, Peter, 75
heroes: justice and, 84, 101, 105, 161, 182, 189, 212, 243; military, 238; movie superheroes, 94
Heston, Charles, 30, 85, 181
High Noon, 74
High Noon Drifter (FPS videogame), 139

Hills Have Eyes, The, 85
horror movies, 94
household codes, 115–23, 127; Deutero-Pauline, 115, 119, 122, 125; Pastorals, 118–20, 125; Paul's letters, 117–19
Howard Kunstler, James, 70–72, 75
How I learned to Stop Worrying and Love the Bomb, 84
How it Ends, 106
hunger, for apocalypse, 110, 247
hunting, 16, 22, 26, 28, 161, 215
Hutchins, Halyna, 107–8

I Am Legend, 95–96
id Software, 130, 140
imagery, apocalypse, 19, 63, 174, 216
imaginary racist, 56
immersive media, 17, 19, 47, 106, 144–45, 226, 233, 236
Immigrants, 6, 46, 51, 65, 73, 150, 188, 202, 231, 240, 252
Independence Day, 91
Indians, cowboys and, 5, 9, 71, 92, 177, 238
Indigenous peoples of America, 22, 139, 236, 246, 249, 258; ancestors, 197, 206; cowboy myth and, 4–10; in *Dissolution*, 77–78; genocide, 210; in racist apocalypse, 238–39; Tinker as writer of, 243; white supremacy and culture of, 260–61
individualism, 4, 51, 214, 223, 244
injustices, 58
interactive media, 17, 20, 106, 136, 154
Invaders from Mars, 85
Invasion of the Body Snatchers, 85
Invisible Empire, of KKK, 52–53
Islamophobia, 89–90, 93, 95, 184, 188

January 6, 14, 21, 215–24, 227–29, 231, 234–36, 2021
Jenkins, Jerry, 52, 67, 167
John Birch Society, 55–56
John Franklin Letters, 55–56

John Wick 2, 132
The Journey (LARP), 228
justice: apocalyptic promise of, 100, 106, 243; criminal justice system, 212; delayed, 13–15, 24; hero takes into his own hands, 84, 101, 105, 161, 182, 189, 212, 243; injustices, 58; NRA, 189; prepper as arbiter of, 159; reinforced with gun, 161; social, 51, 218, 266; white men meted out, 52; widely rehearsed stories of American justice, 24

Kekistan, 216, 222–25
Kennedy, John F., 176–77, 202
kenosis, 227
Killer (videogame), 194–95
Kindergarten Killers (videogame), 190
King, Stephen, 61–63
Kirkman, Robert, 111, 123
KKK. *See* Ku Klux Klan
Kraus, Mike, 78–80
Ku Klux Klan, 21, 23, 69, 92, 175, 180, 203, 211, 218; in *The Clansman*, 53–55; in early Westerns, 82–83; in *Essays of a Klansman*, 63–66; Invisible Empire of, 52–53; lynching, 128; in *The Stand*, 61–63

LaHaye, Tim, 52, 67–68
Land of the Dead, 95
Lapierre, Wayne, 29–30, 99, 180, 183–93, 196, 265
LARP. *See* Live-Action Role-Play
larping, 220, 231; alt-right, 216–19; defined, 229–30; extreme, 21, 228
Las Vegas concert mass shooting, 30, 104, 173, 188, 196
Late Great Planet Earth, The (Lindsey), 59, 61, 64
leaky play, 148–50
Left Behind (series) (LaHaye and Jenkins), 52, 67
Life of a Cowboy, The, 82

Lindsey, Hal, 59, 61, 64
Littleton, Colorado mass shooting, 95
Live-Action Role-Play (LARP), 21, 101, 203–35; *Dystopia Rising*, 227; *Ground Zero*, 96, 227–28; *The Journey*, 228; *Momentum*, 225; pervasive larps, 219, 221, 225–27, 232–33
Lone Ranger, The (TV show), 97
Lone Ranger narrative, 97, 223, 234
Lord of the Rings, The, 93
Lost Cause, 51, 207, 214
Luby's cafeteria, Killeen, Texas, mass shooting at, 89
Lumière brothers, 108–9
lynching, 128, 202, 204, 212

magic circle movies, 221
magic circle of play, 13, 193
make belief/make believe, 13
Malvo, Lee Boyd, 90
manifest destiny, 239, 241
manly media, 111–12
Marey, Étienne-Jules, 108
Marine Doom (game engine), 140
Marjory Stoneman Douglas High School mass shooting, 104, 193
martial arts, Christian, 66
Martin, Trayon, 35, 46, 214, 225
masculine: authority 21, 30; manliness, 51, 116, 120–27; manly media, 111–12
masculinity, 30, 69–70, 110, 132, 148, 165, 168, 170, 216, 224, 266; Christian, 105, 112, 115, 117, 121, 180 (*see also* headship); elemental, 121
mass incarceration, 212, 257
mass shootings: Aurora, CO, 69; blaming people with mental illness, 265; center of American culture, 26; Columbine, 90, 95–96, 133, 140, 204; dark tourism, 35; Dayton, OH, 189; El Paso, TX, 189–90; Las Vegas concert, 30, 104, 173, 188, 196; Littleton, CO, 95; Luby's cafeteria in Killeen, TX, 89; Marjory

Stoneman Douglas High School, 104, 193; McDonalds in San Diego, 86; mythology of apocalypticism, 196; Pulse nightclub, 104, 188; representations of, 97; Sandy Hook Elementary, 30, 69, 99, 185, 189, 195; Sutherland Springs TX, 232; toy guns evoke experience of, 37; Virginia Tech, 96, 184, 193
Matrix, The, 89–90, 105, 146
Max Payne 3 (FPS videogame), 132
Maze War (videogame), 136
McCarthy, Kevin, 190
McDonalds mass shooting, 86
McVeigh, Timothy, 50, 60, 89
media: guns in, 44–45; immersive, 17, 19, 47, 106, 144–45, 226, 233, 236; interactive, 17, 20, 106, 136, 154; manly, 111–12
memorabilia, 41, 107, 111. *See also* souvenirs
mental illness, mass shootings and, 265
Mieseges, Vadim, 90
military: activities, 40, 92; computer projects, 136; heroes, 238; history, 22, 72, 128; perceptual shift from conquering space to managing time, 109; shooters, 142; simulations, 136, 140–41; survival training and procedures, 66, 140–41; US military-industrial complex, 20; violence, 143
military-industrial complex, US, 20
military truths, Christian, 66
Militia, 22, 28, 73, 99, 179–81, 203, 210; paramilitary, 66, 181, 215, 240
millennialism, 52, 141, 244
Momentum (LARP), 225
Monáe, Janelle, 256–58
Moore, Tony, 111
Morse, Theodore, 87, 175–76
Mortal Kombat (videogame), 140, 190–92
movies. *See also* film; *specific movies*: as in the, 9, 12, 77, 88, 104, 132; action, 106; Cold War, 85; cowboy, 9, 83; gun fetish, 87, 189; horror, 94; magic circle, 221;

9/11, 94; superhero, 94; transmedia, 2, 18, 23, 48, 109, 149, 169, 218, 246
murderbilia, 204
mythology: apocalypse, 196; frontier, 2–3, 5–6, 11, 53, 77, 79–80, 131, 137, 162, 172, 174, 176–79
myths: cowboy, 4–10, 19, 50, 83, 234; Kekistan, 227–28; racist, 262

National Rifle Association (NRA), 8, 20–22, 27–34, 49, 56, 81, 99, 112, 215, 232; videogames endorsed by, 174, 192–93
Native American. *See also* Indigenous peoples of America: ancestry, 197; apocalypse, 244; in *Custer's Revenge*, 137; extermination policy, 206–7; gun as deadly antagonist against, 29; militia fought, 210; parallels to Holocaust, 241–42; replay of cultural destruction, 97–98; transformation into barbarians, 8
Nazi, 137, 252; Aryan Nation, 180; Atomwaffen Division, 230
Nazi Christian identity, 180
neo-Nazi, 93
new Christian right, 183
New Testament (the Bible), 115, 181, 185
New World Order, 102–3
nightmares, nuclear, 83–87
9/11, 82, 89, 91–96, 99–100, 141–43, 158, 183, 204
Noir (TV show), 112
non-player characters (NPC), 222, 225
normies, 222
Normistan, 224
Norris, Chuck, 82, 87
Norris, Mike, 101–3
nostalgia, 35, 42, 200–201, 203, 205, 237, 245; frontier, 161; gun, 238; white, 148, 207–10
novels, 12, 15–16, 19, 49–79, 131, 144–45, 231, 255. *See also specific works*; Christian, 52, 59, 61, 67–68, 71

NPC. *See* non-player characters
NRA. *See* National Rifle Association
NRA Guide to the Basics of Personal Protection in the Home, 27–28
nuclear. *See also* apocalypse: bombs, 76, 84, 93, 164, 168; fallout, 67–68, 84, 157, 159; nightmares, 83–87; themes, 84, 143; war, 57, 64–66, 134–35, 227, 241

Oakley, Annie, 49
Oath Keepers, 99, 216, 230
Oklahoma City bombing, 50, 204
Once Upon a Time in the Apocalypse, 107
One Second After (Forstchen), 72
online discussion boards, 17
On the Beach, 84
oppression, Christian mode of, 250
O'Reilly, Andrew, 232
Otherwise Worlds, 258, 259–63
Outlaws (FPS videogame), 139
Ox-Bow Incident, The, 74

Panic in Year Zero, 84
paramilitary, 66, 181, 215, 240
patriarchy, 112, 114, 127, 258–62
Patrick, Dan, 190
Patriot Act, 96
patriotism, 178, 180, 199, 201, 214
patriots, 37, 56, 63, 73, 99, 102–3, 179, 218
Pepe the Frog, 215, 222–23
pervasive games, 193–95, 220–21, 229–30, 233
pervasive game theory, 194–95, 226
pervasive gunning, 194–95
pervasive larp, 219, 221, 225–27, 232–33
pervasive play, 17, 219–21
pervasive story, 2
Pierce, William, 50, 60–61
Pinocchio effect, 195
Playerunknown's Battlegrounds (FPS videogame), 132
play studies: leaky play, 148–50; magic circle of play, 13, 193; pervasive play, 17, 219–21; play frame, 36, 229; play of desire, 35, 205; pleasure of play, 133; theories of play, 36, 148; transgressive play, 219, 221, 224
pleasure of play, 133
pluralism: religious, 22, 253–55; as sustained conversation, 254–55
porn, videogame, 137
Postal (videogame), 87
post-apocalypse, 119, 169
post-millennialism, 52
Pratt, Erich, 179
Pratt, Larry, 178, 181–82
predestination, 29, 45–47. *See also* Calvinism
pre-enactment ritual, 106
pre-millennialism, 52
preppers, 20, 32, 103, 211, 215, 235; accelerationists and, 230–32, 243; as arbiter of justice, 159; Boogaloo Bois and, 231; doomsday, 151–73; *Red Dawn* scenario, 86; survivalists, terrorists and, 88–90; *Take Shelter* for, 98
prophecy, 158–60, 163
props: actual bodies, 14; buying, 17; dark tourism, 204; guns as, 62, 81, 104–8, 131, 240; January 6, 231; material, 145; non-player characters as, 185, 225, 232, 246, 265; people as one-dimensional, 20; sacramental, 107, 132; studies of, 41–43
protective fundamentalism, 245
Protestantism, 45, 181, 186. *See also* Calvinism
proxy objects, 26, 29, 204
Pulp Fiction, 81
Pulse nightclub mass shooting, 104, 188

QAnon, 216, 228–30
Quake (game engine), 130, 138–40
queerness, 250–52, 262
queer theology, 22, 250–52

racism, 32, 46, 51, 53, 137, 188, 207, 212, 223, 242, 248
racist: anti-racist future, 22, 114, 260–61, 266; apocalypse, 128, 238–39, 243–44; backlash, 10; cowboy as white man, 51; defense of civilization, 128; depictions, 8, 53, 55, 58, 70, 82, 125, 209; freedom to be, 224; Great Replacement, 230; habits, 22–23; imaginary, 56; mode of predestination, 45–47; myths, 262; New World Order, 103; racism, 32, 46, 51, 53, 137, 188, 207, 212, 223, 242, 248; rallies, 66; southern, 52; stereotypes, 139; stories, 32, 35, 75, 128; textbooks, 218; theology, 47, 51; tropes, 69, 75; venom, 60
Radar Men from the Moon, 85
Rambo, 88
Rambo: First Blood, 89
Raspail, Jean, 23
Reagan, Ronald, 49, 59, 65, 179
reality television, 151–59, 171
reality TV, 151–59, 171
Red Dawn, 64–68, 77, 85–86, 99
Red Dead Redemption (videogame), 17, 143–44
religious pluralism, 22, 253–55
replica objects, 107
Revelation, 12, 52, 57, 59, 67, 113, 164, 182, 251
rhetorical pleasures of apocalypse, 11
Rhodes, Stewart, 216
Rifleman, The (TV show), 84
ritual: activities, 13, 101; architecture, 3; authentication, 12, 105, 162; confirmation, 107; dismemberment, 205; display, 158, 165–67; enactment, 14, 20, 134, 146, 167; expectation and desire, 50; fetish, 143; guns, 22–23, 26–27, 37, 80, 129, 143, 146, 167, 171; male initiation, 30, 168; objects, 33, 42, 97, 109; play, 148–49; of pre-enactment, 106; of refusal, 26, 262; religious rituals, 220; rite of passage, 58, 77, 165–66; survivalists' play, 33; television, 169; theory, 18, 133–34, 169; videogaming, 129, 131, 134, 141, 148; voodoo, 64

ritualized activity, videogames as, 13
ritualized performance, 103, 133
ritualized story, 14
ritual television, 169
Rival Nemesis (toy gun), 36
Road, The, 15
Robb, Thom, 60
Robertson, Pat, 52, 61, 64, 67–69
RPGs (Role-Playing Games), 2, 13–18, 21–22, 42, 101, 131, 203, 229
Ruby Ridge, 65, 88, 180–81, 231
Rules of Engagement, 90
Rust, 107, 203

sacrament, gun as, 26, 43–44, 106, 107, 167, 234
Sandy Hook Elementary mass shooting, 30, 69, 99, 185, 189, 195
Schaeffer, Francis, 61
Schlafly, Phyllis, 49, 61
Schwarzenegger, Arnold, 86, 89, 92, 94, 138
Scofield Reference Bible, 52
scriptural interpretations, of the Bible, 136, 160, 164, 182, 250
Second Amendment, 10, 47, 73, 176, 179–80
secondary worlds, 190–91
secondary worlds, in videogames, 191
Second Coming of Christ, justice and, 52, 182
settler colonialism, 213, 238, 259, 262
sexism, 75, 114, 248
sexist, 23, 58, 74, 103, 113, 122–23, 224, 260
Shane, 28, 84, 122–23, 163
shitposting, 218, 223–24
Siege, The, 89

Signs, 93
simulations, 20, 134–35, 161, 191; military, 136, 140–41
Sitting Bull, 7
slave patrols, 21, 92, 210–12
slavery: erased history of, 22, 53, 58, 128, 207–8, 210, 213, 238, 242, 256, 258; fetishistic disavowal, 208, 243; in fiction, 62; man behind the gun, 176; terrors of, 209, 211; traumas of, 210, 257; violence of, 127–28
social justice 51, 218, 266
southern racist, 52
souvenirs, 34–35, 80, 177; apocalyptic, 197–214; dark, 35; sacred, 42
Souza, Joel, 107
Spacewar! (videogame), 136
Space Wars (videogame), 131, 139, 144
Spasim (videogame), 136
Spencer, Richard, 218
Spider-Man, 93
spirituals, Christian, 62
Splatterhouse (videogame), 190, 192
Stallone, Sylvester, 238
Stand, The (King), 61–63
stand-your-ground: gun laws, 47, 78; reasoning, 92, 235
Star Wars: Dark Forces (game engine), 131, 139, 144, 146
stereoscopic vision, 233
stereotypes, racist, 139
Stevens, Wallace, 25, 48
storyworld, 16, 129, 143, 145, 147, 192
Sum of All Fears, The, 93
Super Columbine Massacre RPG! (videogame), 94
superhero movies, 94
survival. *See* preppers
survivalism, 33
Survivalist, The, 107
survivalists, 18, 61, 84, 86, 123; apocalyptic, 15–16, 231; in 1980s, 64–65; *Doomsday Preppers* (TV show), 2, 15, 20, 51, 151–73; preppers, terrorists and, 88–90; ritual play of, 33
survival training, military, 66, 140–41
Sutherland Springs, Texas mass shooting, 232

Take Shelter, 98–99
Talking Dead, The (TV show), 112
Tarantula, 84
television, 17–23, 58, 70, 109, 137, 146, 149, 215, 218, 245; *Doomsday Preppers*, 151–71; *Gunsmoke*, 84; *The Lone Ranger*, 97; *Noir*, 112; reality, 151–59, 171; *The Rifleman*, 84; ritual, 169; *The Talking Dead*, 112; *Wagon Train*, 7, 84; *The Walking Dead*, 2, 15, 19, 51, 110–27, 231; *World of Warcraft*, 222
Terminator, The, 86–87, 105
terrorism, 85, 102, 159, 211, 241; Islamic terrorists, 89–90, 93; jihadi terrorists, 89, 93; 9/11, 82, 89, 91–96, 99–100, 141–43, 158, 183, 204; preppers and, 88–90; terror 94, 100, 110, 209
terrorists, 78, 143, 153, 160, 168, 193, 243; in *Amerigeddon*, 101, 102; apocalypticism and, 187–88; cowboys compared with, 87–91; LaPierre on, 183–84; Neo-Nazi, 60–61; 9/11, 82, 91–96
Texas Chain Saw Massacre, The, 85
Thacker, Eugene, 15–16
Them!, 84
theology: Christian, 51; racist, 47, 51
theories of play, 36, 148
theory: critical race, 22, 78, 218, 249, 262; pervasive game, 194–95, 226; ritual, 18, 133–34, 169; trauma, 21; worldbuilding, 190
Thing from Another World, The, 85
Time Machine, The, 93
Tinker, George, 243
Tolkien, J.R.R., 93, 190
totem, 31–32, 37, 109, 171
toy guns, 36–37

transgressive play, 219, 221, 224
transmedia, 15–22, 51, 107, 111, 129–33, 137; fandom, 146–47, 154; movies, 2, 18, 23, 48, 109, 149, 169, 218, 246
transmediality, pervasive quality of, 147
transmedia worldbuilding, 17; videogames as part of, 130, 145–47, 214, 246
trauma, 82, 85, 91, 198–203, 210–14; apocalypse relationship to, 198; of slavery, 210, 257; story, 200–201; theory, 21
Tremors, 88
trope: bad guy with a gun, 184–86, 189– 214, 232, 234, 265; confession to camera, 158–59; good guy with a gun, 3–4, 5, 47, 127, 174, 183–86, 193, 195–96, 225, 232; racist, 69, 75
True Lies, 89
Trump, Donald, 98, 104, 113, 196, 234, 236; Capital riots and, 216–23; "Make America Great Again" motto of, 201; QAnon and, 228–29; on videogames and childhood development, 189–90
truth, 8, 156–59, 172–73, 189, 246, 251
Turner, Frederick Jackson, 3–4, 9, 30
Turner Diaries, The (Pierce), 50, 60–61
The Turner Diaries, 50, 60–61
Turner thesis, 3, 9, 30

Unite the Right rally, 228

vaquero cowboy, 7, 10
venom, racist, 60
videogames. *See also* first-person shooter: apocalyptic videogames, 16–18, 67, 221; *Army Battlezone*, 137; *Battlezone*, 136; blaming videogames for what guns do, 16, 189–90, 193; *Bulletstorm*, 190–92; cowboy myth enacted in, 2, 15; *Custer's Revenge*, 137; endorsed by NRA, 174, 192–93; *Grand Theft Auto*, 132, 144, 190–91; guns, 40, 106, 132–33; *Killer*, 194–95; *Kindergarten Killers*, 190; language, 231; *Maze War*, 136;
Mortal Kombat, 140, 190–92; part of transmedia world, 130, 145–47, 214, 246; porn, 137; *Postal*, 87; *Red Dead Redemption*, 17, 143–44; ritualized activity, 13; secondary worlds, 191; *Spacewar!*, 136; *Space Wars*, 131, 139, 144; *Spasim*, 136; *Splatterhouse*, 190, 192; *Super Columbine Massacre RPG!*, 94; videogame rating system, 192; violent videogames, 15, 20, 48, 104, 130, 141, 149, 189–90, 193; *V-Tech Rampage*, 96; wartime prediction, 134, 136, 140
vigilante, 3, 6, 10, 20–21, 85, 103, 138, 180, 195, 210
violence: military, 143; sexual, against women 53, 62, 64, 106, 214; of slavery, 127–28; in videogames, 15, 20, 48, 104, 130, 141, 149, 189–90, 193
Virginia Tech mass shooting, 96, 184, 193
virtual guns, 39–41, 131–32
voodoo ritual, 64
V-Tech Rampage (videogame), 96

Waco, Texas, 65–66, 89, 191, 231
Wagon Train (TV show), 7, 84
Walking Dead, The (TV Show), 2, 15, 19, 51, 110–27, 231
war, nuclear, 57, 64–66, 134–35, 227, 241
War of the Worlds, 94
war on terror, 82, 91, 96
wartime prediction, 134, 136, 140
Wayne, John, 9–10, 19, 62, 82, 88, 104–5, 138, 179, 237
West, Eliott, 5–6
Western films, 19, 75, 82–83
Western novels, 50–51, 82
white apocalypse, 52, 61, 235
white Christian: conservative, 239; evangelicals, 10; theology, 79
white men, 18, 54, 58, 115, 134, 148, 178, 247; armed, 2, 11, 21, 52, 76, 212, 239; male hegemony, 232

whiteness: as blessedness, 46, 71, 73; idea of "whiteness," 4, 6, 197; as norm, 63, 199, 213, 244, 262

white priviledge, 241–42

whites: as cowboys, 51; in critical race theory, 249; cultural appropriation of, 77; ethnostate, 220, 224; fear of, 73, 212; as martyrs, 60; nationalism of, 181, 222–23, 243; nostalgia of, 207–10; patriarchy, 260; resentment of, 65; as right and might, 30, 236; as settlers, 4, 75; spaces, 212, 239; utopia, 243; as vigilantes, 21

white supremacy, 21–22, 35, 48, 51, 54, 56, 60, 75, 113–15, 127, 133, 146, 148, 180–81, 199, 201, 204–5, 207, 212, 230, 243–45, 254, 266. *See also* Ku Klux Klan; Capital riots costuming, 214–18; culture of indigenous peoples of America and, 241–42, 260–61; "declaration of war" in Ferguson and, 239–40; in *The End of All Things*, 78–80; Otherwise Worlds and, 258–62

white zombies, 69

Willis, Bruce, 82, 87, 92, 105, 136

Wister, Owen, 51

Wolfenstein 3D (FPS videogame), 137

women. *See also* feminism: Black, 257; exclusion of, 58; hatred of, 89; Muslim, 90; Paul's letters on new roles, 116–20; protection of, 120–21; representations of, 62, 71, 74, 122, 123; right to independence, 260; sexual power of, 124; sexual violence against, 53, 62, 64, 106, 214; of the South, 54; stealing, 77, 107; "women's work," 49, 120, 240

worldbuilding, 17, 242, 256, 258–59, 261

worldbuilding theory, 190

World Made by Hand (Knustler), 70–72, 75

World of Warcraft (TV show), 222

World Trade Center bombing, 89, 93, 204. *See also* 9/11

World War Z (Brooks), 69–70

Zimmerman, George, 214

zombie apocalypse, 69–70, 112

Zombieland, 97

zombies, 53 64, 95–98, 260–61; symbolic association to terrorists, 96; in *The Walking Dead* (TV Show), 2, 15, 19, 51, 110–27, 231; white, 69–70

ABOUT THE AUTHOR

RACHEL WAGNER is Professor of Religious Studies and Chair of the Department of Philosophy and Religion at Ithaca College. Her essays have been published in *CrossCurrents Magazine*, *Digital Religion*, and *Religious Dispatches*. Her first book, *Godwired: Religion, Ritual and Virtual Reality* (2012), explores religious experience in the digital age.

www.ingramcontent.com/pod-product-compliance
Lightning Source LLC
Chambersburg PA
CBHW021846090426

42811CB00033B/2161/J